THE
UPRISING

THE UPRISING

an unauthorized tour of
the populist revolt scaring
wall street and washington

DAVID SIROTA

crown publishers / new york

Published in the United States by Crown Publishers, an imprint of the
Crown Publishing Group, a division of Random House, Inc., New York.

www.crownpublishing.com

Crown is a trademark and the Crown colophon is a registered trademark of
Random House, Inc.

Library of Congress Cataloging-in-Publication Data

Sirota, David (David J.)

The uprising : an unauthorized tour of the populist revolt scaring
Wall Street and Washington / David Sirota.

p. cm.

Includes index.

1. Political participation—Computer networks—United States.   2. Blogs—Political
aspects—United States.   3. Business and politics—United States.   4. Internet—Social
aspects.   5. Social movements—United States.   I. Title.   II. Title: Populist revolt
scaring Wall Street and Washington.

JK1764.S5434 2008

973.931—dc22   2008002671

ISBN 978-0-307-39563-4

Printed in the United States of America

Design by Leonard W. Henderson

10 9 8 7 6 5 4 3 2 1

First Edition

To my parents and their parents
—the people who taught me the value of rising up

contents

We hold these truths to be self-evident, that all men are created equal, that they are endowed by their Creator with certain unalienable Rights, that among these are Life, Liberty and the pursuit of Happiness. That to secure these rights, Governments are instituted among Men, deriving their just powers from the consent of the governed,—That whenever any Form of Government becomes destructive of these ends, it is the Right of the People to alter or to abolish it, and to institute new Government . . . It is their right, it is their duty, to throw off such Government, and to provide new Guards for their future security.

—DECLARATION OF INDEPENDENCE, JULY 4, 1776

THE
UPRISING

1

A PORTRAIT OF
THE WRITER
ON A BATHROOM FLOOR

I'M PRETTY SURE I'm still at the Riviera Hotel here in Vegas. I know this not because I can see through the blurry haze of my hangover or think past this pounding headache or feel anything other than the sharp pain of dehydration in my stomach, but because I can still smell the cigarette smoke embedded in the wallpaper.

The Riviera is one of those last hangers-on in Vegas—an aging hotel that still tries to show a little leg and pose as a competitive casino, oblivious to the sleek billion-dollar palaces just a few doors down. Each wing is named after luxurious spots on the French Riviera (I am here in the Monaco Tower)—the names are supposed to make you ignore the décor's distinctly Nixon-era feel. Plenty of twinkling lights surround the faded wall mirrors in the casino—but every fifth light or so is burnt out. Where the registration desks at the newer casinos are adorned with giant fish tanks, or expensive modern art, the Riviera has guests check in at what appear to be bank-teller stations. And forget about amenities. As the clerk barked, "At the Riviera, you can't even reserve a nonsmoking room."

The hotel has a collision-of-two-worlds feeling about it. In a city now dominated by luxury resorts only the wealthy can afford, the Riviera is for the commoner, the everyman. The guests who stay here are the wide-eyed, middle-aged, round-bellied Joneses taking their one big trip of the year from places like Dubuque and Bismarck—they are not the reconstructed-with-plastic nouveau riche from the coast who jet-setted in for the weekend. This is not the place that would host a big pay-per-view prizefight—but it is a hotel where I am not surprised to see a minor-league billiards tournament taking place.

The Riviera is Flyover Country's embassy in Las Vegas—the place where The Rest of Us go when we visit Sin City. That's why it's a damn good place to have the first annual YearlyKos Convention.

This 2006 summer gathering is for those who read, write for, comment on, and are otherwise connected to the weblog Daily Kos. It is a boisterous band—mostly young, middle-class lefties, with some unreformed '60s hippies, '70s environmentalists, '80s anti-Reagan liberals and '90s-era Clinton political operatives mixed in. Imagine a Democratic National Convention and a Star Trek convention having a drunken one-night stand and producing a love child: that is YearlyKos.

Since I have my own blog, I was asked to speak on a few panels. When I checked in to get my convention badge, the volunteer recognized my name and asked me about a blog post I had written a few months back. Minutes later, a woman excitedly introduced herself as "McJoan"—expecting me to know her by her Internet screen name (and I'll admit I did). In another moment, a twenty-something in a seersucker sport jacket covered with political buttons asked for my autograph. I was surprised by the attention.

Here at YearlyKos, I am like an actor who had a minor role in a space movie now visiting a sci-fi memorabilia show. I am Jabba the Hutt's aide with the cream-colored head tumor—now appearing years later at a *Star Wars* revival show. I am the midget inside the Twiki costume at a *Buck Rogers* event. I am the recurring engine room technician on the *Enterprise* now appearing to great fanfare at a *Star Trek* convention.

I am not, of course, Mark Hamill, Gil Gerard, or Bill Shatner. I am second or third tier. The true gods of the convention are people like Markos Moulitsas—the Kos in Daily Kos. Though he's a thirty-four-year-old army veteran and father, he looks like a sixteen-year-old high school sophomore. Not an inch over five foot eight and not a pound over 150, his uniform is after-school casual—at his own convention he could most often be seen wearing baggy shorts and what looked like a short-sleeved soccer jersey.

In just a few short years, Markos went from Just a Dude in his Berkeley apartment posting screeds on a website to a twenty-first-century political boss whom Democratic politicians suck up to and Republican politicians berate.

For a while, the Washington crowd judged Markos by his appearance, downplaying his relevance, pillorying him as an amateur who didn't understand what we're expected to believe is the rocket science of politics. Then, slowly but surely, politicians started seeing him as an ATM machine—a person who, because he had thousands of politically interested readers (the "Kossacks"), could generate fairly serious campaign contributions for candidates. Now, as the brain behind Daily Kos and the inspiration for YearlyKos, he is a major force—a guy whose four hundred thousand daily readership is bigger than that of most major magazines and newspapers. Presidential candidates come to speak to his followers, Senate majority leaders beg his disciples for support, and national party chairmen shake them all down for cash. The politicians want a piece of the action for their own purposes and are more than happy to beg for it.

It was one of these pander-fests that led me to my current place: lying on the floor of the bathroom in my Riviera hotel room, using my sense of smell—the only sense that seems to be fully working right now—to discern where I am. After one (or more like five) too many drinks at a Mark Warner for President extravaganza on the top floor of the Stratosphere Hotel, I am back here at the Riveria, sick—really sick—like freshman-year-at-college sick.

But I want to savor the moment.

I feel like I am in the beginning of *Jerry Maguire*, where pre-TomKat Tom Cruise has the epiphany/nervous breakdown that sets the stage for the whole movie. My own revelation, though, has nothing to do with sports agenting.

From the television across the other room, I can hear CNN's Lou Dobbs. I had fallen asleep earlier, and the show is now in its 4 a.m. repeat, spewing a steady stream of the phrase "illegal aliens" over and over again, and I think I hear something about the Minutemen. I imagine Lou's loyal viewers all over America sitting up watching Lou with me right now, chain-smoking cigarettes, mesmerized by the CNN anchor's rubbery bronze hair—and fulminating along with him.

I can hear a group walk past my room, breathlessly talking about Senate candidates in the upcoming congressional elections. They mention my old boss Bernie Sanders, the socialist lawmaker from Vermont who once got so invested in a legislative fight against Corporate America, he actually helped file a shareholder resolution against the biggest employer in his state.

Meanwhile, on the floor next to me is a creased, pizza-stained copy of the local paper from my hometown of Helena, Montana. The headline blares Democratic governor Brian Schweitzer's skyrocketing first-year poll numbers in a state as red as the Caesars Palace's lights out on the Strip.

I feel a rumble in my stomach and start to move toward the toilet, but lose my balance and overturn my duffel bag, only to have a stack of press releases and campaign literature from New York's Working Families Party spill out onto the floor. The giant "WFP" on the glossy page starts to spin in front of me, and my revelation is born.

It's all connected.

The demagogic Lou Dobbs and his devoted followers . . . the blog nerds outside this hotel room . . . cowboy rabble-rousing politicians . . . urban third parties . . . socialists in Congress . . . big-time lawmakers courting Internet activists . . . the Minutemen . . . shareholder activism . . .

Though I don't know exactly how it all fits together, I know it is all part of something bigger—something antithetical to my past life dealing with legislative amendments as a Capitol Hill staffer, swimming in the inbred politics of Washington and getting frustrated by the blindness of those who can't see past cable-talk-show partisanship.

An insurrection is on—a fist-pounding, primal-screaming revolt from a mob wielding protest signs, ballots, computer keyboards, shareholder proxies, and even, in some cases, guns.

It is an uprising.

Knowing I'm still drunk, I question this epiphany for a moment.

Is this uprising real? Can it succeed? Can it become a full-fledged movement?

Then I puke.

A FEW WEEKS LATER, I'm back in Las Vegas, this time to speak to the national convention of the Bakery, Confectionery, Tobacco Workers, and Grain Millers International Union. Waiting for me at the hotel is the union's president, Frank Hurt, a thickly set sixty-something West Virginian with a warm smile. He gives me a gift bag filled with Twinkies, Hostess Cup Cakes, and Bugles, and I ask, "What's this?"

"Those," he says, "are some of the products our members make."

I feel like an idiot, but Frank says with a smile, "Don't worry about it—most people forget we still make things in America."

The crowd at the convention's main event is huge—about a thousand union members, all wearing the black T-shirts event organizers had handed out. Only two things about this gathering remind me of YearlyKos: It's in Las Vegas, and a lot of fifty-somethings are here, but these fifty-somethings are not the college-educated suburbanites who do politics as a hobby. This is strictly a working-class crowd, with a lot of beer bellies, jeans, and mustaches, and they are here because it's part of their job.

Frank tells me that for many of the delegates, this union convention is their only vacation for the year. "That's why we do it in Vegas," he says. "At least it's some fun."

The speeches from various union members begin to crescendo. One union official tells the members about Congress's refusal to enforce basic workplace protection laws. A smattering of boos.

Next, a rail-thin African-American guy is talking about a labor dispute at his factory, and the angry shouts get louder.

Then a speaker talks about how people in her community heard there were going to be big layoffs because the company is talking about moving overseas. The crowd is now in a full-on froth—one very similar to the froth at YearlyKos when similar speeches about Iraq were given to the throng of middle-class computer geeks, one very similar to the froth Lou Dobbs stirs up every night when he talks about trade and immigration on CNN, one very similar to the froth I had seen Vermont congressman Bernie Sanders whip veterans into at VFW halls in Vermont.

On the plane back home to Montana, it comes to me again. This is all part of an uprising—one that shouldn't surprise anyone.

BY ALL MEASURES, those of us Americans not in the top 1 percent of income earners are under enormous economic pressure and feel totally powerless to influence the government that acts in our name. Public attitudes toward Washington are reaching record levels of animosity never before seen by the country's major polling firms. A Scripps Howard News Service poll in 2006 found "anger against the federal government is at record levels" with a majority of Americans saying they "personally are more angry" at the government than they used to be.

It's the natural reaction from a country that is watching its pocket get picked. Wages are stagnating, health-care costs are skyrocketing, pensions are being looted, personal debt climbs—all as corporate profits keep rising, politicians pass more tax breaks for the superwealthy, and CEOs pay themselves tens of millions of dollars a year.

"There's class warfare, all right," billionaire Warren Buffett recently told the *New York Times*. "It's my class, the rich class, that's making war, and we're winning."

But that may not be true for much longer.

If you took high school chemistry, you might remember that a gas is the most chaotic form of matter—the atoms are bouncing all over the place, and there's no order to it at all. But put a gas under enough pressure, and it will first liquefy into something more manageable, and then it will become an organized solid.

These laws of matter are also the laws of society. We typically exist in a gaseous state. We are all leading our own lives, bouncing around from place to place, watching our sitcoms, working at our cubicles, interacting briefly with each other between doing our own thing. But we change when enough negative economic and political pressure starts hammering down on us—we start to get organized.

The economic persecution of the Gilded Age produced the Progressive Era and the trust-busting crusades of Teddy Roosevelt. The Great Depression inspired an age of unionism and FDR's New Deal. Southern racism spurred the civil rights movement. And today's oppressive class war that Buffett describes is generating an uprising all of its own.

Whether it is shareholders running resolutions against corporate boards, third parties shattering the two-party duopoly, legislators kicking down lobbyists in state capitals, bloggers orchestrating primary challenges to entrenched lawmakers, or armed, enraged suburbanites forming vigilante bands at our southern border, this uprising is not even close to unified. It exists in a liquid phase—a mushy, amorphous state between anarchy and a solid—between chaos and organization.

We will plunge into this fluid for a year, to see what connects and separates the different parts of this uprising. We're going to (try to) find out if a real movement will emerge from the uprising, like the amoeba that once crawled out of the primordial soup.

Our submersion will be one part *Journey to the Center of the Earth,* one part *Heart of Darkness,* and more than one part *National Lampoon's Vacation* (unfortunately, sans swimming in a motel pool with a naked Christie Brinkley).

We'll walk freely into the Montana state senate and Microsoft's cafeteria, and sneak into the U.S. Senate and ExxonMobil's stockholder meeting. We'll go from CNN's air-conditioned studios in Manhattan to the dusty campsite of a quasi-military staging ground on the Mexican border. We'll check out antiwar rallies that feature Sean Penn and strategy meetings that feature an aspiring political boss in the city that brought us Tammany Hall. We'll spend a day with the American government's only self-described socialist, and then we'll spend a day with the man who many think is America's leading nationalist.

And as we traverse the country ideologically and geographically, we'll see how the disparate pieces of this uprising are all part of one enraged backlash—a backlash against the hostile takeover of our government by Big Money interests, the status quo of extreme wealth inequality, the daily reminders of rampant profiteering, and the widespread sense of political disenfranchisement.

This is a populist uprising—and that word *populist* will come up a lot during this adventure. The term is not simply defined by any given issue position. It is instead a "politics that champions issues that have a broad base of popular support but receive short shrift from the political elite," as the *Atlantic Monthly*'s Ross Douthat says. "This explains why you can have left-populists and right-populists," he adds. And it explains why today's uprising is both a left and right phenomenon.

To be sure, uprisings in American history have had only mixed success in becoming real movements. The ones forged in the superheated foundry of economic inequality and war usually get killed off—sometimes with election laws, sometimes with incarceration, and still other times with bullets.

When the Populist Party threatened to undermine the two major parties in the late 1800s, state legislatures swung into action to rig ballot statutes to impede the upstart parties' growth.

When in 1894 union leader Eugene V. Debs led a railroad worker strike against the Pullman Palace Car Company, twelve thousand federal troops were dispatched to crush the uprising and throw him in prison. Twenty-four years later, after almost a million people voted for his Socialist Party presidential candidacy, he was again thrown in prison, this time for protesting World War I.

In the mid-1930s, Louisiana governor Huey Long attacked the New Deal for being too conservative, and launched a Share Our Wealth proposal to cap millionaires' personal fortunes and redistribute the resources to the rest of society. When he started plotting to turn his crusade into a presidential campaign, he was assassinated and his agenda died with him. Thirty years later, when Martin Luther King Jr. started formulating plans for a Poor People's Campaign for economic justice, he and his fledgling initiative met the same fate.

Today's uprising faces its own form of opposition from the politicians, pundits, and business executives who make up this nation's ruling class. There may be less physical brutality, but the stridency from the Establishment is just as pronounced—and the tactics may be more effective in their sophistication.

Opinion columnists—always the Establishment's first warning system—are sounding the alarm. The *Washington Post*'s David Broder issued a breathless jeremiad warning that "a particularly virulent strain of populism has made official Washington altogether too responsive to public opinion." He is ably backed up by *New York Times* columnist David Brooks, who declares that "polarized primary voters shouldn't be allowed to define the choices in American politics" and prays that the "renegades who rail against the establishment [get] eclipsed by the canny establishmentarians."

Washington politicians and political operatives of both parties, meanwhile, have taken to issuing statements insisting that the uprising be ignored. Facing the growing antiwar ferment, Vice President Dick Cheney says the Iraq conflict "may not be popular with the public—it doesn't matter." Facing that same opposition to the war, one Democratic lawmaker tells the *Washington Post*, "I don't think we should be overreacting to public opinion polls," while another tells the *New York Times* that when facing most populist causes, Congress's goal must be to engineer a "Kabuki dance" that tricks the public.

In the suites, conference rooms, and lounges of Corporate America, businessmen frantically read Thomas Friedman's latest book for answers. They find solace in his passages yearning for a future when an elite class of "social liberals, white-collar global service industry workers and Wall Street types [will be] driven together" in a new political party whose mission is to fight against the Great Unwashed mass of blue-collar, working-class stiffs who supposedly "militate for more friction and fat everywhere."

The increasing intensity of the insults proves the hostility is motivated not merely by ideological opposition, but by the fear and paranoia that comes from those in power who see they are losing their authority. The uprising is, after all, a wildfire lit without permission from the political and financial circles that have grown used to controlling everything. It is igniting in the spirit of America's original uprising manifesto, the Declaration of Independence. That document reminds us that the rulers of this country "derive their powers from the consent of the governed"—and "it is the Right of the People to alter or to abolish" the existing order through an uprising when the elite starts wielding power exclusively for its own interests.

Appropriately, our year in the life of the uprising starts about as far away as you can get from the bright lights, caked makeup, canned rhetoric, and bad hairdos of national politics and punditry. It begins like the most truly American of legends: out on the western frontier in a setting where director John Ford would still be able to stage a John Wayne flick without worrying about an urban skyline screwing up his wide-angle camera shot. This is a region that has sparked many of history's best-known and most defiant uprisings.

Welcome, fellow traveler, to the Last Best Place.

2

THE THRILLA IN
MONTANA

I STILL HAVE TROUBLE believing I'm really here, living in Montana. I remember sitting in a downtown Washington, D.C., restaurant after work in 2000 looking down at my stupid suit and tie and my even stupider Capitol Hill badge and telling a friend I was thinking of taking a job with a Senate candidate in Montana. My buddy was indignant.

"You're crazy."

"Why?"

"Montana's really far away . . . like, isn't that near Iowa?"

"Um, I guess it depends on what your definition of 'near' is."

"Well, isn't the Unabomber from out there?"

"Yeah."

"See? You're crazy."

Since moving out to live here full-time in 2005, I've had that same interchange with almost everyone I know, though sometimes the word *crazy* is changed to *insane,* and Iowa becomes Nebraska. The back-and-forth always seems to end with the other person making me promise that I won't become the Unabomber.

The jokes reflect the fact that most people know Montana through pop culture caricatures, from Ted Kaczynski to *A River Runs Through It.*

What they don't know is that this quiet, sparsely populated state known as the Last Best Place is hosting a boxing match with national implications. Call it the Thrilla in Montana.

In one corner is the aging champion—an antitax movement that has long been winning fights in Flyover Country. In the other corner is the young challenger—the populist uprising.

How this challenger fares here in Montana against a fully matured, well-developed movement will give us clues about whether the uprising has a shot to become a national movement itself.

FROM ITS PERCH in the foothills of a quiet residential neighborhood a few blocks from downtown Helena, the Montana capitol building looks like a midsized local bank—not a ring that will host a slugfest over taxes.

To the casual onlooker, the scene in here during these first few weeks of the 2007 legislature isn't much to ogle at. The legislators passing through the beige halls seem jovial enough. But make no mistake about it: this is going to be a brawl because everyone in here hates each other . . . passionately.

Republican legislators hate the Democratic governor, who hates them back. The Democrats, who control the state senate by one vote, hate the Republicans, who control the House by one vote, and the feeling is reciprocated. The Republican House Majority Leader recently told newspapers his "job is to show no quarter to the Democrats," the Republican Speaker of the House's first pronouncement upon being elected is that "it's a war," and the Republican Senate Minority Leader was recently described as a "foaming-at-the-mouth Pomeranian" by a local political columnist. At the same time, the public has long savored a standing hatred for the legislature on principle, according to polls. And, of course, no one has to explain why they hate who they hate. Said one legislator a few weeks back, more mildly than usual: "Some folks just don't like the governor."

Welcome to Big Sky Country, where being angry is known as one of your three god-given rights.*

This is, as my friends reminded me so often, the home of one of the contemporary icons of anger, the Unabomber—and he's not as much of an exception as you might think. To extremists, he is less a villain than the inspirational hometown boy who went off and hit the big time. And here in Big Sky Country, we have all sorts of Unabomber-ish characters, from the Militia of Montana to the Freemen to Prussian Blue—a band reportedly named after the residue found in Holocaust gas chambers and founded by two angelic fourteen-year-old Olsen twin look-alikes who describe themselves on their website as "within the fold of White Nationalist Rock."

This place, in other words, is where the pissed-off come to be pissed off—and this is the sixtieth time the Pissed-Off's representatives will get together officially as a legislature to see if they can chisel all the rage into "progress."

The action starts today, a frigid early January day in a tiny cave of a room in the corner of the top floor of the Montana capitol.

All of about fifty people can fit in this converted attic, better known as the Senate Taxation Committee room. In a capitol complex that has many cavernous, ornate hearing rooms, this space is undoubtedly kept small out of the same desire for privacy and anonymity that, say, a peep show cubby is kept small at an X-rated club. Tax policy has, after all, become the hardcore pornography of politics: no matter what scene you are watching, someone is getting screwed.

This room may be far away from the adult film sets of the San Fernando Valley, but it has been the stage for some really historic lays. We're talking the political equivalent of the Pamela Anderson–Tommy Lee bootleg videotape. The most recent of these was a series of Republican-backed corporate and upper-income tax cuts that then–Senate minority leader

---

*The others being the right to ignore the speed limit and the right to enjoy using a hunting rifle to splatter an elk's brain all over the forest floor.

Steve Doherty once told me was "just another tale of piracy and unarmed robbery here in Montana."

These atrocities are responsible for the birth of a monster known throughout the Montana capitol as the Claw—a monster that is staring up at me from the flyer I was just handed. The paper shows a graph charting the share of total Montana property taxes paid since 1994. From about 1994 to 1999, the two lines on this graph—the blue one for individual homeowners, the magenta one for large corporations—stay together in the middle, creating the arm. But from 2000 to 2005—right when conservatives' huge corporate cuts hit—the lines diverge sharply, with the homeowners' share of property taxes sharply increasing, and Big Business's share dropping. The whole thing looks like a "Y" sitting on its side—or like a claw.

This is the graphical representation of a stunning feat the antitax movement has pulled off—one that should be impossible. They have sold tax cuts for huge corporations and out-of-state landowners to the miners, truckers, ranchers, and various other blue-collar voters who scratch out a living on windswept heartland tundras like Montana. And antitax activists haven't just sold these tax cuts—they have turned them into a populist, election-winning battle cry, like *Braveheart*'s William Wallace screaming "Freedom!" Only instead of getting the peasants to march into battle against the aristocracy, they have convinced them that liberation means handing the aristocracy even more treasure.

But now, out of the gate in this legislative session, Democrats are using the Claw as a weapon for their own uprising. Their William Wallace today is a barrel-chested Tommy Lasorda look-alike named Dan Harrington.

An aging Democratic state senator from Butte, Harrington, is the only member of Montana's 1972 constitutional convention still serving in the legislature.* He is introducing Democratic governor Brian Schweitzer's

---

* The idea of a "constitutional convention" happening in the 1970s—not the 1770s—always makes me laugh. Whenever I hear this convention referenced, I immediately imagine a *Saturday Night Fever* John Travolta wearing his white, bell-bottomed three-piece suit and a seventeenth-century tricornered hat, signing pieces of parchment with a quill.

new property tax plan that would provide a $400 rebate to each resident homeowner, regardless of income or home value.

The proposal aims to hammer down the top talon of the Claw—and it contrasts with the Republicans' plan to further widen the Claw by enacting another flat property tax *rate* cut that sends more of the benefits to out-of-state landowners and corporations.

That Democrats are leading with a tax bill in this legislative session shows they understand the need to face the issue head-on, but shows they also know that if they merely tried to out-Republican the Republicans by proposing even larger tax cuts, they would get outbid and then bashed for not going far enough. So, instead, they are using a $400-for-everyone proposal to try to force a confrontation—one not about *whether* to cut taxes or by how much, but about *who* should receive tax cuts.

And the message is getting through. The state's largest newspapers all previewed today's hearings with a wire story reporting that under the Democrats' bill, "Someone who paid $175,000 for a split-level in Billings or Missoula would get the same $400 check as someone who paid $1 million for a luxury house in one of the state's more exclusive valleys."

"Industrial owners of taxable land and business equipment, such as PPL Montana [the state's big energy company] would get nothing," the story pointed out.

Harrington emphasizes all of these points—and the sedated look on Republican legislators' faces tells me they know they are in trouble. They know their opponents are figuring out how to use class warfare for themselves.

The rebate's cross-demographic appeal is evidenced by the line forming out the door. Representatives from the Chamber of Commerce to the AARP, to realtors, to small businesspeople, to citizens off the street are here to testify in support of the proposal (here in Montana, anyone who wants to testify is allowed to do so). The best of these is the guy speaking right now.

Named Kirk Hammerquist, he's the closest thing to the Marlboro Man I've ever seen—and that's saying a lot, this being Montana, where a visitor from Mars might believe belt buckles, chewing tobacco packs, pickup trucks, and facial hair are prerequisites for residency. Hammerquist, who owns a construction company in Kalispell, has got the whole cowboy look going—jeans, boots, and a mustache.

"I was driving down last night on an ice skating rink," he's says, recounting his journey through the snowstorm that just hit. "And I said, 'why the heck am I doing this?'"

He then answers his question by going into campfire-story mode.

"About 1980, the timber industry was having a tough time in the Flathead, and a lumber company decided to make a statement by paying their paychecks on one Friday in $2 bills," he says. "Do you know what the cash registers looked like in the Flathead Valley for the next eighteen months? They were filled with $2 bills."

I'm starting to get a little lost until he ties it all together.

"I would like to see the same amount of $2 bills sent to absentee landowners or corporate executives in New York and see how long [those bills] would be in Flathead County—they'd never even make it here," he says, contrasting the Democrats' in-state tax cut bill with the Republicans' proposal to give tax cuts to out-of-state corporations.

The line perfectly echoes the criticism Schweitzer and the Democrats have been repeating in the local media. "I know if I get more dollars to a Montana family, they're going to spend it on Main Street," the governor told newspapers during the first week of the session. "I don't want to pick on anybody, but if you have Burlington Northern Santa Fe [Railway], if you give them another $1 million, what's the chances that that $1 million is going to end up in Havre or Livingston or Billings or Kalispell? No, you give them another million dollars, it goes right into their general fund in Fort Worth [at their Texas headquarters]."

Hammerquist continues: "Look, $400 is not a lot, but it's something . . . Talking to my work crew at lunch, asking what they would do with it, they said they'd buy a rifle, maybe buy a washing machine. The best one I probably heard was from an electrician. He said, 'I'd buy studded snow tires for my daughter so I won't worry so much when she drives home from Missoula.'"

He stops for a moment, takes a deep breath, and puts his hand to his temple.

"This state is really becoming a playground of the wealthy—we know it, we can't deny it," he says. "And don't get me wrong, I have nothing against wealthy people—I'm trying my hardest to be one. . . . But to sit there and work on a three- to five-million-dollar home for an owner that is going to be there for a couple of months in the summer . . . and to think the guy that's working with me [putting] all this pride and sweat into that house is going to get less than that person who is going to come play here for a few months—I tell ya, it made me drive all night. I speak for a lot of people, the guys that work with their hands. I had to come down and represent them."

When you shoot skeet, you experience a special feeling the instant before you pull the trigger for a good shot. You know—you just know—that the clay pigeon (or, in Dick Cheney's case, your friend's face) is toast. Kirk Hammerquist, whether he knows it or not, just blew a clay pigeon out of the sky.

Everything about his testimony was perfect. From his "keep it in Montana" nativism all the way down to his clothes and mustache, he used all the Right's populist themes for his own argument. The finish in particular was a thing of beauty. In one anecdote, this Marlboro Man lit a match off his beard and dropped it on a gasoline-soaked effigy of the rich-millionaire-out-of-stater that everyone here loves to hate.

The Republican lawmakers at the committee table sit there with the glassy-eyed look of stoners watching *Dazed and Confused* on a Sunday afternoon. They don't know what hit them.

The panel will pass the bill on a party-line vote, and the Republicans will be embarrassed when they present their counterproposal.

As the *Great Falls Tribune* reports, the GOP is "closely questioned" about "why out-of-state trophy-home owners should share in Montana's largesse" and why the superrich should get more than everyone else.

"As I understand it, the working-class folks in my district would be eligible for about $400, but the generous out-of-state folks who happen to live in my district and happen to measure their houses by acres and build

$44 million homes are going to get a much more generous deduction,"
Democratic state representative Mike Jopek is quoted as saying.

This focus on "out-of-state folks," "executives in New York," and central offices in Fort Worth that runs through the Democrats' message is no
coincidence. It is a carefully calibrated meme recognizing Montana as one
of America's boiling cauldrons of subjugation psychology—a belief that a
place is oppressed by physical and cultural occupation from outsiders. This
belief is crucial to most populist uprisings.

EVERYPLACE OUTSIDE OF America's financial centers has its own
unique strain of subjugation psychology. Being perpetually outraged at big,
powerful, distant elites is being an American in the mythic sense of the
term. It's not that individual people are necessarily nasty to visitors or
tourists or newcomers (in fact, when I moved in 2005, I found that Montanans are among the friendliest people around). It's that the mass public's
collective psyche and the unwritten rules, rituals, and buzzwords of local
political culture is all about backlash—and they reward politicians who
channel the outrage.

The formulaic construction of election candidate rhetoric these days
confirms the universality of subjugation psychology. Everyone has heard
one or another local politician say "For too long, [insert 'politicians' or 'bureaucrats' or 'elites'] in Washington, D.C., have been telling [insert state]
what to do. I promise to fight for a bill that represents [insert state] values
and [insert state] common sense."

In the Deep South, subjugation psychology persists from the Civil
War. In the Midwest, it's all about the belief that the glorious titans of
American industry and the Wise Men of Washington have deliberately left
the region to die a death by a million outsourced factory jobs.

In rural New England, subjugation psychology revolves around the idea
that the Big Boys in places like Boston and New York City don't care about
the rest of their states. This was legendarily proven back in 1998 in Vermont,
when seventy-nine-year-old farmer Fred Tuttle spent just $201 on a suc-
cessful U.S. Senate primary campaign to defeat millionaire Jack McMullen.

Tuttle won simply by pointing out that McMullen had recently moved to Vermont from Massachusetts, and by asking McMullen at a debate to pronounce the name of a Vermont town, Calais—which McMullen said was "cah-lay," but which is actually pronounced "cah-las."

From this anti-outsider subjugation psychology comes nasty euphemisms and nicknames. For instance, there's the penchant in many states for candidates to use any excuse at all to call their opponent "bigcity." If an opponent has lived in, done business in, or even visited a major metropolitan area, they can find themselves being tarred and feathered as "a big-city lawyer" or "a big-city executive"—the implication being that the opponent is a slick, urban phony invading Authentic America.

Similarly, I'm told that in the South, the worst thing you can be called in politics is a "Yankee" (though I'm not sure since I haven't spent all that much time there . . . which probably makes me a Yankee). I do know that in New England, the label "flatlander" is the choice insult for out-of-staters and condemns them to political death.

I had my own personal experience with subjugation psychology when Vermont governor Howard Dean called me a flatlander in front of a few local reporters during one of my first trips up to Vermont as the spokesman for Congressman Bernie Sanders in 1999.* Delayed by a car accident that almost totaled my Jeep, I was late to a press conference and I looked totally disheveled—sweating, unshaven, no sport jacket. Dean said something about telling the "flatlander" press secretary that even though we're in Vermont, people still try to clean themselves up before press conferences.

Everyone laughed at me, the slob who disrespected Vermont by not wearing a jacket, the idiot who thought Vermont was so uncivilized that he didn't have to look presentable.

---

*I didn't quite get how Dean could make me the butt of a joke about flatlanders, considering he grew up on New York City's Park Avenue, and thus is technically a flatlander himself. But, at least in Vermont, it seems that there is some sort of unstated statute of limitations on the flatlander label.

Me, the goddamned flatlander.

It was the same thing when I first worked in Montana in 2000. Everyone, including the candidate I was working for, called me a "city mouse."

"Write up a press release, city mouse."

"Hey, city mouse, what's on the schedule today?"

"Go fuck yourself, you city mouse."

The Rocky Mountain West has a unique—and uniquely intense—brand of subjugation psychology, brought on by its role as America's last and most exploited colony.

This is a place where brutal companies like Anaconda Copper, owned by Wall Street titans, turned Butte, Montana, into one of the nation's largest Superfund sites, first by slashing apart the landscape with copper mines, then by building smelters spewing arsenic, and finally by abandoning a giant open-pit mine that to this day leaks chemicals into the water table. It is a region where for the first half of the twentieth century, National Guard units served as private security forces for out-of-state barons, executing striking miners in epically named conflicts like the Colorado Labor Wars, fought against epically named leaders like Big Bill Haywood.

This stuff is not just ancient history, either. Consider Montana Power Company, once Big Sky Country's economic gem. Just a few years ago, the company's lobbyists convinced Republican governor Marc Racicot and the then-Republican-controlled legislature to deregulate the energy industry, helping the company liquidate its assets in pursuit of a get-rich-quick scheme pushed by the investment bank Goldman Sachs. Local electricity rates in the newly deregulated market soon went from some of the lowest in the nation to the highest. At the same time, Montana Power transformed itself into a dot-com shell called Touch America, which promptly went down the drain, along with thousands of Montanans' retirement nest eggs that had been invested in the company's stock.

The only folks who did well were the folks at Goldman Sachs in New York, and Montana Power's executives, who quietly made off with multimillion-dollar golden parachutes. Oh, and Governor Racicot. He was rewarded for his corporate fealty with a million-dollar-a-year job in

Washington helping the insurance companies pass legislation that makes sure they don't have to pay full medical benefits for miners in Racicot's hometown, Libby—miners who are afflicted with asbestos poisoning from their time digging up vermiculite.

Today's colonial rulers may have different names, but the colonialism persists. If you look at the region's macroeconomic data—with its heavy reliance on natural resource and raw agricultural exports—you may think you were looking at a ledger from the British East India Company, and the oil, gas, mining, railroad, and agribusiness magnates employ armies of lobbyists to make sure state governments continue allowing as much unbridled drilling, digging, and land raping as possible. Meanwhile, with employer intimidation and antiworker statutes having weakened the West's industrial labor movement, the anti-union class warriors who gunned down worker rebellions at the region's coal mines have now reemerged a century later in the region's Wal-Marts. The Rockefellers used militiamen and machine guns to attack working people; the Waltons use lawyers and PR firms. The tactics are more muted, but the goal is the same: maintain control over the colony.

But subjugation psychology in the Rocky Mountain West is more than just a reaction to corporate domination. The last ten years have seen a dramatic population influx—in the northern Rocky Mountain states (Montana, Idaho, and Wyoming), it's been largely coastal white-flighters, while in the southern tier (Arizona, New Mexico, Colorado, and Nevada), it's been those same groups plus Mexicans. And for a region that has been mostly white and working class for the last 150 years, the socioeconomic and ethnic population shifts have caused friction.

Among longtime residents who cling to that untouched Last Best Place spirit, the demographic changes have evoked feelings of physical invasion and resentment. Whether motivated by racism, xenophobia, or just a generalized aversion to change, more and more locals feel encroached on from above and below. They fear coastal aristocrats higher on the economic ladder turning their Main Street into a string of Starbucks and yoga studios, and they also fear that poor immigrants below them on the ladder are going to take their jobs and change local culture. They fear, in short, that their towns are becoming the new Cancuns—places that are both "a playground of the wealthy" as Hammerquist said, and also Latin American slums.

This perception is significantly enhanced by the visuals. From a Mercedes driving through downtown Jackson, Wyoming, to the new wine bar opening in Bozeman, Montana, to taco stands in Greeley, Colorado, locals feel as if the changes are being shoved in their face. Not surprisingly, despising the thought of out-of-staters, cursing at California license plates on luxury vehicles, and ranting about illegal immigrants have become both hobbies and political dialects in Middle America.

The white-flight newcomers also bring their own strain of subjugation psychology. Many of them have put down roots here specifically to escape something, whether it is traffic, liberals, Jews, crowds, black people—you name it, they're fleeing from it and feel persecuted by it. Naturally, then, many come with a libertarian conservatism, adding to the region's anti-everything-ism.

Some of that manifests itself as Republican votes in national elections. For example, George W. Bush won ninety-seven of the nation's one hundred fastest-growing counties in 2004. But at the day-to-day level, that kind of libertarian disposition can be expressed as a Not-in-My-Back-Yard pseudo-environmentalism*—not surprising, considering most newcomers are deliberately fleeing urbanity. But this only feeds the subjugation psychology, because to blue-collar workers, Not in My Back Yard can be synonymous with an assault on their oil rig, timber, quarry, coal mine, and refinery jobs.

For much of the last half century, right-wing activists have succeeded in using subjugation psychology in local politics to make state legislatures

---

*I call it *pseudo*-environmentalism because not wanting an oil well impeding your deckside mountain view doesn't necessarily mean you don't live on subdivided ranchland-turned-suburban-sprawl, and aren't more than happy to drive a nine-mile-a-gallon Hummer up to the new ski resort, which was created by massive clear-cutting.

the pay-by-the-hour motels of the American Right—the dimly lit places where conservative campaigns have been consummated in the most raw and crass ways.

Fifty years ago, conservatives waged a campaign against civil rights, flown under the banner of "states rights" and led by iconic governors like George Wallace railing on Washington for imposing new laws on the country. Next came the state-by-state legislative battle against the ratification of the federal Equal Rights Amendment—a campaign that launched the career of conservative leader Phyllis Schlafly.

More recently, it has been the antitax movement, which has found a home in a Rocky Mountain West that is already hospitable to antigovernment fervor. This place, more than anywhere else, has been the centerpiece of conservative activist Grover Norquist's famed Leave Us Alone Coalition—the term he uses to describe the alliance of antitax, anti-gun-control, antiregulation and anti-environmental groups at the state level. As the *Washington Post* reported in 1987, conservatives had made the "defanging of Big Government" the "driving force behind modern populism"—a right-wing populism trying to impede the government rather than a progressive populism trying to get the government to do more to serve society.

Though this conservative strain of populism was marketed at the national level by Ronald Reagan, the campaigns that weaponized the antitax movement were orchestrated in state legislative settings—the settings that are subject to disproportionately little press scrutiny.

Sometimes the movement promoted racially charged television commercials depicting an imposing government grabbing cash out of your wallet and handing it over to urban "welfare queens." Sometimes it ran so-called Right to Work or tort reform initiatives that demonized union leaders and trial attorneys as driving up business costs and, thus, taxes. Other times the movement authored ballot initiatives euphemistically called Taxpayer Bills of Rights, designed to regressively slash income tax rates for the rich and cut social services for the poor.

All of the narratives propelling the antitax movement cogently explained the quickly destabilizing economy of the "greed is good" 1980s and

the go-go 1990s. Longtime natives were upset that new people were starting to crowd their towns, influence local culture, and drive up the cost of
living. And so the movement gave them latte-drinking yuppies and limou-
sine liberals to blame for raising taxes. Blue-collar types were getting frustrated with economic hardship after losing their natural resource jobs or
seeing their wages decline. And so the movement diverted potential anger
against unfair foreign competition into rage at unions and trial lawyers who
were supposedly driving up business costs and taxes. And/for the white-
flight newcomers? The movement attracted their affection by getting the
government "off their back" in the form of tax "relief," and then appealed to
their revenge instincts by paying for those new tax breaks with social
spending cuts—thus punishing the minorities and the poor that the newcomers were angrily fleeing from. Other parts of the Leave Us Alone Coalition latched onto subjugation psychology in their own ways as well, from
National Rifle Association television ads attacking gun control as an East
Coast scheme to spotted owl–type campaigns tarring and feathering state
environmental laws as job-killing bastard children of tree-hugging hippies.
Montana's recent history shows how successful all this has been.

Once represented in Congress by progressive Democrats like Representative Pat Williams and Senator Mike Mansfield, by 1988, Big Sky
Country had elected its first Republican U.S. senator in modern history—a
come-from-nowhere auctioneer named Conrad Burns, who toppled two-
term incumbent senator John Melcher (D) by portraying him as "a liberal
who is soft on drugs, soft on defense and very high on social programs"—
and, of course, a tax raiser. The race ended with Reagan himself dropping a
bunker-buster bomb on Melcher's campaign, vetoing the incumbent's
wilderness protection bill deliberately to enflame "divides [in] Montana between the conservationists and timber, mining and energy industries," according to the Associated Press.

Six years later, when the smoke cleared from the 1994 national GOP
revolution, Republicans had gained control of the state legislature and the
governor's office. By 1996, Williams was replaced by a right-wing Republican. And four years after that, the Claw first appeared, as big corporations'

share of property taxes plummeted and Montana homeowners' share spiked.

Conservatives had become Montana's political Establishment and the antitax zealotry the state's dominant political ideology, mirroring the similar takeovers throughout the West.

THEN CAME THE phenomenon known as Brian Schweitzer—the barrel of a man whom I'm sharing a drink with right now.

"We've really got them jammed, don't we?" he says, with a self-satisfied smile.

The Montana governor's residence looks like the Brady Bunch's house—sprawling, with a dark-shingled triangular roof. It does not evoke that feeling of history and tradition that a marble-columned governor's mansion in another state might. But still, every time I walk in here, I marvel. Not at the house, but at the occupant, and how he arrived here.

When I first encountered Schweitzer in 1999, Rocky Mountain Republicans were at their zenith. Back then, he was just a fast-talking rancher who had never run for office before. Pugnacious to a fault and able to find humor in almost anything, Schweitzer saw a run for federal office as yet another exciting mountain to climb in the adventure that the *Missoula Independent* has affectionately called "The Life of Brian." Only Schweitzer's ascent to uprising leader hasn't been some Monty Python parody. He is a man who, by his midforties, had developed irrigation projects in Libya, run a dairy farm in Saudi Arabia, conducted ranching business in Argentina, and built a successful mint farm from scratch in northwest Montana. To him, mounting a serious Democratic campaign against a Republican U.S. senator in a Republican state would be another fun challenge.

The year Schweitzer was kicking off his Senate run, my boss at the time, then-congressman Bernie Sanders of Vermont, was leading bus trips to Canada to help seniors buy lower-priced prescription drugs and highlight how the pharmaceutical industry rips off American consumers by charging grossly higher prices on this side of the border. Schweitzer, whom I had met in passing during one of his trips to D.C. to promote his candidacy, soon got in touch with me to tell me he, too, had been thinking of organizing similar trips. By mid-2000, the Canadian bus voyages were the hallmark of his campaign, and by the fall, when I came out to work for him full-time, he was gaining real ground on Burns. He ultimately lost by less than four percentage points.

For most of that first race, political insiders and donors thought Schweitzer was crazy, primarily because, other than Minnesota's Paul Wellstone, no one could remember a non-millionaire, first-time political candidate being elected to the U.S. Senate. His telephone fund-raising calls, which I could hear one side of through the campaign office walls—they were painful.

"I'm running for the Senate in Montana . . . Sh-wight-zer, not Sheister . . . yes, Senate . . . no, not state senate, U.S. Senate . . . right, in Montana . . . yes, you heard that correctly, as a Democrat . . . Hello? . . . Hello? . . . Aw, shit, he hung up."

Still, many people thought he was crazy not just because of the long odds he faced, but because, well, he is crazy.

When you meet Schweitzer, you may think he has attention deficit disorder or is on speed, or both. In one moment, he's beaming like a kid with a new toy, pulling out a vial of biodiesel fuel and using his agronomy background to lecture you about how to solve America's energy problems. In another moment, he'll invite you to come shoot skeet with him—then he'll tell you about his science-fiction-sounding plans to make Butte the first geothermally powered city. And a minute later, his expression will darken, and he'll lean his moonface in toward you and scold you for suggesting he make a short-term political move that he's already plotted a nineteen-step strategy for. "Listen very fucking closely and get your fucking head in the game," he'll snarl before explaining how he's already figured out how to "jam those bastards" ("those bastards" being Republicans, lobbyists, or whoever else is the target of the day).

Working on his original longshot 2000 Senate campaign, I saw a candidate that fully understands subjugation psychology, how conservatives have used that psychology in the West, and how to use it for himself and the populist uprising he now leads.

His 2000 Senate run, for example, was not shrouded in standard Democratic Party talking points about expanding social spending programs—talking points that would have sailed straight into the conservatives' antitax and anti–Big Government buzz saw. Instead, his bus trips and campaign commercials channeled the public's anger at high drug prices into anger at the pharmaceutical industry and an incumbent who took tens of thousands of dollars from that industry. His 2004 gubernatorial campaign against Republican Secretary of State Bob Brown wasn't the bloodless legal brief about management and competence that so many Democratic campaigns have become. It was the go-for-the-jugular attack on how lobbyists had used the Republican Party as a vehicle to perform a corporate takeover of state government—and it worked. Schweitzer was the first Democrat to win a Montana gubernatorial election in sixteen years, and his win came on an election night that saw Democrats get wiped out all over the country. Today Montana Democrats control not only the governor's office, but both U.S. Senate seats, the state senate, and four out of five statewide constitutional offices.

Within weeks of Schweitzer's inauguration in 2005, Republicans vowed to "engage in a crusade to politically destroy him," as the *Missoula Independent* reported. The new governor responded by lashing his name to a legislative agenda headlined by bills to raise the amount of tax write-offs small businesses could take and to prevent legislators from immediately becoming lobbyists. He also championed a bill forcing the state's price-gouging electric utility to buy a certain percentage of its energy from renewable sources—a policy that both was pro-environment and created a guaranteed market for his state's farmers and wind energy producers. Topping it off, he made headlines kicking one of the world's largest railroad companies, Burlington Northern Santa Fe, square in the teeth, telling company executives that unless they immediately cleaned up the environmental mess they had made in the town of Livingston, the state would clean it up and bill them for the work. Montanans loved it, and polls showed that he was one of the country's most popular governors.

The national political pundits who fawned over Schweitzer attributed his success to his sharp tongue, bolo ties, cowboy boots, and eye for good political spectacles—the latter of which is impressive, whether it was his bus trips to Canada, his press conference taking a shot of whiskey to celebrate the state's most famous bar, or his legendary stunt dumping a suitcase full of campaign cash on the capitol floor.

But Schweitzer's flair is the magician's diversion—the pyrotechnics in the right hand that grab the audience's attention for the split second that's needed to really pull off the trick with the left. His true talent is neither the showmanship nor the Buffalo Bill apparel, but the ability to steal the populist mantle from conservatives and position himself as the leader of a new uprising. His tax proposal in that first legislature played to subjugation psychology's "get off my back" instincts, and, because he made sure to use his bully pulpit to call himself a tax cutter at every turn, it helped him avoid being caught in the conservatives' old antitax thicket. Likewise, his challenges to the big out-of-state corporations at the heart of key problems like high energy prices, declining family farm incomes, and environmental degradation created targets for popular blame.

Now Schweitzer and his Democratic allies in the legislature are trying to expand their success with the tax rebate plan that Schweitzer has been crafting for most of the fall.

"This is Huey Long kind of stuff," he says, taking a sip of whiskey. He tells me he's been reading a biography of that famed Louisiana governor who became a national folk hero for campaigning on a radical Share Our Wealth platform.

Schweitzer doesn't have conversations like most people. He alternates between telling you stories and simply declaring things. He rarely asks questions, and even more rarely asks for advice, but not because he doesn't want it or take it. He just gets input by reading your reactions, not by asking for them. If he wants to know your thoughts on an issue, he'll give you his, and then see how you respond. His whole affect is goal oriented—the reason he talks is to get information. Sometimes he wants to see your reaction to a story he's telling; other times, such as right now, he wants the most minute political gossip.

Chatting in the living room of the governor's residence, I can tell he is looking for scuttlebutt on the legislature. I let him know I've been hearing criticism of him from some lawmakers on the left. Democrats who are rightly worried about Republicans' previous cuts to health care and education programs in the name of tax cuts, have been raising important questions about why *their* governor is spending any money at all on more tax cuts.

Schweitzer wants the names of the people who have been whispering. I refuse. He gets annoyed.

"They have to know we need to own taxes if we are going to do all that other stuff," he says. "As long as we don't raise taxes and cut some taxes, we'll be able to do most of what we want to do."

It's certainly true that, at one level, the antitax movement is still winning, since the legislature remains locked in a debate over what *kinds* of tax cuts to provide, rather than whether to cut taxes at all.

But Schweitzer's strategy is a page from the playbook of Saul Alinsky, the radical twentieth-century organizer and modern-day Machiavelli, who was one of history's great uprising architects. Alinsky believed that to be successful, political actors must "start from where the world is, as it is, not as [they] would like it to be." Schweitzer's comment about taxes is made in the spirit of Alinsky's remark. It is an acknowledgment of the specific political landscape in front of him—one scorched from years of antitax crusades.

All of Schweitzer's other proposals—to better fund education, expand health care, and increase investment in renewable energy—will rely on Democrats' using the tax issue to wedge apart the conservatives' antitax movement, which up until now has unified all the different wings of the Republican Party, from the libertarians, to the militiamen, to the country-clubbers.

"Fifteen percent of the Republican legislators are in the red zone, the insane right-wing zone, but the other 75 percent are just regular Republicans," one lawmaker told me before I walked over from the capitol to the governor's residence. "What holds all of them together is a collective hatred of taxation. They've used tax cuts to kill us over the years. But if we get smart and don't allow Republicans to unify around that, they have nothing."

That is exactly what Schweitzer and the uprising are banking on.

A FEW WEEKS after the first clash between the antitax movement and the populist uprising in that tiny attic in the capitol, a Democratic lawmaker invites me along with him on a legislator bus trip sixty miles down the road to the Butte Convention Center, where the Continental Basketball Association is having its annual all-star game. Montana doesn't get many professional sports events, so the Convention Center is bustling—but this is still a Butte affair. A full bar is serving liquor right next to the court, and the mascot of the town's CBA team, the Daredevils, is a guy dressed in a white, star-spangled, full-body Evel Knievel outfit—a tribute to the motorcycle stuntman and Butte native.

Within a few minutes of the game's tip-off, I find myself talking to a short, tubby, thousand-year-old sea dog whose thick white mustache and Coke-bottle spectacles could land him a role as a stunt double for Wilford Brimley. His name is Red—rather appropriate, not because he has red hair (he doesn't), but because old dudes like him always seem to have a spunky name like Sonny or Pop or Doc or, well, Red.*

For thirty years, Red was a legislator from Anaconda—a town just a few miles west of here named after the copper company whose smelter was there. Now, since term limits started in 2000, Red has retired from legislating and is one of the few paid staff members for the House Democrats.

Red is full of the kinds of quips you would expect from any crusty-looking senior who looks like a star from *Cocoon*. "The more these executives and lawyers make," he tells me, in a typical growl between beers, "the stupider they seem to be." (Amen, Red).

---

* Random, slightly related question: Do folks get names like this right when they are born, or do they only get them when they become old?

The game grinds on, and I drift between paying attention to the fairly awful basketball down on the court and paying attention to Red, until he says something that I just can't get out of my head.

"You know," he says wistfully, "there aren't any more really big players on our side."

"What do you mean?"

Oh, sure, he agrees we got Schweitzer.

"But now," he says with a sigh, "it's the right-wing crazies who have all the juice."

His comment lingers in my mind for the rest of the night, and back in Helena the next morning I decide to go up to the capitol to see if Red is right. I want to corner a rank-and-file Republican legislator and see if the GOP has any strategy—or "juice"—at all. I think Schweitzer and the Democratic legislators do—but it's not clear the GOP does. Though they are using their one-vote House majority to stymie the Democrats' tax offensive, their own proposals to hand over new tax cuts to big corporations aren't gaining any public traction.

"They don't care about public traction," my friend and former state senate leader Steve Doherty tells me over the phone when I mention to him what I'm looking to find out. "They don't care because they are the mob."

"What are you talking about?" I ask. "They're still politicians. They have to care at some level."

"No they don't. The mob thinks it doesn't have to care. That's why it's called the mob."

He's referring, of course, to the four Republican lawmakers that lead the House. Folks have taken to calling them "the mob," though for full disclosure: I'm uncomfortable with this nickname because it is an insult to organized crime. Nothing that goes on in the circus that is the Montana legislature is organized, even if some of it is criminal.

Two of the mob leaders, House Speaker Scott Sales and Constitution Party Rep. Rick Jore, are committed members of the antitax movement. These are the guys Red was referring to when he told me about "the right-wing crazies."

For the last few years, Sales was a nobody backbencher so invisible that he was labeled "a political unknown" by the Associated Press. What little notoriety he had came from bills like the one he authored in 2003 to remove provisions in state law that make Ku Klux Klan cross burning a hate crime. Though he had never even headed a legislative committee, he was nonetheless elected the head of his party in 2007 largely on a promise to be better than his predecessors at crushing dissent from moderate Republicans.

Beady-eyed with a tall wave of thinning black hair, Sales would be a good fit for a bad guy in a Coen brothers movie, except that to beef up his authenticity, the Coens would have to tone down Sales's comedy-show clothes. The forty-seven-year-old Republican regularly struts around the capitol wearing an elaborate Howdy Doody costume, complete with tassles and supershiny boots—ostentatious garb that advertises to everyone that he's not actually a real rancher, but instead a semiretired computer-salesman-turned-gentleman-farmer who has only lived in Montana for sixteen years and thinks he's a cowboy because he owns a hobby ranch in the Bozeman suburbs.

One of Sales's first acts was appointing Jore, his ideological soul mate, to the chairmanship of the House Education Committee, despite (or probably because of) Jore's absolute opposition to all public education (no joke). And if you think that's extreme, that's about as moderate as Jore gets.

The first third-party legislator elected to the Montana legislature in almost eighty years, Jore proudly says his beliefs are a form of "fundamentalism." He represents the Constitution Party—an organization that is about as close as there is to an official political wing of the militia movement. The nonpartisan Montana Human Rights Network reports that one of the founders of this party was also one of the founders of Project 7—a group whose leaders were convicted a few years ago for "amass[ing] stockpiles of ammunition, weapons and survival gear in a plot to assassinate officials and foment an anti-government revolution," according to Reuters. Jore has called government workers "tyrants" and has said that America is being overtaken by "liberal socialists [who] have forfeited liberty and justice." Incongruously, he is pudgy, soft spoken, and friendly. If he were an actor, he'd be John Candy—only he wouldn't do teenage comedies—he'd more likely star in films about overthrowing the U.S. government.

"The mob" is rounded out by House Majority Leader Michael Lange and Appropriations Chairman John Sinrud—two balding thugs who could be the "before" models for Hair Club for Men commercials. They are the goons who enforce the conservative lunacy of Sales and Jore. Both equally greasy, stocky, loud, and mean spirited, they are for whatever Democrats are against, and against whatever Democrats are for, willing to be on any side of an issue if it means sticking it to their enemies.

In the face of the Democrats' tax offensive, the mob has lately been retreating to "Big Government" attacks on spending by unilaterally scrapping Schweitzer's entire budget and proposing massive spending cuts. That includes a new initiative to slash the budget of the Department of Public Health and Human Services (read: programs for poor people) from $3 billion to $300—yes, $300.

Republicans seem to be taking the budget hostage with the explicit goal of using it as a bargaining chip to get Democrats to agree to pass their tax proposal, which converts the $400-for-everyone rebate into an across-the-board rate cut—one that gives energy company PP&L Montana $1.5 million, Burlington Northern Santa Fe Railway $1.2 million, and Exxon-Mobil $300,000.

Incredibly—or predictably—they are also digging in to oppose a bill by Senator Jim Elliott (D) that "targets out-of-state residents who have income-tax debts and won't pay them, out-of-staters who get mineral royalty income in Montana, out-of-state companies that welch on their state bed tax or telecommunication taxes, and taxpayers who may be using an obscure trust mechanism to hide income from taxation," according to the *Helena Independent Record*. Put into plain language, Elliott's bill cracks down on tax cheating.

It is a complicated piece of legislation, so when I see Elliott coming out of a committee room, I grab him and ask to speak with him about it. He hustles me into his windowless office on the fourth floor of the capitol.

The place is a mess. Stacks of papers, three-ring binders, magazines, charts, and newsletters are strewn everywhere. Three of the four walls are covered in old news scraps and Xeroxes of well-worn motivational quotes. The other wall, right next to his desk in the corner, is covered by a big magnetic dry erase board that he has made into a legislative tracking chart. Movable patches have bill numbers on them, and along the top, columns designate where the bill is (House, Senate, committee, etc.).

Elliott is a Democrat who represents a Republican-leaning district in Sanders County, which sits along the Montana-Idaho border. Slightly cross-eyed and wearing a hearing aid, he has a grandfatherly way about him in that he is affable and crotchety at the same time. He seems more fit for reading a child a bedtime story than for dueling with oil, gas, and timber lobbyists who despise his tax enforcement bill. But he is a man possessed.

He starts handing me reams of paper about his bill. One of the most telling is a report showing that state auditors in 2005 found that the gap between taxes owed and taxes paid in Montana is somewhere between $178 million and $240 million a year—a 22 percent noncompliance rate. In all, a quarter of the state's economy could be totally "off the books," Elliott says.

As the chairman of the Senate Taxation Committee, he is the lead sherpa for the property tax rebate bill, but I can tell this tax cheat bill is his passion. I can also tell that he intimately appreciates the politics of the populist uprising he is a part of. He gets that the goal is to force the antitax movement to defend tax cheating and regressive tax cuts, and he realizes that, to achieve that goal, he has to avoid the "tax raiser" label. This is why he proposes to take revenues recovered by his tax cheat bill and plow them into new tax cuts for in-state small businesses. Brilliant.

Loaded down with papers from my quick visit with Elliott, I am back in the hall resuming my hunt for a rank-and-file Republican. It is midday, and most of the committee hearings are just letting out for lunch, so in the now-crowded hallway, I have my pick. I introduce myself to a tall, older guy who is wearing a legislator name tag that says Verdell Jackson.

"What is going on with Republicans on taxes?" I ask Jackson. "What's the strategy?"

"Tax reform is one of the main reasons I ran for office," he tells me. "We have to have tax reform, but we have to treat everyone fairly when we do it."

Jackson is tall, has a slight southern accent, and his denim-looking sport jacket is '70s style, but not in an intentionally cool way—in a haven't-bought-clothes-for-thirty-years way. He's a rank-and-file conservative legislator from up in Flathead County—the place that is home to Montana's famous militia movement.

"I absolutely think out-of-state folks and corporations have too much power over our state," he continues. "I also think we need to make sure to keep people from being taxed out of their homes."

I tell him I assume that his other Republican colleagues feel the same way, and he nods in agreement. So are those same Republicans going to buck their leadership and support the Democrats' legislation to pursue out-of-state tax cheats, and the bill to target most tax cuts to in-state homeowners?

Of course not, he tells me.

"That's just an unfair way of doing things," he says flatly.

As far as I can tell, Red is wrong. Republicans don't have a strategy and they don't have any juice . . . at least not yet.

THERE'S A SCHOOL of thought among basketball spectators that says the only important action in a game is in the last five minutes. The same school of thought exists among spectators of state legislatures (granted, a smaller crowd than basketball fans). In, say, a ninety-day legislative session, these observers believe the only real action comes in the last five days.

As something of a traditionalist, I used to believe in the importance of a basketball game's first three and a half quarters, as well as in the significance of a legislature's early activities. But at my ripe old age of thirty-one, I have seen the light. I've watched the Philadelphia 76ers master the art of throwing away big leads in the waning minutes of playoff games, just as I am watching the Montana legislature throw away all of its work over the past three months in an attempt to broker a last-minute tax deal here in the final four days.

As I predicted from the beginning, the whole session is boiling down to a blood feud over taxes. Everything the Republicans have pulled up until now—the move to stall the budget, the proposal to cut state health and social service spending to $300, the House majority leader's recent televised tirade calling Schweitzer a "son of a bitch" who can "stick it up his ass"—all of this theater of the absurd has been aimed at manufacturing a crisis that results in both regressive tax cuts for the wealthy and the death of the bill to crack down on out-of-state tax cheats.

Oh sure, there's been a lot of arguing about education funding levels, and how much of Montana's $1 billion surplus to spend on social programs, but that's all part of the hostage-taking brinkmanship over taxes—the issue that defines this clash.

The mob, backed by every lobbyist in the capitol, has already stomped out a bill that would have forced companies to disclose some of their tax records. Speaker Sales has now gone on to the bigger battle, telling reporters "it's obscene and immoral" that Democrats won't back off their property tax rebate and their proposal to stop tax cheating. Now he is threatening a Newt Gingrich–style government shutdown to get his way.

Specifically, the *Billings Gazette* reports that in these waning hours of the ninety-day regular session, Sales "has refused to schedule key spending and tax bills for a vote in the House" until Democrats "commit to using about $300 million of the surplus" to convert the $400 rebate plan into the GOP's massive tax rate cut aimed at out-of-state corporations and wealthy landowners.

"Their message is the same everywhere—it's all about cutting taxes," says my buddy, Representative Mike Jopek. "It's the one thing that keeps them all together—and it's the one thing still keeping them together here."

In the sunlight out on the capitol lawn, Jopek looks more haggard than usual, and that says a lot for a guy who naturally looks like Al Bundy from *Married with Children*. After three and a half months of the session, and countless four-hour drives back and forth to his farm in Whitefish, he's exhausted, like everyone else in this building.

"They are brainwashed," says Dave McAlpin, the Missoula Democratic legislator, as he walks up to us. "The corporate guys have told the Republicans that killing the [tax cheat] bill is the only thing they care about."

Back up in the tiny House leadership office, I ask McAlpin what the endgame is, because it sure as hell looks like Sales is ready to drive over the cliff. Republicans control the House, and their leaders have been enjoying their role as stonewallers of almost everything Schweitzer and the Democratic Senate have sent them. What once seemed like a worn-out antitax movement that would completely collapse in the face of Democrats' populist uprising now looks as if it is instead making a last valiant stand like a football team's defense on their own goal line. Maybe Red was right, I think. Now that the final days are coming down to taxes—the one issue all Republicans seem to agree on—it's hard for me to see how it all gets resolved.

McAlpin walks out in the hall and brings in a tall guy with a bushy white beard, tinted glasses, and a peace symbol pinned to the lapel of his grayish blue wool sportcoat. For a moment, I think he's resurrected Hunter S. Thompson (he did hang out a lot in Montana, after all). But no, this is McAlpin's fellow Missoula legislator Ron Erickson—and I'm told he's one of the few people who can follow what the hell is going on.

I ask him about Senate Bill 220—Senator Jim Elliott's bill to crack down on tax cheats. Nope, he tells me, it's not the tax cheat bill anymore. That's become energy tax credits. Well, what about the Democrats' property tax rebate? Is that still 405? Nope, that's changed, too—it's in a different bill. After another ten bill numbers, my eyes start to glaze over. All the bills are changing around with no semblance of rhyme or reason.

I can't believe they actually make laws this way.

Totally confused, I go back and track down Jopek. I ask him what he thinks is going on, and he has about as much of a clue about the specifics as me. But he does predict the antitax movement is going to fold.

"You just wait," he says with a laugh. "Sales and Lange and Sinrud are having a great time now in front of the cameras, but you just wait."

Wait for what? They are getting so much attention digging in here, why is the mob going to back down?

"They aren't," he says. "But about twenty of their members are. Remember, this is a part-time legislature. We're going to hit Thursday [one day before the ninety-day session is supposed to end], and about twenty of them are going to say fuck it, we want to go home, and they are going to cut a deal with us."

This is how "lawmaking" works in every divided state legislature. Everyone grandstands, until one side figures out how to cause a mutiny on the other side—a mutiny that provides enough votes for one side to win so they can all go home. The fact that Democrats here have been able to stop the antitax movement by halting the Republicans' regressive tax cuts and playing their own tax game all the way up to the edge—well, it's significant. They've created the clash between old movement and new uprising they set out to generate, and Schweitzer told me yesterday that the polling numbers he's seen on the tax enforcement stuff in particular is "off the charts."

"People are getting our message," he said confidently. "They get that if we let the out-of-staters and the rich guys off, then that means taxes here go up."

We'll see if his optimism pans out.

THIS IS DAY 90 of the legislature—the last day. From the looks of this hearing that mob leader Rep. Sinrud is holding, the hostage taking might be over. It looks like the Republican-controlled House is finally offering up the governor's original budget—tax rebates and all—for a vote. Maybe Jopek was right—maybe the few remaining moderates in the Republican Party had finally told the mob to cut a deal so everyone can go home.

Such wishful thinking . . .

Following Sinrud's saccharine opening statement, Republican Representative Janna Taylor offers an amendment to slash about a quarter of the entire budget of the Montana Department of Revenue so as to hobble the state government's ability to collect taxes. The Republicans may be panicking that they are going to take the blame for forcing a government shutdown, but in their panic, they aren't about to abandon the antitax movement.

When Taylor's screechy voice finally stops, Democratic Representative Eve Franklin of Great Falls starts a fit of parliamentary inquiries. Knowing her, I get the inkling that this is a ploy to stall for time, especially because Sinrud is turning red and starting to fidget. Franklin soon asks for a recess from the committee, which Sinrud grudgingly grants "for three minutes."

Out in the hall, I see my own local Democratic representative, Jill Cohenour.

"Go up to the Senate right now," she whispers. "They are about to adjourn for good."

She says it in a way that suggests it's really big news, but I don't understand why. Rolling her eyes like someone having to explain the punch line of a joke, she says, "Because if they go out, the House Republicans will have to pass our tax bills the Senate has already sent over."

So the battle of uprisings has come down to this: the Democratic-controlled Senate, which weeks ago passed the $400 tax rebate and the tax cheat bill on party-line votes, is going to try to leave its completed work in the lap of the House Republican leadership, which has been stalling everything, thinking that Democrats would cave on the last day to avoid a government shutdown.

The key, then, is for the Democratic Senate to adjourn before Sinrud can reshape Schweitzer's budget bill to eliminate the tax enforcement and rebate provisions, add in the Republicans' regressive corporate tax cuts, ram it through the Republican House, and drop it on the Senate. Democrats want House Republicans to be the ones who have to choose whether to pass the Democratic Senate's bills—tax cheat and tax rebate provisions included—or humiliate themselves by rejecting those bills and forcing a special legislative session to avoid a government shutdown.

It's a race for time.

"Special session," I know, doesn't sound so bad. It may even sound kind of good because, hell, who doesn't like "special" things? But it is an abomination that the public hates. The legislature had ninety days to complete its work, just like every legislature in the past. "Special" sessions have been reserved for unexpected emergencies, not tax fights, and this may be the first time anyone can remember that a special legislative session will need to be called to deal with what is regular, biannual business.

I head upstairs to the Democrats' office just off the Senate floor and go into the back—what they call the "war room."

About fifteen House legislators are glued to two closed-circuit TV sets pushed up right next to each other. The screen on the right shows the Senate floor proceedings; the one on the left is the House Appropriations Committee, where I just came from.

The sound is up on the Senate proceedings, and we can hear Democratic Senate President Mike Cooney doing what sounds like an impression of an auctioneer on a heavy dose of speed. He's whipping through bill after bill, calling for votes. Every thirty seconds a bell goes off to indicate the current vote is finished and the next vote is up.

"Come on, calm down, Cooney," McAlpin says to the television. "You're gonna give it away."

"It" is the element of surprise. Republicans haven't figured out that this race is going on.

I'm stunned that it has come down to this comical game show, with one chamber racing to adjourn before the other chamber passes a bill. But when I take a moment to think about it, I'm really not that surprised. When movements and uprisings clash, brinksmanship inevitably gets involved, even "last one out is a rotten egg" brinksmanship like this.

"Oh shit, what's going on?" McAlpin asks, telling an aide to turn up the volume on the screen televising the Appropriations Committee.

It looks like people are filing out of the room, meaning they may have passed the Republicans' bill. But an instant later, the screen says the committee is just in another short recess.

More legislators are now piling into the war room. It feels like we're watching a sporting event, though spectators at a sports bar know more about what they are viewing than some of these legislators. For instance, a guy with a wild bush of brown hair sitting next to me nudges my arm and asks, "So what's going on here? What's this all about?" Before I can say, "Who are you?" I look down at his chest and see a badge identifying him as a legislator from Livingston. Ah, the joys of a part-time citizens' legislature.

Finally, the screen on the right shows the Senate floor being turned over to Senator Dan Harrington—the Tommy Lasorda twin who originally carried the $400 rebate in those first few weeks of this session.

"Mr. President," he says, slowly rising.

Then, with a dramatic accent on the last word, he says, "I offer a motion to sine die!"—the magic legislative words that in plain English translate into "Shut this goddamned place down for good, mofos!"

Before the last syllable comes out of Harrington's mouth, Cooney leans eagerly into the microphone and says, "Record the vote!" And with that the Senate adjourns, and folks start high-fiving in the war room.

Within thirty seconds, the left screen shows the Appropriations Committee room clearing out as word spreads through the capitol that Democrats have now forced the House Republicans to decide: pass the Democrats' budget, tax rebate, and tax cheat bill that the Senate has already passed, or drive over the cliff with the antitax movement into a special session and toward a government shutdown.

They choose the antitax movement, and the cliff.

THE ROCKY MOUNTAIN region has a history of famous last stands that end badly. The most recent of these came a few years back, when Randall Weaver's family was gunned down by federal agents in Idaho at Ruby Ridge.

That confrontation was preceded by history's most famous last stand of all—the one that took place 131 years ago when a young lieutenant colonel was hacked apart by the Sioux Indians at Montana's Little Bighorn River in a scuffle known today as Custer's Last Stand. They're actually planning to reenact Custer's Last Stand down in Hardin, Montana, in a few weeks. I'm told it's a great event for history buffs, though someone should tell participants that if they want to see a real-life last stand, they should come on up to Helena first.

Jopek's prediction about moderate Republicans peeling off from the antitax movement was wrong. The regular legislative session ended when

House Republicans adjourned without passing the budget. Schweitzer allowed a weeklong break and then called the $39,000-a-day special session necessary to hash out this standoff and avoid a government shutdown.

The special session has picked up where the regular session left off. Only this time, Republicans have lost the will to oppose the $400-per-household rebate. Schweitzer spent the time between the regular session and the special session barnstorming the state bludgeoning Republicans for refusing to go along with his "proposals to cut more taxes for more regular Montanans than we've seen in this state's history," as he said over and over and over again.

The stalemate has narrowed now. "The biggest sticking point in the tax cut bill for many Republicans is provisions aimed at increasing tax collections from nonresidents and corporations," the Associated Press wrote in its story previewing the special session.

"I'm not raising taxes on someone to cut taxes for someone else," Speaker Sales told the AP. The line was a variation of conservatives' now-standard TV commercial attacks that conflate a vote against a proposed tax cut as a tax increase. Only Sales's version is even more extreme. He is saying that merely collecting taxes already owed is raising taxes.

I still can't figure out the Republicans' strategy here. Out of all the issues still in flux—education, social services, prisons—why would the GOP decide to make its last stand a fight to stop a bill allowing Montana to collect taxes owed by nonresidents in order to pay for new tax cuts for local small businesses?

My naïve question is answered when I walk into the hearing room and see more lobbyists here than I even knew worked in the entire state of Montana, much less west of the Mississippi. Strip away all the rhetoric and the posturing as the pressure of a special session does, and you see that the antitax movement is all about shoveling cash to Big Money interests. And Republicans are going to the wall for those interests.

At this hearing to yet again debate the tax enforcement legislation, so many paid shills are whispering in lawmakers' ears, so many notes are being passed, so many executives are lining up to testify at this hearing that I start to lose track of who is supposed to be making the laws and who is supposed to be lobbying for them. It is a tediously orchestrated assault led by none other than Plum Creek Timber, one of the world's largest lumber companies.

Plum Creek executives are at this hearing because the company wants to make sure it is allowed to continue paying almost no corporate taxes in Montana even though it owns a Rhode Island–sized 2,000-square-mile plot of land originally given to it by the government and currently serviced by Montana taxpayers through firefighter and road construction teams. How the company achieved this enviable position is, as Steve Doherty might say, yet "another tale of piracy and unarmed robbery here in Montana"— another tale casting Montana in the role of colony.

Back in the 1860s, the federal government handed over 40 million acres of so-called land grants to railroad companies like Burlington Northern as incentives for them to build cross-continental railways. When Burlington Northern ended up not needing nearly that much land, it didn't just give the acreage back to the public—that would have been too honest. Instead, it kept the land, and bought mills to spin off a new timber business. One became Plum Creek.

But the greed didn't stop there. Seven years ago, Plum Creek used a provision in Montana tax law to declare itself a Real Estate Investment Trust (REIT), which allowed it to siphon most of its formerly taxable income into tax-free dividends for its primarily out-of-state owners. The loophole helps the company pilfer millions of dollars a year from Montana taxpayers, and it is one of the loopholes that Elliott's bill would close.

This is why Plum Creek's vice president Henry Ricklefs is one of the first to speak at today's hearing. He looks like he came right off the golf course at the country club, and his remarks are as sharp as his dress. In this, the final round of the Thrilla in Montana, he lands a barrage of punches, using all the bob-and-weave tactics the antitax movement has relied on since its inception. If I were at a Washington, D.C., seminar run by antitax leader Grover Norquist himself, the lines wouldn't have been any different.

Ricklefs starts out as the Whiner, calling the tax cheat bill a Big Government "assault on Plum Creek," in an attempt to channel subjugation psychology for his own objectives. We should all be outraged that Big Government is threatening to persecute this supposedly poor, honest little company . . .

He then becomes the Enforcer, reminding lawmakers of the company's size and power—the unspoken message being that whoever votes for this bill will be severely punished with campaign donations to their opponents. This muscle flexing started earlier this week when the company ran statewide newspaper ads against the tax proposal.

After that, it's the "double tax" diversion. Ricklefs asserts that, like other businesses, Plum Creek already pays some property taxes—expecting lawmakers to believe that, because of this, the company shouldn't have to pay any of the other taxes that every other Montana business has to pay.

But it is the "antibusiness" plea at the end that is the knockout blow.

"When this body looks at legislation and changes the target very specifically to one company, I would submit to you that it sends a message to business: 'Watch out,'" he concludes in a low, sinister tone. "I would suggest to you that something's going on here more than just tax policy. . . . We have a state that is trying to shine a light on the welcome mat for new business, and at the same time trying to tax in a new way a major employer. . . . That is very disconcerting to business."

The moment he says it, I know the tax enforcement bill is going down.

SCHWEITZER HAS BEEN using his bully pulpit to effectively transform the tax battle into a fight over what kinds of tax cuts to deliver and whether to enforce existing tax laws, rather than a brawl over whether people like paying taxes in the first place. He has also simultaneously played into his state's subjugation psychology by taking high-profile stands against exactly the kinds of big corporations that have been bullying this state since the dawn of time.

Here's the trick: his uprising is anchored in populism—but it is captive-industry populism.

He has taken the highest-profile stands specifically against the bullies who can't kick him in the balls with threats of geographic abandonment that might damage the Montana economy.

Schweitzer's 2005 bill forcing NorthWestern Energy to buy more power from renewable sources and his order to Burlington Northern to clean up its mess in Livingston—these headline-grabbing moves were made knowing that the targets had no real leverage to fight back. North-Western's transmission lines and Burlington Northern's tracks cannot be moved.

When an industry is stuck geographically, its weapon against this kind of populism has always been one or another kind of cash-stuffed envelope. Oil, gas, coal, copper, gold, silver, and timber companies have infamously bought off sheiks in petroleum-producing Middle Eastern countries, bureaucrats in mineral-loaded South American nations, and, yes, legislators in Rocky Mountain states—all to make sure governments let them do what they want.

That worked here in Montana when Republicans were in control of state government, but not so much now. Industries that used corruption to secure themselves are suddenly butting up against a lobbyist-hating governor and a Democratic state senate stubbornly challenging the antitax movement with their own uprising. And so Plum Creek executives like Ricklefs are deftly switching gears by arguing that tax enforcement may not drive the captives away, but it will drive other businesses out of Montana by creating an antibusiness environment. It was an argument I first heard floated on the Senate floor a month ago when a Republican legislator memorably claimed that cracking down on tax cheats was "a witch hunt on multistate corporations" that would supposedly "impose a paperwork burden, a software burden, and a compilation burden on [businesses] that could otherwise be convinced to come here and invest."

The GOP didn't have any substance to back up the charge, of course. But I had a feeling when I heard that line of attack that it would come back again. And now that it's back, I'm sure it's going to take this bill down because it hits Democrats where they know they are weakest.

I recall a long conversation I had at the beginning of the session about energy policy with Evan Barrett, an old political warhorse whose job as Schweitzer's economic development director is to swim in the murky delta where politics and economics meet. During a discussion about the balance between environmental protection and energy development, he told me, "If we move too fast regulatorily, energy companies will go to North Dakota or Wyoming or somewhere else."

Because Montana is not the only state in the region with energy resources like coal, it has no captive leverage and instead has "to first get the companies here, get them invested, and only then create the regulatory structure to make sure they stay here in a sustainable way," Barrett told me as he stroked his wispy white beard.

The situation with the tax enforcement bill and with Plum Creek is obviously different. The timberlands it owns are in Montana and aren't moving—and no one has been able to show in any coherent way how making a captive company pay the same taxes that everyone else pays will hurt Montana's business climate.

However, Barrett's comment is telling. In a state that ranks among the lowest in the country in terms of wages and income, anxiety over the prospect of being tagged with the "antibusiness" label is palpable among all politicians, and the validity of the attack is secondary. The most skilled operatives in the antitax movement, like Ricklefs, know all they have to do is raise the charge a few times to stoke fear.

To their credit, Democrats have worked preemptively to batten the hatches against the "antibusiness" attack, not just by proposing to devote all new revenues from the tax enforcement measures to new small-business tax cuts, but also by obsessively repeating the line that allowing out-of-state tax cheating puts in-state, tax-complying businesses at a competitive disadvantage. And Elliott is wearing a brave face in the committee room following Ricklefs's uppercut. He reminds his fellow legislators that Montana's tax climate was ranked eighth best in the nation by the Tax Foundation, a conservative-leaning think tank in Washington, D.C. He tells the committee that he owns stock in Plum Creek and that "it's OK with me if my company is taxed the way every other company is taxed in Montana."

But I'm still convinced that this bill is going down and that Elliott's efforts won't be enough.

DURING ONE OF my final visits to the Montana capitol, I bought some M&M's from the snack bar right outside the House chamber. Everything was silent. On the wall, someone had posted a print out of a web page titled Profile of the Sociopath—a list of the psychological signs of insanity.

"Someone needs to give that to the mob," I said to Jopek, who looked too tired to laugh.

The special session finally ended with the chest-thumping Republicans caving in on almost all issues. The Democrats' agenda "emerged from the contentious special session largely unscathed," gushed the Associated Press.

Schweitzer's sharpest populist spears—his $400 tax rebate, his bill to freeze college tuition increases, his move to expand anglers' access to rivers—made it. Fumed one Republican lawmaker: "The governor got everything he wanted and then some."

Not exactly.

In the waning moments of the special session, House Republicans pulled their own version of the fast adjournment move that Senate Democrats had used at the end of the regular session—only the GOP passed almost the entire Democratic agenda except the tax enforcement measure, and then adjourned. Democrats had to choose whether to make their own stand: Adjourn without passing the budget because the tax enforcement measures had been stripped from it and force another special session. Or pass the budget sans tax enforcement bill, and go home. Having won on every other fight—including the property tax rebate—they decided to take the bird in hand, ratify the budget, and go home. Not an irrational choice, considering how they won on everything else.

The antitax movement lost on the property tax issue, but in killing the tax enforcement measure, it showed it can still muscle out a win every now and then. The problem for the Right, though, is that winning is getting harder—and coming at a larger political price.

Schweitzer uses the days that follow the special session to trumpet the Democrats' accomplishments, while newspapers dutifully report that the Republicans had blocked the effort to provide a small-business tax cut paid for by closing out-of-state tax loopholes. The Montana Republican Party, so valiant in its last stand, abruptly collapses as soon as the special session is gaveled to a close.

First, they toss Majority Leader Mike Lange overboard, replacing him for not being sufficiently conservative. His sin was not his profanity-laced tirade against the governor that became a national YouTube sensation, but his willingness to meet with Schweitzer to try to iron out a compromise on taxes.

After sacking Lange, the party's Ludicrously Extremist Wing starts publicly feuding with the Merely Ridiculously Extremist Wing, with the former telling reporters "they will recruit primary challengers to oust" the latter. One archconservative, Representative Roger Koopman, says there has been an "unholy alliance" between "liberal Republicans and a liberal gover- nor" and that "the conservative mainstream in the Republican Party [will not] lie down to that."

At the end of May 2007, Democrats sweep local elections in Ravalli County, one of the most Republican parts of the state. The victory comes thanks to Republicans taking subjugation psychology to a cartoonish—and self-defeating—extreme by pegging their campaign to ads portraying local Democratic candidates as John Kerry accomplices and big-city (in this case, Missoula) "liberal tree huggers." In the wake of the loss, GOP senator Jerry Black fires back at Koopman by saying Republicans "need to move toward the middle, in the mainstream"—a damning admission that the party is on the fringe. An exasperated congressman Denny Rehberg (R-MT) chimes in by telling reporters that his party is "kind of tired" and had become "a little lazy."

Mahatma Gandhi said, "First they ignore you, then they laugh at you, then they fight you, then you win." He should have added that if you're not careful, the process can reverse itself, as it has for the conservative antitax movement here in Montana, and lots of other places, too.

Take none other than George W. Bush himself. With two massive federal tax cuts under his belt, he's the antitax movement's poster boy. And yet, *Newsweek*'s 2006 nationwide poll showed that 56 percent disapprove of his tax policies. Bush has regressed from winning on a promise to cut taxes, to fighting the public on the issue. The country is learning that regressive tax cuts whose benefits are targeted to the wealthy mean few tax cuts for ordinary people and depleted budgets, which result in underfinanced social services and crumbling infrastructure.

Facing such public backlash, conservative antitax activists have seen their fate relegated to Gandhi's "laugh at you" phase. In Indiana, Republican Mitch Daniels returned from a stint as White House budget director and Bush's chief tax cut proponent to assume the governorship, and then promptly proposed a plan to raise taxes on the wealthy. When antitax activist Grover Norquist penned a scathing op-ed attacking his former friend Daniels in the *Indianapolis Star,* Daniels responded by telling reporters, "The only Grover they know in Indiana is the fuzzy creature on *Sesame Street.*" Daniels stole the line word-for-word from Ohio's Bob Taft (R), who said almost exactly the same thing after Norquist threw a tantrum and called him an "idiot" who should be "taken out and horsewhipped." Arkansas Republican governor Mike Huckabee soon piled on, pointing out that Norquist has "never been in a situation where he couldn't borrow money so he didn't have to raise taxes or tell old people he's just going to take them out of the nursing home and drop them on the curb." Then, as if taunting him, he said if Norquist "wants to run for governor, there's an election next year in Arkansas—he can get his residency requirements lined up."

Voters are way ahead of these politicians—they are already in an "ignore you" stance against the antitax movement. In 2004, "voters rejected every tax-limitation measure on state ballots" and many states "approved tax increases to pay for specific programs such as schools, roads and mental health," the *Washington Monthly* reported. In 2005, Colorado voters passed a ballot initiative repealing conservatives' crown jewel, the Taxpayer Bill of Rights, which constitutionally restricts state government's ability to raise revenues to invest in public infrastructure. And in the spring of 2007, Idaho governor Butch Otter (R)—perhaps the most antitax lawmaker in the entire Congress during his time in the U.S. House—said he had no choice but to consider a $200 million tax increase to pay for much-needed transportation improvements.

People still intensely dislike taxes, and conservative activists would be only too happy if Democrats forgot that. But America is obviously rejecting the old antitax movement—the one that finances tax cuts for rich people and distant Wall Street bankers with cuts to the services that the rest of society relies on—stuff like roads, schools, bridges, and police departments. And the uprising's success in transforming the tax debate into a populist battle over economic inequality is ripping apart the once durable conservative coalition that supported the antitax movement of years past.

"The Chamber of Commerce, long a supporter of limited government and low taxes, was part of the coalition backing the Reagan revolution in the 1980s," whined Stephen Moore, a Norquist clone who leads a corporate-funded group that finances primary challenges to moderate Republicans. "But thanks to an astonishing political transformation, many chambers of commerce on the state and local level have been abandoning these goals . . . state taxpayer organizations, free market think tanks and small business leaders now complain bitterly that, on a wide range of issues, chambers of commerce deploy their financial resources and lobbying clout to expand the taxing, spending and regulatory authorities of government."

Now as I download my email during the July 4 holiday, I see the political results from Montana are in.

A friend has sent me the *Billings Gazette*'s new postsession statewide poll that shows 64 percent of Montanans approve of the way Schweitzer is doing his job. More impressively, a healthy majority of Montanans approve both of Schweitzer's use of the surplus to better fund social programs and of his tax rebate plan—and very few think it should have been replaced by the Republicans' regressive plan, or made larger. Even Republican voters back Schweitzer's rebate over the GOP legislators' plan.

In this boxing match—this Thrilla in Montana—the new uprising has taken its share of licks, but it has knocked the aging movement down for the count.

3

WHAT KIND OF HARDBALL CAN STOP A WAR?

DURING A JANUARY lull in the first few breathless rounds of the Thrilla in Montana, I decide to leave the front lines of the tax battles and take a trip back to visit another, better-publicized skirmish confronting the uprising—the one to stop the Iraq War.

Just a few months before, Democratic candidates from all over the country hammered the GOP for refusing to put the brakes on the four-year-old conflict that is killing thousands of Americans and Iraqis and is burning through almost a quarter billion dollars a day. The antiwar themes were prevalent everywhere—even in the typically conservative prairie states that I just traversed on my eastbound plane flight from Helena to Washington, D.C. The result was Democrats winning Congress for the first time in twelve years. They won, in other words, thanks to antiwar fervor.

The nationwide opposition to the war is based on a whole host of populist impulses. Some hate the war because they believe lives are being sacrificed to pursue the oil industry's agenda. Some despise it because, without a military draft, the casualties are comprised disproportionately of working-class kids who, in many cases, enlist out of economic necessity. And still others abhor the war because it is draining scarce resources away from pressing priorities here at home.

And yet, the postelection campaign to actually stop the war—rather than just getting candidates to say they would like it to end—seems headed for disaster. The uprising to express the opposition is struggling with dysfunction and disorganization, which is probably why President Bush didn't flinch after an election that humiliated his party. On the contrary, in the weeks after voters went to the polls, he stoically announced plans to escalate the war with even more troop deployments—a "surge" strategy, as the media has labeled it.

The stated goal of this late January 2007 march on the National Mall is to get the new Democratic Congress to use its constitutional powers to block this surge—a seemingly modest goal. Preventing a war from getting bigger after the public overwhelmingly voted in congressional elections to end the war entirely shouldn't be too much to ask. If an uprising can defy the odds and stop the antitax movement in a strongly antitax state like Montana, it should be able to win a fight that most Americans actually support and that an election just turned on.

But it's not that simple, thanks to a fissure between two warring tribes who differ over whether and how to challenge entrenched power.

THE EVENT ON this sunny, frigid day is being organized by United for Peace and Justice, a group heading what progressive activist Matt Stoller has deemed "The Protest Industry"—a clan, says Stoller, "made up of those who decided that participation in the system was immoral" because they "have seen 'compromise' many times before and think they know where it leads."

Everyone from Cindy Sheehan to Naderites to International ANSWER (Act Now to Stop War and End Racism) types to the followers of Lyndon LaRouche to Code Pink is in this tribe. They are the people who have concluded that working outside the system (e.g., marches, sit-ins, pickets, boycotts, etc.) is the only acceptable form of activism, and that working within government machinery, party apparatuses, or conventional politics is both a pointless exercise and inherently spineless.

The Protest Industry is all about loud symbols, and that's no exception among the 100,000 people out here in front of the U.S. Capitol.

Woodstock-era iconography is everywhere. Lynn Woolsey, the liberal Democratic congresswoman from California, is actually doing interviews wearing peace-symbol earrings. The event's official organizers from United for Peace and Justice are doing their best Yasser Arafat impressions by sporting checkered black-and-white Arabian kaffiyehs. The emcee on stage is a guy in a T-shirt with knee-length, white-haired dreadlocks. And the headline speakers are Hollywood celebrities Sean Penn, Tim Robbins, Susan Sarandon, and, yes, "Hanoi Jane" Fonda herself, decked out in a miniskirt and knee-high leather boots.

The walking stereotypes were the first ones on the scene this morning. Some are middle-aged folks with long beards and ponytails who look like they have been sitting on the National Mall since the Vietnam War protests here almost forty years ago. Others are twenty-somethings with Goth-style black T-shirts, lots of earrings, cheek rings, and other assorted face piercings. Interspersed in the crowd are people in various costumes. A guy on stilts is wandering around as a fifteen-foot-tall Abe Lincoln. Another dude is wearing a Grim Reaper costume and a sign that thanks Dick Cheney for keeping death in business this year. This guy seems to have solid theme park experience, as he is actively posing for pictures with people much like a Disney mascot at Epcot Center.

What data there are highlight the outsider views of this Protest Industry. Researchers at the University of Florida and Indiana University surveyed more than three thousand demonstrators at United for Peace and Justice and International ANSWER antiwar marches in 2004 and 2005 and found that almost two-thirds of the protestors said they had no party affiliation or were members of a third party.

Protest Industries exist on both sides of America's political divides (and we'll be visiting one of the conservatives' most famous ones at the Mexican border in a few months), but only the Right's Protest Industry has had recent success in totally vanquishing its Establishment foes. When Republican Barry Goldwater got his clock cleaned in the 1964 presidential election, the Hard Right's Protest Industry blossomed through magazines like the *National Review,* conservative activist Richard

Viguerie's famed newsletters, and Phyllis Schafly's grassroots, state-based campaigns—endeavors that, over time, eroded the standing of moderate Rockefeller Republicans and eventually gave the radical Right full control of the GOP.

The same cannot be said for the antiwar Protest Industry out here on the mall. Despite success in the 1960s and 1970s in creating political pressure to end the Vietnam War, the present-day antiwar uprising remains at arm's length from the Democratic Party and relegated to boisterous but ephemeral displays whose chaos and lack of message discipline reinforce a self-defeating fringe flavor to it all.*

Before the speeches start, I take a walk down the mall toward the Washington Monument and away from the giant stage—a walk into this fringe.

I hit a line of carnival stands for different groups. It is a checkered assortment. For every setup like the Service Employees International Union's, which has a cogently written sign against the war, there is one for a group like "9/11 Truth"—an organization that is demanding that the U.S. government come clean about its supposed masterminding of the 2001 terrorist attacks.

When I walk by the International Socialists' yellow and red display, I notice more and more material about Dick Cheney. The farther down the mall I go, the farther out onto the fringe I am, and the more Dick Cheney I find. He seems to have become a fixation for the hardest of the hard core, the person who is taking over the world and is the explanation for all of the planet's ills. Drought in Oklahoma? Cheney. Terrorist attack in Yemen? Cheney. The Great Chicago Fire of 1871? Cheney. Overflowing Porta Potties at this march? Yup, that's Cheney.

Dick Cheney, mind you, *is* an evil person. But the Cheney fixation in activist circles is so intense, so reflexive, and presented so uniformly at every progressive rally I've ever been to, that the moment I hear a political

---

* By "antiwar uprising," I mean a functioning political organism distinct from the more nebulous broad-based public antithesis to the Iraq War today.

activist say "Dick Cheney," my first instinct is to think the person talking is mildly mentally unstable.*

Which, frankly, is what I think of a lot of people at this march when I talk to them—and not because they oppose the war. This group of protestors may have the same antiwar beliefs as the rest of the country, but this group doesn't look, dress, or even talk like the two-thirds of Americans who oppose the war. And that's the big problem for a Protest Industry needing both to build more mass membership and to pressure a Washington political culture whose decisions are dictated by television.

FOR THE FIRST, oh, 175 years of the republic, the march on Washington was an expression of real power that evoked a response from the political system. In the pre-television era, grassroots organizing, precinct captains, retail politics, and voter turnout operations won and lost campaigns. The more people that could be convinced to physically show up at an organized protest, the more the politicians inside the central government felt pressure to actually do something, because angry throngs were seen as a threat to reelection.

In 1913, for instance, five thousand women marching for suffrage "turned a moderate movement into a full-scale revolution for change," according to PBS's documentary on the march, and ultimately galvanized support for the Nineteenth Amendment that gave women the right to vote. In 1932, twenty thousand World War I veterans marched for medical benefits. President Herbert Hoover was so frightened by the masses on his doorstep that he deployed army infantry units to bayonet and teargas the protestors, leaving scores dead and injured.

---

* It is certainly possible Dick Cheney is trying to take over the world—and I will even go as far as saying that there is some fairly compelling evidence that our vice president would probably *like* to take over the world. But among the Protest Industry, Cheney's world domination fetish is presented not as something that is likely or probable, but instead as a pure fact, which, as evil as Cheney may be, it just isn't.

When television began dominating modern politics in the 1960s, the march on Washington started losing its effectiveness independent of mass media.* By the time the Vietnam War was really raging, the federal government stopped listening to marches based just on the size of the crowd. In the brave new world of election campaigns being duked out through television commercials, Washington learned that a march was only worth listening to if its television imagery competed with politicians' paid campaign ads and the free media exposure lawmakers could generate from a stenographic, power-worshiping press corps. In sum, the Establishment discovered it could basically ignore hundreds of thousands of people on the National Mall.

This is one of the reasons why when 600,000 people rallied in Washington against the Vietnam War in 1969, the war raged on for another four years. This is why when the Million Man March for African-American economic equality descended on Washington in 1995, politicians barely even noticed. And this is why the only recent protests that have resulted in any significant reaction from officialdom have been those ravaged by made-for-television violence, such as the 1968 Democratic National Convention protests or the 1999 riots in Seattle at the World Trade Organization talks.

The system, in short, now rewards visual spectacles over numbers, making it easy for the Protest Industry to conclude that it is more important to have people in front of the Capitol wearing elaborate costumes, walking on stilts, and babbling on about international conspiracies than to have folks just standing here dressed in boring clothes demanding an end to the war. At least the spectacles have a shot to get on television in the age of Britney Spears and *Jackass*.

But this creates a self-defeating problem. While the stunts are more likely to get television coverage, they are also more likely to get precisely the kind of circus-freak-show treatment that defeats the underlying purpose of

---

* Martin Luther King's "I Have a Dream" speech at the 1963 civil rights march defied this trend, because his speech became a media sensation and the 1964 Civil Rights Act was passed soon after.

the event. If the goal is getting as many Americans as possible to join the uprising to end the war, then achieving that objective is not helped by garnering television coverage that depicts marchers, and thus the cause, as totally fringe and therefore culturally repellent to Middle America.

I'll admit right now that if I were a march organizer, I wouldn't be sure how to balance the desire to get TV coverage with the need to get *good* TV coverage, but I'm quite sure the United for Peace and Justice organizers of this event today have not even thought of *trying* to achieve a balance. There's been no basic effort to avoid walking into the worst and most unfair stereotypes that media elites will want to use to describe the uprising against the war.

Sure, everyone here at this rally has every right to use caricatured '60s symbolism, don Arab regalia most Americans (unfortunately) equate with Islamic terrorists, and stress the strong support of Hollywood celebrities. They have this right, but that doesn't mean they are achieving their stated goal of trying to end the war. In fact, it is—quite predictably—exactly the opposite. The lead story on national television tonight—shocker!—will be about Fonda and how her appearance at the march was her first major antiwar declaration since she was humiliated for seeming to publicly embrace North Vietnamese Communists almost four decades ago. That's a perfect story line only if the goal of the march is to convince the 70 percent of Americans who already oppose the war that they definitely don't want to join the organized antiwar uprising.

Really, there's no effort to even hone a basic message. This is supposed to be a rally against the war in Iraq, but as I look out at the sea of signs this morning, I'm sure this event could also pass for a rally demanding (a) the end to a war with Iran that hasn't happened, (b) the impeachment of Bush, (c) the arrest of Dick Cheney, (d) the elimination of the death penalty, or (e) the overthrow of the U.S. government by International Socialists in the name of "regime change." It also could be a rally for more federal funding to rebuild New Orleans, though I suppose it's possible that the signs calling for "Justice for the People of the Gulf Coast" could be referring to the Persian Gulf coast.

Saul Alinsky's advice to activists about "accepting the world as it is, not as [you] would like it to be" means accepting that the reporters, politicians, pundits, and professional operatives who collectively make up today's Washington Establishment want to portray the antiwar movement as a bunch of patchouli-scented hippies, out-of-control college kids, anti-American extremists, and Hollywood elitists—all in order to write off the antiwar uprising. If given the opportunity, the major television networks would preview all their stories about the opposition to Bush's escalation by running a clip from *Cheech & Chong,* a snippet from a Hezbollah rally, and a photo of Jane Fonda under the banner AMERICA'S ANTIWAR MOVEMENT.

What's so infuriating about this scene out here is that Alinsky's words should be especially poignant for the antiwar Protest Industry, whose flamboyant tactics and imagery in the television era became an extremely effective scapegoat that helped Richard Nixon prolong the Vietnam War. He was famously able to deflect public opposition to the war by transforming the 1972 presidential campaign from a referendum on the war into a referendum on the antiwar movement itself. With images of burning flags and garish tie-dye flashing across the nightly news, Nixon rhetorically manufactured a story of himself leading a "silent majority" of millions of regular Americans in a struggle against a petulant and putrid counterculture. And he was wildly successful.

The tactics of the antiwar movement "allowed Nixon to win in 1968 and again in 1972, and a Democratic president would surely have withdrawn [from Vietnam] sooner," activist and journalist Paul Berman told *Salon* in 2003. "There were famous scenes where Nixon specifically ordered that his entourage drive through streets where he knew he'd be attacked by demonstrators because he wanted the right scenes to appear on TV. He presented it to the public: you had to choose between Richard Nixon or some long-haired marijuana-smoking lunatic communist. Guess what. The public chose Nixon."

But that lesson hasn't been learned—at least not by this crowd today. This march will not make wavering lawmakers uncomfortable with supporting the war. In fact, it will probably help them justify perpetuating the war to constituents back home. Politicians from Mom-and-Apple-Pie congressional districts like suburban Kansas City will most likely cite the protest's imagery as "proof" that the only people who want to quickly end the conflict are out-of-the-mainstream rabble rousers, and that in the face of such pressure, Washington must exercise "moderation" and resist the urge to "act hastily"—that is, not act at all.

THIS SAME WEEK I am visiting D.C. for the antiwar march, I have been talking with a group of organizations and apparatchiks who are launching an operation called Americans Against Escalation in Iraq (AAEI)—a coalition of mainly Washington-based advocacy groups pooling cash and staff for "a major, multi-million dollar national campaign to oppose the President's 'surge' proposal to escalate the war in Iraq," as its website says. Within the uprising against the war in Iraq, AAEI and its allies are the other clan, the Hatfield to the Protest Industry's McCoy, the "professional" side of the antiwar effort that stands in contrast to the throng out here on the mall.

They are The Players.

Remember the board game Risk you used to play as a kid? It was pretty frickin' sweet, right? You'd head home from school, flip on *What's Happening!!* reruns, and you and your friends would sit around a big world map, moving armies around, annihilating your opponents, and laying waste to vast stretches of the planet as you strived for world domination—all from the comfortable confines of your house.

That's how The Players see the fight against the war—as a big game of Risk.

You used to play Risk in your wood-paneled basement. The Players conduct their game in wood-paneled offices in Washington. The board game you used to play imagined that world conquest comes not after a long-term battle for hearts and minds, but at the hands of a few mercurial schemers in front of a world map, moving army battalions around to different countries, and thus changing the course of global events. The Players imagine that the war will end not after a massive investment in long-term, on-the-ground local organizing against war, but by the short-term coordination of a few elite actors (political consultants, donors, politicians, and maybe one or two organization heads) in front of a map of media markets and congressional districts, moving money around to television and radio stations to buy attack ads against politicians.

The Players make their moves with campaign contributions, television spots, and PR campaigns—the conventional weapons in a media war—and they are playing their game in Washington and for Washington. They believe the opposite of what the Protest Industry believes: namely, that the only way to effect change is to play an inside game.

Now, it's true—AAEI will spend money on activities outside of D.C., including a whopping $12 million on a nationwide "Iraq Summer" campaign that will orchestrate antiwar protests in the districts of pro-war Republican lawmakers. But while the group bills these activities as "grassroots organizing," they are actually what's known in lobbyist terms as "grasstop" or "astroturf" activities—events designed to look like they are spontaneous, ongoing grassroots organizing but are merely onetime stunts specifically designed for television.

Their goal is to create an illusion to those in Washington that there is supposedly organized, homegrown, election-threatening local pressure on pro-war lawmakers. It is a technique originally developed by lobbyists to manufacture the false appearance of mass public support for corporate-written legislation that has no actual public support—and it is something of a sad commentary. Astroturfing is now being used by organizations that represent the beliefs of the vast majority of Americans, but these organizations have to use the false language of manufactured media coverage to get anyone's attention in Washington, both because that's the only dialect anyone in D.C. speaks, and because no lasting grassroots infrastructure is being built.

AAEI is fairly open about its desire to put on a smoke-and-mirrors show—and nothing more. In a planning document leaked to Washington reporters, the group says its primary goal is to "make a splash in the media"—rather than do the hard work of ongoing grassroots organizing. No permanent institutions are being put in place. No new community organizations are being built, and no existing local organizations are really being strengthened. Little will be invested in hard-core organizing like the door-to-door canvassing or the community organization building that has been key to real movements. Rather, AAEI hires its own temporary staffers to parachute into communities to stage the fireworks.

Of course, engaging in the media war is not, by itself, misguided. As the antiwar uprising's self-designated voice in Washington, The Players are, in fact, somewhat Alinskyian in "accepting the world as it is"—the insulated world of D.C.

Media coverage is important currency in the nation's capital. If you want to influence things here, you have to act with the understanding that Washington is obsessed with what's on television, to the exclusion of almost everything else. And we're not talking about mass-audience television that actually shapes public opinion and that the Protest Industry will be harangued on tonight after the march. We're talking about obscure chat shows that almost no one outside of the D.C. zip code actually watches.

This is a town whose celebrities are people like *Washington Post* columnist David Broder, MSNBC's Chris Matthews, and *Time*'s Joe Klein—people who are known to almost no one out in the country at large, but who are considered influential celebrities inside the Beltway because they appear on these obscure chat programs, from C-SPAN's *Washington Journal,* to Fox News's *Special Report* to MSNBC's *Hardball.* D.C.'s peculiar media obsession, of course, has very little to do with influencing votes out in the country and almost everything to do with narcissism.

Whereas starry-eyed college grads and idealists once came to Washington with dreams of passing the New Deal or stopping the Vietnam War or passing universal health care, they now come looking for a home in what has become Hollywood for Ugly People—a place where dreams are made and broken by one's ability to get on shows like *Hardball*—a must-watch, agenda-setting status symbol in Washington that attracts a total audience smaller than the population of Bakersfield, California, or about one-tenth of 1 percent of the whole country.

Washington's self-absorbed fetishization of tiny-audience television shows might be funny in the same way it is funny to think of Emperor Nero's aides tuning his fiddle as Rome burned to the ground. It might be funny—except that the Iraq War was largely started because of this obsession.

As we all now know, the motive for this war—to apprehend Saddam Hussein's supposed arsenal of biological, chemical, and nuclear weapons before he could use them on us—was fabricated and then sold through a series of televised infomercials. The most famous of these was Colin Powell's made-for-TV case at the United Nations. Hearkening back to Adlai Stevenson's famous Cuban Missile Crisis presentation to the same body four decades prior, Powell supposedly proved that Iraq was capable of blowing the United States off the map—and the media, rather than asking questions, roundly applauded his shameless dishonesty.

But that was just the beginning. Soon fabulous television graphics usually reserved for big-college sports rivalries were unleashed as fantastic March to War effects, replete with custom music and logos. Midlevel military officials, CIA intelligence analysts, and career Pentagon experts were shoved aside by the press corps in favor of far more telegenic pundits with no military or foreign policy experience whatsoever, but who managed to become staples of Beltway television because their pro-war insanity made made for pretty good self-aggrandizing drama.

Neoconservatives like the *Weekly Standard*'s William Kristol staked out beachheads on Fox News sets, while so-called liberal hawks like *New Republic* editor Peter Beinart dug trenches in CNN studios. Almost all of them had avoided military service themselves, but valiantly demanded that other people's teenage kids be sent off to the Iraqi shooting gallery.

These shows served as the bugle call to rally the 101st Keyboard Brigade—the battalion of lesser-known, media-hungry bloggers, columnists, and think-tank scholars of military age who refused to enlist in the invasion they said was so important, yet who demanded America rush to war. Their drumbeat helped create the now-infamous Iraq War echo chamber in Washington that made the historically unprecedented concept of "preemptive war" seem utterly mainstream inside the Beltway.

Now, out in the real world beyond the comfortable confines of the TV studios, it's all gone to shit—all of it. The invasion of Iraq, which started four years ago with happy promises from coiffed pundits, has become a Sunni-Shiite civil war that sends home dead and maimed American soldiers every week. The American public—which polls originally showed was ambivalent about supporting the unilateral invasion—is now firmly opposed to continuing the conflict. Many of Washington's pro-war TV "celebrities" are trying to flee from their previously televised warmongering. Klein of *Time* magazine, for instance, appeared on CNBC a month before the Iraq invasion to state, "War may well be the right decision at this point—in fact, I think it probably is." Now, in 2007, he claims with a straight face that "I've been opposed to the Iraq War ever since 2002."

In light of this, The Players believe that by funneling enough money into organizations like AAEI, pulling enough PR stunts, and putting enough attack ads on television against pro-war legislators in Congress, they can make this antiwar uprising successful without organizing millions of Americans into a cohesive long-term movement. They believe, in short, that if a war can be started because of Washington's obsession with television, then it can be ended because of that same obsession, too.

UNQUESTIONABLY, BOTH THE Protest Industry out here chanting on the mall and The Players scheming in their offices a few blocks from here in downtown Washington are necessary parts of an effective antiwar uprising. The outraged rabble provides the boots on the ground that can pressure lawmakers in their local communities. And that popular ferment could be enhanced by a professional presence playing the Beltway's media game. As blogger Chris Bowers says, "In Washington, D.C., for those who run the government, the public is quite distant and faceless."

"By way of contrast, large donors, consultants, lobbyists, center-right opinion journalists and policy presentations from think tanks . . . are quite real," he says. "While [the antiwar uprising] certainly seems to have public opinion behind us in terms of Iraq policy, and even though we now have a majority in Congress, we seem to lack the political power in those other areas to turn that public opinion into actual, legally binding policy."

The crippling problem for The Players is the increasing difficulty of operating in Washington without being corrupted by it.

If the rules of Washington were written down, the first one would say that anyone wishing to play its games has to sign up big-name political consultants who are perceived to have "influence." That buys you instant credibility with politicians and reporters here—"those folks who write the stories and appear on television and radio to talk about the state of play in Washington," as the *Washington Post*'s Chris Cillizza says. "Like it or not, the opinions expressed by these people tend to set the parameters of the debate when an election year rolls around."

As a Washington pundit himself, Cillizza's analysis inflates his own importance.* But as biased as he is and as much as his statement reeks of elitism, his self-aggrandizing sentiment is religious doctrine inside the Beltway.

This poses an inherent problem for even the best-intentioned advocacy organizations in D.C. The same consultants they need to hire in order to play this incestuous Washington game and influence these people who "set the parameters of the debate" are often simultaneously being paid by the very politicians who should be in their crosshairs. The result is that ideological organizations become fused to the very partisan political structure they seek to pressure.

A look at AAEI's own leadership is instructive.

The group is guided by Hildebrand Tewes, a consulting firm named for its two original partners, Steve Hildebrand and Paul Tewes—both longtime Democratic Party operatives. The firm is one of a relatively new breed of companies that attempts to bring to uprising politics the ease of microwave TV dinners. Don't feel like making dinner? Just throw a Hot Pocket into the

---

* One of the Washington media's favorite hobbies is to write about the importance of the Washington media.

microwave. Don't feel like doing the hard work of local organizing to build a sustaining, durable movement that lasts beyond the issue du jour? Just put together a pile of money to hire a firm like Hildebrand Tewes and you can have your instant "uprising"—one that provides about as much long-term nutrition to your cause as your microwaved junk food provides to your body.

While the firm is supposedly leading an independent antiwar uprising pressuring politicians in both parties, about half its employees—including the firm's two principals—were staffers for the Democratic Senatorial Campaign Committee (DSCC), the reelection arm of the same Democratic U.S. senators that the antiwar uprising now needs to pressure to end the war.

But the conflict of interest only starts there. At the same time Hildebrand Tewes is working with AAEI, the firm is being paid by various Democratic politicians for its services—Democratic politicians that have a vested interest in avoiding attacks from the antiwar uprising.

The consequences of such incestuous overlaps between party and uprising are best exemplified by Brad Woodhouse, the Hildebrand Tewes consultant leading AAEI. He came directly to Hildebrand Tewes after years as the DSCC's chief spokesperson and a mouthpiece for Democratic candidates. This supposed antiwar champion is the same guy who, as a campaign staffer, bragged to newspapers just before the Iraq invasion that the pro-war candidate he was working for (North Carolina Democrat Erskine Bowles) was more pro-war than the Republican candidate. "No one has been stronger in this race [than Bowles] in supporting President Bush in the war on terror and his efforts to affect a regime change in Iraq," Woodhouse fulminated.

Now, just a few years later, he is paid to lead the attack on Republicans for supporting the war—the same war he originally criticized them for not supporting as much as his Democrat.

Woodhouse is no anomaly. His history first emulating a military general urging troops into battle and now posing as a leader of the global peace movement closely mimics how many war-supporting politicians suddenly changed their positions when the political winds shifted. And the way he has been rewarded for his past pro-war declarations with a plum job in the antiwar uprising similarly apes how recent antiwar converts in

Congress are still afforded more Washington media attention and credibility than those lawmakers who originally opposed the invasion. But it is the partisan conflicts of interest, not the hypocrisy, that pose the real problem.

Consider two facts:

1. Democrats now control both chambers of the legislative branch. That gives them full control over Congress's power of the purse, and consequently the ultimate veto power when it comes to the war. No funds for war, no war.
2. Pro-war Democrats under threat of antiwar primaries inevitably stop supporting the war.

The *Baltimore Sun* reports that Congressman Al Wynn (D-MD) originally "voted against the majority of his party by authorizing President Bush to use military force in Iraq." Yet in 2007, "Wynn is one of the war's leading critics." Why the change? Because he faces a tough primary challenge from Democrat Donna Edwards, who is campaigning on an antiwar platform.

Same thing for California congresswoman Ellen Tauscher (D). "She slept fine after her 2002 vote to authorize the Iraq war," wrote the *Washington Post*. But now she opposes it after local activists began floating the idea of a primary challenge to her, and a new antiwar political action committee focused on Democratic Party accountability posted her photo on its website as Public Enemy #1.

Even Connecticut senator Joe Lieberman, the most ardently pro-war legislator in the entire Congress, temporarily buckled when he faced an antiwar challenge in his 2006 campaign. As a *Hartford Courant* columnist noted, "Near the end of the election, Lieberman gazed into cameras and said, 'No one wants to end the war more than I do.'"*

---

* Since winning reelection, Lieberman has gone back to supporting the Iraq War—and more. He's actually called for an additional war with Iran. But the point remains—when he felt his reelection threatened through a primary challenge, he began backing off such ardently pro-war rhetoric.

In light of these two truisms, you would think the central focus of any antiwar organization—whether inside Washington or out—would be on forcing Democrats to use their constitutional power to end the war to do just that: end the war. But you would be wrong.

Almost all of AAEI's "multi-million dollar national campaign" is being spent on television ads or publicity stunts attacking pro-war Republican politicians up for reelection in 2008—people like Maine senator Susan Collins, New Hampshire senator John Sununu, Minnesota senator Norm Coleman, and Senate Minority Leader Mitch McConnell of Kentucky, who Woodhouse spent years attacking at the DSCC. These are Republicans who Democrats (and thus Democratic consulting firms like Hildebrand Tewes) want to defeat in order to retain control of the Senate, whether the war ends or not. Relatively little AAEI resources, by contrast, will be spent on similar ads attacking various Democratic House and Senate lawmakers who have either repeatedly provided the critical votes to continue the war indefinitely, or who have refused to use all of Congress's power to end the war.

Beyond its mission statement, AAEI does not even try to hide its partisan biases. In one classic display, Woodhouse will use his AAEI position to actually defend Democrats when they refuse to stop a war funding bill, saying, "We're disappointed the war drags on with no end in sight but realize Democratic leaders can only accomplish what they have the votes for." No mention of Democrats' ability to use their majority to vote down the spending bill, or to stop any funding bills from moving forward so as to cut off money for the war.

If you believe this ultrapartisan allocation of resources has nothing to do with the fact that the people guiding the spending decisions are former employees of and are still being paid by Democratic politicians, then I'm sure George Bush has another war to sell you. As antiwar Wisconsin senator Russ Feingold (D) has said, the battle to end the war is "us versus them"—not in terms of Republican versus Democrat, but in terms of the uprising versus the "Washington inside crowd that sets the parameters of this debate."

"The Washington consultants—especially those that were part of the previous Democratic administration—come into a room with [the Democratic congressional] leadership and tell them, look, if you propose a timeline or you try to cut off the funding, the Republicans will tear you apart," he said. "The power structure in Washington [is] desperately trying to figure out how to explain why they made one of the biggest mistakes in the history of our country. And that's why you gotta go right at them."

But you can't "go right at them" if your uprising is led by a tightly knit consultant class that has dual loyalties and has been part of the problem from the outset.

As the speeches drone on over the next few hours here at the march on the mall, I get bored and start taking cell phone pictures of famous people. Rather than be depressed by the Protest Industry's self-destructive chaos or The Players' myopia, I figure I can at least email my mom a photo of Susan Sarandon, who is one of her favorite actresses.

Right after snapping a shot of Sean Penn (in which he seriously looks like he's going to punch me), I feel a hand pat my shoulder and I turn around to see Dennis Kucinich, the short, dark-haired, Democratic congressman from Cleveland. I know him from my time working on Capitol Hill, and he wants to introduce me to a towering red-haired runway model who he says is his new wife.

Kucinich is here because a few weeks ago he announced he's again running for president. Wait, let me modify that statement: Kucinich announced he is again pretending to run for president like he did in 2004. I make that distinction because I want to be as accurate as possible. Kucinich is not genuinely "running for president" because he is a smart guy and he cannot possibly think he has any legitimate chance of being elected president.

This reality doesn't necessarily mean his game of pretend is a bad idea.

Though Kucinich is the apple of the Protest Industry's eye, his candidacy draws at best rolls of the eyes from The Players. Try telling someone in

Washington that you support Kucinich for president, and your conversation will go something like this:

"I think I'm backing Kucinich this time."

"Come on, dude, who are you really for?"

"Really, Kucinich. He's been right on all the issues. Health care, the war—"

Cue eye roll and overdramatic, Al Gore–style sigh.

"Dude, come on, really. Stop messing around. Who are you really for?"

Such disdain is echoed even on the big liberal websites, which pride themselves on anti-Washington, anti-Establishment browbeating.

"Kucinich is a joke as a presidential candidate," wrote Markos Moulitsas, the Daily Kos blogger. "[He] represent[s] the cranky left of the party in the primaries."

Markos is not wrong, of course. Kucinich *is* sort of a joke if you believe presidential candidacies should be at least partially related to the goal of actually *winning* the presidency. No sitting House lawmaker has ever run for president and won in modern times, and Kucinich in particular has little national name recognition, doesn't raise a huge amount of money, and polls poorly. There's also the reality that he's just an undeniably weird dude, from the way he always looks like a little kid wearing his dad's oversized suit all the way to the packaging of his legislative proposals. Example: Instead of just pushing for more effective diplomacy, he has a bill to create an Orwellian-sounding Department of Peace.

But what few seem to appreciate—including, perhaps, Kucinich—is that his candidacy is a commentary on the dysfunction of the antiwar uprising itself.

Most understand the Kucinich phenomenon as a sincere antiwar advocate using a faux presidential candidacy both to promote himself and to force major candidates to finally get a backbone on the war, whether he wins or loses. It is this last point that almost nobody in the antiwar uprising talks about because that's where it gets really embarrassing.

The uprising against the Iraq War desperately needs someone—even a short, extraterrestrial-looking dude like Kucinich—in the presidential contest. Why? Because other than the occasional primary threats, the uprising has, up until now, been unable and/or unwilling to force most Democratic politicians to even listen to it.

There is a "cranky left," as Markos wrote. In part, it is the Protest Industry folks who, overcome by cynicism of failed movements of the past, refuse to participate in the kind of highly organized uprising required to stop a war. But it is also millions of people who The Players refuse to try to organize because it takes more than press releases, PR firms, press conferences, and television ads to actually organize lots of people throughout America over the long haul.

Kucinich, therefore, provides a bit of an excuse for both tribes in the uprising against the Iraq War.

For the Protest Industry, the Cleveland congressman's presidential run is reason to continue just showing up for onetime circus-like rallies like this one and not engage in any ongoing organizing because, hell, they've got a presidential candidate making a spectacle out of himself during New Hampshire primary debates! And when Kucinich is berated by *Washington Post* columnists or ignored by liberal writers at national magazines, that just plays into the Protest Industry story line that there's no real reason for antiwar activists to engage in anything more than demonstrations, because they'll just get ignored like Dennis.

For The Players, Kucinich provides similar rationalizations. Seeing Kucinich at a presidential debate talking about the war allows them to feel OK about funneling resources to Washington PR, polling, and political consulting firms rather than spending most of those resources on massive, long-term grassroots campaigns to bring this Protest Industry throng out here on the mall into the fold and perhaps even engage the faceless majority out in the heartland. With a proxy like Dennis in the race getting some media attention every now and again, The Players have an excuse to focus only on their inside game—because, hey, Kucinich is supposedly making sure the outsiders are being included in the 2008 race for the White House.

In short, Kucinich's quadrennial candidacies have become one of the cheap substitutes for better coordination between both opposing camps in the antiwar uprising.

Then again, there's no denying that Kucinich's campaign is also the inevitable by-product of a celebrity-obsessed political media that now gives a mass platform only to people who run for president—and no one else. Delaware senator Joe Biden (D) represents 853,000 people as a senator from the second-smallest state in the country. Almost nobody in America has any idea who he is, and yet because he's running for president, you can't watch CNN, read the *New York Times,* or click over to a liberal political blog without seeing his face or hearing his name. At the same time, AFL-CIO president John Sweeney represents 10 million American workers who rely on his leadership for their wages, health care, and pension benefits, and he can barely get even a throwaway mention in the media (except, of course, when he is endorsing a presidential candidate).*

And that's why, as much as I agree that Kucinich's run for president is quixotic, I still find it odd when folks portray his campaign as entirely pointless. If national politics is the arena in which being on obscure political talk shows is seen as the only way to make change, and if the only way to get mentioned or invited on those shows is to run for president, then isn't having an unabashedly antiwar presidential candidate a necessity for America's antiwar majority to have any sort of voice?

TOWARD THE END OF the march, I bump into Eli Pariser, MoveOn .org's twenty-six-year-old executive director. He and I have been friendly since I worked for one of MoveOn's anti-Bush projects in the lead-up to the 2004 election.

---

*This is no exaggeration: In the first six months of 2007, LexisNexis shows that Sweeney was mentioned in fewer than 200 newspaper articles, while Biden appeared in 5,547 newspaper articles. Magazines were a little better—Sweeney was mentioned in 23 articles, while Biden appeared in 349. But, not surprisingly, TV was the absolute worst. A look at CNN, ABC, and CBS transcripts for the first six months of 2007 shows that while Sweeney was mentioned or appeared all of 1 time, Biden was referenced or appeared 565 times.

As a multimillion-dollar powerhouse and the largest email-based advocacy organization in progressive politics (if not all of American politics), MoveOn is simultaneously invisible and omnipotent. Its ability to be everywhere and nowhere at the same time was supposed to be the bridge among the Protest Industry, The Players, and sympathetic congressional lawmakers.

Email, you see, was going to be the conduit between the insulated Beltway elites and the outside world. It was going to organize all the chaos out on the National Mall into a regimented movement that understood basic political strategy. Raise a whole boatload of cash, sprinkle a little Internet on everything and—*poof!*—there would be a functional antiwar uprising.

But it hasn't worked out quite that way.

After shaking hands and exchanging pleasantries, I ask Pariser why, if he's here, MoveOn isn't officially sponsoring the march? He replies that "we are focusing on local organizing"—as if the organization cannot do both.

Pariser is tall and soft-spoken to the point of seeming aloof. He's dodging my question because he doesn't want to say that MoveOn is too nervous to relinquish message control in front of national cameras. I'd normally call that a cop-out excuse for inaction—but MoveOn has become so iconic, and such a high-profile target, that the guardians of its brand have to make sure to avoid exposing the group to any unnecessary vulnerabilities. Splashing the MoveOn name all over a rally whose major participants include the International Socialists and those accusing the U.S. government of masterminding 9/11 would fall into the category of "unnecessary vulnerabilities."

That said, I certainly believe that Pariser, at least in principle, wants to focus more energy on local organizing. He tells me, "Between 1,000 and 2,000 of our members had 200 meetings this week in congressional district offices"—meetings where local constituents are demanding their representatives vote to end the war.

The district office meetings are really a no-brainer, and, ironically, they pantomime the tactics of groups like the American Israel Public Affairs Committee (AIPAC). I briefly worked at AIPAC during the Arab-Israeli peace negotiations in the late 1990s—well before the organization became a pro-war neoconservative wing of the Bush administration. From that experience, I learned exactly how AIPAC has earned the distinction of Washington's most powerful lobbying organization: through grassroots organizing.

Though most people think campaign donations alone have made AIPAC so significant, the organization really draws its strength from its diligent work organizing Jews throughout the country and getting them to lobby their individual lawmakers on a narrow set of issues. Their theory is simple: put a bunch of politically active people from a community in a room with their congressman, have them make specific demands, and you start to build power. Pariser seems to be suggesting that MoveOn genuinely wants to replicate this from the Left.

Of course, AIPAC has a huge paid staff and major offices on Capitol Hill and in cities throughout the country. MoveOn is about sixteen people with laptop computers and no office at all, despite its massive television advertising budget and membership in the millions.

"Our model right now has strengths and weaknesses," Pariser admits. "The major strength is that we are scalable and that if we focus on replicating a few of the same things all over, we can serve a membership of 3 million people with very little staff. The weakness is that it gets harder to customize our campaigns to each individual state or community."

MoveOn was meant to be the ultimate outside pressure system against both parties, and its leaders pay rhetorical homage to local organizing. But MoveOn is increasingly becoming an arm of the Democratic Party in Washington precisely because the model Pariser describes is far more compatible with The Players' D.C.-centric model than with a truly national effort to build something revolutionary and independent of both parties.

Sixteen people simply cannot organize 3.2 million members in the way the terms *grassroots* and *local* have been understood in the past. That's not a criticism—that's just a mathematical fact, and no amount of technology can really change it.

Unions with even less membership than MoveOn employ hundreds of full-time local organizers to work with potential new members and cultivate homegrown community leaders. MoveOn's model, by contrast, cannot really do door-to-door organizing, institution building, or local leadership development, much less ongoing education. All it can really do is try to make a splash in the media.

This is especially the case since the organization centralizes power and puts most of its resources into a top-down broadcast model in which its headline-seeking emails, directives, and ads come down to members from the organization's leadership. MoveOn could diffuse its resources and decision-making power into more local, less media-greedy endeavors like empowering members to be leaders themselves and build their own uprising institutions. But it doesn't.

Thus the best MoveOn's structure allows it to do is manage its troops the way someone playing Risk manages their armies—and that kind of operation is most compatible, respected, and relevant in the D.C. game because, while it doesn't create long-term power, it creates the perception of it. As MoveOn gets more and more Washington-centric, the organization becomes increasingly vulnerable to the withering pressures of co-option that have pulverized so many other advocacy groups inside the Beltway.

That's why, in 2007, MoveOn opted to join AAEI in support of the group's television ad buys, and onetime grasstops stunts focused almost exclusively on Republicans rather than on, for instance, building local organizations to support primary challenges to pro-war incumbents all over the country.

To be sure, MoveOn has been slightly more willing to be bipartisan in its pressure activities than other groups like AAEI. In May, the organization will buy ads criticizing Michigan Democratic senator Carl Levin and House Majority Leader Steny Hoyer (D-MD) for voting to continue the war. But unlike MoveOn ads blasted at Republicans, the ads against the two Democrats will only be aired on radio—widely known in political circles to be a less in-your-face medium than television and, therefore, far less effective.

Pariser was quoted in a 2005 *Salon* article as saying, "The job of a party is to get elected and the job of a movement is to promote ideas and an ideology." He added that MoveOn is "definitely on the movement side of the equation. We don't want to be the party." As the crowd starts to disperse,

I ask him why, if that is true, MoveOn is generally easier on pro-war Demo-crats than they are on pro-war Republicans. Pariser chafes.

"Democrats in Congress perceive us as going after them a lot," he says. "Even though we may not attack them by name, we send out a lot of material asking people to contact their member of Congress on specific issues—not all of which Democrats like. And so when their offices are flooded with calls and emails, they don't like it the same way the Republi-cans don't like it."

His words today are much more conciliatory than his previous talk of movement building. That change, however, is not just an expression of Washington's conciliatory etiquette. It also reflects a struggle to come to terms with—and reject—the McGovern Fable.

CONSERVATIVES HAVE EXTRAPOLATED Nixon's "silent majority" demonization of George McGovern and cultural critique of the anti–Vietnam War movement into a wild fantasy that supposedly explains every Republican victory in the last thirty years. This McGovern Fable posits that the Left's open confrontation with the Democratic Party may have helped end the Vietnam War, but it also resulted in the 1972 presidential nomina-tion of George McGovern, whose landslide loss in the general election sup-posedly gave Democrats a "national security gap" in public opinion polls. According to the Fable, this gap is singularly responsible for giving America twenty out of twenty-eight years of Republican presidents, and came about not because Nixon ran a smarter race or because McGovern's campaign tactically stumbled, but because McGovern opposed the Vietnam War. (The Fable never bothers to explain how a candidate's opposition to a war that most Americans also opposed at the time was his major flaw.)

The Fable's moral is that Democrats should never oppose war and that the Left should never pressure the Democratic Party, for fear of 1972-style election losses.

"The 1960s and 1970s further cemented the Democrats' image as the party of chaos and disorder," wrote the pro-war Democratic Leadership

Council in a typical 2005 missive employing the McGovern Fable to lambaste the antiwar Left. "1972 presidential nominee George McGovern's tag as leading the party of 'amnesty, acid, and abortion' did lasting damage. At the same time, deep divisions arose within the Democratic Party over the Vietnam War and social instability. That cast further doubt on whether Democrats were the party of social order, even on the bedrock issues."

Of course, as scholar Mark Schmitt has noted, the McGovern Fable is a complete sham. Public opinion data show that the much-vaunted "national security gap" supposedly created by McGovern's 1972 candidacy actually "first appeared in polls in 1967–68, because Democratic President Lyndon Johnson was held responsible for the war itself, not because [Democrats] were associated with antiwar activists."

"The real reason the Vietnam War divided and discredited Democrats and splintered the liberal consensus was because—let's not be afraid to admit it—Democrats started that war," Schmitt wrote in 2006. "Opposition to the war didn't unify or define the party, it divided it. Nixon won the 1968 election because [Hubert] Humphrey was associated with the war [and] couldn't split with LBJ."

In fact, Schmitt points out that in the congressional election immediately following that 1972 campaign, the seventy-five Democrats who won congressional seats were overwhelmingly antiwar.

Yet the McGovern Fable has assumed truism status in political circles. To question it is to mimic Bill Clinton questioning what the definition of "is" is—and to elicit the same hoots and snickers of disbelief.

In hesitating to aggressively pressure Democrats to end the war, MoveOn's leadership is embracing the McGovern Fable's central thesis that Democratic Party unity is, above all else, the path to success. But the organization goes back and forth. Just a few months ago, in fact, MoveOn dared to reject the Fable when the organization backed neophyte Ned Lamont in Connecticut's Democratic U.S. Senate primary in 2006.

Lamont, who had never run for statewide office before, was cast by the media as the politically toxic McGovernite, and pro-war incumbent senator Joe Lieberman played the Well-Respected Washington Insider to be protected and glorified as the Guardian of Serious Foreign Policy.

After Lamont rode an antiwar message to defeat Lieberman in Connecticut's Senate Democratic primary, a throng of pundits, reporters, and politicians took to the airwaves to label the Greenwich businessman the second coming of McGovern, and thus a bellwether of an imminent Democratic defeat in the November elections.

"The Ned Scare" read the headline in the *New Republic,* with 101st Keyboarder Peter Beinart asking, "Does Lamont's victory . . . mean McGovernism has returned?" Senate Majority Whip Mitch McConnell told Fox News that Lamont's primary win meant "the McGovern wing of the Democratic Party is staging a comeback." And *Slate* magazine said, "The Lamont Question" is "Will the Democratic Party repeat the political mistakes of the Vienam era?"

Lamont's willingness to break the Washington taboo and challenge a Democratic incumbent made him the subject of national media ridicule, and most Democratic senators refused to help him, even after he won the primary. But the widespread media coverage his candidacy received converted the bipartisan-backed Iraq War from a less political issue into a clear-cut campaign weapon for Democrats in the 2006 elections—at the very time Democratic campaign strategists were desperately trying to avoid the issue completely.* The Lamont phenomenon horrified Democratic

---

*This is no overstatement. After Iraq War veteran Paul Hackett almost won a special congressional election in an ultraconservative district in 2005 by running against the war, the Democratic Congressional Campaign Committee issued a postelection analysis of the race that made not a single reference to Iraq. Months later, the *Washington Post* reported that House Speaker Nancy Pelosi "said Democrats should not seek a unified position on an exit strategy in Iraq" and "[said that] Democrats will produce an issue agenda for the 2006 elections but it will not include a position on Iraq." She made this declaration even though polls at the time consistently showed Iraq was voters' top priority. This same attitude persisted throughout the campaign—until Lamont became a national sensation.

congressional incumbents—and their fear drove them to make full-throated statements against the war so as to avoid being the next primary target.

Few debate that the politicization of the war into a campaign issue for Democrats was absolutely critical to the party's winning Congress in 2006. That means Lamont debunked the two central theses of the Mc-Govern Fable. He didn't just prove that antiwar primaries help build an uprising to stop the war; he proved that primary challenges from the uprising and opposition to the Iraq War benefit the Democratic Party's electoral prospects.

And yet, here in 2007, MoveOn is tacking back toward the conventional wisdom—back toward the McGovern Fable that prioritizes Democratic Party unity over everything else. Tom Matzzie, who serves both as MoveOn's Washington director and as the head of AAEI, will boast to the *Washington Post* that when it comes to ending the war, "our job is to focus on the Republicans." Not to focus on pro-war lawmakers of both parties, *but on the Republicans.*

Such a posture has generated open hostility from the Protest Industry. For example, when MoveOn's leaders end up deciding to support a Democratic bill funding the war for another three months, Protest Industry groups like Code Pink will quickly attack MoveOn's leaders for supposedly selling out the organization's grassroots membership. *Salon* reports that activists believe that "if MoveOn's millions of members knew the full details of the bill, they would surely oppose it."

But then, the Protest Industry could be ascribing radical views to MoveOn members that they may not hold, nor may ever have held in the first place.

THANKS TO GROSS distortions by right-wing demagogues like Sean Hannity and Bill O'Reilly, many believe MoveOn is a radical outfit. But MoveOn has never really had the anti-Establishment, transpartisan bent of history's movement vehicles.

The organization launched in 1998 with a purely partisan call to arms: an email petition by software developers Joan Blades and Wes Boyd against the Clinton impeachment.

But MoveOn wasn't just about telling Congress to "move on" from one impeachment drive. At a more fundamental level, the organization was originally birthed to defend the Establishment—not to change it. Specifically, people flocked to MoveOn to defend Democrats and the government itself from radical Republican revolutionaries trying to pull a coup d'état.

MoveOn (and The Players) promote a similar institutionalist message when it comes to Iraq—the issue that attracted so many new members to its ranks. Their critique indicts this war's initiation under false pretenses and its mismanagement—but not necessarily the concept of war nor the military-industrial complex as a whole. One thread ties together all the press releases, grasstop stunts, and television ads from most of the Washington-based antiwar groups: a pining not for an end to violence as a legitimate tool of foreign policy or for a significant reformation of America's foreign policy apparatus, but merely for a return to those past eras constantly talked about in Washington—those epochs of supposed bipartisan comity, when wars were A-OK because they were started "legitimately."

Privately, MoveOn's leaders suggest this narrow focus is just a pragmatic decision. Echoing Alinsky's advice to "accept the world as it is," they say that criticizing the Iraq War mainly for being mismanaged, misguided, and initiated under false pretenses is the most realistic way to stop this specific war in Iraq.

But the strategy might leave the potential new activist and the armchair onlooker to logically conclude that all the American casualties and the killing of hundreds of thousands of innocent civilians in Iraq would be acceptable had Bush just been a better military strategist and been more honest about his reasons for starting it all.

Some Democratic lawmakers, in fact, seem to be saying this overtly. With no ideologically antiwar voice in Washington, these Democrats are demanding that their party become ideologically "pro-war"—that is, actually in *favor* of violent conflicts as a standing principle, as long as the violence is managed properly. No joke.

"If we become the anti-war party, that's not beneficial to Democrats in 2008," Representative Lincoln Davis (D-TN) tells reporters, despite polls showing that two-thirds of America wants the White House to start withdrawing troops from Iraq. "The kind of pro-war Democrat that we ought to be [is the one that supports] the war that we fight wisely, the ones that we engage in wisely."

Among The Players inside Establishment Washington, nobody—not AAEI, not the much-vaunted "liberal" think tanks—is making the opposite case, that Democrats have a moral and (as Lamont showed) political imperative to *be* the antiwar party, not just the sort-of anti–Iraq War party. The Players have opposed the escalation of the war in Iraq, but there has been no anti*war* drumbeat—no larger argument is being made against wars as a concept or against the underlying danger of the growing military-industrial complex. This means the next time a president wants to start an absurdly stupid war, he or she faces no ongoing antiwar uprising, and just needs to do what Bush didn't do—dot the *i*'s, cross the *t*'s, and follow proper procedure. Put another way, favoring a narrow criticism of just the Iraq War over an attack on Washington's more general prioritization of war as a foreign policy tool has laid the groundwork for neoconservatives' next harebrained military fantasy, whatever it is, to move forward with little serious Washington opposition.

The absence of a full-throated antiwar uprising is tragic at a time when the country appears more skeptical of knee-jerk militarism than ever before. Gallup's annual World Affairs Poll in 2007 shows that a plurality of Americans (43 percent) now believe "the government is spending too much for national defense and the military"; that percentage includes a majority of both self-identified Democrats and independents, and is far more than the percentages saying defense spending is "too little" or "about right."

Yet, as media critic Glenn Greenwald writes, "The Grand Beltway Consensus, one that encompasses both parties, is that War is how we rule the world. . . . The only debates allowed are how many [wars] we should fight, where we should fight them, and how 'wisely' we prosecute them."

When this particular war does eventually end, both AAEI and MoveOn will undoubtedly claim that their narrow, ultrapartisan Beltway strategies were the key. They are, after all, experts at media promotion, and such a laughable yet easy-to-understand story line will be fairly simple to sell in the same era that has seen politicians and television pundits originally lie the country into the conflict.

But what will be little discussed is the possibility that, by refusing to pressure both Republicans *and* Democrats—by refusing, that is, to embrace a *bipartisan* uprising—their strategies prolonged the Iraq War at a time when Democrats had the constitutional power of the purse to stop it immediately. The partisan blinders allowed this war—sold on false pretenses, initiated without strong public backing, and now despised by most Americans—to go on longer than World War II, at a total cost that experts now say could top $2 trillion.

Then again, perhaps ending the war is not really The Players' foremost objective.

To their credit, MoveOn and AAEI both reject the McGovern Fable's claim that opposing unpopular wars is a bad political strategy. But The Players have not rejected the McGovern Fable's other tenet—the put-party-first dogma. In fact, many of The Players made their careers bashing Republicans in attempts to help Democrats win office, regardless of what those Democrats actually *do* once elected.

The unspoken reality, then, is that The Players may actually not mind the war continuing, because it preserves an effective political cudgel against Republicans. Actually ending the war, after all, means less fodder for the next television attack ad.

Say what you will about these folks marching here on the mall who are demanding an immediate cutoff of war funds: even if these anti-Cheney zealots, pro-impeachment activists, and other assorted Protest Industry followers are utterly disorganized and lack real-world political strategies, at least their activism is about more than just a sporting event. They aren't just out here to help one set of politicians defeat another set of politicians. And just as important, they don't dream of stopping just one war because that's what's considered politically expedient. They dream of changing society's long-term outlook on war itself.

LIKE AN EXOTIC species at the zoo, true campaign junkies all exhibit the same special markings: bags under eyes, graying hair, half-shaven beards (among the males), and expressions of permanent fatigue, like they could fall asleep at any moment because they need to catch up on shut-eye from twenty-five years of late-night envelope-stuffing sessions.

Steve Rosenthal, whom I am having breakfast with in Washington a few days after the march, exhibits all of these telltale signs.

"There's a lot of swirling mass communications going on right now," he says between gulps of coffee. "But it really isn't personalized or organized, and it isn't particularly effective."

He is a rare hybrid of an insider and an uprising guy who got his start (like many fifty-ish movement activists) first as a volunteer for McGovern's 1972 campaign, then as staffer for Ted Kennedy's 1980 presidential bid. He served seven years as the AFL-CIO's political director, and in 2004 ran a group called America Coming Together (ACT)—a one-hundred-million-dollar voter turnout machine that was supposed to give us President John Kerry and leave Democrats with a permanent electioneering infrastructure. It delivered neither: Kerry lost, and almost every major ACT funder—from unions to millionaire donors—decided to pull the plug on the operation less than a year after the election.

Now Rosenthal heads a group called They Work for Us whose mission is to pressure elected Democrats to uphold the uprising's antiwar and economic agenda—and Rosenthal is clearly fed up with the substitution of Washington games for real grassroots organizing.

"It's the same thing I used to say about mail when we did a lot of mail in the labor movement," he says. "What happened over the years was that mail became a lazy way to communicate with people. It's much easier to hire a mail vendor and send out a lot of mail to union members than it is to organize people going workplace to workplace and setting up systems to deliver flyers, and organize weekend walks. That's really hard stuff, and people now avoid doing it because it's hard."

Over eggs, he fills me in on all the different incumbents his group is looking at trying to unseat in primaries and how he wants to "make them sweat and bleed and raise money so they have to think differently about things."

But beneath the strategy talk, he is worried. He fears that even on an issue as pressing as the war, partisan loyalties are going to trump everything. That's not just because of incestuous Washington culture or the McGovern Fable, he says, but also because a lot of the people in the uprising today don't really comprehend how power works.

"What many people don't understand is that these politicians carry more water for you as a result of being frightened," he tells me. "In other words, what are these politicians going to do in the face of a primary challenge? Say go fuck you guys because you might come after me? No, it's going to be the other way around—they'll try to appease us by being better, which is the point."

That's what happened with the Lamont primary and the rest of the Democratic Party. When the uprising backed Lamont over the objections of Democratic officeholders in Washington, those officeholders didn't brush the uprising off—they embraced the uprising's antiwar message out of fear.

The same thing happens at all levels of politics. Back in 2001, Rosenthal helped organized labor in Oklahoma use a primary to vote out an incumbent Democratic state senator who had ushered through a ballot initiative making it harder for workers to unionize.

"Shortly after that, the Democratic leadership in the Oklahoma Senate sat down with the union leadership in the state and said, look, we really want to try to find ways we can work together." Rosenthal laughs as he recounts the story. "It wasn't so much that they were upset about that senator losing, it was that the rest of them still there said, holy shit, we don't want to go through the same type of thing. That's the same thing that can happen on the war."

But, as I will see firsthand during a later journey into the heart of the U.S. Senate, the flip side is also true. If Democratic officeholders know that there is no functional antiwar uprising ready to punish them for their war support, then they will just preserve the status quo—regardless of the television ads against Republicans; regardless of the Protest Industry theatrics on the mall; regardless of the The Players' appearances on obscure shows like *Hardball*; and, worst of all, regardless of American troops dying in Iraq.

4

THE BOSS AND HIS
FUSION MACHINE

REFLECTING ON THE antiwar demonstration as I leave D.C., I'd say at least half of the folks who marched voted for Ralph Nader in 2000, which might lead one to conclude that the people most opposed to the war bear some vague, indirect responsibility for it.

Nader, who remains a hero in the Protest Industry, received nearly 100,000 votes as an antiwar, anticorporate third-party candidate in Florida—a state that George W. Bush (officially) won by just 537 votes. Had Nader not been on the ballot, most agree that enough of those 100,000 votes would have gone to Al Gore to win Florida and therefore elect him president. And President Gore, the theory goes, would never have launched the unfathomably stupid invasion of Iraq that the antiwar uprising now protests.

Then again, Al Gore may never have been in a position to contend for the presidency without the 1992 third-party candidacy of Ross Perot, whose votes came mostly out of George H. W. Bush's hide. Bill Clinton's margin of electoral college victory was provided to him by eleven states that Bush had won in 1988 and that were, in 1992, decided by less than 7 percent—far less than what Perot took out of Bush's numbers in those states. Had Perot not been on the ballot in those states, the theory goes,

Bush would have received the lion's share of those votes in those states and thus won the election—and Gore would never have been vice president nor the Democratic Party nominee in 2000.

The common thread between the Naders and the Perots is the so-called third party, and how it is used every now and again as a momentary tool of presidential-level politics to throw a wrench into one election. But this kind of thing ignores the far more compelling history of American third parties as durable, power-brokering machines operating much farther down the ticket. Away from the camera glare of presidential politics, third parties have, at times, been a mortal threat to the two major parties. That is why they have been so important to past uprisings—and why one little-known third party in New York is so important today.

When I see the Big Apple's imposing skyline from the window of this northbound train from Washington, I am reminded of just how improbable uprisings are in a place like New York. The Empire State—and in particular, that island between the Hudson and East rivers—is the home of an international financial Establishment that doesn't take kindly to boat rockers. Yet in the bustling streets beneath those skyscrapers, and in upstate towns far away from Manhattan, a group called the Working Families Party (WFP) has become the one uprising model with the most potential to convert all the populist anger and frustration into functioning political and legislative authority.

The party certainly struggles with the same tensions that divide the two factions of the antiwar uprising—namely, how to balance the need to stay principled with the allure of Establishment co-option that comes with being inside the halls of power. But where the antiwar Players in Washington have succumbed to that allure with disastrous consequences, the WFP in New York is proving unusually adroit at threading the needle between compromising for insider influence and taking no prisoners for uprising goals.

The question is not whether this scrappy little party can be successful, but whether it can sustain its high-wire act, stay true to its principles, and expand beyond New York's borders—all at the same time.

* * *

"YOU AIN'T GOIN' to gain any votes by stuffin' the letter boxes with campaign documents. What tells in holdin' your grip on your district is to go right down among the poor families and help them in the different ways they need help."

Yesterday's political mail is today's political television commercial, and the man who spoke these words knew a little something about power. His name was George Washington Plunkitt, New York's legendary Tammany Hall boss at the turn of the nineteenth century. He believed the most potent political ammunition was not impersonal mass communications but real organizing, and not through the charities or civic organizations or non-profit groups that today dominate so much of American politics, but through the old-fashioned political party—one based around the most mundane economic issues.

"The trouble is that the party's been chasin' after theories and stayin' up nights readin' books instead of studyin' human nature and actin' accordin'," Boss Plunkitt complained. "The party's got to drop all them put-you-to-sleep issues and come out for somethin' that will wake the people up; somethin' that will make it worth while to work for the party."

With a little updating of details, these could be the words of Dan Cantor, New York's newest party boss, whom I'm headed to see. Only he is not a Democrat like Plunkitt. He is the boss of the Working Families Party—a party created specifically to pressure Plunkitt's Democrats and build an uprising.

After the three-hour train ride from Washington, D.C., up to New York City, I am on a Brooklyn-bound subway reading the *New York Times*. The Metro section's front page shows a big photo of a smiling thirty-seven-year-old man in a dark suit sitting on the edge of a desk in an empty courtroom. He is David Soares, the district attorney of Albany County. District attorneys aren't typically interesting—they are usually careerist lawyers or aspiring local politicians. But Soares is different. He won his position by defeating an entrenched incumbent in a Democratic primary and serving as a battering ram for the WFP. It is a story as improbable as this third party's entire eight-year rise.

When I get to Cantor's row house I congratulate him on the *Times* piece about Soares. He is having breakfast with his wife and he replies by making fun of the bagel I brought with me, asking me, "How can you eat that thing with all that plaque on it?" ("Plaque" referring, I surmise, to the cholesterol in the cream cheese).

Cantor neither looks like a political boss, nor has the pedigree of one. Bosses at least in history book illustrations—tend to be fat, cigar-chomping intimidators. Cantor is more avuncular, like a guy you would want to be the coach of your kid's Little League team. His thin beard, slight build, and black wool overcoat also give him a bit of an unreconstructed-radical look—the look of exactly the kind of troublemaking activist that cigar-chomping party bosses hate.

The stereotypical boss comes up from the street and through the party ranks. Cantor, by contrast, came up as the son of a Levittown auto parts shop owner; matriculated to Wesleyan, the elite liberal college in central Connecticut; and then worked on political causes that tended to give parties a big headache—consumer protests, union drives, the two insurgent presidential candidacies of Jesse Jackson, and ultimately a push to start a third-party movement in America that has rather unexpectedly resulted in the Working Families Party, whose platform revolves around economic and racial justice.

Finishing my plaque-smeared bagel, I leave with Cantor and we walk around the corner into an alley where, in a rusting garage, his worse-for-wear white station wagon lives. He is recounting the Soares story.

"We had wanted to run a campaign targeting the Rockefeller drug laws," he says, referring to New York governor Nelson Rockefeller's infamous statutes enacted in 1973 that mandate draconian sentences for drug users.

The Rockefeller laws aren't seen just as a narcotics issue in New York. Their reliance on punitive measures rather than treatment for narcotics possession and abuse offenses is widely considered to be wasteful and counterproductive in attempting to deal with the drug problem. Beyond that, they are seen as an economic, class, and race issue because many believe they disproportionately persecute minorities and low-income citizens. This makes them the perfect target for a WFP campaign.

"We had two interns in our office that we had to keep busy," Cantor continues, as the station wagon gurgles to life. "So we said to them, find a DA who is bad on Rockefeller drug laws that we could target."

The interns brought back the name of an incumbent machine politician and county prosecutor in Albany. When Cantor poked around some more, he caught wind that one of the prosecutor's assistant DAs, a Cape Verdean immigrant named David Soares, might consider running against his boss. Soares had profound disagreements with his boss on the treatment of drug offenders, with Soares favoring a more treatment-oriented approach.

Cantor admits he wasn't particularly optimistic about the prospects.

"Running a black guy in a county that's five percent black on a platform that the incumbent is too tough on crime is not exactly what you'd first think to call a perfect opportunity," he says as we pull onto the Long Island Expressway headed east.

Nonetheless, the labor, consumer, low-income, and grassroots organizations that comprise the WFP's board decided the race was worth an investment. Bolstered by a cash infusion from George Soros, motivated by the billionaire's keen interest in reforming drug laws, the WFP gave Soares its own nomination at the same time it endorsed him . . . in the Democratic Party primary.

When you hear that one party is endorsed in another party's primary, you—like me—are probably confused. That's because we don't know much about a thing called "fusion."

When physicists in the early twentieth century figured out how to use fusion in molecular science, they were able to build the most powerful weapon in human history: the nuclear bomb. When Boss Cantor and his progressive conspirators figured out how to use this thing called fusion in local elections, they were pretty sure they'd found the political equivalent of the same weapon. But only when Soares and the WFP won that Albany election did New York's political Establishment see the mushroom cloud and start to worry.

HOW DOES A third party like the Working Families Party influence another party's primary? The answer is found in the most famous George Washington Plunkitt quote of all: "I seen my opportunities and I took 'em."

Plunkitt uttered the line to explain his corrupt use of public offices to enrich himself personally. But it could be the motto of the WFP, which saw its opportunities in New York's election laws and took 'em.

The WFP was created in 1998 by major labor, consumer, and grassroots groups to take advantage of New York's election laws, which allow one party—if it chooses—to list another party's candidate on its ballot line and then count all the votes for that candidate together. A minor party, in other words, is allowed to cross-endorse another party's candidate and effectively "fuse" with that party on the ballot—a right that exists in only a few states today.

On New York general election ballots in 2006, for instance, you could vote for Hillary Clinton on the Democratic Party line or the Working Families Party line, and either way your vote counted for Clinton.

This esoteric and seemingly boring little detail at the most molecular level of electoral politics is fusion—and like nuclear fusion unlocking enormous energy from mundane atoms, fusion voting can unlock political power from a mundane ballot, as shown by what was happening at the close of the nineteenth century.

In 1890, when fusion was still legal everywhere, there were at least 450 fusion candidates (i.e., listed on two or more party ballot lines) for the U.S. Congress and governor, and from Oregon to Wisconsin, fusion tickets decided control of state legislatures. By 1892, neither of the two major parties had electoral majorities voting on their ballot lines in three-quarters of all states. Republican and Democratic candidates were being elected to office, but they were being elected, in large part, by votes cast for them on smaller parties' ballot lines.

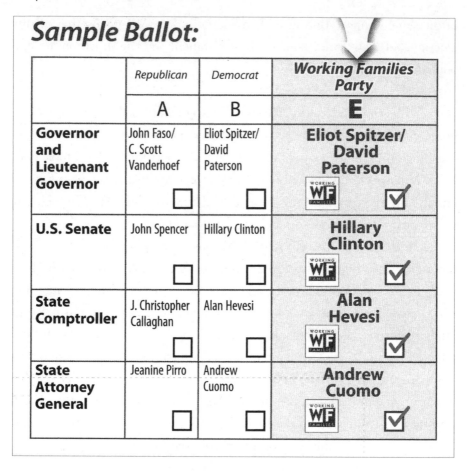

Sample Ballot:

	Republican	Democrat	Working Families Party
	A	**B**	**E**
Governor and Lieutenant Governor	John Faso/ C. Scott Vanderhoef ☐	Eliot Spitzer/ David Paterson ☐	**Eliot Spitzer/ David Paterson** WF ☑
U.S. Senate	John Spencer ☐	Hillary Clinton ☐	**Hillary Clinton** WF ☑
State Comptroller	J. Christopher Callaghan ☐	Alan Hevesi ☐	**Alan Hevesi** WF ☑
State Attorney General	Jeanine Pirro ☐	Andrew Cuomo ☐	**Andrew Cuomo** WF ☑

Fusion's benefits revolve around its ability to bring together—or fuse—culturally disparate constituencies under a unifying economic agenda, without risking a self-defeating spoiler phenomenon where a stand-alone third party candidate like Nader or Perot throws an election to the very candidates they most oppose.

A century ago, the culturally conservative and sometimes anti-immigrant Populist Party (or People's Party) would often use its ballot line to cross-endorse Democratic candidates. The Democratic Party tended to be more urban-based and immigrant-dominated, but it was as progressive on core economic issues like jobs and wages as socially conservative rural farmers. Fusion voting helped make class solidarity more important than cultural division at the ballot box—it helped Democrats overcome their

What's the Matter with Kansas problem whereby rural, culturally conservative, working-class citizens vote against their own economic interests and for socially conservative Republican candidates who represent Big Business.

The formula worked because, unlike the major national parties, which have wide platforms covering every issue, the smaller parties that used fusion voting had distinct and narrow brands. They were either regionally based, focused only on a select few issues, or both. That meant, as in a European parliamentary system, when you voted on one of these parties' lines, you were casting a vote more for the fusion party's platform than for the specific candidates. In a presidential election, a culturally conservative farmer could vote for a Democratic candidate on the Populist line and not feel like he was betraying his feelings on, say, temperance. Meanwhile, an urban immigrant could vote for the same candidate on the Democratic line and not feel like he was endorsing the anti-immigrant views of rural America at the time. Both the farmer and the immigrant voted for the candidate based on economic issues—and by fusing their votes, they were more likely to get people elected who would serve their shared interest.

This is why Republicans so aggressively worked to ban fusion.

"We don't propose to let the Democrats make allies of the Populists, the Prohibitionists, or any other party and get up a combination ticket against us," said one Michigan legislator pushing a fusion ban. "We can whip them single handed, but don't intend to fight all creation." Said another antifusion Republican legislator from Minnesota: "We don't mind fighting you one at a time, but the combination we detest."

President Bush's political guru Karl Rove today tells people his role model is Mark Hanna, the Ohio Republican strategist who helped William McKinley win the White House in 1896 in what historians have called a "realignment" election. The *New York Times* has said Hanna pulled this off by supposedly "moving beyond the party's natural big-business base to appeal to Northeastern and Midwestern immigrants and city dwellers."

But the raw numbers show this "realignment" was not necessarily accomplished through some newly inclusive ideological appeal. It was achieved, at least in part, through a bare-knuckled Republican assault on the election system by outlawing fusion voting—the very tool that was helping working-class urban immigrants and working-class rural farmers form electoral coalitions and elect Democrats.

The scheme worked. Between their election win in 1892 and their election defeat in 1900, Democrats dropped 122 electoral votes—the majority of which were lost in the states whose legislatures had put up obstacles to fusion in the interim. Republicans had masterfully targeted their antifusion legislative campaigns "where the Democrat-Populist fusion candidacies . . . had presented the greatest threat," according to historian Howard Scarrow. And the GOP went on to win almost all of these newly antifusion states in twenty-four out of the next thirty-two years of presidential politics.

DURING THE NATIONWIDE purge of fusion voting at the beginning of the twentieth century, Tammany Hall's Democratic machine passed antifusion laws through the New York legislature after Republicans used it to pick off a few New York City mayoral elections. But because the state Supreme Court struck down those bans as unconstitutional, fusion still survives in the Empire State, as it does in a handful of other places.

In New York's last hundred years, fusion has popped up every now and again as a decisive factor, most famously when the Liberal Party helped deliver John F. Kennedy his margin of victory in New York in the razor-thin 1960 presidential election.

Cut to 1998, when first-term New York Republican governor George Pataki was cruising to an easy reelection victory. Cantor was working as the top organizer for the New Party, which had just lost a Supreme Court case attempting to legally invalidate fusion bans all over the country. Retooling their strategy, Cantor and his fellow New Party organizers joined with New York's big labor unions and grassroots groups to try to use New York's existing fusion laws to secure a ballot line for a new third party—one with a very narrow platform focusing on higher wages, fair taxes, affordable housing, civil rights, and campaign finance reform. The calculation was that the narrower and more populist the agenda, the more sharply the Working Families Party could define itself in voters' minds, and the more clout it could have on its chosen issues.

In its first few years as an official party, the WFP opted almost exclusively to cross-endorse Democrats and avoid running its own stand-alone candidates so as to prevent the Nader phenomenon in which a three-way general election splits the populist/progressive vote and elects corporate-backed Republicans. The goal was simply to build the party's name recognition. In the process, the party demonstrated that its populist economic brand could help Democrats win both votes and legislative battles among constituencies and in districts Democrats usually had trouble winning.

In the 2000 election, for instance, WFP delivered 102,000 votes for Hillary Clinton in New York's U.S. Senate election, and a survey of union members taken after the race found that the use of the WFP line tended to be highest among demographic subgroups "where Clinton received low levels of support overall."

Likewise, in 2001, the WFP's ballot line provided the margin of victory for a Democrat in a tight race for a seat in the Republican-controlled Suffolk County legislature. The winning candidate received 210 votes on the WFP's ballot line in a race he won by 55 votes.

Cantor made sure to use these wins to publicly reinforce his party's narrow agenda. "We want to stand for issues that often don't get heard over the din of money," he told Long Island's largest newspaper after the Suffolk victory. *Newsday* reported that Cantor said he wanted residents to hear the name "Working Families Party" and remember: "That's the party that thinks wages should be higher."

As the party grew, candidates running in Democratic primaries began asking for the WFP's endorsement early. The WFP backing started becoming very valuable in lower-tier primary races, especially in heavily Democratic areas where the primary winner is often the general election winner.

You probably have no idea how to vote in that upcoming five-way Democratic primary race for town council—but if you live in New York, you may know what the WFP stands for, and you will have probably heard through direct mail and canvassing which of those five is the WFP's endorsed candidate. And if you align with the WFP on issues—which you most likely do if you are a Democratic primary voter—then you are probably going to be more likely to vote for the WFP's endorsed candidate.

Same thing in the general election—Democratic nominees ask to be on the WFP's ballot line, knowing that a small but growing segment of unaffiliated voters who don't usually vote Democratic may end up voting for a Democrat on the WFP line—especially since on a general election ballot you see the WFP's name—its seal of approval—next to one candidate in a list of candidates you might not recognize.*

WFP endorsements, of course, come with strings attached: candidates have to fill out WFP questionnaires, submit to town hall meetings with registered WFP members in their districts, and ultimately make concrete pledges to support the WFP's narrow economic agenda. That is, they commit to support the uprising's agenda once in office. The more valuable that ballot line is perceived to be, the more candidates compete with each other for the WFP's endorsement in a bidding war to show who supports the uprising more.

Four years into the WFP experiment, though, "We realized that in order to really take the next step and become a real force, we had to defeat a Democrat in a primary," Cantor tells me.

So the WFP endorsed a primary challenger to a sitting Democratic state legislator in Westchester County who was opposing a bill to prevent cuts to social services for the poor. The ten-year incumbent, who local newspapers said "seemed unbeatable," was defeated by a first-time, WFP-backed candidate in the Democratic primary by twenty-two votes. The WFP assiduously campaigned against the incumbent during the Democratic primary campaign, and its growing name ID and track record made it a credible critic.

The next year, the WFP went even further, successfully running its

---

*You don't see the WFP emblem next to a WFP-endorsed candidate on a Democratic or Republican primary ballot because those ballots only have Democrats or Republicans listed. But on a general election ballot listing all parties, the WFP name is next to its endorsed candidates.

own stand-alone candidate, Letitia James, in a New York City Council race against a conservative Democrat. Her victory was "the first time in about two decades that a candidate won solely on a third-party designation," according to *Newsday.*

Still, New York's Democratic Party was used to strutting around with the hubris of most blue state Democratic parties, and no one was ready to take WFP's frontal challenges seriously . . . until that 2004 Albany district attorney race.

As the primary campaign entered the stretch run and Albany's old Democratic machine started worrying about a loss, things got nasty. The Democratic Party sued the WFP in court, claiming that the WFP's massive field and direct-mail operations for Soares represented illegal meddling in another party's primary.

The WFP successfully fought off the suit and Soares cruised first to a twenty-point victory in the Democratic primary, and then to a general election win. The headline in the *Albany Times Union* could not have been more on the WFP's message: "Primary Win Against Former Boss Sends Shockwaves Through Democratic Leadership."

The successive achievements from the 2001 Suffolk upset to the 2002 Westchester victory, the 2003 New York City Council win, and the 2004 Albany triumph "completely transformed our relationship with the Democratic Party," Cantor says.

"You have to be not just loved but respected. It's best to be both, but if you have to choose, choose respect—and that's what we did," he continues, channeling Sun Tzu. "You cannot build a successful movement until you show you have the ability to defeat a bad Democrat."

Today, the WFP has succeeded in establishing a unique public image. A 2005 Pace University poll showed that the single most influential endorsement in New York City mayoral elections is the WFP's—more important than the state's major newspapers, current or former officeholders, or other advocacy groups. Additionally, the party has established a cause-and-effect relationship between its electoral successes and its legislative victories on behalf of the uprising.

After winning the Suffolk County legislative race in 2001, the WFP convinced that legislature to pass New York's first "living wage" bill, which mandated a $10.25 minimum wage for employees of firms that do business with the local government. Following the 2002 Westchester primary, the state legislature passed a bill helping the town avoid cuts to services. In her first year in office, newly elected city councilwoman Letitia James led the successful fight to block popular Republican mayor Michael Bloomberg's proposals to gut legal services for the poor.

And just months after the state's political Establishment watched in horror as Soares won in Albany, the New York legislature brushed off fears of "soft on crime" attacks and reformed the state's notoriously draconian Rockefeller drug laws—legislation the *Times Union* said the WFP was "instrumental" in passing.

"Democrats are a little bit nervous about us," Cantor says, as we turn off the highway. "They realize they can't take us for granted. But remember—we're not trying to end our relationship with Democrats. We're trying to change it, and for the better."

SOMEWHAT IRONICALLY, Cantor is recounting the Soares race and chest thumping about third-party pressure on Democrats as we are arriving in New York's seventh state senate district, where the WFP and the Democrats are working as one seamless unit in a special election. Last month, a Republican senator vacated his seat, forcing a one-month special election contest to fill the slot. A local Nassau County Democratic politician named Craig Johnson jumped into the race, and WFP quickly agreed to shoulder a sizable chunk of his campaign's field operation.

The strategic theory of the WFP is a modern-day takeoff of how fusion operated in the late nineteenth century. Back then, the Populist Party got the puritanical midwestern farmers depicted in the painting *American Gothic* to vote for the same candidates as the Irish immigrants depicted in the movie *Gangs of New York*. Today, the WFP can be understood by thinking about the sitcoms *The Jeffersons*, *The George Lopez Show*, *Family Ties*, and *All in the Family*. Come election day, the party aspires to create a way for African-Americans like George and Louise Jefferson, Latinos like George and Angie Lopez, suburban liberals like Steven and Elyse Keaton, and working-class social conservatives like Archie and Edith Bunker to all ignore their differences and vote for the same candidates, without feeling like they are selling out their heritage, class, or culture.

If Hollywood producers could pick the perfect setting for a show featuring all of these sitcom families together, they would pick Long Island—a place where WFP has already shown that it can win the Archie Bunker demographic.

In 2002, WFP's ballot line provided 2,900 votes to first-time candidate Tim Bishop (D) in his out-of-nowhere 2,700-vote win over Republican incumbent congressman Felix Grucci. According to the WFP's analysis of the vote, roughly half of Bishop's 2,900 WFP votes came from those who voted Republican or Independent for governor at the top of the ticket,* and then voted WFP for Bishop in the congressional race. Those are ticket-splitting, economic-issue voters, and had there been no WFP line, Bishop would probably not be a U.S. Congressman in a blue-collar district where Republicans have a 50,000-vote edge in registration.

Now the WFP's model is going to be tested in Nassau County—the home of a famed Republican machine that has produced giants like former U.S. senator Al D'Amato (R-NY). It will be tested most in places like the black and Latino section of Elmont, where we are parking the car.

Though it is twenty degrees outside, it is about ninety-five degrees in the Emanuel Baptist Church, and the entire audience is fanning themselves. Looking out over the Sunday morning crowd, I notice two things: most of the women are wearing elaborate hats, and Cantor, candidate Craig Johnson, and I are the only white people in the place. I'm particularly sticking out, because while everyone else is wearing their Sunday

---

*In that race, conservative George Pataki was running on the Republican line, and a right-wing billionaire named Tom Golisano was running an independent candidacy.

best, I'm moderately unshaven, in jeans, and have no tie. I feel like my forehead has the word OUTSIDER stamped on it.

No one seems to notice us at all really, because everyone is riveted by the choir of forty belting out a songs from the front of the room. When the singing stops, a white-haired man in a robe gets up behind the lectern at center stage. This is the Reverend David Parker—the clergyman Cantor told me in the car ride is one of the key players in a race expected to be decided by a handful of votes.

Parker starts out with a fund-raising pitch, imploring his congregation to give generously, and then asking all of those who have given 10 percent of their entire income to the church to stand. Eighty percent of the room stands up.

He delivers a special blessing on the church's givers, and then asks Craig Johnson to stand up in his pew. This is normally when candidates are asked to make a few remarks, so I take out my pen and pad, ready to take down some notes on his speech. But before I know what happened, the whole thing is over.

"Everyone knows what I'm saying when I recognize someone like Craig," Parker says.

A murmur of "uh-huh" goes through the crowd. And then, with that, Parker tells Johnson to sit down.

Cantor is shaking his head, chuckling. "He's not even going to let him talk," he whispers to me. "But that's really fine. Parker just sent the message to vote for Johnson, and that's what's going to be most important for us."

"Us" meaning the WFP, and specifically its canvassing and voter turnout operation in the black community.

"WE'RE HAVING AN actual rally, at an actual *country club*?" Cantor is asking into his cell phone with a tone of disbelief. "Are you serious?"

Yes, apparently the person on the other end of the phone is serious. We're headed from Elmont to an event for Johnson at a country club in the wealthy suburb of North Hempstead.

Suburban country clubs are not exactly strong bases of support for a party whose economic agenda is decidedly, um, anti–country club. The WFP is the party that is regularly lambasted by Rupert Murdoch's *New York Post* as "far left" and that Rudy Giuliani's political aides have attacked as an "ultra-left-wing" organ that supports "gutting the military," raising taxes, and "universal socialist health-care policies."

These caricatures extrapolate the personal histories of WFP leaders like Cantor, with his experience working for liberals such as George McGovern and Jesse Jackson. But like the hippies who shed their tie-dye T's and sandals for button-down shirts and loafers, WFP leaders have shed some of their youthful purity for the more calculating and cutthroat tactics required of New York party bosses. Cantor's take on third-party politics and unmistakable disdain for spoiler parties is a good example of what I'm talking about.

"Third-party politics absent fusion is a fool's errand," he says, rattling off statistics about just how few traditional third-party candidates are elected at any level anymore. "I'm not in this to do fools' errands—I'm in this to exercise real power for our movement."

It is no coincidence that New York politics has been the stepping stone for some of America's best-known Machiavellis, from Boss Tweed to George Washington Plunkitt to Franklin Roosevelt to Robert Moses to Rudy Giuliani to Hillary Clinton. Ascending in a state as big, wealthy, complicated, and brass-knuckled as New York is not for the faint of heart, nor for purists, nor for the obtuse—and that goes for uprisings, not just individual politicians.

For the WFP, wielding power requires many compromises, one of which is an acceptance that the party's focus on working-class issues and working-class voters isn't always going to be the centerpiece of its endorsed candidates' rhetoric. To be a good party boss, you have to be OK with your standard-bearers going from talking like a fire-breathing economic populist in moderate-income neighborhoods to speechifying about social issues at cocktail party events in wealthy suburbs.

This style differs from Protest Industry politics, which focuses more on shaping the discourse. In successful party politics—even third-party uprising politics—the emphasis is on winning elections and passing legislation.

If a WFP-backed candidate is best able to win an election by talking about the issues the WFP has no position on, then that's fine by the party's leadership, as long as the candidate will be a reliable vote for the uprising's agenda in office.

Thus Cantor has no complaints or snarky comments as we walk in to this predominantly white, upper-class crowd here in this country club's bright and sprawling party room that looks like it has held many weddings and bar mitzvahs. Johnson is your classic nondescript midlevel aspiring pol: youngish, tall and beefy, with dark, parted hair and glasses. He is on stage being introduced by an elderly woman whose thick New York accent reminds me of my grandmother.

The topic right now is abortion, an issue the WFP deliberately has no position on. Speech after speech thanks Johnson for his support for a woman's right to choose and hammers his Republican opponent for her position against abortion rights. The speeches have everyone really fired up, though, as Cantor whispers to me, "Reproductive rights are under no legislative attack whatsoever in New York."

But, in Saul Alinsky fashion, Cantor also says, "We have to go to people where they are on the issues they care about if we're going to win elections."

Successful parties are also willing to make enemies out of friends and friends out of enemies at a moment's notice—particularly in dealing with the New York State Legislature.

Thanks to a longstanding mutually-assured-destruction détente, the two major parties used gerrymandering to manufacture a situation whereby for more than three decades, the same New York electorate is represented in the legislature's lower chamber by a Democratic majority, and in the upper chamber by a Republican majority. As a result, most New York state government decisions really are made by just "three men in a room," as the saying in the Empire State goes: the Democratic Speaker of the Assembly, the Republican majority leader of the Senate, and the governor.

That means to get anything done for the uprising, the WFP (like every other political player in New York) has to juggle a bunch of different balls at once. The party must stay in the good graces of Republican state senators while also trying to unseat New York Republicans in other races. It needs to remain on good terms with Democrats while using primaries to pressure them on economic issues. And, of course, the WFP has to keep building its own distinct populist image.

In 2004, the party managed to pull off this juggling act, though not without pissing some folks off. The WFP endorsed an endangered Republican state senator in a wink-and-nod deal with the Republican Senate leadership, which pledged to help override Republican governor George Pataki's veto of a minimum wage increase. The horse trading temporarily enraged Democrats as the WFP's ballot line provided the Republican incumbent with 1,500 votes—decisive in his 18-vote reelection victory.

However, the GOP followed through on its promise, bucking its own governor on Democratic minimum wage legislation traditionally opposed by the Republican Party. The WFP emerged from the battle with the billing of "statewide force" by none other than the *New York Times* (whose editors, as I'll find out later, are no fan of the WFP).

"We made a bet that paid off," Cantor says as Craig Johnson finishes his stump speech to wild applause.

I want to ask him more about this, but we are interrupted by a woman who looks like she walked off the set of *The Sopranos*. She gives Cantor a hug, and I am introduced to Diane Savino, the Democratic state senator from Staten Island. Before running for the seat in 2004, Savino was a state welfare worker, union official, and founding member of the WFP. She talks a mile a minute with a thick New York accent, and she soon picks up where Cantor left off.

"What you need to understand is that a lot of people who consider themselves progressive won't go all out for progressive policies," she says. "That's what the Working Families Party really is for—to not just throw stones, but to force the Democratic Party to start responding in a real way."

But just as the WFP has now been accepted as another soldier on the state's political battlefield, the Staten Island senator reminds me that the

WFP, like any uprising actor trying to straddle the outsider/Establishment divide, will always be tiptoeing through a minefield where one tiny misstep could mean disaster.

"We've thought about trying to create a separate WFP caucus in the legislature," she says. "But it's harder than it sounds because by doing that, you are in a way taking on the Democratic leadership by saying you are separate."

And in New York, she says ominously, "You don't want to be seen as a faction in opposition to the leadership."

That brings up perhaps the most difficult prerequisite of all in exercising third-party power for the uprising: the willingness to make uncomfortable compromises like the one being shoved into my hand by a young campaign volunteer.

The glossy brochure is the standard fare: meaningless slogans ("Real Change, Right Now") and photographs of candidate Craig Johnson in pretending-not-to-pose poses (a full-page spread of the Johnson drinking coffee and talking to people in a kitchen). But one of his bragging points sticks out:

SUCCESSFULLY DEFEATED PROPOSED COUNTY INCOME TAX.

"Yeah, that was the income tax proposal we pushed," admits Alex Navarro with a smile when I ask him about it. He's the WFP's chief spokesman, now on loan full-time as spokesman for Johnson's campaign, and he can admit the irony. "We're backing a candidate bragging about defeating us in his own campaign material, but I guess that's why they say politics makes strange bedfellows."

Strange bedfellows or pushovers?

In 2002, one of New York's most-read liberal weeklies explored the spirit of this question in a lengthy article about the tension between traditional third parties that never fuse, like the Green Party, and fusion parties like the WFP.

"Greens say that the strategy of cross-endorsing Democrats is eternally doomed to fail because the party's more radical views never get publicly expressed by the mainstream candidates," the *Village Voice* reported. "They claim that the WFP merely provides voters the clothespin with which to hold their noses while they vote for the old lesser evil."

Fusion, said New York's Green Party chief, "is the politics of despair."

Taxes are a bread-and-butter issue for the WFP, not some side issue. If the party's leverage stems from giving and withholding its endorsement, ballot line, and all the resources that come with it, why is it backing a guy who has openly defied it on one of its core priorities? Is the WFP's decision to back Johnson "the politics of despair"?

Cantor pauses when I ask the question, and then slowly explains that the WFP's decision to get involved in this Senate race has little to do with Johnson and everything to do with another ball being thrown into the already impossible juggling act that is New York state politics.

That ball is named Eliot Spitzer.

NEW YORK'S FIFTY-FOURTH governor just a few weeks ago began his first term by telling New York legislators: "I am a fucking steamroller, and I'll roll over you or anybody else."

When he was later asked by newspapers if he regretted such a boastful declaration, he snapped, "No. Next question."

In fairness, Spitzer right now has reason to liken himself to heavy streetpaving equipment. His 2006 gubernatorial election campaign very well may end up being officially designated "a fucking steamroller" in even the most staid academic history books.

He won with 70 percent of the vote (and the WFP's endorsement) following two terms doing what was previously considered impossible: relentlessly prosecuting Wall Street crime as a statewide elected official in New York—the home of Wall Street. In the process, he built up his name as the most feared state attorney general in modern American history.

Now, as governor of New York, he is applying the apocalyptic burn-thevillage-to-save-it strategy to one of the largest state governments in the nation, and the WFP—like everyone else—is caught in the middle.

Out of the gate, when Democratic legislators chose an Albany insider over a Spitzer-blessed choice for a plum appointment, things "erupted into an all-out war," wrote the *New York Times*, "as the governor began to visit the districts of fellow Democrats in the Legislature to assail their decision."

Spitzer told a local newspaper that its local Democratic legislator "is one of those unfortunate Assembly members who just raises his hand when he's told to do so, and didn't even bother to stand up and say, 'Whose interest am I representing?'"

And that's friendly compared to what he's trying to do to Republicans.

Before I came up to New York to visit the WFP, a friend in New York politics told me that Spitzer "is going to give Joe Bruno a heart attack," Bruno being the Republican Senate majority leader—one of the "three men in a room" that has run Albany for three decades.

Cantor agrees with the spirit of my friend's comment, explaining to me in the car that Republican governors have refused to strenuously campaign against Assembly Democrats, and Democratic governors have refused to campaign against Senate Republicans.

"For a generation or two now, regardless of who the governor's been, there's been a Republican state senate and Democratic assembly," he says. "A lot of people think both parties liked it that way because they could blame the other for not getting stuff done."

Now, however, Spitzer is breaking the taboo and enlisting all of his allies—and particularly the WFP—in an attempt to break apart the Three Men in a Room détente by putting the full weight of his office behind Johnson's campaign to win this longtime Republican Senate seat in Nassau County. If he wins this race, Democrats will be just a few seats shy of taking control of the entire state government.

The crusade is not a small undertaking, since every individual and institution that is attached to the state's power structure has a stake in preserving the Three Men in a Room détente.

For instance, one might assume that in a supposedly liberal state like New York, the major labor unions would be wholly in the Democrats' corner. But many of them are big financial supporters of both Democrats and Senate Republicans, knowing they need to work through the Republican Senate to get anything done.

Similarly, you might expect that all of the state's Democratic politicians would enthusiastically support a strong campaign to vote out Senate Republicans. Except the détente makes many Assembly Democrats quite happy because they are much more significant players than any of their powerless Senate Democratic colleagues.

More important, under the current system, Democrats don't really face any pressure to actually govern or make good on their stated positions, because they have a Republican foil to blame their failures on. A Democratic Senate would mean that the heat—the *real* heat—would suddenly be on Democrats to deliver. They would actually be expected to pass the progressive proposals they claim they support, potentially fracturing the party along its real divide between economic populists and Big Money appeasers.

With Democrats having failed to win a single Long Island state senate seat in more than two decades, the new governor knows the odds in this race are steep, and he is putting the squeeze on as many groups as possible to back Johnson in the race. Some with investments in the Three Men in a Room détente have said no. The Service Employees International Union's (SEIU) giant health-care Local 1199, in fact, is financing television ads for the Republican candidate.

The WFP, however, said yes when Spitzer came calling, aligning itself not only with a specific Democratic candidate it has substantive problems with, but against Local 1199, one of its most important board members and financial backers.

Does this put the WFP in an awkward position with some of its big labor allies?

"Nope, it happens all the time," Cantor says, swerving us back onto the Long Island Expressway. He doesn't elaborate further, but I suspect from his ho-hum tone that he's telling the truth—and that in such a textured political environment, union leaders may actually want to use the WFP to play both sides of campaigns so that when the election is over, one way or the other, they are guaranteed an avenue of access to legislators.

This bet-covering is exactly what Spitzer aims to end, calculating that, the moment Democrats have both Houses of the legislature, all of the formulas change . . . forever. Republicans will be totally locked out of government, and interest groups won't have a "both sides" to play. There will only be one side. His.

For a small party like the WFP, which itself has relied on winning big gambles, Cantor portrays the decision to back Johnson not as "the politics of despair" but as just another bet that might pay huge dividends for the uprising, and he seems totally at ease with his party's risking its political capital once again.

Some of that serenity comes from Cantor having been through this many times now. Some comes from the fact that if Spitzer gets the Democratic legislature he wants, then the WFP gets to really focus all of its energy on what it does best: pressuring Democrats to make gains for the uprising.

WFP leaders, unlike leaders of progressive groups such as MoveOn and AAEI, understand that the carrot of endorsements is important, but so is the stick of punishment. As much as the WFP gains praise and influence by helping Democrats attract Republican swing votes, the party also gains leverage from Democrats' knowledge that the WFP can often handpick winners of Democratic primaries—or, more threateningly, either withhold its ballot line or even endorse the occasional Republican. Those sticks will get sharper if New York's state government becomes completely but narrowly controlled by Democrats. Why? Because the WFP's ballot line decisions could either preserve or eliminate that control.

But still, something else runs through Cantor's "What, me worry?" attitude—something that comes from the fact that the WFP really had no choice but to make a bet.

"This special election is Eliot's first big move, and we endorsed him for governor," Cantor says. "This is a battle royal. If Democrats win this seat, it's a huge statement by Spitzer that there's a new sheriff in town. If he loses, he'll look like he's got a glass jaw, and we think it is better for our issues if he wins and if we are part of what he's trying to do."

In his eyes, just underneath the Boss Cantor cool, I can see a glimmer of—what is it?—yes, I think it is satisfaction.

"Look, we now have a seat at the table," he says, cracking a smile. "Politicians are coming to us asking us for things because they want something from us. Yes, we have to make compromises. But them coming to us—that's power for our party, which ends up being power for our issues and our movement."

If you didn't hear the last bit about "issues" and "movement," you might think you were listening to George Washington Plunkitt himself.

WE ARE TRAPPED in a Long Island shopping center. Cantor is driving around in circles desperate to find the exit from a shopping center that looks like every other Long Island shopping center we've passed today.

As I watch the dizzying blur of Panera, Starbucks, and hair salons, Cantor is telling me that the WFP's value-add in the Johnson campaign isn't its fusion ballot line, but its organizational acumen and resources.

The party is pouring seventy canvassers and another ten organizers into this race. I tell him that so much staff "sure sounds like a shitload of resources for one state senate race."

"It should," he replies, "because it is. Four million dollars will be spent in one month on this race, and no one is surprised, because this is the biggest legislative race this state has seen in a long time."

Intensity-wise, the Johnson headquarters (which we finally locate in the back of an office park) feels like a presidential campaign, only it is not just white people in here like it is on many presidential races—it's the entire rainbow of races, colors, and ages. Though a Sunday, the office is packed with people. Huge barrels of Dunkin' Donuts coffee are stacked up in the main room, and someone just dumped a garbage bag full of bagels on a table in the middle of the room. People are running around making phone calls, preparing for door-knocking runs, and doing all the unglamorous tasks of local organizing.

When you peel away the allure of the ballot line and the value of endorsements, the scene is what the WFP is at its core: a somewhat chaotic, somewhat ragtag squad of political ground troops in the uprising. Need a crowd for a rally? Call the WFP. Need to canvass the district of a legislator who is getting in the way of a bill? Call the WFP. Need an expert field staff to help increase turnout in a contested election? Call the WFP. You ask Democratic politicians in New York what the WFP truly brings them, and they'll all say one thing: people.

Now it's true—after hearing the Soares story that included the Democrats' suing the WFP—I initially found it difficult to believe that the WFP really would be working right inside a Democratic Party campaign office. I thought at the very least there would be a separate room for WFP folks. But when Cantor introduces me to three young WFP staffers toiling away under the office's wrinkled Nassau County Democratic Committee banner, I become a believer.

"I'll admit it—a lot of people in the party structure are nervous interacting with another party," says Doug Forand, the head of New York's Democratic Senatorial Campaign Committee, who has been dispatched here by Spitzer to guide the campaign.

He looks like George Costanza from *Seinfeld,* and therefore like almost every third-party-hating male I've met who works in professional Democratic Party politics. He's short, wearing khakis, a button-down blue shirt, and glasses, and is both graying and balding. Thanks to Ralph Nader in 2000 and to years inside the Democratic Party machine, these kinds of people either roll their eyes or reach for your throat when you ask about third parties.

But not Forand. Though a Democratic Party operative, he's nothing but effusively complimentary to the WFP. He says that the party, with its specialty in field organizing and get-out-the-vote operations, is critical in a race like this, because most observers believe low voter turnout will benefit Republicans, while higher turnout will help Democrats.

"This campaign is a case study in how we can all work together," he says between barking orders at an underling in another room. "And at this point, because so many Democratic legislators have such close contact with the Working Families folks, they are now seen as a part of the legitimate political landscape."

I press him to see if everything truly is as hunky-dory as he says.

"Look, if you are an entrenched Democrat in a safe district who bene-fits from the status quo, then yeah, you are probably a little concerned about the Working Families Party, because they can make life complicated for you," he admits. "They have the ability to withhold their ballot line, and these politicians know that can hurt. So, at the end of the day, we have more Democratic officials who might go a little more left than they naturally want to because they want that ballot line and they don't want to deal with a primary."

Cantor grabs a bagel off a pile of flyers, and I rib him for putting "a lot of plaque" on it. He chuckles, and again has that twinkle of satisfaction in his eye—not because he's excited to eat cream cheese, but because he heard Forand pay respects to the WFP. He also makes sure to remind me that the WFP–Democratic Party synergy I'm looking at in this office has been made possible by more than just a common interest in seeing one candidate elected. It happened, he says, because the WFP agreed to Spitzer's demands to make this temporary marriage of convenience as smooth as possible. Most important of these was the demand "to not push a Row E message," Cantor says.

Row E is the WFP's official line on the New York ballot. What Cantor is saying is that the WFP's field workers knocking on doors are not telling voters to vote for Johnson on the WFP's line. They are just telling them to vote for Johnson, and he's right—that's a huge concession for two reasons.

First, WFP uses "the Row E message" to develop its distinct brand, which can then be used to attract votes that a candidate might not normally receive—votes from people who may hate the Democratic Party on social issues but are populist on economic ones. The way the WFP gets those in-dependent voters to provide the margin of victory in close races is by telling voters to "vote Row E" specifically to let candidates know that voters want them to represent the working class on economic issues.

When successful, "the Row E message" circumvents vacuous, televi-sion-driven candidate-centered politics to build that critical issue-based coalition between the Jeffersons, the Lopezes, the Keatons, and the Bunkers.

Think back to those 1,300 ticket-splitters on the tip of Long Island who voted at the top of the ticket on the Republican line for George Pataki and then voted down-ballot for Democrat Tim Bishop in the congressional race on the WFP line, giving him his victory. These voters may not have liked Bishop's support for abortion rights, but they probably liked his—and the WFP's—economic positions. Row E gave these voters a way to express that sentiment. The WFP's ballot line allowed them to vote for Bishop's economic stands without betraying their own cultural beliefs.

Second, a "Row E message" is essential to the WFP because the size of the Row E vote can be directly related to how much—or how little—an elected official will support the uprising agenda that the WFP pushes. The more Row E votes a politician gets, the less that politician will ignore the WFP's demands when corporate lobbyists come calling, because they know that if they stray too far, they may lose the WFP's ballot line in the next election and probably lose those votes.

"Organized interest groups exert power by turning out their members and making claims about how many folks they turned out and whom they voted for," Cantor has written in WFP promotions. "But fusion lets everyone—the politicians, the media, and the voters themselves—count exactly how many votes you produced for the candidate running on your line."

So here in the Johnson race, not only has the WFP been muscled into working for a candidate it has serious ideological problems with, it has been pushed into giving up its branding opportunity.

Behold the political horsepower of Eliot Spitzer, the "fucking steamroller."

I'VE LIVED IN a lot of bleak places that are really gray and get a lot of snow. Montana has a severe winter, to say the least. Winter in Chicago, where I lived during college, makes you wonder whether there is a blue sky anymore. But no place that I've ever been is as bleak, cloudy, cold, iced over, and just downright grim as Albany, New York, in February.

Only 150 miles northwest of the East Coast megalopolis, Albany hardly seems in the same state—much less the same universe—as New York City. The sky and the concrete buildings in this town of 100,000 are the same grayish yellow color as the sooty snow that covers the streets. None of the Big Apple's glitz, verve, or bustle has rubbed off on this sleepy state capital, which looks far more Allentown than it does Manhattan. As I walk toward the union hall where the WFP's executive board meeting will be held today, I almost get hit by a car that I couldn't see because the mountains of snow along the curbs are now about six feet high, making the sidewalk and the roads two separate hallways. Even the meters don't stick out.

It has been an eventful few weeks since I hung out with Cantor in Nassau County.

The WFP's gamble on Craig Johnson paid off in more ways than the party even had hoped. In terms of sheer numbers, WFP canvassers knocked on 45,000 doors for Johnson, and roughly half of the 3,600 votes that provided Johnson his margin of victory were cast on the WFP's ballot line. This, despite no proactive advertising behind a "Row E message."

Johnson's victory translated into a media boomlet for the party, as the WFP was widely credited with playing a decisive role in the race. *Newsday* listed Cantor as one of the four big winners in the race. The New York *Daily News* said the WFP "more or less bailed out the Johnson operation" and that the seventy-five field canvassers the WFP donated to Johnson's race "prov[es] as always that there is no substitute for seasoned ground troops." Even former Republican senator Al D'Amato told the *New York Times* that what won the race was the "surprisingly high turnout"—an indirect compliment to the WFP's get-out-the-vote operation.

Before I walked into the linoleum-floored room where the WFP's post-election board meeting is taking place, Cantor promised me that the stats about the Johnson race would be the first thing discussed. But they are only being presented to the crowd of WFP officials by a staffer now, about forty-five minutes into the meeting, because Malcolm Smith just walked in—and WFP leaders want him to see how successful they have been.

Smith is the state senate Democratic leader, which means he has a

little less legislative decision-making authority than the college interns answering phones in a junior Assembly Democrats' office. However, thanks to
the Johnson win, Smith is now just a few Senate victories away from replacing Republican Senate president Joe Bruno as one of the three most
powerful people in the state—one of the three men in the room.

Once the last slide is shown, Smith is introduced by Bertha Lewis, the
executive director of New York ACORN (Association of Community Organizations for Reform Now) and a state cochair of the WFP. As the group
gives him an enthusiastic round of applause, he sits down at a table facing
the room and crosses his hands.

Smith is a black senator from Queens who looks like he's in his late
thirties, but is actually in his early fifties. He sports a thin mustache and is
wearing a crisp navy blue suit, a pink tie, and orange translucent cufflinks.
He has a pronounced New York City accent, and his voice is soft and raspy
like Don Corleone, though he's not here to make WFP leaders an offer they
can't refuse—he's here to deliver a message of unity that plays to the WFP's
vanity, and also a stern warning.

Following the obligatory thank-yous, Smith pumps up the group by
telling them that they should see the Democratic takeover of the state senate as imminent and that they should all feel like they have a stake in that
pending achievement.

"We need your help," he says, striking a note of inclusion that aims
straight for the insecurity that every third-party and uprising participant
lives with—the one that is secretly desperate for any shred of respect from
the Establishment.

But, he quickly adds, the WFP shouldn't expect too much.

"We have to make sure that we are all together," he says, telling the
WFP it has to start looking at the Democratic Party as a kind of domestic
partner, "sort of like [it's] living in your house."

"No matter how much tension there might be over an issue, you know
you aren't going to move out. You know you are going to live together."

He makes a strike on any future disappointment, telling them he
knows that if and when Democrats win the Senate and don't deliver, the

WFP will want to retaliate with their ballot line through primary challenges to Democratic incumbents.

"I'm saying this to you today: Don't do that."

That a senior Democratic Party leader feels the need to visit the WFP and preemptively push back like this is a testament to how strong the WFP has become.

Looking at the facial expressions around the room, I get the feeling that lots of folks are thrown off by Smith's friendly tone and don't sense the pugnacity of his words. But ever so gently, he continues to read them the riot act.

"This is going to happen," he continues, referring to the Democratic takeover and his own subsequent elevation. "And you are going to need to begin to rethink and retool how you are approaching your interests and your desires."

After Smith's speech, the meeting becomes an orchestrated Q&A session. ACORN's Lewis calls on different WFP members who have predetermined queries designed to get Smith to make pledges on the record. This is the highly effective model used by the American Israel Public Affairs Committee (AIPAC)—the model that some in the uprising haven't figured out how to use. Get a big group of influential people in a room with an elected official and put him or her on the spot. It's not rocket science.

The questions run the gamut. Lewis asks Smith to support more affordable housing. A United Auto Workers representative asks Smith about workers' compensation reform. Someone else requests his vote for a bill mandating paid sick days for workers. On almost everything, Smith sounds comfortable—he agrees with the WFP most of the time.

That is, until the last two questions about money—questions that define the WFP.

The WFP is more a sum of its uprising parts than even the major parties and their interest groups. I understood this the moment I walked into this gathering today. In a typical Democratic Party board meeting, people are there as Democrats first, and as their other affiliations second. At the WFP meeting, the seventy or so people packed in here represent their organizations—local public employee unions, ACORN chapters, private employee unions, teachers unions, grassroots groups, you name it. To them, the WFP is the means, not the ends.

Budget fights are one of the key ingredients in the glue that keeps these groups working together as a cohesive uprising. There may be disputes between different unions, and there may be fights over which specific candidates to endorse, but every group here has an interest in seeing public sector services maintained or expanded.* This is why many of the WFP's best-known legislative successes have been battles over social programs—and why Smith is being asked whether he supports Governor Spitzer's new proposal to cut $1 billion out of health-care programs.

"Will you work with us to oppose irresponsible cuts in health care?" asks a guy from the Westchester WFP chapter.

Without stopping for an answer on health care, the questioner goes on to "what drives these cuts: refusal to adequately tax the very richest people in New York."

He tells Smith about the WFP's proposal that would annually tax New Yorkers one day's pay for every $500,000 they make in a year. Anyone making under $500,000 annually would pay no new taxes under the bill. In a state where 44,000 of the wealthiest taxpayers make almost a quarter trillion dollars a year, the plan would raise $11 billion—money that the WFP would like to plow into social programs and into property tax relief for working- and middle-class New Yorkers.

Unfortunately, Spitzer recently took a "no new taxes" pledge (or, as Cantor called it when he started the meeting today, "an idiotic no new taxes pledge"), showing that conservatives' antitax movement has left its scars

---

*Public money as coalition glue is not unique to the WFP. In recent years, conservative ballot initiatives mandating draconian spending cuts have forged together wide coalitions of traditionally antithetical groups that nonetheless share an interest in public investment. Just a few months ago back in Montana, in fact, unions and the Chamber of Commerce partnered up to get one of these initiatives tossed off the ballot.

even here in New York, far away from the libertarian bastions of the Rocky Mountain West.

"Will you support this new tax on the richest New Yorkers?" Smith is asked.

The question goes straight to the issues of corporate power and income inequality, which are just as near and dear to the WFP's heart as budgets, but which the party has had less success with beyond the 2004 passage of a statewide minimum wage increase.

Regarding Spitzer's proposed health-care cuts, Smith is noncommittal but conciliatory, pledging to take up the issue with the governor. Promising to spend money, you see, is politically easy. Corporate interests and the wealthy don't really get offended by spending, and Smith knows that.

But tax increases are different. They are about regulating wealth, which is why taxes are one of the front lines in the uprising, and why politicians like Smith shy away from them.

"I'm just not a tax person—I like to relieve everybody as much as possible of their taxes," Smith continues. "So I can't stand here and say 'Yes, go tax the rich.'"

New York may be a reliable "blue" state, but it is the home of the banking, securities, hedge fund, venture capital, and media industries, to name a few; and that wealth takes time off from power lunches in Manhattan and vacations at the Hamptons to make the elite's economic concerns a priority here in Albany. Taxes are one of those concerns, and this last interchange with Smith reminds everyone in the room how much work the uprising still has in front of it.

ONCE SMITH LEAVES, the rest of the meeting is spent going back and forth between strategizing and lamenting.

During an in-depth presentation on Spitzer's health-care budget, SEIU's political director says, "Spitzer is not taking on business in a way that we think a Democrat should take on business."

SEIU local 1199, which just weeks ago was backing Craig Johnson's

Republican opponent, will soon begin airing television ads against Spitzer himself, chastising his health-care budget cuts.

Later, a guy from the hotel workers union UNITE HERE says he's sure that when the WFP starts pushing its legislative agenda, Spitzer and the Democrats will actually use Craig Johnson as a way to stop them.

"You are absolutely right," Cantor responds. "They will say that if we push too hard on our agenda, we'll pull them to positions that will make Craig Johnson lose his reelection."

Then comes a woman from the Suffolk County WFP chapter—the chapter that helped make Tim Bishop a congressman and was recently credited with flipping the local county legislature to Democratic control for the first time in three decades. She says the party has to get more confrontational. That prompts an older bearded guy from one of the public unions to jump in and say no, the party has to make more deals, which then spurs a guy from the United Auto Workers to remind everyone of the reality at hand.

"Look, Spitzer's goal is to take the Senate and become all-powerful," he says. "He responds to us when he feels that's going to advance his ultimate goal. We have to play that for whatever we can get out of it."

He's correct. As the New York *Daily News* noted, the WFP's decision to back Johnson means "the Working Families Party made a clean break with Joe Bruno and the Senate Republicans after years of playing footsie in order to move specific legislative items forward." This scrappy third party is lashed to Spitzer, at least for now, whether it likes it or not.

But figuring out how to maximize its relationship with the New York governor is only one of the puzzles the WFP has to master in the coming years. If this party is going to be the spark plug of a national uprising, it must come up with ways to expand, not just inside of New York, but elsewhere. And that won't be easy for a few reasons.

As Smith's presentation suggests, the WFP faces opposition not only from Republicans and Rupert Murdoch's red-baiting newspaper network. Some Democratic Party insiders don't care about the uprising, aren't interested in how fusion helps Democrats, and don't like any party—WFP or Greens or whoever—that encroaches on their turf.

"[WFP leaders] need to show Democrats that they don't dilute the [Democratic] party's institutional control over elected candidates," warned a New York Democratic National Committee official in a 2006 *American Prospect* article.

Such passive-aggressive animus becomes more open hostility among elite media voices like the *New York Times* editorial board, which disdains the whole anti-Establishment concept of fusion. In one of a number of similar screeds, the *Times* editors in 2006 offered up a hysterical "last-minute plea" begging voters to avoid voting on any fusion party line. To make their case, *Times* editors pointed out that thirteen years prior, New York City mayor Rudy Giuliani gave a plum city job to the son of the leader of another fusion party who "wound up being sent to prison for embezzling more than $400,000 and for possession of child pornography."

Message from the *Times:* fusion voting encourages pedophilia.

The blowback is predictable. Every uprising that has ever seized power or challenged the status quo has faced moaning, wailing, and crying from those inside the palace walls. And while each threat, flip-off, and attack is not devastating on its own, they take a toll, particularly on the WFP's battle to expand.

When I see Cantor a few weeks after the Albany meeting at a conference of liberal donors in Washington, I can tell he is frustrated. He has been trying to convince national liberal philanthropists to give him money to establish WFPs in the group of states, including Delaware and New Hampshire, that still allow fusion, and to strengthen the fledgling WFP in Connecticut (another fusion state) after Ned Lamont's primary defeat of conservative Democrat senator Joe Lieberman showed the uprising's potential there. Cantor also wants to push fusion legalization ballot initiatives and legislation in other states. Though bare-bones campaigns did come extremely close to passing such legislation in the Oregon and Montana legislatures in 2007, Cantor has not been all that successful in raising the resources necessary to get over the goal line.

"It's just hard on so many levels," he tells me as we meander through the lobby of the Washington Hilton.

One of his problems is the Left's dearth of ideological funders in comparison to the Right. Many very wealthy liberal donors talk a great game about their commitment to liberalism, but a good number of them are basically "starfuckers"—people who make political contributions with little regard for economic issues and with an interest only in getting face time with celebrity presidential or Senate candidates.

"That's what we get from what passes for the Left in this country," New York state senator Eric Schneiderman (D-Manhattan) told me in an interview about the WFP's challenges. "They're all purists until Ted Kennedy will have them to lunch and then they're not."

Cantor, of course, cannot sell donors on celebrity.

"We're the noncelebrity party," he has told the *New York Times*. "What we're doing is not sexy or glamorous. To go door-knocking week after week, month after month, is not for the faint of heart." Nor for starfuckers.

Another problem for the WFP is that many national liberal donors are motivated purely by a partisan loyalty to Democrats, and the effort to build a multiracial, class-oriented uprising vehicle that uses an unfamiliar voting system never makes it onto their radar. Many of these same partisan donors also barely care about the uprising—and, in some cases, these wealthy donors actually disagree with the uprising's populist economic agenda out of their own sense of upper-class solidarity. And at the gut level, when they hear about a left-leaning party that isn't the Democratic Party, they instantly start reliving their anger at Ralph Nader for denying the nation President Gore.

But this may be where the WFP finds its opening with partisan donors.

To fight the antifusion movement in the early twentieth century, fusion party leaders might have told naysaying ideological allies that, "if there had been fusion in 1900, we would have had President William Jennings Bryan!"

Cantor's fund-raising pitch says much the same thing, only updated. "If there had been fusion in Florida in 2000," he tells me he says to donors, "we would have President Al Gore!"

He says fusion would actually disarm Nader-style third-party spoilers by siphoning more of their votes to the Democrat–Working Families fusion nominees. As proof, he points out that when the WFP hit its stride, the New York Green Party lost so many votes that it was stripped of its ballot line for failing to meet minimum voter-support requirements. New Yorkers stopped throwing away their votes on stand-alone spoiler candidates and started voting on the WFP's fusion line.

From there, Cantor makes a strong argument that helping the WFP legalize fusion will allow Democrats to finally break the electoral chains that antifusion Republicans originally shackled them with back in the 1890s—the chains that keep culturally and geographically disparate constituencies from unifying behind the populist uprising on election day. And to make his point, he wields a persuasive December 2005 poll from three key swing states—Ohio, Washington State, and Missouri.

The survey from the respected Benenson Strategy Group used a hypothetical rematch of the 2004 election to ask voters whether they would vote for President Bush or John Kerry, with the option of voting for Bush on the ballot line of a socially conservative third party, and Kerry on the ballot line of an economic populist third party. The result is that Kerry would have picked up far more votes than he would have needed to win Ohio and thus the presidency in 2004.

The survey ran the same test in Washington State, but substituted an antitax party for the socially conservative party. Again, the results are compelling, with Kerry adding nine points to his total margin of victory.

But the most interesting results of the study came from the analysis of the WFP's potential brand appeal.

To the typical Democratic strategist outside of New York, the subjugation psychology case against the WFP probably sounds effective. As the argument goes, the WFP has only been able to succeed because it is supposedly an ultraliberal party in the already liberal state of New York, and its model is therefore not applicable in more conservative states. But according to the Benenson poll, folks outside of New York probably would not even see a WFP in their state as "liberal."

As part of the study, voters in Ohio, Washington, and Missouri were read a description of the WFP as one that fights on "pocketbook" issues "like the outsourcing of jobs to other countries, the cost of prescription drugs, and increasing the minimum wage." Voters were then asked to rate the party on a scale from one to nine, one being extremely liberal and nine extremely conservative. Fifty-seven percent of voters labeled the WFP a five or above. The survey confirmed once again that the pocketbook issues at the heart of the uprising transcend party and ideological labels.

The significance of this result is not lost on at least some national Democratic Party leaders, who already know how the WFP's line in New York has provided the margin of victory for Democrats in many close races. New York's U.S. senator Chuck Schumer, the head of the Democrats' election campaign apparatus, clearly gets it.

"[The WFP] can bring disaffected 'Reagan Democrats' back into the fold," Schumer now tells reporters. "They attract independents, and they provide a place for crossover Republicans."

But, then, what are the costs of working too closely with an Establishment the WFP is designed to pressure? In Washington, the antiwar uprising's deference to Democratic Party leaders has arguably prolonged the Iraq War that the uprising is trying to stop. What would happen to the WFP if it, too, became an arm of the Democratic Party and its partisan national donors? Expanding the WFP model outside of New York clearly could require raising big money from partisan, starfucker donors who might ask the WFP to back off its most confrontational tactics against the Democratic Party. Would such a trade-off be worth it to go national?

And what about the WFP's own members? Will they accept the demands for compromises? Or will the party face the same Protest-Industry-versus-Players split over methods, partisan loyalties, and ideological purity that has weakened the national antiwar movement?

This last question is a very real wild card, as shown by a minor political tremor in 2007. In Rockland County, two top WFP officials announced their departure "because they say the party and its chairman have gotten away from their progressive roots." The local WFP chairman responded by rejecting the notion that "we're getting away from the grass roots," but he also said, "Are we getting a little more realistic as we mature? I think so."

The WFP is attempting to shatter the choice between "realistic" and "idealistic" in New York, showing that a political party can be both while also being part of the bigger uprising. But amassing political power and constructing an ideological uprising is not *always* the same thing—and some progressive WFP loyalists like state senator Schneiderman seem to worry that the party will eventually prioritize the former over the latter.

Citing the fact that the WFP's biggest union members "until very recently, endorsed every Republican state senator in a contested race," Schneiderman told me "success is dangerous."

"I think the WFP are absolutely committed progressives and their intention is good," he said. "But they got into the game, and they wanted to be players and negotiate, and in the Albany scene you feel like you're very important. But if you don't have some clear definition of what you stand for such that it may scare some people away from joining you, then you're probably not going to get much done."

If too many rank-and-file members feel the WFP has lost that "clear definition" of what the party stands for, it could spell trouble, especially considering the party—by definition—is subject to popular control. WFP members can, for instance, override WFP officials' endorsement decisions or even vote out party leaders altogether.

Nonetheless, that air of optimism is always with Cantor, even as we are walking through Washington and he is kvetching to me about fundraising. He has a lot to be proud of. In 2000, he told *The Nation* magazine that he was worried about "how to wag the dog and not just be the tail that gets wagged." By 2003, Democratic operatives were telling the *New York Times* they fear that the WFP is now driving the Democratic Party's decisions. As America's most unlikely political boss, Cantor doesn't forget just how meteoric this rise really has been.

"The problems we have are good problems to have," he says, scratching his beard before we shake hands and he heads off to another donor meeting. "If we can stay true to our agenda, then it's better to have a seat at the table and have these problems than have no seat at all."

5

THE PERMANENT
BARRIER

WHEN YOU COME back to your old digs, everything looks different. A few years back, I visited my old elementary school and was shocked at how low to the ground the water fountains and urinals were. In my memory, they were just the right height. Now they look to me like they were made for hobbits.

It's sort of the same feeling coming back to visit Capitol Hill four years after I left for good. The water fountains and urinals look the same, but everything looks more caricatured—more like a movie set than reality. The imposing size of the Capitol complex, the black town cars, the expensive suits—it all used to seem so mundane, and now it looks so pronounced. It is like a comic book strip portraying the Establishment that the uprising is so disgusted with.

I am back in D.C. this winter of 2007 to visit three lawmakers who come from very different states, but who each ran for office in 2006 promising to represent the uprising inside the governmental institution originally designed to stop uprisings: the United States Senate.

This isn't just my paranoid belief—it is the explicit reason the Founding Fathers established Congress's upper House. Just look at the words of Alexander Hamilton—America's original country club Republican. He fretted not about robber barons or autocratic concentrations of power and wealth, but about creating a nation that might give regular folks the most say over their own government. "Give all the power to the many, they will oppress the few," he said. And let's be clear: he wasn't talking about a majority running roughshod over an oppressed minority—he was worrying about the poor rising up against banks.

Hamilton arose at the Constitutional Convention in 1787 and demanded the creation of a "permanent barrier" against what he called the "turbulence of the democratic spirit." To get that barrier, he said, the country needed an element of its national legislature that would control "popular passions" with its own "permanent will." The result was the Senate—an intrinsically undemocratic organ forever sewn into the U.S. Constitution.

At first, I had decided to visit the "permanent barrier" to see whether this Senate trio will end up being the Three Musketeers or the Three Stooges. I wondered—do they really want to be known as fearless swashbucklers shaking things up on behalf of the uprising and the "popular passions"? Or was that merely their campaign rhetoric, and do they really want to just settle in as stooges for the "permanent will"?

But then, walking up to the Capitol complex this morning, I'm recognizing that what they or any other senator *want* is not the most critical question. What really matters, and what is so little understood, is whether the "permanent barrier" means it is structurally *impossible* to effectively represent an uprising here.

The fortress construction of the Senate office buildings and the swarming security guards tell onlookers this is not a place that should be thought of as open to the public—and certainly not a place where uprisings will be tolerated. This message is reinforced when the armed guards shoo me away from the first three entrances I approach. I'm told I have to go to the entrance for "visitors"—the term used in science fiction to describe extraterrestrial aliens*—which is how Washington lately seems to view the 300 million people that it governs.

---

*Remember the TV series about space aliens called *V*? Right—it stood for "visitors."

Inside, symbolism delineates a caste system. Lawmakers wear gold lapel pins identifying them as Extremely Important People. The well-dressed men and women who wear necklaces with badges and walk *next to* the gold-pinned lawmakers are known to be Important People—usually chiefs of staff, lobbyists, or reporters. The slightly less well-dressed folks with neck badges walking *behind* the lawmakers and who are usually limping under the weight of binders, notebooks, and briefcases are Less Important People—legislative assistants, schedulers, press secretaries, and the rest of the professional drones known colloquially as "Hill staffers."

It is true that merely having a neck badge grants you status in this food chain above the "visitors." That is, as long as your badge is not like the one I am getting—the one stamped with the huge red word INTERN. It might as well have the word ASSHOLE on it, because that's how you are treated as an intern—like a total asshole.

I am being forced to get an intern badge because I was denied an official press pass by the board that issues them—a board controlled by reporters from major newspapers and magazines who have an interest in denying requests like mine.

Right now, the media industry is facing a fairly tenacious uprising of its own thanks to an Internet that empowers more and more of us "visitors" to be news providers ourselves. Like every Establishment facing an uprising, the Old Media hands in Washington respond by trying to create and preserve monopoly control, one that makes public information (i.e., congressional hearings, press conferences, etc.) and public space (i.e., hallways in the Capitol) into proprietary material regulated by a single gatekeeper—the media. Washington reporters who run the press gallery figured out that one way to pull this off is to abuse the power Congress gave them to issue—or deny—press passes.

So I was in a tight spot. Three U.S. senators had agreed to let me spend a few days with them, but Permanent Washington was trying to stop me. What to do?

Become an intern.

I called up a friend who is a congressional staffer and begged him to tell the Capitol security folks that I am his intern.

"Are you serious?"

"Yeah, I really need your help."

"OK, but you have to make some copies for me," he joked. "And stuff some envelopes. And take in the boss's dry cleaning."

Hilarious.

Sitting here in the security office waiting for my intern badge to print out, I feel my career going backward. Twelve years ago as a college sophomore, I was given my first Capitol Hill intern badge, signing up for a summer of indentured servitude. I later became chief spokesman for a congressman, then for the House Appropriations Committee, and now I am back to being an intern. As I put the badge around my neck, I could swear I hear someone laughing.

This is D.C.'s way of punishing me for leaving: tattooing an ASSHOLE label on my chest when I dare to come back for a visit.

JOHN C. CALHOUN HAD Elvis's pompadour about a century before Elvis did. I never knew this until I sat down here in the Senate reception room and caught a glimpse of Calhoun's portrait on the wall. All I knew of the South Carolina senator was that he was Congress's chief spokesman for slavery and against abolition in the 1800s. That his mug now watches over all that goes on in the Senate is probably not a coincidence. The Senate, like Calhoun, is proud of its intransigence and antipathy to change.

"The Senate has a conservatism to it that has often stood in the way of progress," Ohio senator Sherrod Brown (D) is telling me in his gravelly voice. "The old-timers here brag about this institution's inefficiency. They say that it's built to be that way and they're right."

Brown is the first of the three lawmakers I'll be seeing on this trip. I got to know him a few years back when we were both working in the House—he was the congressman from the Cleveland suburbs, I was a staffer for his ideological comrade-in-arms, then-Representative Bernie

Sanders (I-VT). Both of them were elected to the Senate in 2006—but it was Brown's election more than Sanders's that sent shock waves through Washington.

That's because while Sanders won liberal Vermont, a state considered the pot-scented tie-dyed T-shirt of American politics, Brown defeated a Republican incumbent in conservative Ohio, America's sweat-reeking, grease-stained blue collar. His victory shattered the entire Washington myth that Democrats have to split the difference on issues with Republicans and steer clear of the uprising in order to win the heartland. Instead of trying to rebrand himself as a quasi-Republican like many Democrats do in tough states, Brown happily jammed his uprising credentials and his political ideology down everyone's throat.

He started off his run declaring that he was "proud to carry the progressive banner." During the campaign, he boasted to skeptical national reporters that his run was going "to change the direction of the state and the country [because] it can show a progressive Democrat can win in a state like Ohio." And in his victory speech on election night he reminded the public that his entire campaign was about "fight[ing] uncompromisingly for progressive values."

This was something new in Ohio, to say the least.

Brown had built up a populist voting record in Congress and was running a William Jennings Bryan–style campaign in a state that has been the beating heart of Establishment Republicanism for most of American history—a place that Republican presidential candidates have lost just four times since 1948. Ohio gave America the Taft dynasty, which has produced Republican presidents, Supreme Court chief justices, governors, and senators. The state was the launching pad for Mark Hanna, the Republican senator and the late nineteenth century's Karl Rove, whose antifusion campaign helped lock Democrats out of power for the better part of three decades. It was the home of Warren Harding, the empty-suit, knee-jerk conservative that Republican Party elders selected as their presidential nominee in the 1920 convention that was the inspiration for the political phrase "the smoke-filled room." And, of course, Ohio was the place where many believe a right-wing secretary of state used his power over elections and ballot counting to help seal the 2004 election for George W. Bush.

With this history in mind, Brown was criticized by the media and by political "experts" for his willingness to publicly embrace the uprising. And the nay-saying bled into the papers.

Consider the Associated Press story that ran throughout Ohio in the stretch run of the race. Headlined "Brown's Campaign Strategy Questioned," the piece breathlessly claimed that Brown's decision to stress his opposition to lobbyist-written international trade pacts was "a campaign strategy even his supporters call a risk." But there was no mention of the Associated Press's own poll just two years earlier showing that seven in ten Ohio voters blamed these very trade pacts for eliminating hundreds of thousands of Ohio jobs. No, because candidates had never run an uprising-based campaign like Brown's in a state like Ohio, many political experts believed he was destined to lose.

When I interviewed New York state senator Eric Schneiderman (D) about the Working Families Party, he lamented that Democrats "basically killed off the ideological wing of our party" in order to win elections.

"Yet the Republican Party was the party where the ideological wing of the party grew, blossomed, and took control, and they've been kicking our ass ever since," he said. "Democrats still say, 'You don't want to vote against tax cuts, you don't want to be accused of being ideological.' Bullshit! Look who's been beating us! People with insane ideas. But they believe in them."

Brown's unlikely rise to the Senate was run in that lost spirit of outrage and principle—and his win proved Schneiderman's thesis correct. He didn't just win in Democratic strongholds like Cleveland; he won in places like the sprawling Fifth Congressional District along the Indiana border—a place that, according to the *Toldeo Blade,* "has voted Republican in congressional elections since 1938" and twice voted for President George W. Bush.

As much as the pundits, strategists, and consultants in Washington pretend otherwise, Brown showed that if you run an ideological, uprising campaign, you can win—even in most conservative areas, even in the most closely divided and politically important state in the nation.

SHERROD BROWN IS a career politician with a résumé to match. He earned his Eagle Scout badge in 1967, his bachelor's degree from Yale in 1974, and his first public office in 1975 at the age of twenty-one. Because he started out so young, he is still one of the Senate's youngest members, even though he's been an elected official now for more than thirty years.

Psychologically, Brown copes with the two-worlds tension faced by people who are young in human years but old in professional years. Call it Doogie Howser syndrome.

Doogie Howser, as most '80s sitcom watchers know, struggled with the juvenile angst of adolescence while also working as a superstar physician. Sherrod Brown's tension is that of a man who tacks back and forth between youthful, change-the-world idealist and cautious veteran politician.

Only a few months removed from his call-to-arms victory speech, Brown this morning is in the latter mode as he reviews his first few weeks in his new job. Progress and movement building in the Senate "is not going to happen any more than [in] baby steps," he says.

While he has defied the odds by keeping his personal convictions and uprising sympathies intact during a career inside the power structure, Brown's pedigree has made him cautious. He is, after all, a product of a Democratic Party whose current leaders seek not to inspire, but to throw a wet blanket on any potential political wildfires. If the Democratic Party today has a religion, its first commandment instructs politicians to tamp down expectations—or, in Brown's words, to tell voters to be satisfied with mere "baby steps."

I'm not exactly sure when Wet Blanket Politics became gospel among Democrats, but my guess is that if you could peg it to an exact date, it would be sometime between late 1993 and late 1994—the moment Bill Clinton confidently took the mound and served up his universal health-care pro-posal, only to watch it smacked into the upper deck and out of Washington by a big-league cleanup hitter known as the Insurance Industry.

Between the Great Depression and that 1993–1994 era, when Senate leaders crushed Clinton's health-care initiative, a series of American presidents had made successive assertions that seemed totally preposterous at the time, but which amazingly came true. Franklin Roosevelt declared that we could defeat the Great Depression, the Nazis, and the Japanese all at the same time; John F. Kennedy insisted we would put a man on the moon; Lyndon Johnson stated that civil rights would become a reality; Richard Nixon believed we could make peace with China; Jimmy Carter claimed Egypt and Israel could coexist without killing each other; and Reagan said the Soviet Union would collapse. All of these big declarations came true, giving us a sixty-year winning streak.

Clinton tried to make it 7-0 when he insisted that we could have universal health care—and remember, this wasn't nearly as absurd as his predecessors' declarations. After all, every other industrialized country on earth provides medical care to all its citizens.

But when Clinton fired that ninety-five-mile-an-hour fastball over the plate, instead of the sound of a pounded catcher's mitt and uproarious applause for a big win, America heard the crack of K Street's Louisville Slugger as the proposal was blasted out of Washington faster than Kirk Gibson's game-winning home run off Dennis Eckersley left Dodger Stadium in the '88 World Series.

The tragedy wasn't just that one in five Americans were left without health insurance, or that the streak of Great Accomplishments was over— it was that the streak ended in so public and humiliating a fashion.

Hundreds of high-profile industry-sponsored television ads berated the Clinton plan, editorial boards almost universally ridiculed the idea, and after it was over, pundits, pollsters, and lobbyists helped solidify a conventional wisdom that said achieving the health-care goal was impossible and, more broadly, implied that it was idiotic for society to even reach for big goals in the first place.

Clinton certainly got the message. As his health-care plan was sailing over the centerfield wall, he agreed to back lobbyists' job-killing, wage-depressing North American Free Trade Agreement (NAFTA), despite the objections of his old teammates in the uprising and in open defiance of his own campaign promises not to sign such a deal until Mexico "lifted their wage rates and their labor standards and they cleaned up their environment." American Express's CEO gloated at the time that Clinton "stood up against his two prime constituents, labor and environment, to drive it home over their dead bodies." A few years later, Clinton pushed the China trade pact—stripped of environmental, labor, and human rights protections—over the same dead bodies, totally ignoring his own 1992 campaign pledge to not "give all those trade preferences to China when they're locking their people up" (a reference to human rights violations that continue to this day). Though Clinton famously claimed his presidency meant the "era of big government" was over, really it was the "era of big ideas" that had come to a close.

This all happened at the very time Brown was entering national politics. He started out as one of the youngest state representatives in Ohio history and then went on to become a two-term Ohio secretary of state. He lost reelection in 1990, so he opted to run for Congress in 1992, when a Democratic seat opened up near his hometown.

Because the district comprised the heavily Democratic Cleveland suburbs, the primary would decide the election, meaning candidates saw an advantage in brandishing their populist credentials. To distinguish himself with Democratic voters, Brown ran hard for universal health care and against NAFTA, which at that point was being pushed by President George H. W. Bush.

As a freshman congressman the next year, he had a ringside seat to watch how both positions he campaigned on became roadkill. Now a senator in the majority, he exudes a sense of liberation between his bouts of self-conscious punch pulling. As we discuss how he plans to represent the uprising in the Senate, he is optimistic about what's ahead.

"There have been moments when the Senate has responded when the country called on their government to be on working people's side," he says. "The most recent—meaning forty years ago—is what this body did in the mid-1960s. There was clearly a coming together of the public interest in moving the country forward on civil rights, on Medicare, Medicaid—on so much."

But that "forty years ago" refrain lingers.

ABOUT FIFTY PEOPLE are jammed in Illinois senator Dick Durbin's (D) office in the Capitol. It's the usual scene—cameramen in the back, reporters sitting in chairs in the middle, staffers on the perimeter, and senators up front. As an "intern," I am relegated to standing along the back wall.

Normally when a senator walks into a room in Washington, it is like Moses in front of the Red Sea—the ocean parts, and followers fawn. Not when Brown comes in.

Nobody seems to notice him, and those who do see him think he's a staffer or a reporter. That's because he has a youthful, boyish look, while most other senators are in their late sixties and look like they just escaped from a geriatric center; his jacket is perpetually rumpled and lived in, while other senators' aides keep them constantly supplied with freshly pressed suits; his bushy brown hair has no chemicals in it and is tousled this way and that, while most other senators look like they dip their heads in buckets of molten plastic; and he is slightly hunched over, while other senators walk upright with their noses in the air.

Brown's press secretary complained to me earlier in the day about this treatment of Brown around the Capitol. "Everyone refers to all the senators as 'senator,'" she said. "But people just keep calling Sherrod 'Sherrod.'" The horror.

Senator Ted Kennedy (D-MA) kicks off the event by telling the audience that they are joined here by Christian and Jewish religious leaders to demand that the Senate pass a bill raising the minimum wage.

I wince at the scene. The new "thing" is to have Democratic politicians paint every issue in religion and use religious leaders as stage props to counter Republican usurpation of "moral values." But it all looks so . . . manufactured.

I feel this way until Brown starts speaking.

Invoking perhaps the most famous American religious leader of all time, he begins by reading a quote from Dr. Martin Luther King Jr.: "Equality means dignity, and dignity demands a paycheck that lasts through the end of the week."

Princeton's Cornel West has bemoaned the "Santa Clausification" of King, whereby the media has made the civil rights leader into "a nice little old man with a smile with toys in his bag, not a threat to anybody." Yet, as Brown reminds everyone, King didn't get his FBI billing as "the most dangerous man in America" for nothing—he got it because he was building an uprising.

Many Democratic politicians use religious leaders defensively—as shields to validate their own stands. But Brown's words imply an understanding that religious institutions are more than just window dressing—they are integral to movements.

"People of faith, people in the labor movement, people who advocate for children, people in the civil rights movement, people who care about social and economic justice—this is a major step we are taking *together*."

Afterward, walking back down to the Senate chamber, Brown complains to me that "some of these guys call me angry."

He uses the anonymous "these guys" whenever he's talking about people he doesn't like. In this case, he is referring to reporters.

"It fits with their story line," he says. "The thing is, if you talk about economic class, you are automatically called angry no matter what your politics."

He's right, but I counter that I don't see that as a bad thing. Every poll for the last five years has shown that the public is angry—really angry—about everything: the war, the economy, everything. It seems the only place where people aren't angry is inside the comfortable confines of the U.S. Senate—an institution constructed to contradict public opinion through machinery, traditions, and procedures that impose the Establishment's "permanent will."

Because the Senate's rules require sixty votes to do almost anything, almost nothing gets done. Because its terms are six years, senators can defy the public for about five years before they have to start airing campaign commercials to whitewash their record for reelection.

"Look, I think the country would have been better served with a

Senate that's more responsive to public opinion," Brown says. "There is clearly a conservative bias of the institution, a conservative bias toward the most privileged, the best organized, and the best funded."

Recent history confirms his point. Over the last few years, the Senate has been something of a clubhouse for movement conservatives like John Ashcroft and Rick Santorum.

The same cannot be said for aspiring leaders of the populist uprising.

Before the 2006 election, the late Paul Wellstone of Minnesota was the only senator in the last two decades to openly affiliate himself with today's uprising. And unlike the Ashcrofts or Santorums, who were fawned over by the Washington political elite for their movement conservatism, Wellstone was treated in D.C. like the family freak everyone tries to ignore at Thanksgiving dinner. Even new senators who never served with Wellstone casually disrespect his uprising credentials. In a 2006 interview, Barack Obama told me he thought Wellstone was just a "gadfly"—not exactly something people aspire to.

Wellstone's plight was just one of the symptoms of the Senate's built-in "conservatism" that Brown is referring to. So is the chamber's opposition to policies that polls show most Americans support (universal health care, an end to the Iraq War, etc.). It all stems from the fact that, as author Tom Geoghegan has written, the Senate represents "a different country" than the United States of America—a country where "Nevada and California have the same number of people"; a country where democracy doesn't exist in its most powerful legislative chamber.

Think about the "one person, one vote" principle at the core of democracy, and then think of the Senate's numbers. Each state, regardless of population, gets two senators in a chamber where a 41-vote filibuster can stop any legislation. As Geoghegan notes, the 11 percent of America that lives in the 21 least populous states in America are represented by 41 Senate votes. Put more directly, 11 percent of America has the legislative strength to stop Congress from passing bills that the other 89 percent of the country may want. When you boil it down just to the number of voters these senators rely on to get elected, you see that about 3 percent of America's total voting-age population possesses enough Senate representation to stop almost anything. This is the "permanent barrier" in all its mathematical glory.

So even though Wellstone's positions on the major issues like health care, jobs, wages, trade, and education were all majority positions in America, the institution he was in—and which Brown is now in—is the place where uprisings to pass such an agenda now usually meet their end, whether through Republicans' overt opposition or Democrats' Wet Blanket Politics.

Brown is keenly aware of this reality, and he is thinking about how to best navigate such treacherous topography.

Early this morning, one of his aides told me Brown is "considering the Hillary Clinton model"—a reference to how Clinton arrived in the Senate as a partisan icon and worked hard to lower her profile. This has been universally mythologized in Washington as an amazing act of genius, despite the fact that all Clinton really did was stop speaking out on major issues while starting to rake in truckloads of corporate cash and vote for bills supporting the Iraq War. Those minor details of corruption and capitulation were lost in what has become a modern-day fairy tale of a supposed brilliant and ideal "transformation" in courageous pursuit of "bipartisanship."

I ask Brown whether Clinton-style appeasement is what we should expect from him?

He is careful with his words.

"I really do think my building relationships here will help move these people," he says, this time the "these people" a reference to other senators. "But I am going to look at this job unlike probably how many in the past have—that this is an inside-outside job. This is working my colleagues, but it is also helping to organize pressure on this institution."

This is a rare sentiment for a Democratic lawmaker in Washington: a desire to use his office to help spread the uprising's "popular passions."

SINCE THE EARLY 1980s, the Republican Party and the outside conservative movement have been one and the same. The GOP decided that ideology could be a club for bludgeoning Democrats out of office and beating troublesome Republican moderates into submission. The antitax rebellion has been the most effective in places like the Rocky Mountain West, but it is only one star in a constellation of anti-abortion, antigay, pro-gun, Christian fundamentalist, and business front groups constituting the broader conservative apparatus that Republican leaders are perpetually promoting, strategizing with, and pledging fealty to.

With the election of Newt Gingrich as House Speaker in 1994, the ascent of Tom DeLay as House majority leader in 2002 and the ongoing K Street project, whose mission was to insert conservative activists into high-level lobbying jobs, there ceased to even be a distinction between the outside conservative uprising and the inside of the Republican Party—it was all the same machine.

Democrats in Washington, by contrast, have tried to pretend the populist uprising that Brown champions does not exist. Why? Like many things in Democratic politics, the answer goes back to another facet of the McGovern Fable.

George McGovern's 1972 presidential candidacy was seen as an amalgamation of uprising and party. His nomination was the first in the wake of historic reforms (which McGovern himself engineered inside the Democratic National Committee) shoving the nominating process out of the boss-controlled, smoke-filled room and into the voter-controlled public arena of direct-election primaries.

His subsequent loss in the general election was promptly seized on by Democratic operatives in Washington as a rationale to sever the growing ties between the party's Beltway apparatus, which they controlled, and that era's liberal uprising, which they didn't. This version of the McGovern Fable said that Democrats lost the 1972 election because there was just too much democracy in the nomination process, and that the way to ensure a winning presidential ticket was to bring things—at least partially—back into the smoky room, where strategic, if unpopular, decisions could be made in defiance of that era's uprising.

Over the next ten years, these insiders quietly reconstructed their own autocratic power by taking the democracy out of the Democratic

Party. They created "superdelegates"—elected officials and party elites who are given presidential nomination votes just like entire states are, only superdelegates can cast their votes any way they like, while states cast their votes based on the decision of primary elections. This is the Democratic Party's way of subverting its voters' "popular passions" with a "permanent will."

Thus, though you may go to the polls on presidential primary day and think you and fellow citizens have all the say, as of 2004 just 800 "superdelegates" control nearly 40 percent of the votes needed to secure the Democratic presidential nomination. That's 800 elites bound only by their own whims who control the same amount of power over the Democratic presidential nomination as the 12 million registered Democratic voters in the two biggest Democratic states (New York and California).

"General election success" has been the official rationale for shunning the uprising and giving the nominating process this antidemocratic tilt that only the U.S. Senate founders could love—as if only the wise old chin-stroking elders in Washington know who is "electable" and who isn't. (These are, of course, the people who gave us the Mount Rushmore–worthy President Mondale, President Dukakis, President Tsongas, and President Kerry.)

But as *Slate*'s Brendan Koerner notes, the real motivation to limit popular control of the nominating process comes from Washington insiders who are "worried that the populist approach"—which tends to do well in a primary-dominated system—"encouraged insurgent candidates"—the ultimate threat to the Establishment.

As this was happening at the presidential level, the two parties' posture toward uprisings and movements were diverging at other levels of politics as well.

For example, in recent years, influential GOP insiders have quietly encouraged movement conservatives who ran primary challenges against moderate Republican incumbents in places like Pennsylvania and Rhode Island. Though the Republican National Committee made a show of officially supporting the incumbents, there was a wink-and-nod understanding among power players that the primaries were a good thing. Why? Because while these intra-party challenges were ultimately unsuccessful, Republican leaders knew that those moderate incumbents would tilt rightward as they fought to retain their party's nomination. That primary pressure, in other words, would encourage party unity and help prevent politically damaging intra-Republican fissures.

On the Democratic side, it has been exactly the opposite. The corporate-funded Democratic Leadership Council (DLC) ascended to prominence as the designated attack dog against uprising-minded candidates like Howard Dean and leaders like Brown when he was in the House. Beltway pundits such as the *New Republic*'s Peter Beinart openly applauded the DLC's efforts to squash uprising politics, praising it as "an organization of politicians that believes the less beholden politicians are to grassroots activists, the better they will represent voters as a whole."

Brown avoided becoming a political casualty of Democrats' anti-uprising elitism, emerging instead as a spokesman for the populist cause. How he pulled this off has as much to do with his idealism as it does with his abilities to play the Washington game.

Brown bided his time in the House for a decade, carving out niches on economic issues. Often the parties' leadership would agree in their mutual pursuit of corporate money, but maverick Republicans and populist Democrats could form left-right coalitions in opposition. The signature issue for Brown was (and still is) trade, one of the most far-reaching but esoteric issues before Congress, and therefore one thoroughly dominated by corporate lawyers and lobbyists with technical expertise.

But they haven't been able to dominate Brown. As evidenced by his 2004 book *The Myths of Free Trade,* he has perfected the art of at once being able to intellectually challenge the most learned economists and the most influential corporate executives while also distilling the issue for constituents back in Ohio, where globalization has decimated a once thriving manufacturing economy. In 2005, he built a coalition to try to stop the Central American Free Trade Agreement—a pact that expands the very NAFTA trade model Brown was originally elected in 1992 to stop. Despite an intense corporate lobbying campaign to pass the pact, Brown's coalition came within one House vote of stopping it dead.

Unlike less ambitious lawmakers in safe districts, Brown used his uncompetitive reelection races as an excuse to rake in as much campaign cash as possible. Most of his biggest contributors were uprising allies, but Brown, like everyone else in politics, is no saint—he's gotten his fair share of health-care, real estate, and lobbyist money.

Brown was initially courted by Democrats to run for the Senate in 2006—not because of his populist record, of course, but because his diligent fund-raising over the years had left him almost $2 million sitting in the bank. In fact, had he not had that war chest, you can bet his fledgling candidacy would have been cut off at the knees by Washington operatives precisely *because* his uprising allegiances would have been seen as a negative.

It was more than a little hilarious to watch national Democratic Party operatives profoundly uncomfortable with Brown's brand of politics work overtime to help him win his Senate race. But that was Brown's good fortune and smarts. Because Ohio Republican incumbent senator Mike DeWine was so weak, because winning the Ohio race was so necessary for Democrats to win back the Senate, and because Brown had quietly played the fund-raising game for the last decade, he had engineered a perfect situation: decidedly anti-uprising Big Money forces inside the Democratic Party were forced to aggressively support an uprising leader out of sheer self-interest (in this case, winning back the Senate majority). Brown had, in effect, successfully jammed uprising and party together.

Today, what continues to set him apart from most of his Democratic colleagues is his genuine appreciation for the role of the outside rabble rousers, agitators, and activists who comprise the uprising. You can see it right on his lapel, where, just below the glistening U.S. Senate emblem issued to all senators, he has a pin showing a little yellow canary—a symbol of mineworkers' struggle for better working conditions in the early twentieth century. It's sort of a subtle "Screw you, you sellouts" to the other senators we are passing in the hall—and a signal that even though he's a career politician, he actually sees himself as one of the agitators.

"The great social movements, and even the minor undercurrents of social movements, they almost always come from people who were dreamers," he says, as we walk back to his office. "Their ideas begin to take hold, and the public starts listening, and then people begin to move, and then this place moves."

For all this idealism about "dreamers," however, Brown faces the same quandary as other political actors. Just like the Working Families Party leaders in New York find themselves torn every day between compromise and purity, Brown all but admits that he has to carefully dance between uprising leader and calculating pol—and to resist the allure of Establishment co-option that has swallowed up so many others like him.

"There is a natural inclination for all of us in public office to go to those places most comfortable to us," he says. "It's easy if you are a senator or a congressman to spend more time with the wealthiest and the most privileged in society."

It is frigid here out on Pennsylvania Avenue, as I now tag along with Brown to New York senator Chuck Schumer's (D) evening book party. Without saying it outright, Brown lets me know that this is an event he feels he "should" go to as part of his networking responsibilities, but not necessarily an event he wants to go to.

We reach Hunan Dynasty—the dumpy Chinese restaurant a few blocks from the Senate office buildings where much of D.C.'s after-hours business gets done over Lo Mein. The room is packed with lobbyists from just about every major industry—Big Oil, Big Pharma, Big Insurance. Thankfully, we only stay here for about fifteen minutes—enough time for Brown to make sure Schumer knows he was there.

Walking toward his apartment on Capitol Hill after the sordid scene, Brown is again trying to pump himself full of optimism.

"I'm telling you, these guys have really changed because of the [2006] election," he says—"these guys" in reference to Democrats in Washington.

I tell him I didn't really see that at the Democrats' lobbyist lovefest in the restaurant, but he insists that "the progressive movement is making it easier for members of Congress to be progressive, both because members see the results of the election and because the progressive movement is holding people's feet to the fire."

Before I can contest his claim, we are being interrupted by a tall guy who stops Brown to say hello. He reminds Brown that he is the lobbyist for Anheuser-Busch and they exchange "good to see you's." Walking again, an awkward silence lingers, as if I had just seen something I wasn't supposed to see.

"I'm not going to stand here and tell you there aren't Democrats addicted to corporate money—there are," he says. "But the hope is that the progressive movement can wean them off that mother's milk by showing them there is a different way. And I really do think that's going to happen."

Baby steps, I tell myself. Baby steps.

IF YOU SEE Montana senator Jon Tester standing next to another U.S. senator, the first thing you will think is, "Wow, Jon Tester really doesn't *look* like a senator."

Tester, the second lawmaker I am visiting on this D.C. trip, wouldn't disagree with you. In one of his most effective campaign advertisements in 2006, he offered up a hearty dose of subjugation psychology, telling voters, "I don't look like the other senators, but isn't it time the Senate looks a little bit more like Montana?"

But boy, as I see Tester bounding into fellow Montana senator Max Baucus's office this morning in the Hart Senate Office Building, it just hits me again—this guy really doesn't *look* like he belongs here.

Tester and Baucus are here early this morning for their open-invitation coffee klatch with constituents. The weekly event is shticky—but it serves a purpose in letting them both meet as many Montanans visiting D.C. as possible in one shot.

Seeing the two together is like watching Arnold Schwarzenegger and Danny DeVito in *Twins*—the differences couldn't be more pronounced. In terms of outward appearance, Baucus is the senatorial average: average hairstyle (side brushed silver); dress (Brooks Brothers–style, conservative blue suit and gray tie); height (5'10"-ish); build (170s?); and career path (professional politician).

Compare that to how Tester's whole image gives him the look of a Las Vegas pit boss circa 1964. This career family farmer sports a military-style flattop; wears a dated, brownish suit that looks at least fifteen years old; fronts a turquoise and orange tie with a gold and diamond pin; and with a huge barrel torso, tree-trunk-thick arms, and hands the size of those giant foam glove signs they sell at stadiums, he is just about the largest human being I've ever been around.

Max Baucus dressed up in a full Bozo the Clown costume could be mistaken for nothing other than a U.S. senator. If Tester were to don an old blood-and-grass-stained Green Bay Packers uniform and one of those helmets with a single bar across the face, you'd swear he was an offensive lineman from NFL films' 1952 "frozen tundra at Lambeau Field" video.

Yet, to draw a distinction only with Baucus is to understate Tester's utter singularity here in Washington. The contrast between him and just about everyone in the Senate is so profound, it's hard to believe he really *is* a U.S. senator and not one of the badgeless sightseers taking a Capitol tour. And judging by our first conversation this morning, Tester may not fully accept it himself.

When I ask him how the move from his farm to Washington went, he complains that "all my city clothes are here in D.C., but I haven't moved my work clothes here."

When I remind him that his "city clothes" are now his "work clothes," he cracks a grin and says, "Oh yeah, I guess you're right."

FORGIVE JON TESTER for being a bit dazed and confused. He hasn't been on the careful, plodding, straightforward march of a career politician like Sherrod Brown. His path to Washington was the equivalent of the magic bullet theory: the trajectory is so statistically unimaginable and unfathomably improbable that recounting his ascent to uprising leader can make you sound like a crazy person, and yet his story is 100 percent true.

Lots of politicians pretend to be small-town farmers. They use the rural estates they own as an excuse to don a flannel shirt and chew a strand of hay in their TV commercials.

Tester, on the other hand, is an actual real-life farmer, with a two-fingered paw to prove it.

Born in Big Sandy, a town of about seven hundred in north central Montana, he has spent most of his fifty years working an eighteen-hundred-acre patch of high prairie that was originally homesteaded by his grandfather. Some of the biggest events in his life have been quintessentially farm stuff. At age nine, for instance, a meat grinder sheared off the three middle fingers on his left hand, making his wave look like the surfer's thumb-and-pinky "hang loose" sign. At thirty-nine, he converted his family plot into an organic farm, shrewdly betting that, in the face of agribusiness mergers, the best way to stay afloat was to find a niche market.

Tester is as devoted to this farm as the typical career politician is devoted to holding public office. Walking out of Baucus's office and to a committee hearing, he tells me he's still planning to till his land as a full-time lawmaker, and that if this new D.C. gig gets in the way of the farm, he might drop the whole senator thing entirely.

"That farm is two generations of work," he says. "Divorce is not an option."

Tester's political career started after 1997—an infamous moment in Montana history. That was the year the state legislature, bowing to Wall Street demands, deregulated its energy industry, which had been providing Montanans some of the lowest-priced power in the nation. It was one of the most controversial and greedy moves in a state psychologically scarred by a long history as America's most exploited natural resource colony.

The next year, Tester decided to turn his anger about deregulation into a run for a state senate seat that just opened up in Big Sandy. Despite the district's strong Republican tilt, he won.

By 2003, he had become the state senate's Democratic leader, and after the 2004 election, when Democrats took back the majority thanks mostly to the good fortune of a favorable redistricting map, Tester became Senate president.

Up until then, Tester's political story was filled with standard forms of good luck—a timely open seat and a helpful redistricting map, but nothing particularly unbelievable. It was in 2006 that Tester got swept up into the uprising and things got crazy.

Term-limited out of the legislature, Tester decided to throw the Hail Mary pass and declare his candidacy for the U.S. Senate against Republican Conrad Burns. As if defeating a three-term Republican incumbent in a strongly Republican state was not enough of a challenge, Tester was also facing a Democratic primary against state auditor John Morrison, a statewide elected official and wealthy trial lawyer.

Establishment money quickly lined up behind Morrison, a Baucus-ish candidate whose grandfather had been governor of Nebraska and who had been groomed to be a politician since birth. Few could imagine Tester winning the race—but those few were Internet bloggers like Markos Moulitsas of Daily Kos and Jerome Armstrong of MyDD who loved Tester's rural populism and his real-guy-ness. Suddenly, and largely without any effort of his own, this prairie farmer and his underdog campaign was the darling of the largely coastal and urban Netroots. And as Tester admits, they carried him.

"Early on in my campaign, what kept me in the race was probably the blogs," he says. "They were able to raise the campaign awareness out there—they were able to raise me some money and keep me alive."

At the same time Tester got this unexpected Internet boost, Montana's progressive community coalesced around him out of a disdain for Morrison's aloof, almost patrician affect. Bumper stickers and pins depicting the silhouette of Tester's distinct flat-topped head were all over college towns like Missoula and Bozeman. The farmer from Big Sandy had become the uprising candidate.

Still, many of his own supporters in Montana worried that he would lose the primary. Talking with him four months before the primary at the Montana Democratic Party's 2006 Mansfield-Metcalf dinner in Helena, I told Tester that in a recent meeting in Washington, then–Senate minority leader Harry Reid asked me if there was any way to avoid a primary.

I suggested to Tester that he at least think about waiting until 2008 to run for the U.S. House.

"It's not a bad suggestion, and I'm not gonna lie, I have thought about it," he told me. "But I'm going to win this primary, I'm going to win the general, and that's what's going to happen."

Morrison continued to enjoy billing as the runaway favorite until a few weeks before primary day, when Montana's largest newspaper chain published a story about his having an extramarital affair. The headlines were a deathblow to Morrison and a stroke of almost divine intervention for Tester.

Though polls in the last week of the race still showed things tight, and though most Democratic Party operatives in Washington were still fully expecting a Morrison victory, on primary election night, Tester destroyed his opponent, 61 percent to 35 percent.

The general election was arguably an even bigger climb. Burns hid his nasty personality behind that same folksy Gomer Pyle act I had watched him employ in 2000, when I was working for Brian Schweitzer's failed Senate campaign against him. Using his seniority and his position on the Appropriations Committee to raise big campaign contributions from Washington special interests, Burns had built up a massive war chest for a barrage of TV ads.

From the day after the primary until the November 7 election, you couldn't turn on a television or a radio for more than about a minute in Montana without being hit with an ad calling Tester everything from a terrorist sympathizer to a Hillary Clinton fan. One ad even tried to make fun of Tester's weight, manipulating a photo of his head to depict him actually eating houses and cars while a voiceover claimed he would tax Montana to death.

But again, Tester benefited from almost unimaginably good fortune. Over the summer, details began leaking into the press about Burns's association with Jack Abramoff, a Republican lobbyist who had been convicted on bribery charges. The more news that dripped into newspapers, the less Burns was able to use his "aw shucks" crap to absolve himself and the lower his poll numbers fell. And the stories added urgency to Tester's uprising message railing on corruption, lobbyists' influence, and the general stench of rot leaking from Washington.

Nonetheless, the race was happening in Montana, still one of the most Republican states in the country, and on election night, the results were too close to call. Only on the afternoon of the next day was Tester declared the winner by less than 3,000 votes out of almost 400,000 cast—and his victory sealed the Senate majority for Democrats.

Months removed from that unwavering confidence he expressed to me during the primary, Tester today acknowledges his own self-doubt with a smile after I tell him what an idiot I felt like for ever encouraging him to think about backing out of the Senate race.

"You've got nothing to apologize for," he says, as we get back to his office. "I'll admit it: in my heart I really didn't figure on winning either the primary or the general, so it's still taking some time to get used to all of this."

IT IS EASY to see why Tester is not yet "used to all this." For a real small-town kind of guy, it can be unnerving to find out that most of his Senate Democratic colleagues don't just look different from him—they really seem totally uninterested in, and perhaps even willfully ignorant of, the workings of his state and what moves people there.

To be sure, he was forewarned in April of 2006 that this would be a fact of life in Washington. In that month's *New York* magazine profile of Senator Schumer, the high-profile New York Democrat portrayed himself as culturally in tune with the heartland—at the very same time as he went into a vigorous defense of the Patriot Act.

"There were some in our caucus that wanted to let the Patriot Act lapse," Schumer says. "To let it lapse would be a disaster, particularly for our Democrats in red states."

Schumer, the supposed guru, apparently was unaware that many of the most politically important "red states" hate the Patriot Act because it infringes on basic privacy. In Montana in particular, Republican and

Democratic state lawmakers near-unanimously passed a resolution condemning the law and encouraging the state's law enforcement officials to
refuse to comply with it. When some months later Republican senator
Burns took Schumer's rhetorical lead and criticized Democrats for trying
to weaken the Patriot Act, Tester fired back by saying, "Let me be clear: I
don't want to weaken the Patriot Act, I want to repeal it."

He then aired what became one of the most effective advertisements
of the entire campaign—an ad attacking Burns for refusing to repeal the
Patriot Act.

Tester's reward for his election campaign is a full-time job with people
like Schumer, who despite their self-promotion as political gurus, clearly
don't care to learn about Middle America or the uprising that Tester comes
out of.

While some freshmen Democratic senators like Virgina's Jim Webb
appear to find the elitism and disconnectedness of Washington wholly infuriating, Tester seems to find it all incredibly hilarious.

He is perpetually laughing at everything and cracking jokes with
staffers. It's not that he thinks his job is a joke—whenever he talks about
substantive issues, he instantly gets a stern look on his face. It's that he
thinks the entire Capitol Hill scene—the "shit show," as one of his trans-
planted Montana aides calls it—is a scream.

It's easy to see what's so funny as we start out at a Small Business
Committee hearing this morning on something about "procurement."

When we walk in, Senator John Kerry is just finishing up a monotonous
recitation of numbers and nomenclature. Maine Republican senator
Olympia Snowe picks up where he leaves off, and when she concludes her
remarks, there is an uncomfortably long silence because Kerry is falling in
and out of sleep. Startled when he realizes everyone is waiting for him, he
forces a "thank you, Senator Snowe" through a giant yawn and then quickly
hands the floor off to Tester, presumably allowing him to get back to his nap.

Through all the acronyms and governmental terms and "distinguished
colleague" pleasantries that have been thrown around up to this point, I

can't really understand what in the hell is going on in this hearing, and I have no idea how Tester, just weeks removed from his life as a full-time farmer, could possibly get any of it, either.

But when he leans forward into the microphone and speaks, I wonder if the real problem is that too many people here are "experts," and not enough people here are like Tester. His major political experience was as a part-time lawmaker in a Montana legislature, where deliberations are, ahem, less formal. That may deprive him of some of the expertise of the career politicians around him now, but it also gives him a better view of the real-world applications of what's being discussed.

"Look, I don't know a lot about procurement," he starts, with the word *procurement* coming off his lips with a hint of nervousness, as if it were unfamiliar. "But here's what I know: there are businesses that don't have the wherewithal to take on a massive federal contract—so it seems to me the size of the contracts you are offering are the real problem."

In rapid-fire questioning, he asks for an inventory of all the programs available to veteran-owned small businesses, and the size of those programs. For the first time in two hours, I understand what this hearing is supposed to be about.

"ONE OF MY frustrations here at this point in time is that they take real pride in being slow," Tester says, leaning back in the chair behind his desk.

We are back in Tester's windowless temporary office in the basement of the Russell Senate Office Building. Business equipment is strewn everywhere, including a video teleconferencing machine with a sticker on it marked "Inheritable—Burns—Tester." The harsh fluorescent lighting gives the place a police interrogation room motif.

Tester just finished up a meeting with a guy from the Montana Humane Society who came by to say hello. The senator seemed overjoyed to see someone—anyone—from Montana, and when asked how he was settling in, he said with a chuckle, "We're still not adjusted and, god willing, we never will be fully adjusted."

But when, after his meeting, we start talking about Iraq, he becomes dead serious. Like Sherrod Brown, who yesterday complained about the Senate's suffocating sclerosis, Tester takes a jab at the system he's just entering.

"They call it 'deliberate,'" he says as he uses his left hand to air quote. "But the Senate is slow. The prime example is what's going on with the Iraq War right now, and the escalation by the president. He came out with that escalation proposal shortly after we got sworn in. We're just getting to a resolution now, weeks later. It's nonbinding and after that we'll see what happens. It just takes a lot of time, but maybe I'm more anxious than most people are."

His eighty-seven-year-old mother has been calling him every day about the war, imploring him to "get this thing shut down," but Tester says of Congress: "The way it's set up right now, it's very difficult to do that when we have a president in the White House that feels so strongly about killing people."

So, I ask him, how can it be stopped?

He first says flatly, "Elect a new president."

But that's a cop-out, I say. He just got elected on an uprising platform not only against corruption, but against the war, and Congress ultimately could stop the war with its power of the purse . . . if it wanted to. Isn't there a way the antiwar uprising can help someone like him stop the war? And if so, how? By running primary opposition to pro-war Democratic incumbents?

"I don't think there's anything wrong with primaries," he says, acknowledging that he thought Ned Lamont's antiwar challenge to Joe Lieberman was "useful."

This is a controversial view in Washington.

Generally, defending primaries—at least openly—is the ultimate form of apostasy here. You can do anything in D.C.—sell your vote, become a paid lobbyist for an industry you used to regulate, get fellated by an intern in the Oval Office, but none of that elicits more public vitriol from politicians (particularly Democrats) than broadcasting one's support for primary challenges to incumbents.* That's because, as candidates like Lamont and organizations like the Working Families Party have shown, primaries are among the uprising's most potent weapons against status quo political cultures.

Of course, Tester's opinion of primaries is hardly black-and-white.

"The risk [with a primary] is that you are taking a proven electable commodity and you are replacing them with a commodity that may not be electable after the primary," he says.

But he says again that he thinks primaries can be very positive, and he has said the same thing to his Senate colleagues.

In one of his first closed-door meetings with Senate Democrats, Tester says a senator who had recently experienced a tough primary gave a stern speech saying that Democratic bigwigs in Washington must start taking more punitive steps to crush primaries before they happen. This colleague offered up the tired claim that primaries weaken the eventual nominee for the general election.

"Well, I got up and said, 'Hey folks, the primary I went through made me a stronger candidate,'" Tester recounts, adding that the room went totally silent. "And then I reminded them I wouldn't be here if there wasn't a primary, because they tried to pick another candidate!"

At this he cracks a smile, reliving the pleasure of what must have been a great "fuck you" moment.

"Look, I get the motivation for not wanting primaries," he says. "Elections are a real pain in the ass, they cost a lot of money, they take a lot of time, they take a lot of energy, and, quite frankly, they are mentally taxing. But on the other side of the coin is you also have the ability to hold incumbents accountable for past voting records and influence them on future voting records—that's what it's about. That's democracy."

---

* As mentioned earlier, there have been some recent exceptions to this general rule on the Right, but those primary challenges were very quietly orchestrated with and vetted by GOP higher-ups—they were not unauthorized primaries from true outsiders like Lamont.

* * *

LATER IN THE day after a Senate floor vote, Baucus is on C-SPAN discussing the controversial corporate tax cuts he attached to a minimum-wage bill. I ask Tester what his strategy is for working in the shadow of his state's senior senator. How can someone represent the uprising in the shadow of an obstacle like that?

This is a big question that goes, indirectly, to whether Tester really will represent the uprising. Baucus has been in Congress for more than three decades. In the words of the *Nation* magazine, he is "K Street's favorite Democrat"—a reference to how Baucus has used his position as chairman of the Senate Finance Committee to become Corporate America's go-to guy for its antitax, antiregulation, and pro-outsourcing agenda. At a more granular level, Baucus's office has become, bar none, Congress's most effective in-house job training program for the corporate influence industry. Baucus staffers learn the legislative ropes working for him, and then typically go out and become high-paid lobbyists.

Every position Tester takes will be compared to the Baucus operation in the local press. How will Tester represent his populist economic and anticorruption platform in the shadow of Senator K Street?

"I have to walk a fairly fine line with Max," he says in a low voice, his eyes darting to the side, as if he's whispering a secret to me. "But, look, when it comes to actual votes, I will do what I need to do."

Easier said than done. Tester's campaign rhetoric against special interests, lobbyists, and the intersection of money and politics was superheated. But these are the very forces of corruption that run this place. They have not just infested his Montana colleague's office—they have infested the whole city. Turning his uprising campaign into action is going to take more than a little bit of strategy—and guts.

Before I can ask another question, our interview is broken up by a meeting with two guys from a nonprofit that provides job training services in Bozeman. It's the usual affair—the locals tell the senator and his legislative director they are looking for his help in securing a federal grant in the upcoming budget, and the senator pledges support while the legislative director furiously scribbles notes. Nothing is out of the ordinary . . . except for one thing.

As Tester is hamming it up and telling these guys he's going to do his best to help them get their grant, the word *earmark* comes up in passing. That's what the request really is: they want Tester's help in "earmarking" federal money for their work . . . months after Tester ran a political campaign attacking earmarks as the ultimate symbol of corruption.

I decide not to say anything, mainly because Tester is not doing what his opponent Burns did, which was earmark federal money for political campaign contributors. But now sitting here at the end of my day with Tester, I'm thinking back to what Brian Schweitzer told me.

Just after he was elected governor, I asked Schweitzer—another burly populist from Big Sky Country—whether he would ever want to be in the Senate.

"No, because then I'd become a *senator*," he said with a sneer, and he declared that once you get to D.C., the combination of distance from home, Washington's go-along-to-get-along attitude, and corporate pressure changes you, even if you are the most sincere person. What he was effectively articulating was the common belief that it is intrinsically impossible to represent the populist uprising in a place like the Senate.

At the time, I didn't think he was being totally fair, though I also didn't think he was entirely wrong. One thing I do know: if anyone is going to definitively prove or disprove his hypothesis in the coming years, it will be the farmer-senator from Big Sandy.

WHY IS BERNIE Sanders arm in arm with Alan Greenspan?

This is what I am thinking as I walk up the short corridor to Sanders's new Senate office and see the Vermont lawmaker exiting his with a tall, balding, droopy-faced guy that I swear is the former Federal Reserve chairman.

Could Sanders have changed that much since moving over from the House to the Senate just a few months ago? He's got the same shock of white hair, ruddy face, and Buddy Holly glasses that is his distinctly retro look. But has he fulfilled the Schweitzer prophecy? Has he gone Senate on us?

I start to feel beads of sweat on my forehead. I'm getting really upset and nervous. How could this be? How could he be hanging with Greenspan?

When I worked for Sanders seven years ago as his spokesman in the House, our best annual media hit was "The Greenspan Hearing," as it was known in the office—the annual congressional testimony by the then-Federal Reserve chairman. Every lawmaker on the panel would kiss Greenspan's ass—their own televised genuflection to Wall Street. Every lawmaker, that is, except the distinguished—and decidedly pissed off—gentleman from Vermont.

My first experience with this was sitting behind Sanders at a 2000 committee hearing when, to the shock of other lawmakers (and, frankly, me) he dressed down the Federal Reserve chairman for sugarcoating economic data. At the same hearing a year later, Sanders, hollering, demanded Greenspan "tell the American people why you think not raising the minimum wage, maintaining a disastrous trade policy, and giving huge tax breaks for the rich works for the benefit of the average American." Under prosecutorial inquisition, Greenspan admitted he wanted to abolish the minimum wage entirely, sparking a flurry of unflattering headlines.

By 2003, these encounters had taken on something of an Ali-Frazier cult following in the House, with everyone—reporters, committee staffers, and lobbyists—buzzing before the hearing with speculation about whose teeth would get knocked out this round. Only that year, it wasn't a refereed World Boxing Association spar—it was an Ultimate Fighting Championship smackdown, with Sanders pounding Greenspan senseless in a one-sided, knee-on-the-throat shitbeating.

He started off telling Greenspan he was "way out of touch with the needs of the middle class and working families," and "that you see your major function in your position as the need to represent the wealthy and large corporations."

"You just don't know what's going on in the real world," the Vermont lawmaker said, his voice rising. "The country club and the cocktail parties are not real America. The millionaires and billionaires are the exception to the rule."

He then listed statistics detailing how millions of Americans are losing their health insurance, wages are decreasing, unemployment is growing, and CEO pay is skyrocketing. Realizing he had to pose some sort of question to the Federal Reserve chairman, Sanders slowed and started yelling in staccato.

"DOES . . . ANY . . . OF . . . THIS . . . MATTER . . . TO . . . YOU? Do you give one whit of concern for the middle class and working families of this country?"

Greenspan nervously chuckled in that way you used to giggle and then wet your pants out of embarrassment when your first-grade teacher scolded you in front of the whole class.

So why, just a few weeks after being elected to the Senate, is Sanders hanging out with Greenspan?

"David!" Sanders exclaims as I approach him. I'm a hugger—when I see most people I've known for many years, I instinctively go in for the hug. But not with Sanders. It's not that he's overly formal. On the contrary, he's the guy whose uniform is the tattered thousand-year-old navy sport jacket and a rumpled sweater—and who is universally known as "Bernie" in Vermont. It's just that he's, well, not the warm, huggable type. (As I heard one guy in Vermont put it, "He's a person of the people, but not a people person.")

I end up getting the patented Sanders nonhug hug—one arm around the shoulder that seems like an embrace but somehow keeps you at arm's length. He says, "I want you to meet Michael Copps, one of the most important people in America."

Whew, it *is* the old Bernie.

Copps, a dead ringer for Greenspan, is a commissioner at the Federal Communications Commission (FCC), and Sanders isn't kidding—he has been one of the most important (though unrecognized) uprising figures in the last few years. Don't laugh—it's really true.

The FCC may sound like the federal government's very own bureaucratic hell à la Initech from *Office Space,* but its jurisdiction regulating the media—and specifically regulating media ownership—makes it one of the most powerful agencies in the United States. Copps has used his position as one of five commissioners to help fuel the improbably successful uprising to delay the Bush administration's attempts to gut existing laws against rampant media consolidation.

In a town where celebrity and proximity to celebrity is the prerequisite for "important" status, Sanders's understanding that this virtually unknown commissioner is "one of the most important people in America" shows how the Vermont senator is far more different—and far more committed to the uprising—than even his position as Congress's lone independent suggests.

A CONFESSION: WHEN I applied for a job in Bernie Sanders's office eight years ago, I didn't actually know I was applying for a job with Bernie Sanders, and had I known, I might not have applied.

Some background: When I applied for the job, it was 1999 and I was a twenty-three-year-old in an entry-level position with the American Israel Public Affairs Council. I was desperate for a way out, but I didn't think any politician would hire me because, just a few months prior while working in one of my first jobs out of college, I had been fired from a low-level position on a local political campaign.

Nevertheless, when I read a want ad looking for applicants in a "progressive" congressman's Capitol Hill office, I sent off a résumé to the anonymous P.O. box listed. About a month later, I received a call from a Jeff Weaver in Sanders's office asking me to come over to the Hill for a visit. The name "Bernie Sanders" was familiar only because he was always mentioned as Congress's only self-described socialist.

I didn't remember applying for a job in Bernie Sanders's office, I told Weaver.

"We listed it as 'progressive,'" he replied in a mildly annoyed tone, as if he'd had to say it before.

It is standard for Capitol Hill job listings to have anonymous contact information, so as to prevent a flood of calls. However, I was pretty sure anonymity was used for the Sanders job listing in order to avoid turning off applicants who might never apply if they knew they would be working for Congress's only official independent and a—*gasp!*—socialist. The word still sounds a little too East Germany for modern-day Washington.

When I was (improbably) offered the job, I had a bit of a panic attack.

What the hell *was* a "democratic socialist"? Was I really going to work for one? If I did, would I be able to work in Democratic Party politics—or American politics—ever again? Or would I be relegated to running campaigns for politburo candidates in former Soviet satellite countries?*

On the other hand, having recently been fired, did I really have a choice if I wanted to work on Capitol Hill?

I took the plunge.

Up until August of 1999, I was your typical brainwashed suburban Democrat. Democrats were great, Republicans were evil, and that was about as complex as it got for me. I carried this simpleton mind-set into my work with Sanders, until about a month into the job, when I made my very first trip up to Vermont.

As the US Airways prop plane from D.C. swung back and forth in a gusty breeze over Lake Champlain, my white-knuckled fright subsided momentarily when Weaver told me I'd be accompanying Sanders to a Vermont town meeting during my visit. I chuckled at the term "Vermont town meeting," thinking of ultraconservative Pilgrims in an Independence Hall–like building being stirred into an angry froth by a stern-faced preacher demanding the local witch and warlock be burned at the stake.

Funny, the scene at St. Michael's College in Burlington was a lot like that.

Though no one was wearing black shoes or hats with gold buckles on them or eating a big Thanksgiving turkey with Indians, a throng of seven hundred middle-aged IBM workers that summer evening was whipped into

---

* I hear campaign work in Romania and Bulgaria is a great career builder.

a frenzy by a congressman—my new boss—delivering an economic sermon on the mount. Long arms in the air, he verbally crucified Big Blue for its recent decision to slash promised retirement benefits. He specifically laced into IBM's CEO Lou Gerstner for paying himself $14 million a year while telling workers their pensions "were not worth the paper that they had been written on."

Between standing ovations and Sanders's repeated promises to use every power at his disposal to stop the cuts, IBM employees stood up to vent their frustration with ever-increasing ferocity.

"It is nothing less than corporate-sanctioned greed!" shouted one worker in an outburst that was followed by wild cheers.

That this meeting of white-collar Republican-leaning tech workers was organized by America's most famous socialist convinced me just how little I—and many others—understood about the guy I was now working for. At the beginning of the night, these folks were the antithesis of what you would expect to be a welcoming audience for a congressman derided as a "leftist" or a kook by the media. They were a murmuring group of buttoned up, golf-on-Saturday, church-and-football-on-Sunday Rotarians. After about an hour with Sanders, they were a fist-pumping mob of radicalized rage—an uprising that went on to organize itself and successfully fight IBM's cutbacks.

They had fallen under the trance of one of Sanders's special uprising spells: the ability to package complex economic issues into us-versus-them, you're-with-me-or-you're-against-me choices. In this particular case, he cut straight through the spin from IBM's press flacks and contrasted the pension cutbacks with IBM's profits and its CEO's paycheck. On other complex issues—from trade to drug prices to agricultural subsidies—it's the same method, and his fight-for-the-little-guy consistency has given him the haloed straight-shooter image that every politician dreams of—the one where people say "I may not agree with him on everything, but I know where he's coming from."

His proponents applaud his use of red-meat issues and his overarching rhetorical style as populism—channeling people's anger into political action against the designated villain of the moment. His longtime haters, such as the right-wing editorial board of Vermont's *Caledonian-Record,* deride this as "classic demagoguery"—manipulating emotions and fanning the flames of deep-seated frustrations. In truth, it is both, and that is Sanders's other magical talent: positioning.

We tend to think of that word *positioning* as something bad—John Travolta in *Primary Colors* telling one audience one thing, and then another audience the exact opposite.* But there's a difference between duplicity and positioning. The terms don't *have* to be synonymous, and positioning in particular doesn't *have* to be a nefarious endeavor.

Duplicity is selling something different to different audiences. Positioning, on the other hand, is the art of selling the same thing to different audiences. Without the latter, broad, coalition-based uprisings cannot exist—and Bernie Sanders knows that better than perhaps anyone in politics.

Sanders is a Jewish New York City transplant with a thick Brooklyn accent in a rural French Catholic state whose subjugation psychology is notoriously hostile to urban outsiders (the "flatlanders"). He was a perennially marginal candidate for the tiny, anti–Vietnam War Liberty Union Party during the 1970s. He was the longtime mayor of the liberal bastion of Burlington in the 1980s. This résumé does not necessarily help politicians win statewide in Vermont, thanks to the state's more conservative, working-class areas.

Yet, Sanders won Vermont's lone congressional seat in 1992 and has since become his state's most popular politician. His success has rested on his ability not just to win huge margins in Vermont's liberal enclaves, but to consistently overperform in its New England Yankee conservative

---

*For two good nonfiction examples of such negative positioning, see Bill Clinton's telling voters he'd never sign NAFTA until Mexico improved itself and then lobbying Congress to pass the bill letting him sign NAFTA, or George W. Bush's telling voters he is a "compassionate conservative" who cares about inner city schools, and then refusing to better fund those schools.

pockets—places like Vermont's staunchly Republican Northeast Kingdom. A look at one of the state's most conservative counties is instructive.

In his second House reelection campaign during what became the 1994 Republican takeover of Congress, Sanders won almost 52 percent of the vote in Orleans County, a Republican area that sits along the Canadian border. Comparing those numbers with a generic, run-of-the-mill statewide race, the Democratic candidate for lieutenant governor that year pulled in just 44 percent in the county. Sanders ended up winning reelection by a tight margin, while the Democrats' lieutenant governor candidate lost. This trend became more pronounced in future years. In 2000, Sanders received 70 percent of the vote in Orleans County, besting even Republican senator Jim Jeffords's 66 percent. Meanwhile, Democratic candidates for president, governor, and lieutenant governor lost the county. And in 2004, Sanders again won 70 percent, while the Democratic candidate for governor won just 33 percent of the vote in the same county.

This same thing has happened in most of Vermont's most conservative areas. And Sanders pulls off the feat all while happily telling people he's a socialist and proudly presenting himself as a leader of the uprising. How? Through positioning. He makes sure the uprising crusades he spends most of his time on can be packaged to different audiences in different ways without compromising his underlying objectives and without deceiving people about what he is pushing.

An issue like pension protection is a classic example. In the years that followed that first town meeting I attended, Sanders championed legislation to stop the kinds of schemes IBM and other corporations were using to rip off workers. He also bought shares of IBM stock for the explicit purpose of attending the company's stockholder meeting and publicly confronting Big Blue's CEO over the issue.

The crusade was billed in the national media as "liberal," and to left-leaning voters in Vermont, Sanders presented his efforts as an altruistic cause helping families in need. But at the same time, he also pitched his campaign to culturally conservative voters in the Northeast Kingdom as a punitive measure bashing the same class of Big Money elites who had decimated the area's industrial economy. That's positioning: same campaign, same legislation, different packaging.

Sanders employs such skills to advance all of his other signature issues.

In liberal Brattleboro, Sanders's work fighting "free" trade deals is about improving human rights for desperate workers in China—a Save the Children message that would make Sally Struthers smile. In blue-collar conservative Derby, it is about saving jobs—a "screw Wall Street" message that would make Lou Dobbs applaud. In liberal Winooski, Sanders's focus on reforming the International Monetary Fund is about relieving poverty in the Third World. In more conservative Barre, it is about cutting off taxpayer handouts to already-wealthy corporations. In liberal Montpelier, Sanders's work preserving media ownership rules is about stopping Fox News and Rush Limbaugh from taking over the airwaves. In St. Johnsbury, it's about protecting local, family-owned news outlets from being taken over by multinational interests.

Sanders's trick in all of this is his embrace of—or "don't ask, don't tell" posture toward—the diverse motivations of those supporting uprising causes. Whatever brings them to his side, he's glad to welcome them as allies.

When he holds one of his town meetings on media ownership in a conservative area, Sanders knows that many folks attend and support the cause because they hate the supposedly "liberal" media. That's fine with him, even though he himself is a liberal and thinks the media is too conservative. Similarly, I remember well Sanders's performance at a 2000 rally at the Capitol, stoking the anger of enraged union workers and demanding congressional Democrats stop President Clinton's push for the China free-trade pact. He told the crowd to "duck your head, because the lobbyist money is flying all over the place." He shared that stage with people like Pat Buchanan, whose opposition to the pact grew straight out of xenophobia.

This kind of cold calculation for uprising ends hasn't been employed in any comprehensive way in decades. But Sanders's tactics provide a significant, if isolated, example of how cross-marketing and coalition building can still work for the uprising even in a stultified legislative arena.

Rolling Stone's long 2005 profile of Sanders praised him as "the amendment king of the current House of Representatives": "Since the Republicans took over Congress in 1995, no other lawmaker—not Tom DeLay, not Nancy Pelosi—has passed more roll-call amendments (amendments that actually went to a vote on the floor) than Bernie Sanders," wrote the magazine.

How could this be possible? How could the federal government's lone socialist not just propose, but pass more amendments than anyone in a Republican-controlled Congress? Because partisan politics, to Sanders and other true uprising soldiers, is not a linear continuum—it is a circle. He comprehends that in many cases, a powerful paradox is at play: the more progressive one's agenda, the more opportunity to attract support from the lunatic wing of the Republican Party, as long as you are willing to avoid applying purity standards and accept that different people come to the same issues with far different motives. (This is why, for instance, one of Sanders's longtime allies during his time in the House was Texas congressman Ron Paul—the ultra-right-wing Republican and former Libertarian Party presidential candidate.)

On top of this, Sanders learned early how to manipulate the sausage-making process that is congressional bill writing. He discovered that while Congress's restrictive rules prevent House members in the minority from bringing their stand-alone bills to a vote, those rules provide loopholes that let anyone offer amendments, as long as they are germane to underlying bills already being voted on.

So, when the Justice Department's appropriations bill came up, Sanders offered an amendment limiting the government from spending money to enforce some of the most intrusive provisions of the Patriot Act. The bill passed the House over the objections of the White House, thanks to support from both Democrats and archconservative antigovernment Republicans.

When the bill appropriating money for corporate subsidies came up, Sanders proposed changing the bill to prohibit the government from funding a multibillion-dollar subsidy to Westinghouse Corporation for the construction of a nuclear facility in China. His proposal passed over objections

from an army of lobbyists thanks to votes from progressive Democrats who
want the money redirected to domestic priorities; fiscal conservative
Republicans who want to cut all government spending; national security
Republicans who don't want to help a potential adversary develop its nuclear capacity; and xenophobic Republicans who hate Chinese people.

This kind of cold calculation is straight out of Saul Alinsky's *Rules for
Radicals*.

"It is futile to demand that men do the right thing for the right
reason—this is a fight with a windmill," Alinsky wrote. "The organizer
should know and accept that the right reason is only introduced as a moral
rationalization . . . therefore he should search for and use the wrong reasons to achieve the right goals. He should be able, with skill and calculation, to use irrationality in his attempts to progress toward a rational world."

Most politicians think appearing on a cable screamfest like *Hardball*
or getting a photo op next to a presidential candidate makes them important. But everything Sanders does in the legislative arena understands that
the way to best represent the uprising inside the halls of Congress is to
find ways of making the Establishment turn on itself and do what it exists
to prevent. And if that means exploiting procedural loopholes to wring, co-
erce, or otherwise elicit support for a status-quo-challenging political
agenda from ideological enemies, then so be it. Better to win than to fight
with a windmill.

STILL, THE ULTIMATE problem for Sanders has always been his minority status. Twelve out of his fourteen years in Congress have been under
Republican rule. Thwarting the GOP's iron grip can make room for baby-
step successes like his amendment victories, but it cannot close the deal
because, in the Republican Congress, when his uprising legislation passed,
it was usually killed behind closed doors in the House-Senate conference
committee negotiations.

But now, for the first time, I am visiting with Bernie Sanders the senator, one who caucuses with the new Democratic majority. No longer does he
have to look for parliamentary loopholes—under Senate rules (as opposed to

more restrictive House rules), any senator can try to amend anything to any bill, without having to be a legislative contortionist. The only limitation is the mutually assured destruction component of it all: senators know that whatever stunts they pull—whether controversial amendments or filibustering—can be pulled right back on them by anyone else.*

It is this conflict between Sanders the tenacious bomb thrower and Sanders the tactician who understands how power works that will determine whether his elevation to the Senate is a significant elevation for the uprising or merely for one Vermont politician.

This conflict has been on the mind of Sanders's chief of staff, Jeff Weaver, well before Sanders destroyed Republican millionaire Rich Tarrant in Vermont's 2006 U.S. Senate race. A St. Albans, Vermont, native and a former Marine reservist, Weaver has worked for Sanders for fifteen years. He is stocky, wears silver-rimmed glasses, and has a cue-ball-shiny head. While only in his early forties, his beard is white—probably from working for Sanders for so long.

He came to Capitol Hill from an activist background—like so few Capitol Hill staffers, but like so many of Sanders's closest allies. As a college student in the mid-1980s, Weaver was thrown out of school for staging protests demanding Boston University's right-wing college president (and soon-to-be failed gubernatorial candidate) John Silber divest the university's stock holdings in companies that did business in apartheid South Africa. Among his protests, Weaver hung banners outside the college dorm room opposite Silber's office window.

He is the yin to Sanders's yang. Where Sanders is perpetually scattered,

---

*This explains why the Senate—and not the House—is called a "club." In the House, there is no restraint on hatred between the majority and minority party because there are few procedural consequences for hatred. The minority party can get steamrolled and there's no way it can exact punishment. In the Senate, on the other hand, everyone is nice to each other because having even one archenemy means you may never get even your most mundane priorities, like local spending, passed without someone trying—and being able—to screw you.

frenetic, dour, and emotional, Weaver is methodical, calm and basically happy-go-lucky about Capitol Hill goings-on in the same way Jon Tester seems to find all of it funny.

"The difference between the House and Senate is not just that we're in the majority," Weaver says, sitting across the table from me in the Senate's subterranean cafeteria. "It's that we have more input from the start of legislation rather than at the tail end like in the House."

For the first time in my week in the Senate, I am hearing something encouraging about the potential for concrete uprising influence here in D.C. Because any senator can grind the progress of Congress to a halt, the Senate leadership has to talk to—and try to accommodate—each individual senator *before* introducing any bill. An effective senator will seize on that opportunity to advance his pet causes.

The only obstacle for Sanders is that this form of power has never been his forte. His gift has been finding legislative seams and then going outside the Congress to organize the uprising to bring a public, pan-ideological groundswell of pressure aimed at wedging those seams apart. But the Senate rewards insider, behind-the-scenes, decidedly nonuprising machinations—the "Hillary Clinton model," if you will.

"The key for us is to choose three big issues that we tell the leadership that we will shut the entire place down over," Weaver continues. "Everything else, we have to negotiate on—but we've got to figure out what the three are that we will stop everything for and organize around."

ABOUT FIVE TOTAL reporters are here at Sanders's press conference on veterans' health care this morning. I am only sort of surprised—that small number was standard for Sanders's press events when I worked for him in the House a few years back, but I thought it might get a little better with his move to the Senate. Apparently not.

Sanders is in the middle of his usual Bernifesto, as his friends call it. It is a speech that can be applied to anything, really, as it focuses on universal truths:

"It is an absolute outrage that we are giving tax breaks to millionaires while cutting back on [insert federal program]. In the richest country on earth, it is immoral to throw [insert mistreated segment of the population] out on the street."

In this case, the federal program is VA medical care (which Bush is proposing to slash), and the mistreated segment of the population is veterans. Tester follows Sanders with his own speech, affably referring to his new Senate colleague as a "comrade" (maybe Sanders's democratic socialism is rubbing off on his fellow freshman), and then the press conference is over.

Afterward, as we walk back to Sanders's office, the Bernifesto continues in private, now taking aim at the media.

"If Barack Obama or Hillary Clinton walked down there for that press conference, you'd have fifty reporters looking for their quote of the day," he is fuming. "But this is a class issue, and the media doesn't cover class issues—they cover celebrity."

Sanders has identified a substantial obstacle to the uprising—one that goes way beyond arcane rules and Senate etiquette. No media audience on Capitol Hill is interested in most of the economic issues that today's uprising is based on. This is not for lack of material. Most of what Congress actually does (when it's not renaming post offices) is deal with economic issues, because most of what Congress does is collect and spend money. From whom it collects money and on whom it spends money is, fundamentally, a class decision.

But trying to discuss class issues, even with the microphone of a U.S. Senate seat, is maddeningly difficult thanks to a Hollywood-ization of the Beltway media in recent years. Capitol Hill is filled with scores of reporters whose beat is "politics"—usually interpreted as "politicians"—and relatively few reporters whose beats are substantive like, say, "veterans affairs." Journalists, in other words, are now experts on individual personalities rather than experts on issues. The result is a glut of horse race election coverage, gossip columns, and celebrity profiles, and a dearth of stories accurately reporting major decisions and legislation with context.

In decades past, the mavericks—whether the Robert LaFollettes of the Left or the Joe McCarthys of the Right—could count on being able to generate media coverage for their uprisings if the substance of their causes were compelling. But this mainstream media conduit closed as broadcast TV cut its news-gathering investments and as opinion peddling and news-as-infotainment came into vogue. In a media culture that prioritizes cost cutting, it is far cheaper to produce personality content about a senator's likability than it is to actually dig up and cover real news.

In this vacuum, the conservative movement built up its own direct conduits: magazines, newspapers, radio stations, and ultimately Fox News—an entire network designed to amplify all the causes in the conservative movement. But for everyone else on the political spectrum, all the people who aren't Hollywood celebrities or presidential candidates who pundits say have a "decent chance" of being elected, the microphone is stuck in the off position.

ALL OF THIS said, Sanders is nothing if not incredibly, incessantly, almost annoyingly persistent in selling the uprising's agenda—and I'm not just talking about selling it to the media.* I'm talking about selling it one person at a time, to anyone he can make listen to him. Among his targets are the people he can summon to his office who won't say no because he's a U.S. senator—people like, say, the Bush administration's highway officials, whom he is meeting with now.

They look like Bush types: One is a middle-aged dude dressed in a dark suit with slick black hair; the other is a conservatively dressed woman who introduces herself by mentioning that before getting her government job, she "worked in the trucking and rail industry"—the industry that she now oversees as a government official. Beautiful.

---

* Though, as his press secretary, I was ordered to send more than one press release to *Washington Post* editors about Bernie's international economic reform legislation that I knew would be immediately discarded. I imagined them setting up a fax machine that released my faxes straight into the trash.

The Sanders treatment in these settings tends to be a chess match—one in which he toys with his opponents before going in for the kill. These visitors make their first move by telling Sanders that "all eyes will be on the highway trust fund"—the massive federal pot of money that builds roads, and that the Bush administration has considerable control over. Message to Senator Sanders: we can mess with your roads in Vermont if you become troublesome. The woman refers to a potential increase in "discretionary programs" for highways—another reminder to Sanders to use his position to increase funding for their fiefdom, or else. Sanders replies, "I thought they were called earmarks . . . ," eliciting an uncomfortable laugh from these folks who literally fund the bridge to nowhere.

Now it's time for Sanders's moves. Ever the fix-the-potholes mayor of Burlington, he asks innocently where the highway trust fund gets its money, and they say from the tax on gasoline.

"So it's fair to say that fuel efficiency *isn't* in the trust fund's best interest?"

The meeting soon ends.

Next up, two executives from Goodrich's facility in Vergennes, Vermont, and the company's Washington lobbyist. This meeting begins with a similarly aggressive chess move as the executives mention that the company employs 720 people in Vermont. Message to Senator Sanders: mess with us on anything, and we can easily make at least 720 of your voters extremely angry at you by blaming you for anything we decide to do, like, say, slashing wages or eliminating jobs.

Sanders asks where the company gets most of its work. "We're not really a tire company anymore," says the lobbyist, a sixty-ish guy with a deep voice and what looks like bad reddish brown hair dye. "We do mostly aerospace work and get our business from the government."

"So," smiles Sanders, moving his rook into position, "you are a socialist enterprise, then."

Chuckles all around, and then curt good-byes.

Now, after a brisk walk over to another office building, we are in a Senate Budget Committee room. Testifying are three Establishment economists—one from the investment bank Bear Stearns and two from the Peterson Institute for International Economics. I don't know exactly what the topic is, and I don't think Sanders does either. But that's not important, because the Bernifesto is applicable in any setting like this and is about to be fired up with velocity previously reserved for the Greenspan Hearing.

All politicians have a special place where they most shine. For some it is the endless grip-and-grin chicken dinners. For others it is the backroom world of wheeling and dealing. Sanders's sacred place is the Hearing Room.

To Sanders, the Hearing Room is not a place for prim games of chess. It is a big shark tank, with him as the Great White. When the clack of the gavel starts the proceedings, it is like a whistle signaling feeding time. Any topics, no matter how esoteric, and any witnesses, no matter how scholarly, inevitably end up as morsels of blood-drenched chum.

Usually, the witnesses don't know they are about to become food— they don't know it until Sanders's questions begin and they see the dorsal fin peek out of the water. They always look completely bewildered by the attack, thinking something along the lines of, "What the fuck? I thought this was a routine hearing on Commerce Department regs." Then, when Sanders moves in for the kill and the question starts crescendoing, I imagine they can hear *Jaws*'s two-note theme song.

Sanders starts his inquiry today by pointing out that "we were told by Corporate America and by Presidents Reagan, Bush one, Clinton, and Bush two" that "free" trade deals were "really going to be a good thing for America in the sense of creating good-paying jobs in this country, reducing our trade deficit, dealing with immigration, et cetera, et cetera." In fact, he says, "this has not happened."

"So my dumb-bunny question is: In the midst of all that reality, of the decline of the middle class, the increase in poverty, the loss of good-paying jobs, the growth of our trade deficit, why is anybody continuing to defend our current trade policies and why are people not saying, 'Excuse me. It has not worked. We need to rethink them very fundamentally'?"

The first witness is Fred Bergsten, whose official biography boasts that he is "the most widely quoted think-tank economist in the world." With a smug smile, he says the problems "cannot really be attributed to the trade agreements."

Sanders pivots to a hypothetical.

"If you're an employer in North Dakota or in Vermont and you can move to China and hire people—hardworking, good people—at fifty cents an hour, you don't have to worry about unions, you don't have to worry about environmental protection, why would you not do that? Why would you not?"

Bergsten doesn't back down, abruptly claiming that "the reason you would not is because the productivity of those Chinese workers is, in most cases, equally lower than their wages."

Now Sanders has them. His voice rising, he snaps, "I don't believe that." Bergsten, sensing danger, cuts back in, making a palms-forward "stop" gesture, and says, "I will grant you, in some sectors, it is not true."

But it is too late. There's blood in the water.

"The people who run companies like General Electric are not dummies," Sanders starts lecturing. "If I'm paying somebody fifty cents an hour as opposed to fifteen dollars an hour or twenty bucks an hour, I can compensate for that. If you work half as effectively, I still make a lot more money. And the proof is in the pudding, all right?"

The other economist who hasn't said a word until this point now feels the urge to raise his hand, thinking it is safe to go back in the water.

A bad decision.

"I don't think it's a fair characterization to describe the U.S. as headed in the direction that you're saying," he says. "This is a vibrant economy that's growing fast, that's creating a lot of well-paying new jobs."

This is Sanders's signature topic. Anytime anyone—and especially some Establishment shill—starts going on about the booming economy, the teeth gnash and the death lunge comes.

"Manufacturing jobs are in decline in the United States. Is that correct?" Sanders asks with a snip in his voice.

Yes, the panel agrees.

"Service-industry jobs," he goes on, "pay substantially less than manufacturing jobs?"

The previously silent economist who has now picked this fight says, "No, I don't think that's correct."

Cue the *Jaws* music.

"Service-industry jobs working at Wal-Marts do not pay less than working at General Motors?"

The economist digs in and says that's right, and says he defines "service industry" jobs as anything from reshelving at Wal-Mart to investment banking at Goldman Sachs. And with that, Bernie Sanders has tricked this three-headed chimera into embarrassing itself.

"I guess, then the problem is, working at Goldman Sachs, they're going to get a fifty-million-dollar bonus," he concludes. "Can we equate that in the same category as working in McDonald's? That doesn't make a lot of sense to me."

Bergsten stammers that because of "free" trade, "we gain a trillion dollars a year."

But Sanders swats that away, pointing out that "my constituents don't gain part of that—most of that trillion goes to people very much on the top."

Bergsten meekly responds, "That may be for the next debate . . ." but Sanders is soon out the door. He's eaten enough feeder fish for one meal.

"This is a very conservative Senate," Sanders says, looking at the floor.

The gears in his head are cranking away as we walk through underground tunnels to the motorized cart that ferries people back and forth from the Russell Senate Office Building over to the basement of the Capitol. He's thinking aloud, and I just happen to be here listening.

For the entire week here, in the winter of 2007, an Iraq War resolution has been dominating the news. Since Republican senator John Warner of Virginia announced his interest in some sort of bipartisan bill rebuking President Bush's proposed escalation of the war, Senate Democrats have been working feverishly to attach him to something—anything—concrete so as to isolate Bush and other Republicans. The problem is how much of their soul—and 2006's antiwar election mandate—Democrats will have to sell in order to get a deal with this one Republican. It looks like a lot. Warner's proposed language meekly states opposition to Bush's surge plan—but only to his specific plan, not to the general concept of militarily escalating the war.

"Right now there are not the votes to even pass a nonbinding resolution against the war," Sanders says, working through his position on the resolution. "This speaks to the very conservative nature of this institution. So the question is, what do you do from there?"

No "right" answer exists at this moment, especially for someone like Sanders—a person whose career started within the uprising against the Vietnam War, and who, in recent years, has loudly opposed the Iraq War.

But Sanders knows Congress's numbers all too well. Democrats were handed the majority in 2006 because they pretended to support the antiwar uprising. Polls continue to show the public is strongly against the war, and wants congressional action to end it. Yet, between all the party-line Republicans and a kowtowing faction of conservative Democrats, the majority of lawmakers in Congress are still pro-war.

Sanders doesn't like this reality, but he accepts it. Now he has to figure out whether he will vote for or against the resolution, should it come to the floor. If he votes for it, he knows he will be complicit in a congressional sleight of hand designed to trick voters into thinking something was done to end the war, when in fact nothing at all was really done. If he votes against it, he knows the Senate is so closely divided his vote could send the resolution down to defeat and give Bush a pass.

"There's a lot of language in this bill that is bad," he says, talking to the wall, refusing to make eye contact with me. "So what you are faced with is—does it make more sense to support it for the Democrats' argument or does it make more sense to say no for all the apparent reasons that it's a bad resolution?"

On the elevator up to the Democratic caucus meeting where the issue will be hashed out, I reiterate the point Weaver made to Sanders before we left the office: that eight months ago thirty-nine senators voted for a bill concretely demanding a withdrawal of troops from Iraq; since the last election, the new Senate probably has nine more votes for that position; and some might ask why the Senate, after the 2006 election, seems to now be retreating from that ironclad withdrawal position in favor of a debate about even weaker nonbinding resolutions?

Bad call.

"David, I'm trying to figure out the best thing to do here," he says to me in that same exasperated tone he used when I screwed up a press release as his spokesman. "There are two sides to the story. I mean, it's not a strong resolution period, but there are two sides to the story."

STANDING OUT IN a hall of the U.S. Capitol waiting for the senators' closed-door meeting to break up, I imagine this is how it feels to stand outside the Vatican waiting for smoke signals indicating the election of a pope. The place is packed wall to wall, but it is quiet like a library. Everyone—staff, reporters, security guards—is whispering, as if a monumental decision were being made in there.

That senators are debating whether to support a nonbinding bill that, by its definition, doesn't actually *do* anything seems lost on everyone, as does the fact that a good number of the Democrats in there originally voted for the war in the first place and have repeatedly voted to continue it. If Kabuki theater were a Broadway act, this whole scene would be up for a Tony. It wouldn't win, though, because the drama is based not around a compelling story, but around a navel-gazing tragicomedy whose sole purpose is to make the actors on stage feel important.

Shouting starts rising from the back of the corridor like the sound of an oncoming wave cheer at a stadium. Senators are now pouring out into the hall and being accosted by reporters.

Illinois senator Barack Obama fights through the crowd, refusing to answer whether he will hold out for something stronger than a nonbinding bill. Louisiana senator Mary Landrieu stops to hold court about how the watered-down Warner proposal supposedly "sends a very powerful signal that we want a new direction." It is a signal that most Democrats have agreed to vote for Warner's bill and not demand more.

I hear someone ask Virgina's Jim Webb, "Did MoveOn's endorsement of the bill sway senators' positions?"

I can't find Sanders, so I take the elevator back down to the Capitol basement, where I know I'll catch him when he heads back to his office. Tester happens to be there, and he tells me that it's true, MoveOn did endorse the nonbinding bill, and that the Democratic leadership actually read MoveOn's press release to the caucus as a way to pressure progressive senators like Sanders and Wisconsin Democrat Russ Feingold to support the bill.

I don't get it, I tell Tester. After an antiwar election, antiwar marches, antiwar petitions; after the full Senate just months ago came within striking distance of a strong stand against the war—why, after all that, would the Senate Democrats endorse a bill that legislatively retreats from the goal of ending the war?

"Because remember what I told you yesterday—the Senate is a 'deliberative body,'" he says, sarcastically making air quotes with his hands. He's not happy about it either.

Fine, I think. Let's just say you excuse the lawmakers themselves for being "deliberative." Let's just say you chalk up their surrender to legislative machinations. What about the uprising? What about MoveOn? Why would *they* throw their weight behind a bill that does nothing?

"Hi Jon, how are you," says Sanders to Tester as he comes up behind us, the Brooklyn accent making the greeting sound like *"ha wah ya."*

Sanders looks even more pained than he did before the caucus meeting, and when we get away from the hubbub, he starts venting about the very question I've been struggling with.

"I'm being put in a difficult position on this thing, instead of the conservative Democrats," he says, slicing at the air with hatchet motions. "In June it was a debate about how strongly to say 'end the war'; now it's a debate over how weakly to say 'don't escalate the war.' And now I've got to figure out the role I want to play."

I can feel where his frustration is coming from. This is politics—everyone gets put into bad positions. But the uncomfortable situation he's in now is not just a product of his status as a politician or even as a progressive in a majority conservative institution—it's due to the capitulation of the outside uprising.

In the weeks leading up to this debate, MoveOn's leadership refused to make big, confrontational demands on Democrats to hold the antiwar line. They opted instead to endorse the weak resolution as a way to potentially humiliate Bush. In the process, they deserted the uprising's true allies in Congress like Sanders, Brown, and Tester. The Players, in other words, behaved as if continuing the partisan war was more important than ending the Iraq War—and today's collapse is the result.

Sanders, though refusing to single out any one group, explains the consequences: "It makes it that much more difficult to fight in this very conservative institution without loud voices and pressure coming from outside this institution."

This is the gravitational dynamic that the conservative movement has mastered, but the populist uprising has yet to fully grasp. Right-wing think tanks and activist groups exist to place uncompromising pressure on Congress. They take positions far to the right of where Congress has the votes to go. That outside pressure emboldens conservative movement allies on the inside to stand firm, which pulls the inevitable legislative compromise closer to the Right's objectives. The most recent example of this came during the debate over the war itself. It's not an accident that neoconservatives basically pushed for a wholesale American takeover of the entire Middle East and ended up with one of their big goals: an invasion of Iraq.

The uprising has learned none of these lessons when it comes to Iraq. Getting all Democrats and enough Republicans to vote for binding legislation to end the war requires two things: instilling fear of electoral reprisals in Democrats who may consider voting to continue the war, and obligating politically endangered Republicans who say they are against the war to put up or shut up.

A nonbinding bill accomplishes precisely the opposite: lawmakers of both parties can claim they voted for something to end the war, even though they didn't—while leaving the antiwar uprising's strongest advocates like

Sanders out in the cold. Worse, when Democrats go unpunished for refusing to hold out for something stronger, they will feel free to ignore the uprising in the future—and on every issue.*

When we get back to Sanders's office, CNN is airing an interview with
Democratic senator Carl Levin, who is citing MoveOn's endorsement of
Warner's nonbinding, do-nothing Iraq bill to defend the Democrats' decision
to support it, too. The legislation, he says with a straight face, "would be a
very dramatic statement of senatorial disagreement with the president."

People are dying in Iraq, America's reputation in the world is being soiled,
the vast majority of the country wants to end the war, and top Democrats are
claiming a dramatic "statement of senatorial disagreement" would be a victory.

Sanders is deflated. His white hair is mussed from his nervous habit of
rubbing his head when deep in thought.

"The fundamental question is how you mobilize the Democratic base
around progressive politics," Sanders says, taking off his jacket and sitting
down at his desk. "Those two things—the Democratic base and progressive
politics—are not necessarily the same."

This statement could sum up why Sanders has officially remained an
independent, despite now biannual overtures from Democrats for him to
formally affiliate with their party. The uprising has always been his
calling—not the Partisan War. He explains this to me by discussing his old
Vermont counterpart, Howard Dean.

When I worked for Sanders, the two of them never really got along.
Dean was a career politician, and even though he called himself a Democrat, he was much more in the New England Republican mold: moderately
progressive on social issues, Wall Street–friendly on economics. Dean had
much more in common with Vermont GOP senator Jim Jeffords than he

* Days after this sorry display, Democrats fail to muster the necessary procedural votes to have a full-on floor debate about the war. A few months later,
Democrats will give Bush a blank check to continue the war for the whole
summer, and a few months after that, various Democratic lawmakers will
propose more nonbinding bills to give Republicans even more of an excuse
to avoid supporting a real end to the war.

ever did with Sanders, yet he was hailed as the populist presidential candidate in 2004.

"If there's a lesson of the Howard Dean campaign," Sanders says, "it is that the younger generation's definition of 'progressive' is anyone who rips apart the other side. Dean was a moderate, yet he became the progressive candidate for president because people get off on stridency."

Dean, as Sanders acknowledges, has experienced a legitimate transformation since his days as governor. He is now using his position as Democratic Party chairman to embrace the Working Families Party's methods of melding uprising and party. In particular, he is spending more resources on grassroots organizing in all fifty states, which has raised the hackles of Washington consultants hostile to expenditures on anything other than expensive television ads in a select few congressional districts.

But Sanders's point is a good one, even if it is a taboo.

Whether it is economic issues or the Iraq War, there remains an enormous gap that mortally threatens the uprising. On one side of the abyss are the partisan warriors in institutions like the U.S. Senate and in offices throughout Washington, D.C. who claim to act in the uprising's name but who care about one thing and one thing only: party power. On the other side is the actual uprising happening all over the country. It is this chasm—and the partisan warriors' attempts to pretend the chasm doesn't exist—that might prevent the uprising from making the gains necessary to become a full-fledged movement and overcome the status quo's "permanent will."

"People keep saying political consciousness is so high right now, but it's not," he says as a dark expression washes over his face. "People know we have a moron in the White House, and that's about it. And if that's the only thing people know, if that's the only thing people get organized around, then we're in for some real trouble."

6

MAD AS HELL, AND NOT GONNA TAKE IT ANYMORE

I F YOU MADE a list of buildings that symbolize raw, unadulterated, bone-crushing power, One Time Warner Center would definitely be on there, just below the Pentagon, the Notre Dame football stadium, and that grotesquely large Wal-Mart superstore on the outskirts of your town. The $1.7 billion fortress on Manhattan's Columbus Circle is no ordinary building. This is one of the world's largest media companies attempting to physically belittle the manhood of its competitors—and not just with the regular "how big is yours" height and girth measurements. No, the Time Warner Center is *two* massive erect phalluses, not just the usual one.

It is a gray, snowy Albany kind of day here in New York City, which makes entering at the bottom of this behemoth feel like a mishmash of scenes from *The Empire Strikes Back,* as the Big Apple's Albany-ness casts it perfectly in the role of the ice planet Hoth. Trudging up Fifty-eighth Street with a stiff wind and wet sleet in my face has me craving the warm innards of a freshly gutted Taunton (or at least a Starbucks). The Time Warner Center's front lobby is all midlevel Death Star drones, with a wall of gray-suited security guards sitting at computer consoles behind a granite counter. If they were wearing the black-and-white storm trooper uniforms, they wouldn't look out of place.

After providing my ID and bags for inspection, I am instructed to pass through a mini-tollgate, which opens when a guard behind it mystically waves his hand, presumably summoning the telekinetic powers of the Force.

An elevator ride later, I arrive on the fifth floor. The cavernous, high-ceilinged CNN newsroom is dotted by clusters of desks next to floor-to-ceiling windows that look down on a frozen Central Park below. You can't turn your head more than ten degrees without seeing a plasma TV screen.

I see my buddy Slade Sohmer walking toward me from the back corner. He looks the same as he did back when we were drinking buddies in college—his brown hair hasn't turned gray, his sideburns haven't gotten any shorter, and he still wears a perpetually bemused smirk, as if he just heard a dirty joke.

Probably because I barely remember Slade 100 percent sober and/or dressed in anything more formal than a T-shirt, I am still stunned that he's now the top assistant to Lou Dobbs—the buttoned-down, pinstriped, ultra-serious former corporate sycophant who now, each night, invades America's living room as a fiery ball of Huey Long populism, Howard Beale "mad as hell and not gonna take it anymore" outrage, and Hulk Hogan point-at-the-camera bluster.

I first emailed Slade a few months ago asking to spend some time with Dobbs, the television anchor who most overtly associates with the uprising. Slade told me he wanted to help, but that he probably couldn't because CNN's PR people would be nervous about someone reporting from inside *Lou Dobbs Tonight*.

Then, a day later, Slade called me back and said he figured out a way to make it work. "We're just not going to tell corporate," he said. So this day is an unofficial journey into the core of CNN's most controversial operation.

The Lou Dobbs for President bumper sticker adorning the wall of the office explains why the show has such an edgy reputation. Leveraging his status as one of CNN's first on-air reporters and the corresponding editorial control (some say fiefdom) that he has built from such long service, Dobbs has shattered the division between reporting and opinion—a weighty feat at a network that tries to create a staid image as "the most trusted name in news." In the process, Dobbs has established an uprising beachhead inside the media Establishment—one whose inner workings I hope to see during this visit.

For his efforts (and to the great consternation of many media, business, and political elites), Dobbs has attracted a devoted following. Between the winter of 2005 and the winter of 2007 when I am visiting Dobbs, his show's ratings have jumped roughly 40 percent. In the last two quarters, *Lou Dobbs Tonight* has been CNN's second-highest-rated evening program after *Larry King Live,* but that doesn't tell the whole story because Dobbs's earlier six o'clock show time naturally has fewer viewers to draw from than King's prime-time slot. Comparing apples to apples, in the first three months of 2007, *Lou Dobbs Tonight* has been the CNN evening show closest to achieving the number one rank in its time slot.

Dobbs's program is nothing like the slew of substance-free pundit shows that Washington vomits out to America every night. Instead of creating a show focused on the Beltway's internecine inside gossip, *Lou Dobbs Tonight* designs its program for the average person. Not surprisingly, its audience is much larger than that of shows like *Hardball**—and Lou Dobbs himself is much more influential in actually altering the broader political debate raging outside the nation's capital.

Dobbs's rise has not been gradual—it has corresponded with his recent transformation from power-worshiping journalist to political televangelist. And depending on your perspective, his influence on the uprising and impact on America is either a crusade to save the country, or to destroy it.

---

* For example: According to Nielsen, in the first quarter of 2007, Dobbs's audience was double the audience of *Hardball* and *Scarborough Country* combined—an astonishing statistic, considering Dobbs's show is in the 6 p.m. hour, which generally has far fewer viewers than *Hardball*'s 7 p.m. hour and *Scarborough Country*'s 9 p.m. hour.

* * *

It's about 10:30 a.m., and Dobbs is not yet here—no shock, considering the roads from his farm in north-central New Jersey are said to be impassable because of snow (nothing to worry about, I'm told—Dobbs's driver has never failed to get him in for a broadcast). So, the morning editorial meeting for tonight's show is going on without him.

When walking into executive producer Jim McGinnis's office, you are first met by a closed gray door. Taped to this door is a spoof of a World War II ad showing a smiling soldier drinking coffee with a line at the bottom that says, "How about a nice big cup of shut the fuck up." Below that there hangs a sign reminding visitors to "think before you say something stupid."

Behind this door, the office is cramped. Eighteen people are assembled, with some, like correspondent Kitty Pilgrim, forced to sit on the floor. On the air, *Lou Dobbs Tonight's* tone may be all testosterone all the time, but it looks like off the air in the New York studio, women outnumber men by more than three to one.

McGinnis is sitting at a cheap wooden desk. Hovering over him is a poster of an airbrushed Dobbs with the motto "Straight talk on power and the powerful," and along the shelf behind him he has taped two cartoon postcards—one that depicts Dobbs as Tony Soprano, another as Jimmy Stewart in *Mr. Smith Goes to Washington.*

McGinnis is *Lou Dobbs Tonight's* target demographic: factory-worker beefy, porn-star mustache, and wearing a JC Penney-ish navy-blue-and-green-striped plaid work shirt. I'm surprised he's not wearing a leather handyman belt with wrenches and hammers and tape measures hanging off it, and if he were fixing the leaky pipe under your kitchen sink, he'd definitely be showing plumbers' crack. I actually suspect he's showing said crack to the folks sitting behind him as he leans over a speakerphone blaring the voice of Casey Wian, the show's hypercaffeinated Los Angeles correspondent.

Panting into the phone with sheer excitement, Wian is recounting the latest about the two border patrol agents, Ignacio Ramos and Jose Compean, who were convicted for "wounding a suspected drug smuggler" at the

Mexican border "and trying to cover up the shooting," according to the Associated Press. When watching *Lou Dobbs Tonight*'s ongoing coverage of the controversy, you might conclude that Ramos and Compean are today's Sacco and Vanzetti—the famed immigrants at the center of a wrongful-conviction cause célèbre during America's last immigration wave in the early twentieth century. There's just one (huge) difference: while those protesting the execution of yesteryear's tandem argued that America was unfairly scapegoating immigrants, Dobbs's protest of Ramos and Compean's incarceration implies that today's duo was convicted because America is *too* sympathetic to immigrants.

Dobbs's campaign is having some success. Conservative talk radio and websites are now calling for the release of the two border patrolmen, who, they say, were just doing their job.

Their attention has created a feedback loop to the show. At one point, McGinnis cuts into Wian's breathless report on an uncooperative government spokesman to cite as backup evidence a story from conservatives' best-known conspiracy-theory-laden website, WorldNetDaily (though, to his credit, he does question the veracity of what he read).

With Wian clicking off, McGinnis starts going over what "the network has for us"—a reminder that *Lou Dobbs Tonight* really is its own separate entity that gets to pick and choose from what the rest of CNN is offering. Today, the show might do an interview with CNN White House correspondent Ed Henry about President Bush's press conference. But, in the spirit of journalism's "if it bleeds, it leads" axiom, McGinnis says, only "if Ed gets into a flurry with Bush." Otherwise, the show will air something else.

Such autonomy is a big part of why *Lou Dobbs Tonight* has been able to break journalistic barriers by mixing "news, opinion, and debate," as the announcer tells viewers at the beginning of the show. Dobbs has been an on-air personality at CNN since 1981. Following a tangle with management in 1999 that prompted him to leave the network, CNN executives begged him to come back. Reese Schonfeld, who cofounded CNN with Ted Turner and became its first president, believes that was when Dobbs consolidated his power. "When they brought him back, he became totally independent," Schonfeld told the *American* magazine. "He knew they needed him more than he needed them."

The Dobbs empire is now a staff of roughly forty, including a core group of beat correspondents who report exclusively for the show and take their editorial orders from Dobbs—and no one else at CNN.

"We couldn't do this on a daily basis if I was reliant solely on the network for reporters," McGinnis tells me once the meeting is over and everyone has cleared out of his office.

By "this" he means the bird-dogging of specific stories night after night into recurring themes with their own special graphics at the bottom of your television screen. Bill O'Reilly or Sean Hannity might spend a week or so following a *National Enquirer* headline like, for instance, Anna Nicole Smith's death. Dobbs, by contrast, spends month after month after month on themes like "War on the Middle Class" (translation from Dobbs-ese: kitchen table economic issues); "Exporting America" (job outsourcing); "The War Within" (drug and alcohol addiction); "Dangerous Imports" (toxic stuff coming in from China); and, most famously, "Broken Borders" (illegal immigration). The themes and the specific slants they represent are as integral to the show as the personalities reporting them. As one CNN correspondent told the *New Yorker,* Dobbs's reporters "are expected to file reports within [the show's] editorial point of view."

McGinnis acknowledges that a "large portion of what we're doing is tied to Lou's personality, his outrage, and his passion"—but the charismatic anchor is only one ingredient in attracting the show's sports-fan-like following. The other, clearly, is the deliberate use of repetition to define a narrow, machete-sharp issue focus—one that creates a unique identity beyond just the Lou Dobbs cult of personality.

"The rap against television news has always been that it has a short attention span, and inside the industry people think that if you do a minute-and-a-half package on something—well, we're on record about that, we don't have to do anything else on it," McGinnis says. "But we've got a lot invested in the stories that we do. Sure, I get accused of being a broken record at the morning editorial meetings with the rest of the network, but we do reporting that is relentless on a story until that story finds a conclusion."

Calling the Dobbs's broadcast merely "relentless" is like calling Cujo merely "agitated." In both cases, "rabidly ferocious" is more like it. Not only do reporters hit the same story lines over and over again, but rarely do ten minutes go by on a regular broadcast before Dobbs turns to the camera to tear into whatever villain is at the heart of the specific story line that day. His columns on CNN's website deride Bush and Congress for "telling working folk to go to hell." And lately, his correspondents have been joining in on the act during the anchor-reporter banter. "It's really amazing that 80 percent of all the new things that are coming in are from China," Pilgrim said on air last year after a story deriding free trade. "And no one is noticing!"

The clear goal is to get viewers to associate specific topics with this specific show and consequently to "increase the audience's intensity," as CNN's president has said. It is a well-trodden, niche-focused route to building a devoted viewership in this age of saturation media. People who love fixing stuff around the house watch Bob Vila. People who are into cars listen to those two clowns from Boston on NPR's *Car Talk*. I'm into tropical fish, so I was psyched when my dad got me a subscription to *Aquarium Fish* magazine. It's all about providing content for a niche audience. Dobbs just seems to have found a very popular niche.

But there's another unstated goal of *Lou Dobbs Tonight* that rarely gets talked about in the scores of shallow magazine profiles of the CNN anchor—a goal that aims to build something more than just a Lou Dobbs fan club or a one-topic audience. The dogged pursuit gives the show the feel of an ongoing, never-ending campaign, as if the objective is to transform television watchers into followers. Put another way, *Lou Dobbs Tonight* is the closest thing America has to Uprising Television.

This path, known to fans as "advocacy journalism" (and to detractors as "propaganda"), is less traveled, mostly because it tends to make risk-averse ad sponsors nervous. But it is not entirely unique in American history.

During the nineteenth century, for instance, America's media was dominated by the penny press—newspapers whose news copy, not just their editorial page, openly pushed the agenda of the political organizations they affiliated with. And by openly, we're not talking about Fox News's slanted journalism that hides behind Orwellian "fair and balanced" claims to objectivity. We're talking about papers that flaunted their political affiliations right in their mastheads (the last vestiges of this era remain in the names of papers like the *Arkansas Democrat-Gazette* and the *Waterbury Republican-American*).

With the rise of new technologies in the early twentieth century, advocacy journalism became affiliated with talk radio. Out of the Sacco and Vanzetti era came Father Charles Coughlin, a Catholic priest who in the 1930s used radio to stir up ethnic and racial hatreds, becoming one of American history's most infamous xenophobes and the nation's first right-wing talk radio star. At his peak, Coughlin encouraged listeners to participate in an uprising, resulting in mass protests by Coughlin followers railing against Roosevelt administration policies.

Today, we have Rush Limbaugh, another right-wing icon whose audience is more than just casual listeners—they are self-proclaimed members of the conservative movement who even have their own nickname (ditto-heads). His appeal, like Coughlin's, is not just his ideology or his bombastic antics, but the way he creates the perception of community. You listen because you want to get the *real* story about the ongoing battle that you and your buddy Rush are fighting in the trenches.

Same thing, interestingly, with a completely different media personality—Howard Stern (who told his radio audience in 2007 that he is "fascinated" by Dobbs). For years, Stern has used the non-tits-and-ass segments of his show to attack his competitors in the morning entertainment/pop culture radio genre, and to organize mass public rallies to taunt local shock jocks when he overtook them in the ratings.* The technique is

---

*When I was a teenager, one of the most memorable events in Philadelphia was the rally when Stern overtook local DJ John DeBella in the morning ratings. Stern staged a public "funeral" for DeBella in front of a throng of fans in a downtown park. A few of us considered skipping school to go to the rally, but we wussed out.

hilarious in its juvenile, color-war-at-summer-camp theatrics—and it creates a camraderie between broadcaster and audience. To be a Father Coughlin or Rush Limbaugh or Howard Stern listener is to have a special identity that goes beyond mere interest in the substance of what these hosts talk about. To regularly tune in is *to be a part of something,* and the opportunity to experience that feeling of solidarity appeals to many in this, the *Bowling Alone* era of social isolation.

Never, up until now, have these methods that meld media and uprising been applied to an endeavor as mainstream as *Lou Dobbs Tonight.* The next closest thing is Fox's *O'Reilly Factor,* but Bill O'Reilly is at best a pure cult of personality, and more often a slapstick spectacle who draws a gawking audience the same way a movie like *Jackass* draws rubberneckers who just can't believe someone is going to, say, put his nipple in a RedLine office stapler.

Here we are, in an office in CNN's studios—the aorta of supposed "objectivity" at the heart of Time Warner's media empire. And yet McGinnis is at one moment referring to "the show's position" on given issues like immigration, and at another saying the White House's decision to back off the potential sale of U.S. ports to the United Arab Emirates "is a victory" for *Lou Dobbs Tonight,* which for weeks eagerly slashed the proposal apart with the possessed, joyous-in-anger vengeance of Leatherface in *The Texas Chainsaw Massacre.* The show takes positions because it sees itself as an active participant in the uprising, rather than an observer—and Dobbs wants you, the viewer, to join in.

McGinnis says his entry into advocacy journalism was "not an immediate conversion," because he had been working for years in more traditional media. However, he certainly has a personal connection to the issues Dobbs focuses on—some more surprising than others.

Connection to the working-class jobs and wage issues? Check. McGinnis is Irish-American by birth, though "don't tell Lou I called myself that," he says, laughing about Dobbs's America-first mantra and his criticism of those who flaunt their dual nationality.

He grew up the son of an independent salesman in Chagrin Falls just outside of Cleveland, Ohio, and after graduating high school, he worked in Erickson Tool's factory.

Connection to the anti-elite outrage that courses through the typical *Lou Dobbs Tonight* broadcast? Check. Unlike many high-level producers and reporters today, McGinnis is not an Ivy Leaguer or hotshot journalism school product. After his stint at the factory, he went off to Xavier University in Cincinnati, got a first job in the NBC mailroom at Rockefeller Center in New York, and eventually landed a low-level gig at CNN's *Moneyline* in 1989, where he slowly but surely worked his way up. Expressing his own subjugation psychology, he snipes at the "trust fund kids who come into this business" and says, "I don't see a lot of people coming with varied backgrounds, and that makes the media and its perspective very inbred."

Connection to the immigration debate? Check. The forty-five-year-old McGinnis tells me that he is "married to a former illegal alien"—a Brazilian woman who "came up here and overstayed her visa." He is quick to say that she "started the citizenship process before her visa expired" and "when we were courting, if you can use that phrase anymore, she was still in the process of trying to become legal." But yes, it's true: the head producer of *Lou Dobbs Tonight*—the show that has lately made attacking illegal immigration its central thrust—is married to a former illegal alien.

I ask McGinnis whether he is discomfited by Dobbs's focus on immigration and the accusations by some that the show is racially charged. Absolutely not, he says.

"When it comes to immigration, some people say, 'Well, you guys are just against brown people and you don't like Hispanics,' and they're always shocked when they actually listen to what is said in the pieces we report," he says. "The reality is, when you do have a government [like Mexico's] basically using your country as a safety valve and telling its citizens to circumnavigate the laws of the neighboring country, that's an issue that people here need to discuss. Some folks say, 'Well, you're racist to talk about this'—if that's the truth, then we can't have discussions on a whole host of issues out there that need to be discussed."

But while the show disavows any racist sentiments, it shares the "don't ask, don't tell" quality of the uprising—that Alinskyian tactic of avoiding the "fight with a windmill" by accepting support from all comers.

Just like progressive Bernie Sanders accepts without question conservative support for his initiatives, just like the Working Families Party sometimes makes common cause with Republicans, McGinnis acknowledges, if ever so subtly, that *Lou Dobbs Tonight*'s ratings may be benefiting from some of the uglier human emotions that are boiling in a population under increasing economic stress. "We both reflect and, yes, tap into some of those feelings that are out there," he says.

Lou Dobbs Tonight succeeds at "tapping into" its viewers' outrage as much by choosing to cover controversial issues as by intentionally isolating story lines from one another. For example, the show discusses trade policy as purely an issue of American sovereignty and job outsourcing, while immigration is presented as a separate issue of national security and cultural invasion. Dobbs, though, rarely explains how America's rigged trade policy actually increases Mexican poverty, thus driving more and more Mexicans to come over the southern border looking for a better life. Even though this interaction between trade policy and immigration is absolutely essential to understanding the two issues, Dobbs rarely focuses on the connection; the complexity and "help-the-poor-foreigners" message distracts from the frothing nationalism that has been the CNN anchor's route to better ratings.

McGinnis nonetheless insists the show does not specifically intend to "tap into" racism and anti-Hispanic xenophobia and repeatedly states that the show is "factually based." But notice the phrasing: rather than "factual," he says "factually based"—the same kind of terminology used to describe, say, historical fiction.

Clumsy wording? Definitely. Did McGinnis mean to subtly imply a distance from the truth? Absolutely not. But is it a Freudian slip inadvertently hinting at a problem CNN higher-ups may be worried about? Perhaps, considering the fiasco in the coming months when Dobbs himself gets the Lou Dobbs treatment on CBS News's *60 Minutes*.

During a profile of Dobbs, CBS's Leslie Stahl will ask the CNN anchor about his show's stunning claim in 2007 that poor border security and illegal immigration have contributed to seven thousand cases of leprosy in the United States in the last three years. Stahl will point out that, according to the U.S. government, there have been seven thousand leprosy cases in the last *thirty* years, and no data exist about how many of those cases involve illegal immigrants. Dobbs will tell CBS that "if we reported it, it's a fact." The next week on his show he will reiterate the claim. This will result in a flurry of criticism from nonpartisan groups like the Southern Poverty Law Center and from the *New York Times,* whose top business columnist will harangue Dobbs for "mix[ing] opinion and untruths" and for having "a somewhat flexible relationship with reality."

McGinnis insists he is genuinely concerned about properly "calibrating" the show's content so that as it pushes an uprising agenda, it doesn't actively feed xenophobic and racist impulses, even inadvertently. "Through history we've seen certain rises in populism and sometimes it's ended very badly," he says. "You get into the nativists and things like that and it's very ugly, and I think that, while we are, as journalists, chroniclers of life and times, we also have a certain responsibility."

Many Hispanic rights groups scoff at the mere notion that *Lou Dobbs Tonight* tries to fulfill such a "responsibility" or even thinks about "calibrating" its focus. They say the show is at minimum overly demagogic and more often a microphone for racist propaganda, with Dobbs playing Father Coughlin.

The National Council of La Raza, a leading Latino rights group, has called Dobbs "the darling of the anti-immigrant movement." An immigrant advocacy group in Arizona has called Dobbs "the number one cheerleader of all who want [to] bash the undocumented." Citing the show's decision to air interviews with activists who have ties to white supremacist organizations, Mark Potok of the Southern Poverty Law Center said in 2006 that Dobbs "puts people with connections to hate groups on his show without revealing those ties, seems to endorse racist conspiracy theories, and describes anti-immigration vigilantes as 'great Americans.'"

The cantankerous Dobbs, to his credit, constantly invites his critics on his show to air their grievances. Following the *60 Minutes* report, for instance, Potok will be invited on the program to debate Dobbs over the leprosy charge. That's the thing with Dobbs: if you are a willing sparring partner ready to face rabbit punches, groin kicks, elbows to the face, and all the other rhetorical street-fighting techniques of cable television, then regardless of your position on an issue, he welcomes you into *Lou Dobbs Tonight*'s steel cage with a hearty "let's get ready to rumble."

Such an eagerness to spar with opponents is rare among those in Dobbs's position. Most often, media personalities either refuse to recognize their detractors or berate them without giving them the opportunity to respond. Dobbs's enthusiasm for the fight is more than just his being thin skinned. He feels so passionately about his causes that he wants to convince everyone—even his most vocal critics—of their worth. The behavior shows he is not just trying to be another televised "shock jock." It indicates that he has much bigger uprising goals.

This is exactly why he scares so many people.

To SEE LOU Dobbs swagger into the offices of *Lou Dobbs Tonight* is to see Darth Vader striding the terminals of the Death Star, periodically interrogating, ordering, and scaring the crap out of subservient underlings. I first viewed this in 2006 when I visited the newsroom before I appeared as a guest on the show. He had his jacket off and his tie loosened, and he was hovering over a cowering reporter demanding she get an on-the-record quote from the White House about an immigration issue. (Luckily, the invisible throat choke was never administered.)

Today, the sixty-two-year-old anchor is wearing a black suit over a black sweater and a tie, the dark colors adding to his general Vader-ness. I can almost hear "The Imperial Death March" as I see him leaning over a short bald dude, barking out what kind of graphic transitions he wants between tonight's segment on the latest bloodshed in Iraq and the following piece.

When the tirade ends, he walks by me with a short hello and tells me to go into his office and take a seat while he meets with my friend Slade out in the hall. I can hear snippets of the conversation, mainly because it is punctuated by loud outbursts that sound like they are designed for everyone in the office to hear. *Murmur, murmur* . . . "Don't even talk to me about Bush, I can't even say the word Bush!" . . . *murmur, murmur* . . . "Barack Obama is conducting himself like an outright phony" . . . *murmur, murmur, murmur* . . . "Max Baucus is behaving like an idiot, but then again, he's not all that bright" . . . Some television personalities become different people once the cameras shut off. Not Lou Dobbs. As long as he is awake, the Lou Dobbs show is going on—the public only gets to see the most controlled hour of it once a night.

If you had never seen *Lou Dobbs Tonight* and miraculously found yourself beamed into Dobbs's office, you might think you were in a Wall Street executive's corner suite. His big desk sits in front of a giant window overlooking Manhattan. Lining the room are pictures of Dobbs and his kids playing golf and riding horseback in lush green places far away from the rust-colored factory communities and desert-brown border towns that dot the typical *Lou Dobbs Tonight* broadcast.

For years, Dobbs's romance with the Wall Street lifestyle was not just confined to office motifs and family photo albums—it was the central theme of *Moneyline*, the first CNN show he anchored and his original claim to fame. A typical segment, which aired on July 4, 2001, was titled "Hail to the Chiefs." It featured Dobbs stating that corporate executives "are as powerful as politicians, as recognizable as celebrities, and always on the line."

"We look to them for inspiration and innovation," he said.

Dobbs was the guy who "liked to boast about flying around with Henry Kravis, Robert Mosbacher, and other top financiers," according to *Washington Post* reporter Howard Kurtz. He was the guy who made paid appearances in promotional videos for investment firms like Shearson Lehman Brothers and Paine Webber. In short, Lou Dobbs—with his pressed pinstriped suits and that slick head of Howdy Doody orange hair—was the guy you thought of when you heard the term "Corporate America."

This power-worshiping Dobbs of old—if he were still around—would likely be invited on *Lou Dobbs Tonight* by the new Dobbs to serve as a typical

weeknight's featured guest/human sacrifice on display for televised disem-
boweling. It was the new Dobbs, after all, who, just three short years after
praising rapacious CEOs as an "inspiration," chastised those "who simply
look at [the American economy] as a convenient piggy bank to loot, and the
worker be damned."

When Dobbs comes in, sits down, and leans back in his chair, I am
struck by how well he cleans up for the spotlight. In the poster out in the
lobby, he has the taut, slightly tan skin, and brawny physique of a middle-
aged cover model for *Cigar Aficianado,* but here in his office before makeup
time, I can see his splotchy complexion and his everyman gut. Up close, he
looks like *Happy Days*'s Richie Cunningham, only forty years, fifty pounds,
and two embittering factory layoffs later (which, as a demographic, is probably a large segment of his viewership).

I start out our chat by making small talk about the presidential campaign, and he's instantly off on a rant about how disgusted he is that the political system is dominated by Ivy League elites with "sparkling résumés
based on privilege or good fortune." He wonders why none of the candidates are just regular folks.

"We have some wonderful people in this country, wonderfully tal-
ented, principled, smart people, who got to maybe a state university, who
perhaps have worked a significant portion of their lives, who have done
something beside make a billion dollars, who perhaps taught school or ran
a plumbing business . . ."

His rant isn't necessarily insincere. As the son of a propane salesman
and a bookkeeper in rural Idaho, Dobbs grew up around exactly the kinds
of people he is describing. But let's not forget—his career as a television
personality making millions of dollars a year was aided by a sparkling,
Harvard-gilded résumé and by more than a little good fortune.

Contradiction is a consistent thread through the Lou Dobbs story,
which has seen him go from Big Business stooge to Big Business antagonist
and from Establishment spokesman to anti-Establishment prophet. Yet,
Dobbs denies there's any contradiction at all.

Calling himself "a spokesman for the outrage," he says, "Throughout it all, I've held the same ideals. It's just that until the last six or seven years, I truly believed the system was working—and what I can't comprehend is why so many people cannot see that the system is now broken."

Earlier this morning, McGinnis pinpointed for me exactly when he believes Dobbs's metamorphosis began. "It was the Enrons and the World-Coms and the immense greed at the top," he said, referring to the corporate scandals in 2002.

However, fitting for a guy who grew up in the antigovernment Rocky Mountain West, Dobbs also was particularly angry about Arthur Andersen's collapse—but not primarily because the accounting firm's executives helped misstate corporate earnings. No, McGinnis said Dobbs believed that federal prosecutors, by shutting down the whole company, unfairly punished all of Andersen's rank-and-file workers for sins committed only by those at the very top.

"The government's choice to cast everybody in the same light at Andersen came together with that issue of greed at Enron. The fact that nobody was really looking out for the common people who were getting crushed in all of this had a profound effect on Lou," McGinnis said.

Some critics claim that Dobbs's dramatic and public change of heart was a coldly calculated move to increase his show's ratings. But his transformation was probably like most things in life—a mix of both principle and opportunism.

The rough spots Dobbs hit during his change suggest principle. For instance, while the emerging populist Dobbs began railing against specific companies that outsource jobs as part of a new "Exporting America" segment, the old Dobbs continued to publish a financial tip sheet that often promoted the same companies. The clumsiness of falling into such an easily avoidable conflict—one that was inevitably exposed and ridiculed—indicate a person who was truly torn between two perspectives. You would think someone who had a supercalculated master plan to change his whole image in pursuit of ratings would be calculated enough to prevent such a predictable embarrassment.

Then again, Dobbs's own explanation about his change is a little too convenient. Was Lou Dobbs really just a naïve Little Red Riding Hood innocently skipping down the gold-paved streets of capitalism, only opening his eyes to the real ways of the world after unexpectedly encountering the Big Bad Wolf called corporate greed?

"I have to believe that Lou Dobbs is ranting nightly about 'cheap overseas labor' as a pure ratings play," wrote conservative *Wall Street Journal* editorialist Daniel Henninger. "It's about the money. And it makes perfect sense: companies outsource to protect their market share, and Lou attacks outsourcing to protect his market share."

Such critics point to the fact that when Dobbs first came back to CNN's *Moneyline* in 2001 as his old corporate-genuflecting self, his ratings were flat. Only when he began his transformation into a populist firebrand did his viewership start to increase significantly.

Looking out at Manhattan here in his office, Dobbs concedes that the ratings change corresponded with his own change, but nonetheless laughs at the theory that his transformation was a contrived ratings ploy. And when he explains why, I agree it actually *is* pretty funny.

"I can't imagine any journalist walking up to the executive producers of any one of the network evening newscasts and saying, 'You know, I think we should cover the outsourcing of jobs, I think we should cover the impact of free trade, the fact that our trade gap is rising faster than our federal budget—that's the way to get ratings,'" he tells me. "If I were interested in ratings, I would cover Anna Nicole Smith and Michael Jackson. But I don't."

And when he says "I" he means "I"—not the network-wide "we." That independence has been vital to creating a show that caters to the uprising by indicting Corporate America from within Corporate America. There's no way anyone other than Lou Dobbs could get away with the kind of show he runs at CNN. From the issues the show focuses on to the controversies it creates, *Lou Dobbs Tonight* is the anomaly in what has long been a conservatively run network. Dobbs has only been able to create and sustain such a show by using his giant personality and his impressive ratings to demand total autonomy from the rest of the network. It is no exaggeration to say that Dobbs and his team shape and dictate their show every night—and that CNN merely turns the cameras on and beams it out.

"I am the managing editor, and that's not a title in our case," he says, in his signature General Lou Dobbs authority voice. "I have absolute editorial authority over the broadcast."

Dobbs is definitely proud of his power and the fact that he's managed to create his own uprising outpost inside the belly of the beast. And once in a while, he lets everyone know it.

For example, on the day Anna Nicole Smith died, CNN's Wolf Blitzer did the customary cut to Dobbs to preview his upcoming show. Dobbs promised stories about Iraq, immigration, and the federal budget. Then, veering off script, he looked into the camera at Blitzer standing in front of a four-way split screen of Anna Nicole Smith photos and said, "There will be no reporting beginning at the top of the hour on the passing of Anna Nicole Smith—we hope you'll join us. Wolf, back to you."

Blitzer's stunned expression was the same as if he'd been told on national TV to kiss Dobbs's fat white ass—which was basically what happened.

"Sometimes there's an audience worth not having," Dobbs says. "That's the judgment I make, and I have both the responsibility and the luxury of not having to appeal to the so-called lowest common denominator in television. I want an audience that commits to participating in this democracy and to ignoring wedge issues."

I can't believe I am hearing this, and I tell Dobbs so. Especially with immigration—his signature topic—he is Mr. Wedge Issue.

"When I talk about a wedge issue," Dobbs says, "I mean one on which you can throw out any number of positions and not anything is going to happen in Washington, D.C., on that issue—nothing—because there is no bona fide commitment on the part of either party to pursuing a resolution of that issue and it is only there for the purpose of a campaign and to drive votes and excite a base."

But isn't that the Lou Dobbs formula on immigration? Isn't his MO about exciting a base of economically depressed working-class voters and directing their anger at an ethnic minority group and a seemingly unsolvable issue?

The room feels hotter after I pose this question, as if someone just jacked the thermostat up to 105 degrees.

"There is a group of people who would like to believe that somehow debating illegal immigration, the security of our borders or our ports, is somehow racially inspired," he says, annoyed and tapping his hand on his desk. "But there's never been an issue of race introduced into this discussion by me."

Some of Dobbs's toughest critics grudgingly acknowledge that, at least rhetorically, the CNN anchor has not made bigoted remarks. "Dobbs has steered clear of the racist comments," acknowledged the Southern Poverty Law Center.

But these same critics say his one-sided focus on the wedge issue of illegal immigration—and his one-sided take on the issue—fuels anti-Hispanic xenophobia, because most illegal immigrants are Latino. He might respond to them with a "my best friend is black" answer by citing his own marriage to a Mexican-American. Or he might point to his move a few weeks ago to become a lifetime member of the National Association of Hispanic Journalists. But he does none of that. Instead, he normally responds to them, as he is to me right now, that for him, the issue has nothing to do with race or even legal immigration levels—it is all about border security.

"If we are to have a national debate and a national dialogue and a decision about national policy and we make a judgment that we're going to raise immigration levels—let's say that we double them, let's say that we triple them—sign me up," he says. "There is nothing in me that is a restrictionist whatsoever, and I realize that separates me from others who are against illegal immigration on the basis that there is too much immigration. I don't believe that. I do believe that we're not in control of our immigration policies or what's happening in this country. And that leaves me in despair."

But whether or not Dobbs is, in his heart, a racist is less important than figuring out what he's trying to "tap into," as his producer McGinnis put it, and how he's been so successful.

THE LOU DOBBS phenomenon is, at its root, backlash politics. He exposes our messy, unfair, chaotic, out-of-control world, from our Swiss cheese borders to our lobbyist-rigged trade policies to a persistent narcotics problem. And viewers respond because it successfully "taps into" their desire to resurrect our collective memory of the ethereal, fuzzy Golden Age of America's past—that sepia-toned simpler time when national security was ensured; citizens were educated, engaged, and drug-free; politicians were "statesmen"; the working stiff made a decent wage; and, above all else, laws were followed.

This last point is probably the most important of all. In an unfathomably complex world where the click of a mouse in a Tokyo skyscraper can eliminate an Ohio city's entire job base, or where a ragtag band of bourgeoise Saudis can kill three thousand Americans in a few hours, Dobbs seizes on a frantic public's desperation for more *control and order*.

That's really what Dobbs's whole immigration schtick is all about. Whether his audience is workers worried about losing their jobs to undocumented laborers, suburbanites who fear a cultural takeover of their neighborhoods, or even legal immigrants who want others to have to go through the same ordeal they went through to become naturalized, the base emotion drawing them to Dobbs is a pining for a mythological past when control and order dominated.

The whole posture comes from Dobbs's innately authoritarian disposition. He is the guy who says that if he reported it, it *is* fact. He is the strongman who comes right into your living room every night to tell you that he's out there protecting you from the lawbreakers, whoever they may be—and that is comforting to a public fearful of the ever-increasing chaos outside.

"I don't believe there is too much immigration," as he told me. "I believe that *we're not in control* of our immigration policies or what's happening in this country."

In the coming months as the debate over a bipartisan immigration bill hits Congress, he will ratchet this up to brazen sloganeering, at one point airing a graphic at the bottom of the screen that says "Enforce the Law," when reporting on the bill's provisions.

That Dobbs's themes reference a Golden Age of safety, equality, control, and order that never actually occurred doesn't matter—because thanks to fairy-tale-laden high school history books, conservative politicians, Hollywood, and, yes, Lou Dobbs, the memory of such an era has been manufactured and implanted in America's collective brain à la *Total Recall.* America remembers experiencing a utopia our nation never actually experienced.

Of course, on *Lou Dobbs Tonight,* this nostalgia formula is never explicitly stated. But in the discussion we're having now about what he's trying to accomplish, he alludes to it.

"This country has always had elites," he says. "But those elites, for the most part, worked in the national interest and for the common good, were united in understanding of our national ideals and values, and worked diligently and virtuously."

The language leads me to believe he is going to start telling stories about the Rockefellers or the Carnegies, who high school history books lead us to believe were such benevolent elites, even though they made their fortunes crushing unions, degrading the environment, and generally wreaking havoc on the planet. But instead Dobbs starts reminiscing about the antiwar and civil rights movements of the 1960s, complaining "that energy is lacking now." His objective, he says, is to reawaken people in the same way they were awakened forty years ago to strive for lofty goals.

But Dobbs implies something different on his show. The famous movements in the 1960s were never about resurrecting a past era—they were about the country's desire at that time to reject the odious parts of its history (Vietnam, Jim Crow laws, etc.) and create something entirely new. Dobbs, on the other hand, is all about rejecting the path we are headed on, and bringing back what we once (supposedly) had.

Pundits typically portray 1960s-flavored, create-a-whole-new-future movements as "liberal" and enlightened while painting bring-back-the-past movements as "conservative" and Luddite, which is probably why Dobbs continues to be labeled a conservative (albeit an unconventional one). But such binary pigeonholing occurs mainly because the national media is almost solely focused on the simplistic narrative of recent presidential politics, where this binary meme has occasionally fit.

On the right, Ronald Reagan dreamed of America as a "shining city on a hill"—a nod to a famous sixteenth-century Puritan vision—and then during reelection, he told voters it was "morning in America *again*"—two references to the past. Similarly, George W. Bush promised to "*restore* dignity and honor to the White House."

Meanwhile, Bill Clinton was labeled a liberal, in part, for positioning himself as a *New* Democrat who would provide a "bridge to the Twenty-first Century." These candidates won (or in Bush's case, "won"), because those were the directions the country was looking in at the time.

But chronological aspirations—hoping to resurrect a better past or hoping for a bright new future—are not tethered to one ideology on the Left or Right, as evidenced by the 2006 election.

Facing a public angry at a new war, and a newly awful economy, the Democrats' most high-profile uprising Senate candidates were not those who talked about creating some fantastic new Epcot Center economy, but Sanders, Brown, and Tester—that is, a 1930s style socialist from Vermont, a 1940s-ish New Deal Democrat from the Midwest, and a 1950s-looking farmer populist from Montana, all of whose progressive, left-leaning campaigns were rhetorically rooted in reconnecting with an idealized past. Similarly, the Democrats' key House candidates who won in Republican districts largely ran against trade deals that had decimated their local economies, invoking an idealized past when said trade deals hadn't yet been signed.

In the media, the same thing is happening, as evidenced by a quick comparison of Dobbs and *New York Times* columnist Tom Friedman—two men who enjoy roughly the same prominence, but not the same grassroots following.

Friedman is the modern icon of supposedly "liberal," forward-looking sophistication, publishing books trumpeting a brave new technological world that lets educated elites devise Internet-based schemes to plumb the world's impoverished villages for the next call center headquarters. But, though Friedman's entire outlook is aimed at creating a new future, there's nothing necessarily liberal, forward-thinking, or sophisticated about his advocacy of job outsourcing and his veneration of low-wage labor, no matter how many times he makes up silly-sounding terms like "the world is flat," no matter how many columns he writes about his "interesting" conversations with oddly loquacious strangers in foreign lands, no matter how cool and efficient and cheaply made he tells us the latest iPod is.

Dobbs, by contrast, is billed most often as a "conservative" because his baseline narrative is about restoring a past zeitgeist of control and order. Yet there's nothing ideologically conservative about his rants against lobbyist-written trade pacts, outsourcing, and exorbitant executive pay packages, nor about his advocacy for higher wages and better benefits for blue-collar workers. He may be hearkening back to a Golden Age of America's past (that never really existed), but he's also channeling history's most outspoken left-wing populists (who most certainly did exist).

Between the *New York Times* columnist and the CNN anchor, only Dobbs can claim to be remotely connected to any sort of grassroots uprising (sorry, Tom, the elites who meet once a year at the ski resort in Davos are not grassroots nor an uprising). That's not because the country is more ideologically "conservative" (polls show the exact opposite). It is because people have seen pay-to-play politics rig the economy to shift more and more wealth to fewer and fewer people—and that pisses folks off. Dobbs's enraged, propagandistic portrayal of a mythic, idealized past ultimately taps into tangible memories of a very recent past—one that might not be the utopia of our dreams, but one that most certainly did happen and that was at least somewhat better than today. It turns out that people are far more interested in reclaiming that past than they are in reaching for the science-fiction fantasy of technological nirvana dreamed up by Tom Friedman.*

Many people—liberals and conservatives—can remember feeling at least a little more secure before 9/11, and are angry that they don't feel as secure today. Many people can remember feeling at least a little more hopeful about the economy a few years ago, and are angry that NAFTA and Enron and massive job outsourcing and huge industrial layoffs and government corruption and lying politicians have destroyed any reason for optimism. And many people are looking for someone or something to administer a little payback on the road back to stability.

That's where *Lou Dobbs Tonight* comes in—but unlike the typical backlash voices on right-wing radio that make their living picking on the disenfranchised, slandered, and/or generally powerless (minorities, gays, socialists, etc.), Dobbs's show plays the role of trophy hunter: The bigger and more imposing the target, the better. All of the entities in Dobbs's crosshairs are very powerful, very wealthy interests. That's true even on an issue like illegal immigration, which he tends to lay blame not as much on poor Mexican migrant workers looking for a better life as on American companies looking for exploitable labor to employ.

"I love it when people say I rail and rant against corporate power," Dobbs says. "How could you not?"

These are not positions that make the Establishment comfortable—especially from a person whose ratings and reach are actually impacting major public policies. In just the last year, various movers and shakers have told newspapers that on many issues like trade and immigration, Dobbs is almost single-handedly driving the agenda. One lawmaker told a magazine

---

*This reality seems to genuinely irritate Friedman, who recently lashed out at Dobbs by calling him a "blithering idiot" who is part of "a political class not making sense of the world for people." For his part, Dobbs responded that Friedman's "name calling would bother me more if he were anything more than a tool of international corporatism and a card-carrying member of his own Flat Earth Society." (*New Yorker*, 11/27/06)

that he regularly hears his congressional colleagues say, "You do this, Dobbs will go after us, or if you do this, it will play well on Dobbs."

Yet, attempting to guard his role as a journalist, Dobbs denies he is trying to be overtly political.

"I'm not calling for a revolution," he says, putting his jacket on and getting up to head off to the makeup room. "But I am calling for all of us to demand change."

I want to ask what the hell the difference is, but he's already out the door and on his way over to his studio.

HERE IN THE *Lou Dobbs Tonight* studio, we're about five minutes away from showtime, and Dobbs is behaving like he's on speed. He wants to know if I have any more questions for him, and I ask him why he's been attacking House Speaker Nancy Pelosi (D) over her request for one of the military's Boeing 757s to transport her between Washington and her San Francisco congressional district. Dobbs has been hammering away at her move for the last few days, saying it is proof that she wants to waste taxpayer cash for her own benefit. I tell him the Associated Press reported that to get all the way to California, she needs a plane much larger than her Illinois-based Republican predecessor used.

"I don't give a shit what the Associated Press reports," he says, getting so close I can smell his makeup. "That [smaller] plane can fly 2,700 nautical miles, which is well over the 3,000 miles needed to get to California. We did our own investigation, and besides, there are plenty of planes available to the 81st Airborne Division other than a 757, which she requested."

I tell him Tony Snow, the White House press secretary and not exactly a Pelosi ally, said her request was totally justifiable. This makes him laugh in a Dracula, *muh-ha-ha-ha,* I'm-about-to-use-your-jugular-as-a-straw kind of way. "Are you saying that a man who travels on Air Force One to Bush's fund-raisers would have an interest in pointing out excess?"

With this, he wheels around and heads for the anchor desk, where Kitty Pilgrim and correspondent Christine Romans are seated. I have no idea whether he is right or wrong about Pelosi's plane, but I'm not even interested because I am overpowered by the vintage Dobbs authoritarianism. This man has absolutely no shred of doubt about anything he does, and has a temper that can be set off pretty damn quickly.

As the camera guy starts counting down the seconds until the show goes live, Pilgrim compliments Dobbs on his sweater/jacket combo. "I'm like Mr. Rogers," Dobbs says with a laugh. "I have a gentle, calm demeanor." At this, Romans and Pilgrim start guffawing too, as if it's the most hilarious thing they have ever heard. Like the show's viewers, they know it's never a beautiful day in Mr. Dobbs's neighborhood.

EARLIER THIS MORNING, Jim McGinnis told me that the joke around the office is that *Lou Dobbs Tonight* is all about "truth, justice, and the American way." But it's only a joke for how cheesy it sounds—because watching Dobbs here in his studio and hearing both his on-the-air and off-the-air remarks, I can see that he really does believe that he is the ultimate defender of those principles.

In the first segment, longtime CNN Pentagon correspondent Jamie McIntyre is reporting that U.S. military commanders are now contradicting the Bush administration's latest allegation that Iran's government is spearheading an operation to arm Iraqi insurgents. McIntyre, usually a very businesslike, old-school reporter, mimics the Dobbs gusto. "It's really a textbook case of how not to conduct foreign policy," McIntyre says with disdain.

The words could have come from Dobbs himself, who quickly wraps himself in the flag by concluding that "in a difficult fight, one expects far more of our military leadership, as well as our civilian leadership, perhaps, than our dedicated men and women in Iraq in uniform are receiving."

Now we're on to CNN's Capitol Hill correspondent Andrea Koppel—daughter of Ted Koppel, one of Washington's most esteemed guardians of traditional, nonadvocacy journalism. She is reporting on the nonbinding congressional resolution against President Bush's plan to escalate the war in Iraq. But unlike with McIntyre, when she concludes, Dobbs is not satisfied

and demands to know whether anyone in Congress discussed what to actually do in Iraq, and what the real-world ramifications of President Bush's
"surge" will be.

Koppel is knocked off balance. "Sure. I mean, Republicans have talking points," she says.

But Dobbs cuts her off. "I was talking about really the more specific
consequences with some considerable specificity," he says.

With a grimace, she responds, "No, not really."

Her expression telegraphs displeasure, as her own anchor has
backed her into a corner because he didn't like her softball reporting. Before she can get another word in edgewise, the TV-anchor euphemism for
"sit down and shut up" comes, as Dobbs closes with a curt "Andrea,
thank you very much."

Now in a commercial break, Lou is berating Pilgrim. Perhaps still annoyed with Koppel, he's questioning whether Pilgrim's upcoming story
reaches the level of message discipline he expects from his own reporters.

"What the hell is your story about?" he demands, as he reads the script
of her piece on big banks marketing their credit cards to illegal immigrants.

She defensively replies, "Don't worry, you'll be fine with it."

When the story runs, Dobbs is a little less angry because he undoubtedly likes the beat-up-the-big-corporation quality of the report. Pilgrim, a
full time *Lou Dobbs Tonight* reporter, knows what her boss wants, and during the on-air banter after her piece runs, she dutifully lobs alley-oops for
the big man to slam-dunk. By the end of the segment on the company's
business with illegal immigrants, Dobbs has posterized Bank of America for
engaging in "the worst kind of obfuscation" and has dunked on the company's spokesman for "going through some nonsense claptrap."

The rest of the show just keeps dialing up the outrage. There's a story
by veteran CNN reporter Jeanne Meserve about the National Football
League rejecting a Border Patrol recruitment ad as "too controversial" for
the Super Bowl. Dobbs throws down his pen on the desk in disgust, telling
the audience that the NFL "ought to be ashamed of itself" and then, pro-
wrestler-style, turns to the camera and challenges "anyone from the NFL,

from the commissioner, on to whoever you want, come on [the show] and explain to us how it's controversial to support the men and women who are serving this nation in such a critical national security role."

Later, there's a report from *Lou Dobbs Tonight* correspondent Lisa Sylvester about the Bush administration's failure to pursue fair trade policies with China. "Promises made, promises not kept," Sylvester says as Dobbs smiles approvingly. Between the hard-hitting rhetoric and grainy, black-and-white photos of individual cabinet secretaries, the report could pass for an election year attack ad, affirming the nature of the show as an ongoing campaign for the uprising.

During the last commercial break, Dobbs goes unusually quiet and takes a deep breath. "It's a good thing I don't have a heart condition," he says, putting his hands to his temples. "Every night these people piss me off."

He uses "these people" the way Ohio senator Sherrod Brown uses the term, referring not to his reporters, or the camera crew—but to the big, faceless powers that be: the royal These People.

After almost an hour of the merciless shock-and-awe display that is a typical Lou Dobbs broadcast, I'm sure his viewers are angrily muttering the same thing. And that, more than anything else, is why this man has been so successful in bringing thousands of viewers into the uprising—and why his influence keeps growing.

7

MAINSTREAMING
THE MILITIA

FINE PRINT IS never really "fine." Oh, it's small. But it's rarely "fine" in that flippantly affirmative "yeah, fine" way we typically use the word. It's usually altogether not OK in any way at all, like the software documentation that says when you install the computer program you will be giving up all your private information, or the microscopic drivel at the bottom of your credit card bill letting you know you will be paying a 500 percent interest rate.

I guess that's why it's fine print—because they know if you read it, you won't think it's fine.

Our impulse to avoid reading the fine print is the same impulse to quickly turn the TV off when we inadvertently happen upon the Discovery Channel showing footage of eyeball surgery. We don't want to look because it's just too terrifying.

But on this warm, early spring day in 2007, I look at the fine print because I figure if I'm going to an armed encampment on an international border, I better know what rights I am signing away. And sure enough, I'm scared shitless.

The California Minuteman Civil Defense Corps sent me this "hold harmless" agreement a week ago, but I am only getting around to reading it right now, already on the plane heading toward San Diego. The first—and really, only—thing I notice on the paper is that the word *death* is mentioned four separate times.

One of these references comes in a list of "risks of bodily harm" that include "physical illness caused by heat and/or cold and poisonous herbs and plants, poisonous snakes, or injury from wild animals, exposure to elements, drowning, dehydration, death and Acts of God." Another comes in a passage about the "risk of physical confrontation with illegal aliens attempting unauthorized entry into the United States of America," which, the agreement tells me, "may result in physical violence and/or conflict, resulting in possible serious physical injury, and/or possible death."

As I said, the fine print is rarely fine.

I chew some peanuts, swallow, and sign the documents. I've already paid for this 1,200-mile trip from my home in Montana, and I want to see what the uprising against illegal immigration is really all about . . . even if it kills me.

The Minutemen, you may have heard, are those gun-toting guys who patrol border areas looking for people trying to sneak into the United States from Mexico. The members of the organization, named after the Revolutionary War militias, have been labeled everything from patriots, to vigilantes, to racists. From afar, they seem the type of die-hard, self-righteous Republican foot soldiers who have Arizona senator Barry Goldwater's words painted on their bedroom wall: "Extremism in the defense of liberty is no vice," Goldwater said. "And moderation in the pursuit of justice is no virtue."

But something more than just mundane Republican politics is at work out here on the right edge of America's populist revolt. With the help of provocateurs like Lou Dobbs, conservative ideology has mixed with feelings of economic anxiety. Though these people patrolling the border see different enemies and are plagued by paranoia, they too exhibit the pure, unadulterated frustration prevalent throughout the rest of the uprising.

That's why I asked to tag along with the organization for the first few days of its monthlong patrol known as Operation Stand Your Ground. It is why I am now driving east on Interstate 8—away from the ocean, the resorts, the golf courses and all the other reasons people travel to this part of Southern California.

This is a long way from Lou Dobbs's studio and snowy New York City. I am hurtling toward a desert region known in California as the Inland Empire—the central, noncoastal, and ultraconservative part of the state. My destination is a dusty swath of scrub brush between San Diego and Mexicali, Mexico—a place that almost nobody deliberately visits. Nobody other than Mexicans coming over the border, and American weekend warriors trying to catch them.

Because the Southern California megalopolis is the largest American population center directly adjacent to Mexico, San Diego County's sixty-six-mile international border is one of the most-trafficked routes for the millions of people who each year illegally enter the United States. The *Santa Cruz Sentinel* reported that in the first half of 2006, U.S. Border Patrol agents said they arrested more than 85,000 illegal immigrants on this border and they said "for every one they arrest, some estimate three to 10 get away." And that's just along the border. The *North County Times* reported that in the first half of 2007, 650 illegal immigrants were arrested inside the county itself.

Immigration, therefore, is never far from any political debate here. If the state legislature isn't considering proposals to bar illegal immigrants from receiving government benefits, political candidates are campaigning to stop illegal immigrants from getting driver's licenses. Just last year, the area's suburban voters elected a lobbyist for an anti-illegal immigration advocacy group to Congress.

As I speed east, San Diego's skyscrapers give way first to sprawling strip malls and then to vast, sandy nothingness. About an hour into the drive, a huge sign rises from the desert floor advertising the Golden Acorn Casino—the landmark I was told to look for as a signal that this is my exit. I pull off onto a thin winding road headed south toward Mexico—toward the staging area for an endeavor birthed from the same angst present in the rest of the uprising, but expressing itself in an extreme way. Here, on the border, the uprising is aimed at physically and culturally sealing America off from the continent to its south.

CAMP VIGILANCE SOUNDS like a Civil War–era outpost on the western frontier or a fortified special ops base in a hostile region of Iraq. But this headquarters of the Minutemen is actually just a section of a shabby RV park called Outdoor World in the desert town of Boulevard, California.

I roll up next to a gleaming white Cadillac with a Secure Our Borders bumper sticker. The parking lot is adjacent to an ancient one-story brick building that was, 150 years ago, a stagecoach depot. Hearing voices inside, I enter.

In front of a smoldering stone fireplace stands a short, pudgy, goateed guy with a black Minuteman baseball cap and a gray sweatshirt that reads ACLU: ENEMY OF THE STATE. Upon closer inspection, I can see the C in ACLU is a Soviet hammer and sickle.

A map of the area stands on an easel off to the man's left, and he is making a presentation to an assembled crowd of about twenty-five white, graying, fifty-something men, most in jeans, cargo pants, or camouflage. This must be Carl Braun—the head of the California Minutemen.

"There's no need to be armed in camp," he is telling everyone. "A lot of new people come here and want to carry their piece in camp, but that's not necessary because someone will always be armed guarding the camp."

He then points to me, tells the group I am here to do some reporting, and makes a crack about how the media is always portraying the Minutemen as lunatics.

"We're going to install a Gatling gun on top of Camp Vigilance for these media people," he says. "We'll have the marines coming in saying, 'See, they are crazy vigilantes!'"

Everyone finds this very funny. I don't get the joke.

Pointing to the map, Braun spells out where different teams will be stationed tonight along the parts of the Mexican border where there is no fence at all. He has a soft, slightly hoarse voice that remains very even—not angry or animated. He implores everyone to take pictures if they see Mexican military near the border because, he asserts, that would be a violation of the 1848 Treaty of Guadalupe Hidalgo that ended the Mexican-American War. This treaty, which gave the United States most of its southwestern territory, actually says that both Mexico and the United States have "the entire right to fortify whatever point" they want on the border, but I don't pipe up to correct him.

Braun tells everyone that tomorrow during daylight hours we will be going to a town called Jacumba, where some semblance of border fence has already been constructed. There the group will be replacing hand-sized American flags that the Minutemen previously tied up but that have been torn. A big guy in a red-and-black checkered flannel shirt with dark blue jeans says that on his last patrol he saw a Mexican on the other side of the border pull down one of these flags and wipe his ass with it. This becomes folklore throughout the weekend, and Braun responds that, not to worry, "We'll be having a ceremony to dispose of the flags that have been desecrated."

Folks file into an adjacent room, where a picnic table is being set up for dinner. Braun comes over to me, introduces himself personally, and thanks me for making the trip. When I tell him I have been hearing a lot about his group's activities and wanted to see their work for myself, he stops me and makes sure I understand who they are.

"Remember, we're the Minuteman Civil Defense Corps, and we have absolutely no affiliation with any of the other Minutemen groups," he says.

The uprising against illegal immigration, Braun explains, is a loose coalition of groups, many using the Minuteman brand, but not all of them are officially connected.

For instance, the Minuteman Project is run by Jim Gilchrist, the Southern California rabble-rouser who in 2005 ran a spirited third-party race for Congress in Orange County (just north of San Diego). The project focuses on what Braun says is "internal vigilance"—political lobbying and public protests at day labor centers inside the United States that help some of the 7 to 20 million illegal immigrants in the United States find work.

There is the San Diego Minutemen, a local, independent spin-off of the Minuteman Project that tries to document which employers in that city have pledged to hire only documented workers.

But most famous of these is the group I'm with now—the Minuteman Civil Defense Corps, which runs volunteer patrols on the Mexican border aimed at helping the U.S. Border Patrol apprehend illegal immigrants as they enter the United States.

The group is the brainchild of Chris Simcox, an activist who comes across in the media as a mix of John Wayne and David Koresh. Immediately following the 9/11 attacks, he left his job as a private school teacher in Los Angeles and moved to the desert town of Tombstone, Arizona. There, he bought the local newspaper and transformed it into a pamphleteering operation that distributes screeds against illegal immigration. In 2002, he published a missive calling for the formation of an armed militia at the border, and the Minutemen started to take shape. Simcox began touring the region whipping up support for his activities, sometimes with ludicrously hyperbolic assertions.

"There's something very fishy going on at the border," he told one crowd in 2003. "The Mexican army is driving American vehicles—but carrying Chinese weapons. I have personally seen what I can only believe to be Chinese troops."

In his appearances on Fox News and in speeches around the country, Simcox claims the Minuteman Civil Defense Corps is actually helping to physically close the 1,900-mile U.S.-Mexican border. "We're going to seal that border as citizens, from the Gulf of Mexico to the Pacific Ocean," he told the Congressional Immigration Reform Caucus in 2005.

Braun, however, admits that's a wild overstatement.

"This is a political protest," he says, taking off his hat and wiping his brow. "We suffer no illusions that we're down here and we're sealing these borders. I mean we know we're not. The Border Patrol uses us as a force multiplier to help them, and we're very, very effective when we're here. But we all have lives. And when we're done down here, we go home, and there's no one here to watch the border anymore."

It is PR politics disguised as direct action—but direct action is not the objective, like it is in other cogs of the broader uprising.

For instance, union organizers and shareholder activists use collective action and stock holdings to try to force corporations to change. Like others engaging in direct action, they are not looking to exercise Republican democracy by pressuring a third party (i.e., the government) to act on their behalf. They are trying to attain uprising goals without the help of an intermediary.

The Minutemen border patrols, on the other hand, are merely a gesture. It seems like their sporadic patrols are closing the border, and they market themselves as truly strengthening national security. But, as Braun said, their primary objective is to humiliate the intermediary—in this case, the U.S. Congress—into action. It is a conservative Protest Industry working outside the system, pressuring Congress to build a wall between Mexico and the United States, deploy tens of thousands of federal troops to the border, and punish corporations that continue to hire illegal immigrants.

"We're out here embarrassing the government," he says. "Every time we come out here, we're embarrassing the government."

DINNER IS A smorgasboard. Everyone has brought their own food and tossed it on a big table that serves as a community buffet. Candy bars. M&M's. Tostitos. Loaves of bread. Soup. It looks like someone robbed a convenience store and dumped the booty in the middle of the room.

The sun has gone down, and so has the temperature. As I huddle by the fireplace trying to warm up, a guy wearing a camouflage jacket, khaki shorts, and a Minuteman hat walks up and introduces himself as Rick.

The first thing that strikes you about this fifty-nine-year-old is his pale, light blue eyes. The next thing you notice is his white curlicue mustache.

Rick came down to the border today from his home in Bellflower—a middle-class town nestled between Los Angeles and Long Beach. He tells me he owned a landscaping business for twenty years, and he got involved in this part of the uprising because he got sick and tired of trying to battle it out with other businesses that employ low-wage illegal immigrants.

"They don't gotta pay workman's compensation, no liability insurance," he says. "I just can't compete with them."

Rick speaks in a low voice, and when he wants to make a point, he pauses, looks around, and then moves closer to you, speaking out of the corner of his mustache as if he's letting you in on a secret that's too controversial to speak out loud. He does this when he tells me that his answer to the immigration issue is simple: throw the bosses in jail.

"We need to lock up people hiring illegal aliens," he says. "And when employers see on the TV other employers going to jail for hiring illegal aliens, it'll shut it down."

Before I get any crazy ideas that Rick is some kind of Big Business–bashing lefty, he tells me he recently finished off a four-year stint on the Bellflower school board as a conservative Republican. He proudly boasts that "the teachers union fucking hated me" and refers to one educator whom he had a dispute with as "a total liberal . . . probably a goddamned lesbian."

Rick's story is the emblematic tale of the Minutemen—the one that they have all, in one way or another, lived.

He grew up just south of Los Angeles in the port city of Long Beach. Out of high school he took a blue-collar union job making ejection seats for fighter planes manufactured at Douglas, the California defense contractor that later merged with Boeing. Like almost everyone here, he enlisted in the military and served in Vietnam. He became a sniper in a special air force unit whose number is emblazoned on his white pickup truck's license plate.

"We're part of the 5 percent club," he says, cracking a smile. "We're the 5 percent of the country who goes and defends the country while the other 95 percent sits on their fucking ass and bitches."

His postwar career building a small business unfolded at the same time Ronald Reagan as California governor, and then president, was bringing conservatives' antitax movement into the political mainstream—and it brought Rick into the Republican Party. "I hang out with business guys now," he tells me—referring not to the Warren Buffetts, but the local Chamber of Commerce types.

214 | T H E   U P R I S I N G

It's the same story for most of the Minutemen and their sympathizers. They started out in the white working class, pulled themselves up the economic ladder, and don't understand why everyone else hasn't done the same—and doesn't look the same. They are the real Reagan legacy—the people who may have started out as working-class Democrats, but who so internalized all the leave-me-alone ideology, subjugation psychology, suburban neurosis, and white flight-ism of the Right's campaigns that they have become the most reliable Republican votes of all.

Their modest beginnings certainly give them a genuine sympathy for populist, fight-for-the-little-guy economics (as long as they aren't the ones who have to pay higher taxes). But even as they have climbed the ladder, they still see themselves as the little guys "being squeezed from above by the economic elites, and from below from the multicultural hordes that are sucking the lifeblood from the productive middle," as social commentator Bill Berkowitz has written.

That sentiment is leading more of them to leave their Main Street Republicanism for the extreme end of the uprising: the Minutemen. This transition is logical within the context of modern-day conservatism.

Right-wing politics has thrived by using fear and resentment to divide socioeconomic classes along racial, cultural, and geographic lines. The big problem for working-class whites, Ronald Reagan basically said, was working-class black "welfare queens" stealing their tax dollars and inner-city gangs preparing to break into suburban bungalows, rape women, murder men, and steal hubcaps off pickup trucks. The big problem for yuppie midwesterners, George W. Bush says, are middle-class East Coasters who want to legislate secular hedonism and take away their guns. The themes and the villains change, but the story line stays the same: a set of people in the economic class just below you is taking your stuff and threatening your way of life—and if those people are dealt with harshly, your troubles are over.

This panicked story is woven right into the rant Rick is delivering between sips of coffee from a Styrofoam cup. Except in his story, the villains are not blacks, or people living in New York City or Hollywood celebrities—they are dirt-poor Mexicans risking their lives to cross the vast desert border and enter the United States.

"Over 50 percent of the people who come over the border want to rip this country off," he claims. "Half are coming up here because they are drug dealers and they are going to rip the system off one way or another . . . another 25 percent come up here because they want the bennys—they can have their kids, they can be on welfare, they don't have to work."

As if trying to show me a softer side, he says, "Sure, maybe the other 25 percent are looking for a better life or a good job."

"But I see three-quarters who are coming up here that are just using the system or trying to steal from us."

Of course, whether such theft is actually happening is the subject of much debate.

In late 2004, a local newspaper in San Diego published a story about an anti-illegal immigration group's report claiming California's roughly 3 million illegal immigrants cost taxpayers nearly $9 billion a year. But in December 2006—just a few months before I am visiting the border—the Republican comptroller of Texas touched off a national firestorm when she released a study showing "that undocumented immigrants in Texas generate more taxes and other revenue than the state spends on them." The comptroller's report said illegal immigrants "put about $420 million more into state coffers than they take out," according to the *Washington Post*.

Rick doesn't want to hear it. He's convinced illegal immigrants are costing him and his fellow taxpayers jobs, wages, and taxes, and he's unswayed by any debate over numbers. He wants a harsh crackdown on employers.

Rick's involvement in the uprising here at the border is evidence that he is not a low-information voter—this is a serious investment of time in a political cause. And so the contradiction of him simultaneously describing himself as a staunchly pro-business Republican while demanding Congress hammer business highlights something deeper than mere ignorance.

As the world has gotten infinitely more complex over the last thirty years of technological change, America's public discussion about the world has gotten more simple. Issues like foreign policy, globalization, and immigration have added all sorts of gray shades to the political landscape. But with so much complexity and so many conduits of propaganda (newspapers, radio, television, blogs, email lists, etc.), the only messages that break through to an overwhelmed public are the most crisp sound bites and the most simple explanations. The discussion has devolved to a fifth-grade civics class just as the world needs a PhD seminar on economics and sociology.

For someone like Rick, this dichotomy has created a terrifying fog—one that eliminates any sense of security or control. He sees complex demographic shifts make whites a minority in his town. He watches global economic forces stress his business. And he witnesses his country struggle with the asymmetrical threats of global terrorism. But he, like all of us, has become addicted to simple answers—so addicted, in fact, that he barely notices when those answers conflict with each other.

When we talk about the environment, for instance, he says, "This country is being destroyed from within by its own government." He says regulations from the Southern California Air Quality Management District and the federal government's Environmental Protection Agency "are running business out of this country faster than you'll ever know." Yet he complains that smog is destroying Los Angeles.

When we talk about his time at Douglas, he says the company moved many of its operations from Long Beach to China.

"We're losing our jobs, and these are good-paying union jobs," laments the same guy who was just ripping on unions.

Right after saying it's time to arrest corporate executives who hire illegal immigrants, he's railing on "these politicians who're banging on large industry, saying big business is bad."

Listening to the others commiserate over dinner at Camp Vigilance, I know Rick's rhetorical U-turns are common here. I can also tell that the Minutemen are all vaguely aware of and uncomfortable with the contradictions. You can hear their discomfort in their exasperated declarations, like when Rick at one point says, "Republicans and Democrats are both whores because it's really about one thing to them—money."

The beacon of light that cuts through the haze for these folks is the Minutemen, an amateur club that is about trying to do something—anything—to make sense of it all. And what better way to get some semblance of control and form an uprising than to hone in on emotional issues like cultural change, security, and territorial integrity—all the issues woven into immigration.

To these fifty- and sixty-somethings, the threats they fear above all else are the ones that are most complicated, persistent, and seemingly omnipotent: crime and an amorphous feeling of insecurity. The U.S.-Mexican border, which is largely unfenced and unguarded, is the perfect representation of those problems for these guys. Like Lou Dobbs, they see its porous quality as a symptom of a lack of control over the very lines that delineate America, physically, ethnically, and geopolitically. And to them, the "broken" border between the United States and an impoverished, crime-plagued country with a very different culture arouses specific fears of a menacing invasion.

Rick's particular fear is drugs and gangs. He says he lives down the street from members of the Mara Salvatrucha, or MS-13—the famed Latin American gang that is now growing in the United States. "These are bad news motherfuckers," he says, leaning in and lowering his voice again. "These guys are hard-core criminals and they will kill you and me in a second and not even think about it."

I have heard about this gang. In 2005, the *Washington Times* reported that the Minuteman Project's Gilchrist was telling his members that MS-13 operatives have been sent into the United States to target Minutemen for retribution. At dinner, I overheard someone say MS-13 has offered up a $10,000 reward for anyone who kills a Minuteman. Where the rumor started and whether it is true is anyone's guess—but the men around the table reacted with both fear and excitement, clearly a bit pleased to be important enough to have a bounty on their heads.

Rick, though, isn't happy at all—he is seething as he describes MS-13. He is convinced they are flooding over the Mexican border, along with huge drug shipments—and he is sure they are coming here because "they know that our justice system is so lax and liberal" that even if they get appre-hended, "you can actually live better in jail than you can out on the street."

"When those MS-13 guys walk down the street and look at me and my son, I think, 'I could fire three shots and you three would be dead in three seconds, you and all your buddies,'" he says, and with his sniper back-ground, I believe him.

But are gangs really what he fears? Or has he really joined this uprising because he fears a Latino cultural invasion?

I ponder this as we stand by the fire. He hasn't said anything overtly racist. But is Rick a racist for so reflexively equating illegal immigration from Mexico with violent crime and drug dealing?

Experts say MS-13 now has 50,000 members in the United States, most of whom probably came through Mexico. And it is undeniable that smugglers carrying illegal drugs flow over the border every day. But so do tens of thousands of Mexican peasants just looking for subsistence jobs and a better life.

Before I can ask the question tactfully, he has read my mind.

"I'm not a racist or a bigot," he says, as the fire crackles in the back-ground. "If you want to come here and you want to come here legally and be an American citizen and love this country and speak English, I'll help you."

I want to follow up, but he says he has to go to his trailer to prepare for the first patrol of the night. I tell him to stay safe, and he jokes that com-pared to what he's been through before in the military, this stuff is not too difficult. I force a smile, but my mind can't shake his last comment.

I'm sure he and his fellow Minutemen don't think of themselves as racists or bigots. And in the strictest definition of "racist," they probably aren't, because most of them probably don't consciously believe they are racially superior to others.

But their paranoia about everything—crime, security, getting ripped off—it all has metastasized into a broader fear of foreignness—the textbook definition of xenophobia. Notice Rick's qualifications: He'll help you if you prove to him that you love this country and speak English—that is, if you show that you aren't strange or foreign.

Though the Minutemen's xenophobia isn't restricted to feelings about Latinos, they probably find Latinos most easy to focus on because they are the ones coming over the border. As the *Orange County Weekly* said, the Minutemen espouse "an anti-immigrant ideology that attempts to link Mexico with every perceived foreign threat—not just Chinese communists, but also al-Qaida operatives and Latin American guerrillas."

Rick's perspective is similar to that of Simcox, the Minuteman Civil Defense Corps founder, who has publicly attacked illegal immigrants for supposedly "refusing to assimilate." This nationalist xenophobia's natural target is Mexicans, because they represent the kind of cultural change that terrifies a domestic population under increasing stress. Mexicans (as opposed to Canadians or Europeans) not only look different from white Americans, they speak a different language, possess different cultural mores, and often come from an economic strata that up-from-the-bootstraps whites particularly disdain, because they see themselves as having surpassed it.

So why does change completely petrify more and more Americans? Because change is accelerating at the very same time all the things that were supposed to lessen change's negative impacts are being stripped away. Globalization, job outsourcing, and economic instability are speeding up at the same time the government is slashing programs that provide a social safety net.

Meanwhile, new technologies like the Internet and cell phones that allow us to experience more and more of our lives in physical isolation are disconnecting us from each other at the same time we are experiencing the effect described in Robert Putnam's book *Bowling Alone,* whereby the old institutions of "social capital" (PTAs, community clubs, granges, etc.) that brought us together and helped us deal with change are now crumbling.

The fear this change and this safety net erosion sows, of course, has an economic benefit—namely, worker productivity skyrockets as people are frightened into working harder and harder just to maintain their status. But it also sows xenophobia—an impulse, as I'll find out, that went from latent to overt here on the border thanks to 9/11.

AFTER SETTING UP my tent outside the stagecoach house, I go back to the fireplace and pull up a chair with a few guys who are sitting around drinking beers and shooting the shit. They are all casually dressed, suburban types. As they chuckle at a joke, someone notices what looks like a small marijuana water pipe on the ground. Everyone laughs even harder, feigning outrage, pretending they don't know whose it is.

I can't help but laugh out loud with them, though probably for different reasons. Many of them, like Rick, are here because they say they want to stop drug dealers from coming over the border—and I'm sure they do in theory. Yet here they are giggling like college freshmen when they see a buddy's pot pipe.

Their chortling tells me that for all the hype about the Minutemen's stern image, and for all the life-or-death significance of the immigration issue, most of the rank and file don't take themselves or their time out here too seriously. From the name Camp Vigilance to all the ex-military guys involved in the Minutemen, I expected the scene here to be very regimented and stiff, but it all feels like a bunch of guy friends out on a hunting trip—only instead of hunting deer, they hunt people. It is one-half political activism but also one-half Old Milwaukee beer commercial, which is probably by design.

Any effective organizer in any uprising past or present will tell you the campaigns that attract the most loyal followings are usually those that make the activism fun for the activists. As a '60s-era antiwar organizer once told me, "Half the people who went to protest marches against the Vietnam War were there just to smoke weed and get laid." So, sure, a few of these guys here at the border never crack a smile, and there's no doubt that Minuteman leaders like Simcox and Gilchrist work hard to portray themselves as stone-faced hard-asses. But for the most part, the grunts who make the trek out to places like Boulevard or Tombstone make their journey at least as much for the camaraderie as for the cause.

I feel a tap on my shoulder and turn around to see Braun. He tells me to meet him out front, because we're going out for a quick patrol and tour of the border.

I walk out the screen door and see a trailer office—the kind you might find on a construction site. The banner hanging off the side shows a pencil drawing of a guy in a tricornered hat with a rifle slung over his shoulder, binoculars in one hand, and a walkie-talkie in the other. This is the communications center, which monitors four security cameras inside Camp Vigilance and keeps in constant CB contact with the Minuteman teams when they go out for patrols.

Three middle-aged women—the first women I've seen here—are standing outside talking. One of them relates an anecdote about how a few weeks ago the Minutemen helped Border Patrol catch a group of illegal immigrants. Another jokes, "The illegals all look alike, don't they?"

They all laugh, but stop short when they see me walk by toward Braun's truck.

Soon after we veer off the highway and onto the dirt road, I see Braun's hand moving down underneath the dashboard and then I hear two loud clicks of something opening. Out comes a pistol.

We have turned off the public road and onto private land along the border. The owner, Braun says, has given the Minutemen permission to patrol the property and carry firearms out in the open. Braun handles the weapon comfortably—a familiarity that probably comes from his years serving as a military police officer in the air force. In a paintball kind of way, Braun and most of the other guys here seem to enjoy being part of the Minutemen as a means to relive their days in the service. The nostalgia goes farther than folks wearing holstered guns, too. For instance, the Minutemen regularly speak in acronyms. Braun always refers to his organization's "SOPs"—standard operating procedures. And on the CB, everyone is referred to by a code name.

Braun, though, is a bit different than the average Minuteman grunt. As we drive south in the darkness, I pick up that he didn't relish his time in the military as much as, say, Rick did. "I enlisted in the army to escape the draft and I burned my draft card in basic training," he says. He laughs at himself, adding, "A whole lot of symbolism, but not a whole lot of effect."

He points to a set of bright lights on the horizon and tells me they are part of a maximum security Mexican prison in the middle of the desert. He doesn't know if anyone has escaped from there and tried to hike over the border, but he does say he's certain that Middle Eastern terrorists have tried to enter here.

I ask why he is so sure, and he says because "I've seen 'em."

He tells me about the real catalyst that took the Minutemen from the hobby of a few gadflies like Simcox to a national organization with 10,000 members, including 2,000 in California alone. It started back in the winter of 2005, with a series of stories that have become legend in Minuteman circles.

"The Border Patrol found a mosque, a makeshift mosque, about a half mile that way," he says, pointing off to our right.

He pulls the truck off to the side of the road, and we jump out onto the desert floor. With the moon shining, we can make out the border fence about five hundred yards away, as well as the silhouette of an ancient, inactive volcano known as Boundary Peak. Out in the distance we can see the glow of the Mexican town of Jardines del Rincón, and we hear coyotes howling. Braun points out spots along the border that have no fence—and starts recounting the circumstances surrounding this mosque story. Back in 2005, he says, he and a group of Minutemen heard people screaming at each other at around 2:30 a.m.

"We looked in our night vision scope and we saw three guys just walk across the part with no fence," he says, leaning against the truck's bumper.

"Now, I've heard Arabic spoken before," he continues, reminding me that his sons, who are serving in Iraq and Afghanistan, speak the language. "So I call down on the CB to another one of our guys and I told him you have three guys coming your way. And I ask him: 'You were in Desert Storm, tell me what language they are speaking.' And he comes back and says, 'I've got bad news for you. They're speaking MSA—Modern Standard Arabic.'"

In just the first night with the Minutemen, I have heard this story recounted at least five times, and each time it is told a little differently. I ask Braun why this hasn't been reported and he says that, in fact, a congresswoman had already confirmed it publicly.

But when I later look into these allegations, I will inadvertently find myself wading into the murky whirlpool of conspiracy theory where politics, right-wing media, and the Internet froth.

Braun is correct that, right after his 2005 border patrol, North Carolina congresswoman Sue Myrick (R) held a press conference to announce that federal authorities had arrested "three al-Qaida members who came across from Mexico into the United States." But what Braun doesn't say is that within days of this announcement, Myrick was humiliated after her local paper investigated the claims and found they were entirely false.

Similar details emerge about the mosque that these supposed Arabic-speaking border-crossers allegedly constructed. Days after Myrick's press conference, Texas senator John Cornyn (R) told the fringe right-wing website HumanEvents.com that "he has seen anecdotal evidence of Arabic belongings" discovered near the border. Yet when pushed on whether that means terrorists have crossed into the United States through Mexico, he was forced to admit that "I don't have any information that it has actually happened."

Right around the same time, Texas congressman John Culberson (R) issued a press release saying a top al-Qaeda terrorist was being held in a jail in a Texas border town after being apprehended trying to come into the United States through Mexico. Culberson appeared on Fox News to trumpet the revelations in advance of a congressional debate over immigration, and the story was spread by websites like WorldNetDaily (the same conspiracy theorist website that I heard Lou Dobbs's producer cite in a morning editorial call).

But just a few weeks later, the *Houston Chronicle* reported that the law enforcement authorities Culberson said were holding the supposed terrorist refuted his entire story. "Congressman Culberson has two or three stories confused," said the local sheriff. "We have no terrorist in our jail."

All of these myths emerged in that winter of 2005—the very time the Minuteman Civil Defense Corps started to really take off. And that's no coincidence, Braun acknowledges, after he points out a Border Patrol helicopter slowly scanning the ground off to our right.

"Most of the people that are here, 95 percent, I would say, for them, this is a national security-slash-safety issue."

Whether or not a racist outlook makes these guys see the border primarily as a "national security/safety issue" is hard to say. But what's most important in understanding this uprising is understanding that when you strip away the (not insignificant) questions about personal motives, you see that the Minutemen are really the first militia to emerge from the burning wreckage of 9/11.

MILITIA CULTURE AS a contemporary phenomenon is much different— and much darker—than what the Founding Fathers were talking about when they referenced militias in the Bill of Rights. Today's militiamen are not the happy-go-lucky Paul Reveres of the eighteenth century.

In the 1980s and 1990s, militia culture bloomed most famously in places like the Rocky Mountain West and Pacific Northwest. Some militias were overtly white supremacist, others were antiglobalization separatists. But all of them found unity in a hatred for a federal government they believed was aiding global bogeymen like the Trilateral Commission, the United Nations, and the theoretical One World Government—bogeymen that were supposedly plotting to take over America.

This anti-Establishment ideology, while extreme in the case of militias, is another common thread throughout the uprising on both the Right and Left. Both sides—like more and more Americans—agree with those like Lou Dobbs who say the two-party system is broken, and believe Washington is totally unresponsive to those it governs. As Braun says, "Our government's for sale."

He picks up a pebble off the ground and flings it out toward the dark abyss that is the vast open border. "The middle class is getting squeezed out of the whole equation."

Extreme elements of the Left express these sentiments as pure chaos—the most famous recent example being the anarchists who committed acts of violence during the otherwise peaceful protests of the 1999 World Trade Organization meeting in Seattle. The extreme Right, by contrast, has established well-organized militias by attracting membership and support from people desperate for a sense of empowerment in an unstable world that makes them feel economically and culturally helpless.

Militia culture has bubbled underground for years, and the United States has a sordid history of extremists immersed in that culture (remember the Oklahoma City bombers?) turning their antigovernment ideology into violence. But when those planes hit the World Trade Center on 9/11 and scaremongering became the norm in the years afterward, paranoia and militia culture were given an unspoken boost of legitimacy. As Scripps Howard's 2006 poll showed, "Widespread resentment and alienation toward the national government appears to be fueling a growing acceptance of conspiracy theories" surrounding the attacks. And whether consciously or not, many conservative-leaning Americans probably thought that perhaps those guys who arm themselves and practice military ops in advance of the apocalypse aren't that crazy after all.

The Minutemen were able to bring militia culture into the mainstream. They have a cause and charismatic leaders like Simcox and Gilchrist who seem to offer a more palatable, salient militia ideology, and one with a rationale—border security and the War on Terror—that combats charges of racism and extremism. The organization succeeds in taking militia culture from public access documentaries and tiny-circulation newsletters to a staple of the Establishment media and a growing force in the halls of power.

Flip on CNN, Fox, or any other network, and you will often run into Minutemen when the immigration issue comes up. With politicians today worshiping television, such exposure naturally translates into political cachet.

Not only have California governor Arnold Schwarzenegger and Texas governor Rick Perry publicly endorsed Minuteman patrols in their states, but the Southern Poverty Law Center (SPLC) reports that more than twenty U.S. congressmen attended a Minuteman rally in September of 2005 with founder Chris Simcox. Six of them "actually signed up with his organization, strapped on handguns, and participated in Minuteman patrols in October, along with Arizona Republican gubernatorial candidate Don Goldwater," the report stated.

That same year, the Associated Press ran a story headlined "Border Volunteers Should Be Deputies" detailing how Colorado senator Wayne Allard (R) told a congressional hearing that the federal government should consider giving Minutemen official police powers. His declaration was eagerly followed up on by Texas congressman Culberson—the same frothing fearmonger who wrongly claimed al-Qaeda terrorists had been captured at the border. According to the *Brownsville Herald,* Culberson authored a bill proposing to hand over up to $6.8 billion to "volunteer militias" like the Minutemen and grant them authority "to use any means and any force" that is already granted to state and federal law enforcement officials. His bill drew a stunning forty-seven Republican cosponsors, though it was never passed into law.

Polls show this campaign to make militia culture legitimate in the public's mind has been remarkably effective. A 2005 Rasmussen survey found 54 percent of Americans have a favorable opinion of the Minutemen. A 2006 Fox News poll found a plurality of Americans believe the organization is just "concerned citizens" and not vigilantes.

The Minutemen have muscled their way into legitimacy in no small part by playing up the terrorism stories Braun and his comrades constantly harp on—and it doesn't really matter whether the folklore is actually accurate.

In a post-9/11 world saturated with oversimplified talking points, horror stories just have to *sound* true in order to serve a national-security cause. We learned this lesson with the neoconservatives and the Bush administration's claims about Iraq's supposed WMDs. And we are learning it today with the anti-immigration faction of the uprising.

As just one example, take Senator Cornyn's claims about the supposed

"Arabic belongings" found at the border. When pushed, he said he didn't feel the need to present any hard evidence supporting his allegations that al-Qaeda is coming over the Mexican border. Instead, he just said he knows crossing the Mexican border "is easy to do"—expecting that alone to be adequate proof of terrorist infiltration.

This isn't to say that the wide-open U.S.-Mexican border poses no legitimate security concerns. Far from it. Most experts agree that the border is a vulnerability.

In 2004, *Time* reported that "a key al-Qaida operative" in Pakistan told interrogators that he had considered a scheme to "smuggle nuclear materials to Mexico" for transport into the United States. That same year, the Central Intelligence Agency issued a threat report identifying the Mexican border as a potentially serious national security vulnerability. In 2005, the Associated Press reported that one U.S. immigration official told a Mexican court that smugglers have "continued to help Hezbollah-affiliated migrants in their effort to illicitly enter from Tijuana." The concern was echoed in 2006, when FBI director Robert Mueller confirmed to Congress that federal law enforcement officials had broken up a Hezbollah smuggling ring in Mexico.

Nevertheless, the gap between the facts of these stories and the folklore that surrounds them has been deliberately widened by the activists building this anti-illegal immigration uprising.

That same 2004 *Time* report made sure to point out that the terrorist's claim was "unproved." But that didn't stop *Human Events* editor Terrence Jeffrey from publishing a nationally syndicated column citing the incident as proof that al-Qaeda will soon "pull off an attack on the United States using weapons of mass destruction smuggled across our southern frontier." Incredibly, Jeffrey made the claim even though he admitted that a senior U.S. official explicitly told him: "We do not have any evidence to suggest that they have or are carrying out this kind of plot to use Mexico."

The 2005 Associated Press dispatch reported that it was not clear exactly what "Hezbollah-affiliated" really meant, and that it was possible the smuggler in question was using the permeable U.S.-Mexican border to help innocent Lebanese refugees seeking political asylum from their war-ravaged country. Similarly, the *Albuquerque Tribune* reported that in his testimony about the Hezbollah story, FBI director Mueller "told [Congress] that most reports about alleged terrorists crossing the Mexican border have not proved to be true." But that didn't stop right-wing activist Jerome Corsi from jumping onto Fox News in a joint appearance with the Minuteman Project's Gilchrist to declare that "we've had Hezbollah agents that came across the border with Mexico," nor did it stop the conservative website Newsmax.com from publishing a story headlined "Hezbollah Invading U.S. from Mexico."

Because these examples of misinformation involve a few grains of truth, they are tame compared to the wild-eyed alarmism that increasingly dominates the immigration debate. The "reporting" from right-wing clearinghouse WorldNetDaily is typical. The conservative website has posted stories with headlines like "Islam on March South of Border," equating the religion's relatively modest inroads in Latin America with a menacing threat to American national security. When the *El Paso Times* reported that Iraqis seeking shelter from the war were coming into the United States through Mexico, WorldNetDaily used the article to run a story headlined "Iraqi Terrorists Caught Along Mexico Border." This, even though the *Times* reported that "none of the Iraqis [coming from Mexico] have been linked to terrorist activities."

Watchdog groups worry that the intensifying media frenzy around the border security issue has helped groups like the Minutemen use fear to further legitimize militia culture. As Mark Potok of the Southern Poverty Law Center told *Time* magazine, the Minutemen "have found an issue with racial overtones and a real resonance with the American public and they are exploiting it as effectively as they can."

That success, says Potok, has had consequences that reach way beyond the issue of border security. His watchdog group told *Time* that the rise of the Minutemen "seems to have reinvigorated members of the antigovernment militias of the 1990s" as well as neo-Nazis and the Ku Klux Klan.

In 2006, the SPLC counted about 800 racist groups operating in the United States—a 5 percent boost in just one year, and a 33 percent jump from 2000. In that same *Time* piece, a leader of a Nazi organization in Ohio said his group has taken a page out of some Minutemen groups' playbook and started physically harassing immigrants at day labor centers. This, said the Nazi leader, helped his organization forge new ties with the Klan, which, of course, already has some experience using the immigration issue for its racist cause. As the *New York Times* reported back in 1980, KKK leader David Duke conducted "a Klan border patrol against illegal Mexican aliens."

Staring out at those prison lights on the horizon, Braun seems genuinely hurt when I ask him about charges of racism, and about concerns that the Minutemen are encouraging the ugliest human instincts.

He starts for the first time telling me a little bit about his personal life. He grew up in Toms River, New Jersey, has been married twice, and—to my admitted surprise—he earns his living in San Diego as the head of a firm that helps companies find qualified minority and women candidates for job openings.

"This is not a debate about race, [and] if it were a debate about race, I couldn't be involved," he says. "I'm a diversity recruiter, for godsakes. I dedicated my entire career, twenty-five years of recruiting, to help women and minorities break through the glass ceiling of Corporate America. If this were about race, Carl Braun wouldn't be a part of it."

Amid the crackling of the CB, I press him. "Fine," I say. "Even if you aren't personally a racist, isn't this organization fueling racism by channeling so much of the uprising's general anger specifically at one ethnic group?"

"There are three hundred groups [that do border operations], and I can't account for what everybody says and does," he replies, with a hint of anger. "Yeah, there are people out there that just say the damnedest things. I look at them and go, 'Get off my side.'"

He insists that the "SOP" of the Minuteman Civil Defense Corps is to weed out racists and white supremacists by interviewing people before they are allowed to join the organization. He says, "We're very concerned about the people trying to make the trek across" the desert from Mexico; that when they find an illegal immigrant in need of water or medical attention, they are there to help; and that "if the tables were turned and we were in [the Mexicans'] place, we'd probably be doing the same thing" by trying to get into the United States.

But something about the way he declines to address "what everybody says and does" on the race question reminds me, yet again, of that look-the-other-way tactic so prevalent in other parts of the broader uprising—the one that pretends not to notice that support may be coming from the more odious corners of society.

Braun's day job gives him a compelling alibi to charges that he personally is a racist. But he clearly comprehends that the uprising he leads benefits from racist passions in the rank and file—whether stated or unsaid. His careful language deliberately avoids confronting the parts of the Minuteman coalition that he knows are crucial to its growth and success.

Braun employs this same bob-and-weave strategy when we discuss the Minuteman image. Just as he complained about the charges of racism while being careful not to necessarily offend racists, he complains about the Minutemen's being portrayed as lawless vigilantes meting out harsh frontier justice—but he also knows that the spaghetti Western image benefits the organization and its recruitment.

Seeing nobody trying to cross over the border out at Boundary Peak, we are now back in the truck heading home to Camp Vigilance. Braun says, "As much as the media likes to portray us as the bogeyman, we're not the bogeyman, [and] we're not a bunch of crazy nuts."

Many think the Minutemen are physically rounding up illegal immigrants and shooting them if they run. And there have been sporadic reports of confrontations between some volunteer border patrol groups and Mexicans. In 2005, the *Arizona Daily Star* published a front-page story documenting how sheriffs' deputies were reporting that "vigilantes" have been abusing illegal immigrants. "Illegal entrants have reported being kicked, shouted at, bitten by dogs and had guns pointed at them," the paper stated.

In 2006, the Associated Press reported that the Minuteman Project was investigated by Arizona law enforcement officials after a Mexican man "told authorities he was held against his will" by three of the organization's volunteers. The SPLC has also reported that one prominent anti-immigration leader who was an original member of Simcox's organization "secretly urged the nation's largest neo-Nazi group to launch a campaign of violence and harassment" against Mexicans coming over the border.

It is true, however, that the same Associated Press noted that Border Patrol officials say Minutemen generally "have remained peaceful." And Braun insists the Minutemen really are just a big neighborhood watch. "We report, observe, and direct," he says.

He insists that the firearms they carry are only for self-defense, and there's no denying that the border is a dangerous area. In February of 2006, Homeland Security secretary Michael Chertoff told Congress that the number of violent incidents aimed at U.S. Border Patrol agents had doubled in a year. In February of 2007, the New York Times reported that stepped-up "efforts to stop smuggling and illegal immigration have led to increased violence along the southern border" as both drug dealers and human smugglers seek to continue their operations.

But the Minutemen, Braun asserts, try to avoid confrontation at all cost.

"When we see people coming over the border, we call Border Patrol—that's our SOP," he says, adding that they always call the Border Patrol to alert them before they go out on their own patrols because they see their efforts as "cooperative" rather than confrontational.

All of this may be true, but don't be fooled: the Minutemen have actively cultivated the organization's paramilitary reputation, and the vigilante image is not an accident, despite Braun's protests to the contrary.

Minutemen are typically photographed by the media wearing military garb, brandishing weapons, and scanning the border with binoculars. They have received attention for overly aggressive behavior, sometimes bordering on harassment. In late 2006, for example, a liberal Arizona state legislator received death threats from people claiming to be Minuteman members after she proposed legislation to legally restrict the organization's activities.

Meanwhile, the highest-profile leaders above Braun often openly encourage the macho depictions. In that 2002 call to arms in his Tombstone newspaper, Simcox urged citizens to form "a committee of vigilantes." In 2003, he suggested to the *Los Angeles Times* that the Minutemen are looking for a firefight, declaring, "If [people crossing the border] fire on us, we'll fire back." In 2005, Gilchrist was quoted in the *Orange County Register* as saying, "I'm damned proud to be a vigilante."

The image serves three purposes. First and foremost, it gives the Minutemen an edginess that attracts media attention and therefore helps their political protest gain traction. If they really did try to brand themselves as merely a peaceful neighborhood watch, they probably would not be a regular feature on Fox News.

The vigilante image also serves to heighten the perception—and maybe the chance—that there will, in fact, be a physical confrontation at the border. Braun says this is absolutely not the goal, but he also says he believes that "for this to be raised to the level that the government has to do something about [the border], there's gotta be an incident."

Finally, the reputation serves as a niche marketing tool pretty obviously directed at recruiting a specific demographic: the weekend warrior looking for the occasional glory of law enforcement, the thrill of clandestine special operations, or the chance to relive their military service.

Braun denies this, of course. Pulling the truck past an armed watchman back at the gate of Camp Vigilance, he says the Minuteman Civil Defense Corps does not want to attract "Rambos" because "that's not what we're about." As proof, he tells me that after a speech he recently gave to a Republican audience in Santa Barbara, he was approached by a guy who said he was interested in joining the Minutemen because he wants to "go down there to the border with a high-powered rifle and shoot them all and put them all in a mass grave."

"I said, 'I'm sorry, we don't have that kind of policy,'" Braun recounts, and he told the guy he was not welcome in the organization.

Why the bloodthirsty lunatic even thought of the Minutemen when he decided he wanted to "shoot them all and put them all in a mass grave"— well, I'm not sure that bothers Braun. Skilled in the art of looking the other way for his uprising, he might say that he just can't account for what everybody says and does.

UNZIPPING MY TENT in the morning, I recoil at the burst of frigid air not yet warmed up by the sun. I might have slept longer, but the commotion over at the stagecoach house woke me up. So I bundle up in a sweatshirt and head over to see what all the fuss is about.

"Thirteen illegals," I hear a tall guy excitedly telling Braun. "We saw thirteen coming over the border and we called in Border Patrol to get 'em."

Still bleary eyed, I grab a granola bar, a glossy magazine sitting on the couch, and a cup of black ooze that is supposed to be coffee. I walk back outside, and sit down on the steps to just chill for a few minutes.

It is a crystal-clear morning, and for the first time I can see how brown the whole landscape is. The area looks like a huge sheet of coarse sandpaper.

I watch Rick taking supplies out of his aging RV and putting them into the back of his pickup truck. He is wearing a white T-shirt, jeans, work boots, and green suspenders that hold up a holster for his pistol. A few guys walk by eagerly talking about the "catch" last night. Everyone looks happy. I, on the other hand, keep imagining people trying to trek miles across this bleak terrain by foot, only to become tracking targets for suburban California thrill seekers.

My stomach turns.

I flip open the magazine I have in my hand and realize I am holding a wrinkled copy of the October 2006 edition of the *New American*—the official publication of the John Birch Society, one of the nation's oldest and most famous white supremacist groups.

The magazine's lead story pushes the theory that the American, Mexican, and Canadian governments are secretly planning to legally unify the three nations and construct a continent-spanning NAFTA superhighway. This is another verse of folklore I've been hearing about all weekend.

Certainly, something called the Security and Prosperity Partnership (SPP) exists, and its motives are definitely suspect. As journalist Chris

Hayes found during his extensive investigation for the *Nation* magazine, the SPP is "far more ambitious and more nefarious than its architects claim," with its objectives not just security and prosperity but "deregulation by stealth and the imposition of U.S.-style 'war on terror' security measures on Canada and Mexico."

That said, as Hayes has also shown and most major news organizations have confirmed, absolutely no hard proof exists suggesting that the SPP is creating a supernational North American Union or that a privately owned NAFTA superhighway connecting all three nations is being planned.* These news reports, though, have only served to fuel the myth—because naturally the myth says all of this is being worked out in secret, and the more denials, the more proof that they—the royal They—are hiding something.

Shit, I think as I thumb through the pages. It's too early in the morning for conspiracy theories.

A brown Honda CR-V rolls up and out bounds a pear-shaped computer programmer named Steve—the only guy here with long hair. A fifty-six-year-old British ex-pat who enlisted in the English navy as a teenager, he has glasses that make him look like a young Ben Franklin, except Steve isn't wearing knickers and ruffles—he's wearing loose cargo pants and a filthy gray T-shirt that reads MOTHERS AGAINST DRUNK KENNEDYS. He sports four small stud earrings, and one arm is tattooed with a wizard, the other with a snake.

He tells me to get in because we're heading over to the border town of Jacumba, so I hop into the front seat. Dangling from the rearview mirror

---

* In his definitive investigation, Hayes has found very concrete evidence that the Texas state government is proposing a $185 billion Trans-Texas Corridor comprising "4,000 miles of highway, rail and freight corridors, the first of which would run up from the border through the heavily populated eastern part of the state." But while he concludes that this "Trans-Texas Corridor is very, very real" he also found that "there's no such thing as a proposed NAFTA Superhighway," in that there is no privately owned, trinational, continentwide highway being built (*The Nation*, 10/15/07).

is something called a "Backwards Bush" clock counting down the time before President Bush leaves office—a strange ornament for a guy who, like everyone here, twice voted for Bush (and judging by his T-shirt, hates Democrats).

"Bush certainly hasn't changed Washington, he's become a part of it," Steve says when I ask him what the clock is all about.

"What's that mean exactly?" I ask.

"Well, he's behind closed doors trying to join three nations together under the banner of SPP."

I guess it isn't too early in the morning for conspiracy theories, after all.

Militia culture has long pointed to the supposed NAFTA Superhighway and the SPP as a grand conspiracy—it fits into the One World Government fears. And as militia culture has gone mainstream through the Minuteman uprising, so has the North American Union theory.

Back a few months ago in Montana, the legislature overwhelmingly passed a Republican resolution opposing "the North American Free Trade Agreement Superhighway System" as well as "any effort to implement a trinational political, government entity among the United States, Canada, and Mexico." Similar resolutions have been introduced in a third of all state legislatures, as well in Congress, and some major political candidates are starting to make their opposition to the phantom superhighway a central part of their campaigns. In 2006, for instance, Democrat Nancy Boyda unseated incumbent congressman Jim Ryun (R) in an archconservative Kansas district by lambasting him for supporting bills that she said would bring the superhighway through Kansas City.

America has always had its share of conspiracy theorists—some outlandish, others more realistic. Some believe aliens landed at Roswell. Many believe there was more than one person involved in the JFK assassination. And a few, like the group I saw at the antiwar march in Washington, believe the U.S. government orchestrated the 9/11 attacks.

The difference with the North American Union theory is its connection to a bigger political ideology—one that steals from both the Left and

Right in the same sort of way Ross Perot did in the 1990s. This ideology is partly nationalist and vaguely pitchfork populist; mostly libertarian but also a bit fascist; more comfortable with equal-opportunity xenophobia than targeted racism (though there is some of that); and, above all else, grounded in a belief that both parties' Establishments secretly collude with moneyed interests in a treasonous plot to oppress regular folks and undermine America's sovereignty.

This ideology is obsessed with all the issues under the globalization umbrella (immigration, trade, etc.), and for understandable reasons: as economist Jeff Faux's seminal book *The Global Class War* shows, most globalization policies are indeed crafted and enforced in secret, and designed to enrich a tiny handful of superwealthy financiers making up a transnational elite. High-profile gatherings of this elite in posh locales only support the theories. What better proof of a conspiracy than the Establishment retreating to Davos, Switzerland, every year for a closed-door confab to conspire about global economics?

As it relates to domestic politics, this anti-Establishment uprising ideology is pulling Steve and many traditional conservatives away from the Republican Party. "I was a Republican, but I certainly am not now," he says. "You get people who say what they think you want to hear, then once in office they forget what they promised you." Last night, Braun said much the same thing about Bush: "I voted for the man twice, [but] I'm absolutely incensed at what he's done at the border."

But Bush's refusal to build a fence separating Mexico and the United States and his position supporting a path to citizenship for illegal immigrants already inside the United States were merely the final push out of the Republican Party for people like this. The bill of particulars against the GOP from the right side of the populist uprising is long. As religious conservative leader Richard Land has said, "There are significant differences between social conservatives and economic and defense and libertarian conservatives." Immigration is one of those big differences.

Sure, many of the Minutemen and their sympathizers still end up voting Republican in general elections because they are loath to vote for

Democrats. But they are expending other political resources like volunteer time and small-dollar campaign contributions outside the Republican Party and on uprising endeavors.

For some like Steve, that means helping third-party protest candidacies. He worked for the 2005 congressional campaign of the Minutemen's own Gilchrist, who ran unsuccessfully in Orange County as the nominee of the same American Independent Party that nominated segregationist Alabama governor George C. Wallace for president back in 1968. (The party's leaders here in California are lately trying to formally absorb Minuteman chapters into their party structure.)

For others, going outside the Republican Party just means coming down here on weekends and tying little American flags on steel posts at the Mexican border like a group of Minutemen in front of us are doing right now.

Steve pulls the car off to the side of the dirt road, and we walk out into the now-hot sun. The brown dirt and sand crunch under my feet, making a cloud of dust as I walk. I reach down to pick up what looks like a pebble but is actually an old bullet casing. I throw it toward the border and see off in the distance what looks like a tall stick with underwear on it. Steve says it probably is one of the infamous "rape trees" where Mexican women are sexually abused by "coyotes" (aka Mexican smugglers who help illegal immigrants get to the border).

Last night, I heard one Minutemen describe this part of the border as a "fence," but that is like referring to the Beatles as thespians. Sure, John, Paul, George, and Ringo made a few silly movies, but actors they were not. Likewise, some makeshift slats line this dirt road, but this is no barrier.

The border here at Jacumba consists of six-foot-tall rusted metal poles driven into the ground with two steel beams welded horizontally across. The beams are about two feet apart from each other and have markings on them like 9040 USS CARNEGIE USA 1952 and OH 8521 ILLINOIS 1919 USA. Steve says this is old railroad track.

And that's it—that's the "border"—a few pieces of metal that probably wouldn't obstruct cattle, much less humans.

Steve leans over and picks up one of the flags the Minutemen had tied to the poles. He shows me that the flag's wooden stick has a label that reads "In honor of U.S. Border Patrol Agent Nick Greenig killed in the line of duty 3-14-2006."

The flags, though a seemingly small gesture, serve a number of purposes for the Minutemen. They are a simple fund-raising tool, which is essential for any fledgling uprising. Braun told me last night that "people who want to help us make a contribution asking us to dedicate flags with their names, the names of fallen border security agents, or the names of Iraq war vets on the fence."

As I watch Eric, a white-bearded eighty-two-year-old Minuteman, tying up Old Glory on another pole, I see that the flags are also a camera-friendly backdrop for photojournalists covering the organization. Eric, a veteran of the Battle of the Bulge in 1944, is smoking a pipe and wearing a Disabled American Vets hat with gold wings on the bill. The image of him ambling along the border with his trusty black Labrador retriever surrounded by fluttering flags would make a professional political consultant smile.

But the flags are not all about public relations with the outside world. They also make the Minutemen themselves feel that what they are doing is a solemn duty. While their border patrols make these guys feel like they are on the front line of a war, the vista of little flag memorials staggered one after the other out here in this frontier setting does a decent job of manufacturing the gravity of, say, Arlington National Cemetery or the battlefield at Gettysburg.

About twenty minutes into our stop here in Jacumba, a white Border Patrol SUV rolls up. Steve waves hello, then exchanges a few pleasantries with them, and they drive off. When they are gone, Steve tells me the Minutemen have "a very good relationship with Border Patrol," but I'm not so sure.

Yes, this brief exchange seemed friendly enough, and, yes, Camp Vigilance's constant telephone contact with the Border Patrol has probably smoothed relations. But law enforcement officials have told the Associated

Press that though the Minutemen have basically been peaceful, they have also "continued to unwittingly trip sensors that alert the agency to possible intruders, forcing agents to respond to false alarms." Border Patrol "said volunteers' footprints have also made it difficult for agents to track illegal immigrants."

But again, as Braun said, this is more about "a political protest" than about actually sealing the border, so it's not clear the Minutemen really care that their activity may sometimes disrupt the work they claim to support.

FINISHED WITH THE flags at this spot, Steve tells me to ride with a quiet retiree named Ed over to the O'Neill Valley—a place that the Border Patrol has said is "commonly used as a pickup point for both illegal aliens and illicit narcotics." Back in 2000, for instance, authorities made arrests in the area and seized almost a half ton of marijuana being smuggled into the United States from Mexico.

This first part of our drive is relatively silent, giving me a chance to take in what is something of a moonscape. The sandy desert looks less brown and more white here, and this valley is even more desolate than Jacumba and more isolated from any semblance of civilization.

We pass a yellow warning sign in Spanish showing a picture of a sun, mountains, a cactus, and a snake. The word *agua* (water) is marked with an X. I don't speak the language, but it is easy to tell the sign warns people coming over the border of a hazardous environment that is claiming more and more lives.

The Government Accountability Office reports that the number of people who have perished trying to cross the border has doubled in just the last six years to almost 500 deaths annually. Braun last night told me the Minutemen are "very concerned about the people trying to make the trek across" and that one of the social services of his organization has been its efforts to get food, water, and medical attention to illegal immigrants lost in the desert. But as Reuters points out, many experts believe the death rates along the border are increasing because Border Patrol and Minuteman activities are "forcing migrants to take more dangerous, remote routes to cross into the United States and pushing up the number of deaths" in areas like the O'Neill Valley.

Ed turns the maroon pickup truck from the paved road onto another dirt road that heads along a steep hill toward the border in the distance. The desert floor next to this hill is littered with shotgun shell casings and Miller Lite cans. Ed tells me that locals use this place as an unofficial shooting range, and we soon come upon groups of people taking target practice. One guy wearing acid-wash jeans, sneakers, and no shirt is standing under a cheap plastic canopy firing a pistol at a human-shaped target while his friend, a fat goateed dude in a tank top, sits in a lawn chair drinking beer.

I can't believe we're in the same state as San Francisco hippies and Hollywood lefties, but then I remember what a friend who worked in California politics once told me. "Most people think this is a superliberal state," he said. "But in California, when you drive twenty miles east from the coast, you teleport yourself from Berkeley to Birmingham, Alabama." Only, in Birmingham, he said, "it's a little less extreme."

"There are at least some black and brown people down in Alabama. You can't say the same for California's Inland Empire—there's nothing but pissed-off white people there."

Now that I have finally used some small talk to break the ice with Ed, I am finding that he is a different kind of Minuteman—the kind who seems like less of a motivated crusader and more like someone who just fell into the uprising as a hobby. When I ask how he first heard about the Minutemen, he says, "It was Sean Hannity, as a matter of fact," referring to the ultraconservative Fox News personality.

After seeing a Hannity piece on illegal immigration, "I started snoopin' around." He mentioned what he saw to "a couple of ladies" he met at a square dance, and they put him in touch with the Minutemen.

I almost laugh when I hear him say "square dance," but I remember that Ed is seventy years old and grew up outside of Minot, North Dakota, so I guess his recreational dance activities aren't that shocking. Also, he's got a pistol at his side, so probably better not to mock him.

Ed would be a great model for one of those close-up black-and-white portraits you see at art galleries. His face has a lot of folds in it, and he's wearing silver-rimmed square sunglasses. He's ex-military like most of the others, but he and his family are careerists, not just temporary enlistees or draftees. He served thirty years as an air force crew member on a C-141, his son is a military civil engineer who "goes out in hostile areas and builds runways," Ed says, and his grandson is in an air force special operations unit.

He tells me his first wife was Mexican, insists his decision to join the Minutemen "is not a race thing with me, it's a terrorist thing," and then, as evidence, tells me the story about the mosque supposedly being found around here—the same story I've been hearing all weekend.

Approaching the border now, our discussion drifts into economics, and he voices many of the same contradictory feelings that Rick voiced yesterday afternoon. He complains that where he lives in Lake Arrowhead (an Inland Empire town eighty miles east of Los Angeles), legitimate businesses cannot compete with employers who exploit low-wage illegal immigrants. But Ed doesn't believe any tension exists within the Republican Party between Big Business that exploits these workers and anti-immigration conservatives like him who want the border closed.

"I don't think there's a lot of big corporations out there wanting the illegals to come over here so that they can hire 'em so that they don't have to pay 'em high wages."

When I tell him that the U.S. Chamber of Commerce—Big Business's most important Washington lobbying group—has been pushing for an immigration policy that includes what someone like him would deem "amnesty," he categorically refuses to believe it.

"Oh, I don't know about that," he says. "I don't think so. I think most people in America want the government to crack down on these companies."

Polling data suggest he's absolutely correct about that, but I reiterate that I am talking about political lobbies like the Chamber of Commerce, not "most people in America."

"Well I'm a little confused about the political lobbies 'cause I really don't know what they are thinking, quite frankly," he concludes.

His sentiments are the classic symptoms of Partisan War Syndrome— a state of mind antithetical to uprisings. Those afflicted display an inability to reconcile personal ideological differences with allegiance to their party.

Ed has the standard Minuteman view of the world: build a fence, put military troops on the border, and crack down on businesses that employ illegal immigrants. But, almost unconsciously, he refuses to believe that such positions are at odds with his Republican Party whose corporate financiers want to preserve a steady supply of exploitable low-wage labor.

Ed's partisan blinders are not deliberate political calculations like they are among Washington operatives in the antiwar uprising. They are a trait of a typical citizen in a country where the media's "red versus blue" narratives encourage everyone to think like partisan automatons.

That said, his involvement in the Minutemen's uprising is itself a revolt against Partisan War Syndrome, because the organization's campaign is almost entirely ideological—not partisan. It is, as Braun said, an effort to "embarrass the government," no matter which party controls the government. Such a with-us-or-against-us uprising outlook comes straight from the very top of the Minuteman structure, as I found out when I talked to Al Garza, the Mexican-American executive director of the Minutemen's national office.

Garza, a former Riverside, California, private investigator and a rifleman in Vietnam, is visiting Camp Vigilance this weekend. While he chainsmoked outside the stagecoach house earlier this morning, he told me, "We're monitoring each and every congressman" on immigration legislation.

"Each and every representative that votes a yea on amnesty and nay on border security will be fired," he said, adding, "They work for us."

Ed reaffirms his Republican loyalties a few times on our drive in the O'Neill Valley. But he also acknowledges that his "confusion" about the political lobbies motivated him to join the Minutemen. His ongoing involvement in the organization is not really about party ties or even the specific immigration issue. It has more to do with a kind of low-grade desperation.

"I thought, I haven't done a darn thing for my country here in the last few years," he says, explaining why he finally signed up for the Minutemen. "I thought maybe it's about time I got off my lazy butt and went out and *did something.*"

He adds that's basically the outlook of everyone here.

"The guys that I know in our group are just pretty much a patriotic bunch of guys that want to come down here and *do something.*"

He says the last two words with a tone that is the verbal equivalent of slamming his fist on the dashboard, and the words hang in the air. Joining the Minutemen is his way of taking some action in response to the emergency that is the state of the world today. For many—whether Minutemen, Working Families Party organizers, or antiwar protestors—such a desire to do something is the reason to get involved in the uprising in the first place.

But why is this organization and this specific cause the beneficiary of these guys' restlessness?

I wonder this as Ed starts using the same anticorporate rhetoric that I've been hearing all weekend from everyone else. He's specifically going off about gas prices and ExxonMobil's recent profit reports. "They're telling us that they have to raise the price of gasoline because of supply and demand, and I say, okay, I'm not against you guys making money. I mean that's what companies go into business for is to make money," he says.

"[But] I got a feeling—and it's only been recently that I've been kind of getting this feeling—that they've been profiteering."

He tells me his wife owns ExxonMobil stock. Yet instead of, say, using those stocks to channel his anger into something like shareholder activism (more on this soon), he is out here at the border. What does that say? Does it say there aren't enough other uprising vehicles to harness his anger? Does it say that vehicles like consumer advocacy / protest groups are poorly marketed?

Maybe none of the above. Maybe all it says is that this particular vehicle is just the most visceral and easy to understand—the activist response to pop culture's worship of simplification in the face of complexity. The Minutemen are, after all, an organization that allows participants to immediately behold the illusion of results in a society whose problems are so seemingly immense and immovable that activism can feel like a waste of time.

Ed, for instance, can't drive to ExxonMobil's headquarters and do anything more than get turned away by the private security guards there. But he can drive down to the border, pick up a few flags, point Border Patrol agents toward a few illegal immigrants running across the desert, and maybe add a few yards of makeshift barbed wire to the decrepit excuse for a border barrier.

He knows he can do this because the Minutemen have aggressively marketed themselves in a way that—tactically, at least—might have made the late Saul Alinsky proud. "The organizer knows that his biggest job is to give the people the feeling that they can do something," Alinsky wrote in *Rules for Radicals*. "People hunger for drama and adventure, for a breath of life in a dreary, drab existence."

That is what the Minuteman Civil Defense Corps does for its members, and it's fair to say that most groups on the Left have not figured out how to manufacture the same kind of excitement that might channel the frustration of people like Ed into class-unifying activism and away from this sad intraclass battle between middle-class Americans and working-class Mexicans.

Ed finally pulls the truck over at the top of a big hill and we get out. The border "fence" here is different from Jacumba's only in that the poles in the ground are a bit higher and some are riddled with bullet holes—but the space between the horizontal railroad tracks is just as wide.

With the *rat-a-tat-tat* of shooting-range gunfire echoing through the desert, I ask Ed whether he thinks a better-fortified fence or any amount of border security would really stop illegal immigration. He has a puzzled look on his face, as if I have just asked him whether the sky is blue. So I try to explain what I mean by asking whether he had ever considered that the real issue at the heart of illegal immigration is widespread poverty in Mexico?

Since the passage of the North American Free Trade Agreement in 1993, millions more Mexicans are living in poverty. Isn't that the real problem causing so many people to risk their lives sprinting across a desert looking for a job and a better life? How about the increasing death rates along the border as border security increases—doesn't that show that illegal immigrants aren't being deterred by interdiction methods? In other words, doesn't all this show that if you don't deal with the systemic economic problems in Mexico, trying to seal the border is like trying to put a Band-Aid on a huge flesh wound?

He looks out across the fence and thinks for a second.

"Yeah," he starts slowly, "The biggest problem is that the country over there is impoverished. There's a lot of money in Mexico, but it's all concentrated with a few people."

So, I say, aren't efforts to build a twelve-foot fence just creating a market for thirteen-foot ladders? Shouldn't the Minutemen be lobbying Congress to support antipoverty initiatives in Mexico? Shouldn't lifting up the country to our south be the real priority?

"I don't know how we'd do that," he says, still speaking slowly.

Braun said much the same thing last night, agreeing that "the only way that we can address this is to help these people where they live," but saying that "the trouble with making investments in Mexico is that it's run by about 5 percent of the population, and when the money goes down there, it gets sucked off and it's gone."

Mike, a Minuteman from San Diego, went even further when I interviewed him earlier today. He told me he believes "Mexico is due a revolution," but that illegal immigration is preventing one. "The people that come to this country are escaping rather than making a change in their own country," he said.

If this "revolution" did occur because America seals the border, it is entirely possible that "Mexico erupts and we have a destroyed nation on

246 | THE UPRISING

our southern border and even greater illegal migration," as *Mother Jones*'s investigative reporter Charles Bowden has said.

Indeed, it is a complicated situation with no easy answers—and yet with the Minutemen, the reflex is to simplify—to revert to leave-me-alone-ism.

"It's Mexico's problem," Ed concludes, picking up another flag off the ground. "I'd go with the fence. Even a twelve-foot fence is gonna slow down an awful lot of people from coming over."

WHEN I FIRST saw Ron last night, I thought he could have been the original model for the lumberjack on Brawny paper towels. He was wearing a red-and-black-checkered flannel shirt and dark blue jeans, but sitting with him back at Camp Vigilance, I realize it wasn't just his garb that reminded me of the Brawny man. It is this Minuteman's overall largeness.

He's probably six foot five and 250 pounds. His white hair is combed, and he wears a shiny ring with an American Gold Eagle coin in it. The coin is at least the size of a quarter, if not a half dollar, but wrapped around Ron's huge finger, you might think it was smaller than a dime.

He is sitting in a lawn chair outside of his polished white Winnebago describing the ins and outs of the mining machines he used to market as a salesman for Dresser Industries, which ten years ago was acquired by Halliburton—the oil company that Vice President Dick Cheney once ran and that has been at the center of multiple overbilling scandals surrounding its work in Iraq.

"They have a very famous name now," Ron says with a chuckle. "Perhaps not so famous . . . infamous."

He is using words like *crush* and *pulverize*—words that sound particularly threatening coming from someone as physically imposing as him, even though he's talking about drill bits and minerals.

I can hear a twinge of a Midwest accent in his voice, and he tells me that, yes, he grew up in Chicago as the grandson of Polish immigrants. But he quickly adds that his father changed their family's name from Damchek to a more Anglo-sounding surname. "It was important for him to not be part of an ethnic group but rather be an American, because he was a proud American," he explains.

That aside might make Lou Dobbs and Chris Simcox both stand up and applaud. Dobbs rails on Americans who flaunt their hyphenated heritage. Simcox rails on those who "refuse to assimilate." And Ron makes sure I know that he thinks the way to be a "proud American" is to downplay one's ethnicity.

Ron's family was "hardcore Democrats," he says, but that had a different meaning back when he was growing up in the Chicago of Richard J. Daley, the autocratic mayor who, when faced with the civil rights and anti-war uprisings of the 1960s, made the words *crush* and *pulverize* political tactics rather than just mining terms.

With his in-laws and siblings serving in the police and the military, Ron's family were classic Daley Democrats—the white ethnic working-class voters who cheered on their mayor's "speak softly and carry a big stick" disposition that resulted most famously in his decision to unleash a barrage of violence against anti–Vietnam War protestors at the Democratic National Convention in 1968. Much of the country was horrified by the televised melee, which investigators later deemed a "police riot." But many Daley Democrats cheered.

"Daley ordered police to go around and crack some heads," Ron reminisces, with an approving tone. "He was not exactly a liberal."

With white flight, the Daley Democrats in Chicago and similar cities have since migrated from urban centers to suburbs and exurbs. They have become Reagan Democrats—or, as they are now called, hard-core Republicans. They have made that political shift, and some are now joining uprisings like the Minutemen in no small part because they pine for the "crack some heads" ethos.

This is one of the qualities that keeps working-class Americans voting for the Republican Party, gives Lou Dobbs's law-and-order mantra such currency among television viewers, and brings white-collar businesspeople like Ron to the border. In an America whose culture says no problem is too complex for an oversimplified answer, the use of violence, force, and "strength" is becoming the simplest answer of all.

Ron, for instance, talks like a Fox News anchor when the subject of the Iraq War comes up, asserting that "the cost of freedom is high" (there is actually a Fox News show called "The Cost of Freedom").

"We have shed our blood for the freedom of Americans," he says, parroting Bush administration rhetoric. "What happened in Iraq was necessary. All the evidence showed [that] they had weapons of mass destruction and that they were a haven for people that want us all dead. . . . We have got to preserve our own security and our own safety and the only way to do that is to fight the enemy in their backyard, not in ours."

That no WMDs were found and that the 9/11 Commission has roundly discounted claims of a Saddam Hussein–al-Qaeda connection—that's not important to Ron, nor to the other Minutemen here. They want some revenge—and Ron's rhetoric is the most gentle.

Braun, for instance, told me just an hour ago in his truck that when it comes to Iraq, "the only thing, in my opinion, that the Arabs understand [is] force."

"We're talking about people who are somewhere between 700 to 1200 AD in their brains," he said. "And the only thing that's going to knock them back into oblivion again is brute force."

Rick, the former sniper in Vietnam, was even more direct when we chatted last night.

"If I could run the war, I'd have us take the gloves off," he said. "I'd say here's the deal, this is what we're gonna do: we're gonna go slaughter 'em, we're gonna kill 'em by the thousands. We're gonna make 'em surrender, we're gonna teach the world a lesson. When you got to war, you go to war."

What I didn't comprehend until talking to Ron, though, is that these guys really don't differentiate much between the Iraq War and their activity on the border. To them, it is all part of the same fight to protect America as they know it—white, English-speaking, and, above all else, free of dark-skinned people who they fear are either Mexicans attempting a cultural takeover, or Middle Easterners plotting a terrorist attack.

Ron tells me he's down on the border because "We don't want the enemy here, we don't want another 9/11."

Out in the O'Neill Valley a few hours ago, Ed said, "We can't allow our country to have wide-open borders. It won't be America anymore."

I'm now back in the truck with Braun heading back out to the border, and the Minuteman leader tells me he believes America is experiencing an "invasion from the south" and that "we are behind enemy lines here [in] California."

"All we can do is hope to survive here, and I mean that sincerely," Braun says. "This state is overrun, and we've lost it. What can we do now? Well, we can try and maintain a foothold here. We can try to save states like Montana and Idaho and Georgia and everywhere else from the ravages of illegal immigration."

His concerns reflect the Minutemen's new growth strategy far away from the border. According to Census Bureau data, minority groups make up an increasing share of the population in almost every state in the nation. Latino populations are expanding from Southwest states with a long history of cross-border integration and into the heartland. These new-growth areas are far less diverse and far less accustomed to Latino culture, meaning there is a greater potential for stoking anti-illegal immigrant fears. It is easier to be afraid of something you've never been exposed to than something you have.

This is why the national training coordinator of the Minutemen told a local television station in Kansas City that most of the organization's new chapters are popping up not in border towns, but in "areas like Sioux Falls, South Dakota, and Omaha, Nebraska, which are only now experiencing the demographic change that occurred generations ago in traditional gateway states such as Texas and Arizona." And it is why Senator John McCain will tell the *New Yorker* during his second presidential campaign, "You probably see more emotion in Iowa than you do in Arizona on [immigration]. I was in a town in Iowa, and twenty years ago there were no Hispanics in the town. Then a meatpacking facility was opened up. Now twenty percent of their population is Hispanic. There were senior citizens there who were—'concerned' is not the word. They see this as an assault on their culture, what they view as an impact on what have been their traditions."

Braun parks the truck at a border area known as Red Rocks—an expanse of improbably balanced boulders right out of the Road Runner cartoons. The picturesque landscape is ruined only by a rusting and rickety barrier dividing Mexico and the United States. This section is more of a wall than a fence. Here, the poles support ten-foot-tall sheets of corrugated metal rather than widely spaced crossbeams. Braun tells me the sheets are surplus mats for planes and tanks that used to be laid over swampy rice paddies in Vietnam. Sure enough, one is marked KAISER STEEL 1968.

He shows me a stretch of rock where the steel wall abruptly ends and just some strands of barbed wire continue. The Minutemen put that barbed wire up, he says proudly.

I walk up to the makeshift fence and find myself standing in a huge pile of garbage. I had previously read reports about how nonprofit groups are worried that the border region is becoming a major environmental hazard. Now I see what they are talking about—and it is a huge bummer, not just because of the degradation of the landscape, but because of the stories each piece of garbage tells.

I see blue-and-white wrappers from what looks to be a package of Mexico's version of Oreos. I kick an empty bottle of water with a Spanish label on it. Underneath the rubble is an empty can that probably held preserved food. I pick up a small piece of cloth that Braun says illegal immigrants wrap around their shoes so as to blur footprints and make it more difficult for Border Patrol to track them.

The trash pile tells the tale of people fleeing and starving. It is its own monument to desperation. And yet to Braun, the pile warns of an oncoming confrontation.

He says Mexicans coming over the border "know that if they shoot one of us," that Minuteman is "going to be replaced five to one, ten to one, twenty to one by that guy who is going to be down here with an assault weapon looking for something to shoot," he says. "It's going to turn into a bloody mess and may turn into a civil war."

"We don't want that to happen," he adds. "We don't see violence as the answer to this thing."

A long silence ensues as a light breeze wisps through the brush. Braun's dark premonition weighs down the silence. And then he says, "We're on the front lines of this whole thing down here and we are watching our country slip away."

"Not on my watch . . ." he says, almost in a whisper.

It is this sporadic rhetoric about war and about a country supposedly "slipping away" that suggests the Minutemen and the anti-Establishment uprising they represent are not easily pigeonholed. They are a kaleidoscopic mix of earnest fear, confused paranoia, and ugly instincts.

On the border among the tumbleweed, the sidearms, the trailers, the CB chatter, the incessant military jargon, and the piles of imported trash, globalization's harsh economic consequences and the understandable distrust of a corrupt government have simmered into a boiling stew of cultural xenophobia—one made even hotter by the ever-heightening fears of terrorism.

Here at the southern border, the right edge of the uprising is at once predictable and shocking, spontaneous and calculated, uniquely American and uniquely frightening.

8

DILBERTS OF
THE WORLD, UNITE

I CAN'T SLEEP, but I probably wasn't going to sleep anyway because this contraption we're flying on from Helena makes a deafening sound the entire time it's in the air. It's that humming noise that overlays all those old black-and-white films depicting World War II bombing raids. According to the flight attendant, this Alaska Airlines twin-prop is actually called a Bombardier.

Up here at twenty-five thousand feet, the weather is beautiful. Blue skies, bright sun, and Mount Rainier's snowy peak lancing the thick blanket of clouds below. It is a bright, pleasant vista compared with the typical Seattle winter day I find on the ground when we land. The penetrating gray makes everything colorless—the buildings, the skyline, even people's clothing and skin are gray, as if you are actually *in* a black-and-white movie.

My cab is now plowing through what feels like never-ending—though politely quiet—congestion on I-5. Having grown up on the East Coast, I got used to traffic jams as places to vent frustration—honks, swerves, and middle fingers. But out here, the Pacific Northwest's generally understated disposition translates into muted road etiquette. It puzzles the hell out of me.

How can you people stand this? I wonder.

Because they are here for the Great Jobs—the high-tech jobs. And the good life.

Immigrants flowing into New York's Ellis Island in the early twentieth century dreamed of gold-paved streets and a subsistence wage. A century later, the new arrivals to this fast-growing metropolis on Puget Sound fantasize about information superhighways and stock options.

I guess visions of computer screens and big salaries take the edge off, which might make this corner of the country seem like an unlikely place for the uprising.

Then again, I'm here to visit with a person who used to have one of those Great Jobs and came out of the experience as one of the uprising's most important figures. He's a guy named Marcus Courtney, whom I've never met before, but whose email list I've been on for probably a decade. He is the president of a group called the Washington Alliance of Technology Workers—or WashTech for short.

The fifteen-hundred-member organization's name implies its mission: the word *alliance* sounds like a grassroots advocacy group, like MoveOn; the term *workers* suggests a traditional union, like the United Steelworkers. WashTech, as I will see, is both.

No matter how much I rack my brain, I can't remember why I got on Courtney's listserve—but I know it had something to do with his group's work in the 1990s trying to alert the world to the reality that the much-ballyhooed technology boom was not going so well for everyone.

Back then, dot-com celebrations were happening everywhere. From Silicon Valley, to Boston, to Austin, to Portland, to Seattle, the geeky Lambda Lambda Lambda frat brothers from *Revenge of the Nerds* were suddenly big men on campus, starting new computer companies, swimming in cash—partying, as Prince might say, like it was 1999 (and it actually *was* 1999). As the kegger raged upstairs, though, little WashTech was shrieking from the bottom of a well in the basement about an impending economic massacre.

Sadly, very few were listening. Now the party's over—and a white-collar uprising is on.

If, like me, you have not heard much about all this, do not blame yourself. We live in a media environment that trumpets the price of the Apple iPhone as big financial news and adultery as major political news. But the fight WashTech is contributing to is hugely important for two reasons—one is obvious, but the other we're not supposed to discuss at all.

First the obvious: the white-collar sector is growing fast. Between 1977 and 2004, the number of professional and high-skilled workers in the United States more than doubled. Today, the U.S. government classifies almost 28 million Americans as highly skilled professional or technical workers and predicts that roughly one-third of all employment growth between now and 2012 will be in the white-collar sector (whether that holds true as outsourcing accelerates is a big debate—more on this later).

In contemporary American history, though, sheer size is no longer the primary determinant of change. The better gauge is demographics, which brings us to the second reason this white-collar uprising is so significant. Though it is taboo to even say it, let's just admit it: if American politics and culture still react to the mass public at all, they react almost exclusively to the upper-middle professional class, and to almost no one else. That's not a good thing at all—in fact, it's pretty awful. But it is absolutely true.

For example, many historians believe antiwar pressure during the Vietnam War only started changing public policy after the draft lottery was created and upper-middle-class parents began worrying about their kids being sent off to battle. Business misbehavior was rarely a congressional focus when CEOs were cutting blue-collar wages. But when Enron's collapse hit the stock market and undermined the retirement savings of the upper middle class, lawmakers raced to pass corporate accountability legislation. Housing affordability and predatory lending received little attention in Washington when only the working poor couldn't pay the rent. But only now that mortgage defaults are roiling Wall Street is the problem deemed a crisis.

So this white-collar uprising is not just about professional office workers and their individual fight. It is also about whether an uprising can flourish in the very demographic that the Establishment most responds to—a demographic that also happens to be skeptical of collective action.

By 9:30 A.M. I am in a Starbucks in the University District with Courtney. Sitting here in an outpost of one of the city's most famous companies makes me feel simultaneously as Seattle as a visitor could possibly feel, and as much of a hokey tourist as someone coming here should feel when they go corporate for a cup of joe in a town that seems to have an independent coffee shop on every corner.

Courtney is wearing jeans and a blue button-down shirt. His face is round, and he is in the same balding phase Bruce Willis was experiencing in the first *Die Hard* film—the one where he keeps his remaining hair short so as to obscure what's going on up there.

He is a storyteller, like many old hands in the labor movement who rose through the ranks in the one-on-one work of convincing people to join a union. And the story Courtney is telling me now, like lots of labor tales, is the kind that emulates Teddy Roosevelt's famous "Man in the Arena": "The man whose face is marred by dust and sweat and blood; who strives valiantly; who errs, who comes short again and again . . . who spends himself in a worthy cause, who at the best knows in the end the triumph of high achievement, and who at the worst, if he fails, at least fails while daring greatly." It could be WashTech's motto.

In 1993, Courtney was one of the many starry-eyed college grads who migrated to Seattle just as the tech boom was moving into warp speed. He was searching for one of those Great Jobs and found one first at Adobe and then at Microsoft in technical support.

The hitch was that his Great Job at Microsoft turned out to be not so great. He was one of roughly 6,000 employees at Microsoft known as "permatemp" workers—an employment classification whereby a company pays a temp agency middleman for someone's full-time, indefinite labor. The designation covers up to a third of all Microsoft workers in the Seattle area (and thousands more at companies like Boeing)—and it has obvious advantages for employers. Most important, a company doesn't have to pay regular benefits (health care, pension benefits, or stock options) to "permatemps" no matter how permanent such employees are.

"I didn't come to Seattle to organize or to be political," Courtney says. "I came to be a computer programmer."

But Courtney grew up in Butte, Montana—the home of the underdog, from the radical Industrial Workers of the World challenging the copper barons a hundred years ago, to Evel Knievel—the daredevil motorcycle stunt man who made long shots his own personal trademark. To a Butte guy like Courtney, everything is political—especially the underdog causes.

"Around the middle of 1997, me and my officemate, who was another contractor, one day we're talking about work and how we weren't getting any kind of real raises or cost of living increases, and I was like, 'this permatemp stuff is kinda bullshit,'" he recounts. "The contract agencies are ripping us off. I was like, god, I wonder if there's an organization to help us."

So he started telephoning state agencies, labor councils—anyone who would take his call.

"Everyone was totally fucking clueless," he says. "All anyone knew about the new economy was that people make a million dollars, and no one had any idea that here in Seattle—the place where everything is supposed to be booming—a huge percentage of the employment is contracted out."

Courtney and two others began building an email list of fellow permatemps and other high-tech workers who were chafing against the situation and interested in getting more politically active.

In December of 1997, their efforts were bolstered when the *Seattle Times* published a front-page story about how Microsoft used its political connections inside Washington State government to secure a regulatory change exempting high-tech companies from having to pay "temporary" computer professionals time-and-a-half for overtime.

"At this point, a bunch of us have had a few meetings, but there's nothing formal going on," Courtney says. "But when this story breaks, the Washington Department of Labor and Industries gets flooded with angry emails and calls."

It was a screwing of bipartisan proportions. The rule change was approved by the administration of Democratic governor Gary Locke, and it was designed to bring the state's labor regulations into conformity with federal law, which was changed by the then-Republican Congress. The *Times* also noted that the local labor movement had left the permatemp workers out to dry, as two Washington State unions supported the rule change after it was revised to make sure their own members were protected.

For the uprising, the whole episode was like a match being dropped into a pool of gasoline. Sold out by both political parties, and ignored by organized labor, "we decided to get serious," Courtney tells me.

From the flames of outrage, the Washington Alliance of Technology Workers was born, with Courtney scraping together enough money from a few sympathetic national unions to work full-time on the project. The organization's mission is straightforward: to get high-tech workers to vote to form unions at their workplaces so that they can collectively bargain for wages, benefits, and job security with employers.

Out of the gate, Courtney was thinking huge: he wanted to unionize Microsoft, and within a year of WashTech's launch, a majority of permatemps working on Microsoft's tax preparation software, TaxSaver, had signed a petition formally requesting union representation as a collective bargaining unit—a big move.

Microsoft is a lot of things—and one of them is a master of shell games. According to the *Wall Street Journal,* this is a company that, through the creative manipulation of tax loopholes, uses "a law firm's office on a quiet downtown street" in Dublin, Ireland, "to house an obscure subsidiary that helps the computer giant shave at least $500 million from its annual tax bill." Evading a few workers with the same kind of legal sleight of hand was a cakewalk.

The company countered WashTech's union drive by citing the status of the workers as permatemps—the very status that they were rebelling against—as the rationale to claim that the company had no statutory obligation to listen to the union.

"Issues of collective bargaining are issues between employees and their employer," said a company spokesman at the time. "In this case, the employers are the staffing companies."

Roughly two-thirds of all permatemps had been working full-time at the company for more than a year. And yet Microsoft was saying that because the company was paying the workers through a temp-agency middleman, it had no obligation to talk to those workers about employment issues.

The *Seattle Times* reported that when the workers and WashTech began the Byzantine process of trying to collectively bargain with four separate temp agencies, the agencies claimed that because the workers were merely "temps," they were not "an appropriate bargaining unit under the federal labor laws." Courtney and his colleagues were, in other words, caught in no-man's land—call it Dilbert's Purgatory.

"Permatemps were getting the worst of all worlds," Courtney says, taking a sip of coffee.

When it came to wages, they were considered high-level computer professionals, and thus not entitled to overtime pay, thanks to the state ruling and change in federal law. When it came to benefits, they were treated as mere temps unworthy of the health-care coverage and stock options. And when it came to basic union rights, they were treated as "a second class of subordinate workers," as the former chairman of the National Labor Relations Board said at the time. They had none of the organizing privileges that other company employees enjoyed.

The public face of Microsoft and many tech companies is not the scowling, white-haired, scotch-drinking, Old Money industrialist of ages past. But just because the boss wears khakis, sneakers, and a Hawaiian shirt on Fridays doesn't mean he isn't a boss—and bosses, whether their names are Rockefeller or Gates, know the best way to bust a union is to lay everyone off. That is precisely what Microsoft did in March of 2000. Just months after the TaxSaver union drive started, the company announced it was terminating the software project and firing all the permatemps working on it.

Fortunately for WashTech, that very same year saw groundbreaking strikes at Verizon and Boeing, both of which helped keep this new white-collar uprising going.

Verizon workers already unionized through the Communications Workers of America (CWA) and the International Brotherhood of Electrical Workers engineered an eighteen-day walkout that yielded major wage concessions. Same thing with the thirty-eight-day strike by the Boeing members of the Society of Professional Engineering Employees in Aerospace. Both moves made big news. One *Seattle Times* headline blared: "Strike Heralded as Dawn of New Age; Unions Look to Bring Professionals into Fold." Another read: "Strike at Verizon Gives Hope to Organizers in High-Tech Industries in Puget Sound Region." And Courtney, by this time a skilled uprising leader, told reporters, "We can point to [the strikes] and say there are the same issues . . . and [show] how the unions have shaped solutions."

In 2000, two months after the Verizon strike ended, WashTech launched a union drive at Amazon.com's four-hundred-employee Seattle customer service center. This was a far more traditional fight than the Microsoft battle because the Amazon workers were full-time employees and there was no permatemp shell game to be played. And company management reacted in a far more traditional—but equally as cutthroat—way.

The *San Francisco Chronicle* reported that Amazon CEO Jeff Bezos "came out swinging against the idea of unions at his company." Picking up the tactics of the notoriously anti-union Wal-Mart, Amazon management began forcing employees to attend meetings disparaging the concept of unions. The company then demanded "customer service representatives send an anti-union message to customers who inquire about the organizing campaign," according to *In These Times*'s labor reporter David Moberg.

But the final blow came just twelve weeks after the organizing drive started, with Amazon closing its entire Seattle customer service operation and mowing down all four hundred workers. Where did the jobs go? To the union-free subcontractors of Northern Ireland and India, of course.

Courtney takes a deep breath, and sighs. This is the low point of the story.

"The labor movement had zero interest in really addressing the freelance contingency economy," he says, his face starting to scowl. "It was like five people and just a few organizations in America were trying to organize the entire information economy."

At this, he names a handful of WashTech-like organizations all over the country that are engaged in the white-collar uprising, and when he mentions the Alliance@IBM, I finally remember: I got on WashTech's email list in my very first week on Capitol Hill. Thrown into that job as congressman Bernie Sanders's chief spokesperson in 1999, we had four days to prepare for that town hall meeting—the one in which hundreds of IBM workers came out to discuss how to prevent the company from slashing their pensions. During all our preparation for that meeting, we kept finding material from this fledgling little group named WashTech on the other side of the country.

Before I can mention our common bond, though, Courtney is starting to boil.

"It was and still is the Helen Keller style of organizing," he says. "If labor leaders stumble into something, they will look at it, but otherwise they are blind. I mean, we had to beat down the door to get them to pay attention, and we were trying to organize the largest fucking tech companies on the planet."

The Communications Workers, he acknowledges, was the one union that came through in a big way, investing in WashTech in those dark days after the two failed union drives.

Courtney used the resources to build his organization's "at large" membership—workers who are not covered by any union contract, but who are sympathetic to WashTech's cause and pay eleven dollars a month in dues to support the organization's work. Courtney remained visible in the local media as an increasingly effective advocate for tech workers.

But despite growing the organization's email list, swelling its at-large membership to a few hundred, and becoming a national media voice for the uprising, WashTech still desperately needed to successfully unionize a workplace to prove that it could be a fully functioning, contract-negotiating force inside a workplace, and not only an outside political advocacy group. In short, the group needed a break, and it finally got one in 2005.

That year, 900 call center workers at AT&T Wireless in suburban Seattle voted to form a union and affiliate with WashTech.

As of mid 2007, WashTech has roughly 1,500 total dues-paying members—1,100 at AT&T, and 400 "at large." It also has an email list with 17,000 subscribers.

Whether WashTech's work can expand the white-collar uprising beyond that, however, is very much an open question.

Certainly, the conditions seem ripe.

Between 2000 and 2004, 221,000 American tech jobs were eliminated as offshore outsourcing accelerated. In 2005, the U.S. Census Bureau reported that household incomes had failed to increase for five straight years, with the most significant income decline occurring in the upper-middle-class income bracket—the one that includes many high-tech workers. That same year, the Institute of Electrical and Electronics Engineers reported the first drop in median income for tech workers in the thirty-one years it had been producing annual wage and salary analyses. And WashTech's own survey of Internet technology (IT) workers found that the majority said their health-care premiums had increased and their wages had either remained flat or dropped.

As these trends have intensified, WashTech's membership has grown, as has traffic at websites like Mini-Microsoft—a blog that a Microsoft employee set up to let colleagues discuss work-related issues, and that has publicized internal documents showing how Microsoft executives were jacking up their pay while leaving workers' wages flat.

Nonetheless, there are reasons why only between 2.0 and 5.5 percent of high-tech workers are unionized—reasons that have little to do with concrete economic factors.

"Many people in these industries say, 'I hate unions' just on principle," Courtney tells me as we walk out of Starbucks. "But these same people will then go over to the Mini-Microsoft website and voice their complaints because they know the company is reading the site and has changed its policies accordingly."

"In other words," he says, "that site has become one of a number of virtual union halls, with workers, in a way, collectively bargaining. That website, our regular meetings, our organizing drives—all of this is building into a real movement."

WHEN COURTNEY AND I part, he tells me to come back to see how WashTech works on a day-to-day basis, and so now, a few weeks later, I have returned to the Pacific Northwest to meet with a bone-thin red-headed communist named Todd Tollefson, who is greeting me here at the airport on yet another gray Seattle day.

Tollefson is Courtney's top organizer at WashTech and I'm not red-baiting when I call him a communist. "Card-carrying member of the Communist Party USA," Tollefson tells me with a smile, as we sit in the quiet traffic on I-5.

Soft-spoken and preternaturally chipper, he moved out to Washington State from Minnesota nineteen years ago as a grunt for Citizen Action, the grassroots group that runs local canvasses in support of liberal causes. Though he says he "didn't really know what a union was" when he first started there, he ended up trying to organize Citizen Action's own door knockers into a union—and incredibly, he was fought by Citizen Action's leadership, some of whom were labor leaders. "I learned a long time ago, David, that a boss is a boss is a boss," he says.

From there he took a job with Shuttle Express, the airport limo service in Seattle. But he had an ulterior motive in taking the job—he was a "salt" for the Teamsters, who were relying on him to infiltrate the company to start a union drive. Unfortunately for Tollefson, the job didn't last long enough for his organizing campaign to get off the ground. After backing one of the company's vans into a Jaguar carrying musicians Courtney Love and Kurt Cobain in 1994, he was fired.

Tollefson found more success in the late 1990s. As an organizer for the Service Employees International Union's local out here, he success-fully unionized social workers at a big home-care company in Seattle, and did the same at a hospital in Yakima in the southeastern corner of the state.

Now as a six-year veteran at WashTech, he is applying his hammer-and-sickle dogma to the brave new world of organizing high-tech workers ("Dilberts of the world, unite!"). That has required him to work in WashTech's hybrid model as both a traditional union, with collective bargaining, contract negotiations, and organizing drives, and a grassroots advocacy group with its at-large members and legislative lobbying work. He certainly runs the traditional workplace campaigns aimed at getting workers to sign petitions asking for a National Labor Relations Board–sanctioned election (the crucial step needed to officially certify a union). But he also now recruits at-large members to join WashTech "just like getting folks to join an organization like Greenpeace," he says.

Driving along Seattle's Lake Union, we bank right and pull into a parking lot under a short box of a building that sits directly under the interstate.

"What you have to understand is that there are two kinds of people that join our union," Tollefson says while we walk up a flight of stairs to WashTech's office. "A few are philosophically aligned with the concept of unions. But most aren't—they are just really gung-ho on changing things in the high-tech industry on issues like outsourcing, immigration, and wages."

Tollefson is describing the outlines of the same constituency that has become key to today's uprising everywhere. These are swing voters, but they aren't the socially liberal, economically conservative suburbanites—the "Office Park Dads" or the "Soccer Moms"—that pundits always say are the key "swing" demographic in presidential elections. They are folks whose libertarianism have in the past led them to vote Republican and dislike unions, but whose self-interested proletarian sympathies on issues like wages and health care are now pulling them in a populist direction. And that group increasingly includes high-tech workers.

According to a national poll commissioned by WashTech in late 2003, 73 percent of IT workers describe themselves as either Independents (32 percent) or Republicans (41 percent)—a demographic that is typically hostile to both the ideology of the labor movement and the concept of collective action. However, an overwhelming majority of this same GOP-dominated group told pollsters they support strongly progressive legislation to expand unemployment benefits and to prohibit government contracts from being given to companies that outsource jobs.

So, when it comes to economic issues, while tech workers may be slightly more affluent and may wear whiter collars, they are the long-lost political cousins of the socially conservative, economically populist manufacturing workers who made Ohio's Sherrod Brown a U.S. senator, just as they are an Internet-age, Frappuccino-drinking version of the old fashioned beer-guzzling Archie Bunker demographic that the Working Families Party has brought into the uprising in New York.

WashTech's office, in many ways, resembles that WFP campaign headquarters I visited a few months ago, only with a more pronounced labor motif. Grainy pictures of old-school labor leaders like César Chávez, Eugene Debs, Elizabeth Gurley Flynn, and Samuel Gompers adorn the walls. *People's Weekly World*—the socialist newspaper—sits on the front table right when you walk in. This could just as easily be the union office for the muscle-bound longshoremen working at Seattle's port as it is the home of the group representing pocket-protector-clad software geeks.

Tollefson sits down at his small desk in the corner and prints out driving directions. In a few minutes, we will be heading out to do some one-on-one visits with WashTech members at Microsoft—part of Tollefson's membership maintenance duties. He tells me the theory behind the "at large" membership efforts is all about building "critical mass."

"If we get enough people involved in WashTech as just an advocacy organization, and those people talk to the people they work with, we could get to a point where we have enough strength to do a full union organizing drive at many of these places," he says.

With management continuing to abuse the permatemp designation, ratcheting up outsourcing, and scaling way back on stock options, the prospects for a formal union drive at Microsoft must be pretty good, right?

"In the long term, yes, but in the short term, no," Tollefson says. "It's a huge company, and everyone there is still like 'I'm going to be rich one day because I work at Microsoft and I don't need anyone's help getting ahead.' But there is something deeper going on. They are starting to get really angry about their wages and their work situation. The problem is that when they think union, they think garbage men and Teamsters—and they just don't see themselves that way."

Tollefson is touching on a psychology that all of organized labor struggles with today—not just the WashTechs that aspire to unionize white-collar workers. Since the dawn of capitalism, owners have had a financial interest in vilifying unions so as to deter workers from joining them and demanding better wages, benefits, and job security. But it has only been in the last thirty years that hating the very *concept* of unions, solidarity, and collective bargaining has become a legitimate outlook in the public at large—and that transformation did not happen by itself.

Today a constellation of Washington front groups, law firms, consultants, and politicians make their living publicly berating and crushing unions. The Center for Union Facts, for instance, runs expensive ad campaigns attacking union leaders. The National Right to Work Committee lobbies for laws that restrict unions' ability to collect membership dues. Jackson Lewis is a major law firm that specializes in helping corporations stop union drives. It runs annual seminars entitled "How to Stay Union Free." And senior congressional leaders now use the same rhetoric to attack unions that they use to vilify terrorists. For instance, in 2003, then-House majority leader Tom DeLay called the labor movement a "clear and present danger" to the United States. Likewise, in 2005, Representative Charlie Norwood (R-GA)—who was then heading the U.S. House's subcommittee on labor law enforcement—called unions "enemies of freedom and democracy" that use the same "tyranny that Americans are fighting and dying to defeat in Iraq and Afghanistan."

This aggressive onslaught inevitably reinforces public-opinion-shaping media coverage that is already biased against unions. If it isn't *The Sopranos* depicting the labor movement as an appendage of the mafia, then it is elite Washington reporters portraying organized labor like the horse and buggy—a hilarious anachronism to be laughed at and banished to the historical scrap heap. "It was as if I had wandered into the industrial economy's version of Jurassic Park," sneered reporter Matt Bai in the *New York Times* after visiting a labor union facility. "'Welcome to Laborland, U.S.A., and please be careful—there are actual union leaders wandering around.'"

Despite all of this, a majority of Americans still tell pollsters that, if given the chance, they would vote to join a union. Though the propaganda has certainly mainstreamed anti-union ideology, the public still seems to fundamentally understand that without unions, most of the social progress we take for granted would never have happened. As unions say, "We're the people who brought you the weekend."

Such good feeling persists even in the white-collar world, even among tech workers who, as Tollefson said, initially "just don't see themselves" as potential union members. Center for American Progress labor expert Jim Grossfeld's focus group research in 2005 found that even those rank-and-file professionals who say they do not want to be in a union, and who see unions as antiquated, nonetheless acknowledge that unions probably can help with the traditional struggles over wages, health care, and pensions.

Groups like WashTech, however, haven't been able to expand these persistent positive feelings about unions and the low-grade white-collar uprising into a more mature movement because they face the Fantastic Four: a quartet of pernicious and dishonest story lines that play to tech workers' unique self-image and that discourage full participation in the uprising.

The story of the white-collar uprising will be the story of whether groups like WashTech and its organizers like Tollefson can overcome these obstacles, each of which I will see firsthand today.

It is easy to mistake Redmond, Washington, for a college town like Palo Alto or Madison. College towns revolve around universities, while Redmond revolves around Microsoft—but the bucolic scenery and bustle is just the same.

Pulling onto the Microsoft campus, we pass a sign for valet parking for employees. Tollefson tells me the service exists because as new construction has taken over old parking lots, the company doesn't want employees wasting their work time searching for places to put their cars. This seemingly insignificant situation is one example of why union activity at tech companies is so difficult. Before even getting to go toe-to-toe with the Fantastic Four, organizers like Tollefson have to find ways around physical barriers in order to get their message out.

"There is no workplace whistle or shift changes or even a set way people come out to their cars," he says, turning off the car in one of the few empty spots in the back of a self-park lot. "That makes it harder to distribute union organizing materials and run a real campaign because people are just so spread out."

The way many tech companies have set up their workplaces also poses complications.

"Union drives are all about workers talking to each other, but Microsoft's workplace is set up in very small groups," he says. "Folks here work on individual slices of big projects in small teams, so workers end up knowing only about five or ten people."

True, the short-lived uprising at Microsoft's TaxSaver division back in 1999 showed how the smallness has at least some advantages. The group working on the project was so tiny, they only needed about sixteen workers to legitimately petition as a certified bargaining unit under federal labor law. However, because the team was so small and was working on such a minuscule slice of a project, management had no problem amputating it from the rest of Microsoft when the union drive got going.

The TaxSaver experience explains why WashTech's work building a broad at-large membership is so important, and why it has to be done through the microtargeted, one-on-one meetings like the ones we are headed to today. The union has to plant as many seeds as possible in as many different peer groups as possible before it reaches that "critical mass" of penetration Tollefson was talking about earlier.

When I look across the cavernous wood-and-glass cafeteria here at Microsoft's Redmond West campus, I can make out this thinly sliced team structure in real time. The room is crowded with people from all different ethnic backgrounds carrying trays of food to long tables. The high ceiling in this A-frame, ski-chalet-style room makes the conversations echo, turning the words into one ongoing thrum of background noise. But watching who is talking to whom, it is easy to see that the crowd is actually many different microcrowds of three to five people, with little conversational crossover.

As I survey the scene, I barely notice a bushy bearded guy sidle up to our table and sit down. He is wearing beige cargo pants that are slightly too short on him and a green button-down shirt with the top two buttons undone. When Tollefson sees him, he says hello and introduces him as Doug.*

Hailing from the town of Bingen along the Columbia River in southern Washington, Doug started out as a commercial diver off oil rigs but had to give it up after a head injury. Unemployed and ultimately relying on a food bank, he never thought he would stumble into computer work. But a teacher at a job training class was impressed with how quickly he had zipped through a basic computer course. Motivated by the compliment, Doug went on to teach himself more about computers and the tech industry, first landing himself a job as a computer game tester at Sierra Online, and then as a permatemp at Microsoft testing software.

Doug was one of WashTech's original at-large members and when Tollefson asks him about how his efforts to recruit new members are going, he is despondent.

"Maybe I'm not the most persuasive guy in the world, but I've been talking to folks off and on for the last six, seven years, and I haven't actually gotten that many to join," he says.

This is not because his coworkers are so happy. At twenty-five dollars an hour with no health-care benefits or vacation, he and the permatemps at his level aren't exactly living large for their skill set. But the reason he's had such trouble is because of the Marlboro Man Fable—the first and most powerful of the dreaded Fantastic Four.

Doug says that while tech workers like him certainly have complaints about wages and benefits, they do not see unions as being congruent with

---

* Doug is a fictitious name—he requested I use a pseudonym so that he is not blacklisted by his employer.

their more deeply held beliefs in what he calls "rugged individualism"—that Marlboro Man spirit that says everyone is a lone cowboy who can tough it out on his own.

"One of the successful things the high-tech industry has done is to have sold people on the idea that if you just struggle all by yourself, you can be Bill Gates, too," he says. "That's kind of what we sell in our whole country as the rugged individualist, the self-made man. There's no such thing, really, but that's what lots of folks believe."

And for a reason: in a diverse country of three hundred million people divided along race, class, religious, and ideological lines, the one thing that our culture teaches everyone to believe is the Marlboro Man Fable and its cousin, the rags-to-riches story. The legend of the individual working hard and becoming fabulously wealthy all on his own isn't just one of many American dreams—it has become *the* American Dream. And paradoxically, at exactly the times this dream becomes particularly difficult to achieve, our pop culture kicks in to make it seem totally realistic by lionizing the tiny few who defy the odds.

At the beginning of the twentieth century, America experienced the Gilded Age—a time when a handful of moguls became incredibly wealthy while millions of Americans languished in poverty. But there were the Horatio Alger dime novels to keep everyone thinking they, too, could be the next Rockefeller or Carnegie. During the Great Depression, Hollywood's "Golden Age" films trumpeting the glamour of wealth served as the distant mirage of water to a population marching through a desert of destitution. During the 1980s, the idolization of billionaires by shows like *Lifestyles of the Rich and Famous* and magazines like *Fortune* told Americans that if they just kept their head down through stagnating wages and growing wealth inequality, they too might make it big. And today, political rhetoric is drenched in the up-from-the-bootstraps pablum of "rugged individualism." It has taught America to believe that all good things spring from the Marlboro Man's leave-me-alone libertarianism.

Factwise, of course, Doug is right—the promised benefits of "rugged individualism" are largely a fiction.

Most "rags to riches" stories are not what they seem. Many major corporations that are supposedly the shining beacons of rugged individualism and free enterprise rely on massive government subsidies paid for by taxes on everyone else. Similarly, many of the entrepreneurs deified by the media as successful Marlboro Men did not start out penniless—they had huge financial and familial advantages. Microsoft's Bill Gates is known in the American zeitgeist as the tech industry's very own Marlboro Man, supposedly having made it out in the computer frontier all on his own. Except, he was born to a very wealthy Seattle family headed by a father who was a prominent attorney, and a mother who served on the board of major banking, insurance, and telecommunications corporations.

Meanwhile, an avalanche of evidence has destroyed the very idea that America's devotion to "rugged individualism" has made the nation particularly blessed with the kind of socioeconomic mobility that might make "rags to riches" stories more common.

In 2004, the *Economist* wrote that there is "growing evidence that America is less socially mobile" than the world's industrialized socialist countries like Germany, Sweden, Finland, and Canada. In 2005, the London School of Economics found that the United States offers the least chance for upward economic mobility when compared to seven socialist countries in North America, Scandinavia, and continental Europe. That same year, the *Wall Street Journal* reported that "despite the widespread belief that the U.S. remains a more mobile society than Europe, economists and sociologists say that in recent decades the typical child starting out in poverty in continental Europe (or in Canada) has had a better chance at prosperity."

The gulf between the Marlboro Man Fable and reality is one of the most combustible ingredients in today's uprising. People's experiences of stagnant wages, rising health-care costs, skyrocketing personal debt, and decreased retirement benefits indict the Fable in a far deeper way than even the best uprising leader could. However, as Doug says, the awakening these facts should elicit has been slow in coming in a white-collar world that matured during the go-go 1990s when the Marlboro Man Fable seemed to be validated.

"We've trained people to sneer at unions and look down on people working together to accomplish things," he says. "Microsoft is a big success story. The first employees of Microsoft all became millionaires, and a lot of the folks here still think that's going to happen to them."

The Marlboro Man Fable poses the toughest challenge to WashTech out of all the Fantastic Four's story lines because it drills directly into white-collar workers' psychology—specifically, their belief "that interests of employers and employees are the same," as sociologist Seymour Martin Lipset found in his groundbreaking research on the subject.

Blue-collar workers are more comfortable with acknowledging the labor-versus-management divide, and all of the problems that come with such a divide. But tech workers tend to see themselves as part of the management class, pride themselves on getting ahead on their own, scoff at the idea that they may need help, and do not want to see a difference between employer and employee. As one labor official told the *Sacramento Bee,* professionals "don't hate the boss, they want to be the boss." And if they acknowledge that employer-employee distinction—if they acknowledge that there is something to rise up against—they must admit to themselves that they are different from the bosses they aspire to be.

To understand these attitudes, consider one of the last union elections to make nationwide headlines. Back in 1977, a young insurgent named Ed Sadlowski ran for the presidency of the United Steelworkers. The *Atlantic Monthly*'s James Fallows has recalled how just before the vote, Sadlowski "said in a *Penthouse* magazine interview that he didn't think people were meant to work in smelters and hoped the day would come when they didn't have to." At the time, it was considered a controversial statement. How dare a union leader imply that working in a smelter is undesirable?

But that's the thing: many of today's white-collar workers came from modest backgrounds, are self-taught, or are the first in the family to go to college. They clawed their way into the industry specifically to avoid the smelter—and they therefore see themselves as the proud, real-life manifestation of the dream Sadlowski articulated.

They have chosen their occupation—they have not been forced into it like a strapped Chicago Southsider was forced into the blast furnace at the steel plant. In fact, they see just being in their line of work an accomplishment unto itself, not just for its financial rewards but for the status it imparts. And the status is supposed to mean a secure job that pays such generous benefits, affords such a good lifestyle, and attracts such professional respect that one shouldn't need a union. As labor expert Jim Grossfeld found, "White-collar workers believe that unions, as stereotyped, are appropriate for people with 'jobs,' but unnecessary for people with 'careers.'"

"You know, I just don't know what it's going to take," Doug says. "I just don't know how to change people's minds and make them realize that we're all in this together."

DURING THE CAR ride out to the Seattle suburbs for our next meeting, I keep thinking about something Doug said right before we left the Microsoft campus. Tollefson asked him how work had been going, and he replied that things are "okay," but he didn't seem particularly upset about his wages—he was most despondent about his work life.

"Working in the industry has just become a ho-hum job now," he said. "This is what's killing Microsoft. It's not the smartest guys who get hired who are all scrumming to make something happen . . . it's becoming a purely extractive company now. They get people, they suck out of them what they want, and then they throw them away, and that hurts institutional knowledge and innovation here."

He lamented that "things have really changed around here," noting that when he first started "we had a kegger every Wednesday and if you worked after six o'clock, you'd get free dinner."

But, he said, "That's all gone now. Even the paper towels in the bathroom have gotten crappy."

The train of thought reminded me of how WashTech president Marcus Courtney told me at Starbucks a few weeks ago that he sees huge uprising potential from the fact that "a lot of educated professional people love the work but now hate their job."

I didn't really understand what Courtney was alluding to when he said it, but listening first to Doug and now to Chuck,* I am starting to grasp it.

We are here in Chuck's living room in suburban Seattle. He is sitting on a piano stool in front of an ancient organ. No lights are on; the only thing illuminating the room is the gray sky from the window and the glow from a wood stove that is heating the house. The crackle from the fire is interrupted by Chuck's voice and the periodic screeching of his pet parrots from their cages in the kitchen.

Chuck is short, stocky, and wearing black jeans and a tight black T-shirt. A relatively new WashTech member, the fifty-something's cue-ball bald head gives him the look of Mr. Clean. He has worked for Microsoft "about nine of the last eighteen years," he says, proudly showing us his "five-year Microsoft clock"—a desk timepiece he received after five years as "a blue badge"—the lingo used to describe (officially) full-time Microsoft employees.

Now Chuck is a permatemp—and he's currently out of work, thanks to another of Microsoft's shell games. He did not lose his job or get fired. In the wake of a recent court ruling that nailed Microsoft for abusing the permatemp classification, permatemps like Chuck are now forced to take one hundred days of unpaid leave from Microsoft to "prove" they are really just temporary workers, even though many are rehired by Microsoft right after the break. The whole game has helped bring previously apolitical people like Chuck into the uprising by pissing them off.

Chuck is at a higher skill level than Doug. He doesn't test software; he writes it. He taught himself computer programming with a Tandy computer back in the 1980s and was a code writer for Vista, Microsoft's new graphics-heavy operating system released in late 2006.

As Tollefson asks him questions about his time at Microsoft, Chuck's grievances sound much like Doug's parting words. He, too, reminisces about the good old days—the days "when Bill Gates and [current CEO Steve] Ballmer came to meetings of very low-level groups, just to show up and say hi and see how the company was doing."

---

* Chuck is a pseudonym.

Now, he says, "A lot of people are simply unhappy with their working conditions."

When he says "working conditions," he is not referring to sweatshop-like facilities or overcrowding or a lack of air-conditioning—he is talking about what he believes is flawed management that prevents him from being a happier, more productive, profit-generating worker for the company.

"There is no interest there in making things more efficient or easier to do so that we can get more work done and increase productivity," he says. "On the Vista project, it was so conspicuous that people weren't getting work done. It wasn't just like it was a few dissatisfied people."

Microsoft is no different than most tech companies in that it started out with the Entrepreneurs in the Garage model—little management oversight and lots of free-flowing creativity. Chuck says that as the company has grown into a global powerhouse, a new top-down employee review and oversight system has drowned workers in bureaucracy. And he pines for a return to that creative culture.

"When I first worked there many years ago, Microsoft was unequivocally leading the way in enabling people to work, in getting barriers out of the way," Chuck says. "There was a very vibrant dynamic with a lot of productivity going on. We were breaking new ground, solving new problems for the very first time. It was high growth."

Now, though, he says it is a mess of red tape. As an example, he says what used to be a simple system of "checking in" to access and edit program code has become a nightmare—all in the name of better management.

"I used to spend probably 90 percent of my time on the job actually working on the code, and checking it in was a very small part of my week," he says. "That ratio was more than inverted in my last group. It was very common to do two hours of work and then spend over a week to wrestle it through the check-in system."

In other words, he is most angry at management not because they aren't paying him well, but because he feels they are getting in his way of doing a good job and doing the work he loves. This specific dissatisfaction is perhaps WashTech's best chance to break through the Marlboro Man

Fable. If WashTech can sell itself and the concept of collective action to white-collar workers as the vehicle to bring back the glory days, improve the workplace experience, and better the company, it has a very real shot to build its uprising. As labor expert Jim Grossfeld's research showed, "White-collar workers are fundamentally optimists [who] like their jobs [and who] do not respond to the argot of struggle, but to the language of advancement." He wrote that the professional workers who have joined unions "do so less to win economic security than to protect their autonomy and, with it, the integrity of their professions."

Take nursing—a white-collar profession that has seen union membership rapidly grow, even as overall union membership in America has declined. The California Nurses Association's expansion is due in large part to its sales pitch as not only a traditional union that helps nurses secure better pay, but as a vehicle to help nurses do their jobs better. For instance, the union successfully organized the University of Southern California's hospital by telling nurses that union membership would give them "a say in how the hospital operates," as the *Los Angeles Times* reported.

"It's not only about the money," one nurse said of her decision to support the union. "It's about quality patient care, which is very important to nurses."

WashTech can make the same kind of pitch. It can also show tech workers that unions have a strong track record of benefiting companies' bottom line and improving workplace efficiency.

At the 2004 conference of industrial relations researchers, nonpartisan academic experts presented a broad survey documenting "a positive and statistically significant association between unions and productivity." Earlier research by the New York Federal Reserve Bank found that unionized companies are 27 percent more productive than their nonunion counterparts. University of California labor expert Harley Shaiken says this is because unionized workforces mean lower turnover, stronger job training, and more standard communications conduits between employees and management.

But, echoing Doug, Chuck says, "There's still just this broad cultural antipathy toward the idea of unions" in the tech industry, and it is being sustained not solely by the Marlboro Man Fable, but also by the Legend of Job Security—the second of the Fantastic Four.

As we've seen, good corporate PR and workers' own career ambitions make white-collar culture predisposed to view the boss and the company as inherently benevolent. Out of this, many workers believe they don't need a union because they think such benevolence will ensure their job security and protect them from the outsourcing buzz saw. WashTech's own 2005 poll showed that about half of all tech workers surveyed do not believe outsourcing will affect their jobs. This, even though simultaneous polls of high-tech executives show that most of them are planning to radically accelerate outsourcing in the coming years.

But whereas surmounting the Marlboro Man Fable requires changing deep psychologies and self-images, breaking through the Legend of Job Security is a much easier task for the uprising, thanks to the harsher and harsher realities that are becoming impossible to ignore.

Princeton economist Alan Blinder reports that up to 42 million American jobs could be outsourced in the coming years. He says jobs based around personal services that "cannot be transmitted through a wire" may be impervious to outsourcing pressures. But, impersonal services like software programming—well, that's another story . . . a story prepackaged every evening on *Lou Dobbs Tonight* and one that Chuck says many high-tech workers are now starting to really get a handle on.

"A lot of full-timers who have been at Microsoft a long time are finally believing that sometime in the next few years, five years maximum, some whole division is going to show up one Monday morning and their card keys aren't going to work," he says. "And they're gonna have been laid off and their work will have been sent to India."

Such an epiphany is thanks, in no small part, to WashTech's work.

WashTech's website, newsletter, and legislative advocacy focuses heavily on outsourcing issues. It has deftly played its role as information conduit to expose outsourcing practices in provocative ways that aim to grab workers by the lapels (or BlackBerries) and shake them into collective action.

For example, WashTech has leaked internal Microsoft documents proving that company managers are encouraging those under them to hire foreign workers. In 2004, the *Seattle Post-Intelligencer* reported that the organization leaked details of confidential agreements between Microsoft and Indian outsourcing companies. WashTech "said [the documents] debunk the popular notion that only lower-level technology positions are vulnerable to outsourcing."

"[This is] the smoking gun that says to all Microsoft employees, if you think Microsoft management is somehow creating immunity around a certain set of occupations so that they won't be offshored, you better think again," Courtney told the paper.

The rhetoric dovetails with national news and local stories in Seattle that stoke fears of outsourcing. In 2003, the Associated Press ran a story on its national wire about soon-to-be-laid-off high-tech workers who were being asked to train their foreign replacements. The next year, Seattle University released a study showing that 80 percent of the region's tech companies were outsourcing jobs.

The union is using its megaphone to focus attention on these concerns, realizing that as globalization politically unifies owners of capital across international borders and linguistic barriers, it also has the potential to ideologically unify white-collar and blue-collar workers across cultural and occupational lines. More specifically, WashTech is making a bet that while tech workers may not want to see themselves as "garbage men and Teamsters," as Tollefson told me in the car, they understand that layoffs are layoffs, and they will be inclined to join WashTech and the uprising if only for self-preservation. Outsourcing, therefore, may be the catalyst that gets tech workers to see through the Legend of Job Security and past their management-class solidarity to recognize the existence of the labor-management divide.

For its part, Microsoft (like most American tech companies) is doing its best to preserve the Legend of Job Security and hoodwink its workforce into continued sedation. The company's shenanigans were best exposed a few years ago, thanks to WashTech.

Back in 2003, WashTech leaked internal Microsoft slideshows proving that the company's top brass was telling midlevel managers to "pick something to move offshore today" because in India, you can get "two heads for the price of one." Yet, when the Associated Press asked Microsoft about this, the company denied it had any plans to slash its U.S. workforce. When in 2004 WashTech exposed Microsoft's contracts with outsourcing subcontractors, the company issued a nondenial denial, saying, "This is not a departure from the way we've always done business."

WashTech's outsourcing campaign is a fragile balancing act. As it fights off the Marlboro Man Fable by positioning itself as the instrument to improve tech companies' efficiency and bottom line, it is simultaneously attacking the Legend of Job Security with a more traditional us-versus-them campaign. But Chuck's *harrumph* after he talks about outsourcing suggests the two-sided strategy can work.

"It just . . ."

His voice trails off for a moment, and the parrots start a back-and-forth screech song.

"It's just fuckin' corrosive."

"What specifically?" I ask.

"Everyone feels that they're being lied to a lot."

That's music to a union organizer's ears.

THIS IS IT. We're going in.

Years of devoted *A-Team* and *MacGyver* watching have made me dream of uttering those dramatic words, and I almost do as we park the car.

There it is—Building 32 at Microsoft's main campus.

We step out into the drizzling rain. I am humming the *Mission Impossible* song as the glass doors get closer. Will there be motion detectors? What about retina scans? Will there be full body X-ray machines? Or what about fingerprint identification? And how is Tollefson planning to get us by all that?

The door opens. Tollefson walks up to the reception desk and signs our names onto a clipboard. A security guard waves us in with no questions.

Wait, wait. Hang on here. *This* is the notoriously anti-union Microsoft?

"They let us come right in to talk to folks that we know," Tollefson says. "They don't try to block us. They know that if they did, it would make us seem bigger and more important."

Damn. I was all ready for my retina scan.

I was also ready for the place to look like the lab of a mad scientist—beakers, boiling chemicals, wall-sized computer screens, the works. Instead, it resembles an Ikea catalog.

The colors are neutral, the furniture is modern-style, but everything in the place looks cheaply made—like, if you dare sit in that chair over there, it might collapse.

I follow Tollefson through a hallway and around a corner into an open space with two couches. It reminds me of the common area in my freshman-year college dorm. Waiting for us here is a thickset, dark-haired guy named Rennie Sawade—a permatemp who is one of WashTech's newest members.

We greet in hushed tones as other Microsoft employees walk by—some with the blue badges, others just permatemps. The meeting feels secret, even though we are holding it right out in the open.

Tollefson takes a seat on the couch and starts by asking Rennie what motivated him to join WashTech a few weeks ago. He replies that he has recently started posting a regular podcast to his personal website about what it is like to work in the white-collar world. "When I was looking up articles for my podcast, I kept finding stuff on your website," he says in what is almost a whisper. "And I figured, well, you know, I should probably support what I'm preaching and support the union."

Rennie's soft voice has a slight midwestern accent ("Da Bears") from his time growing up in Michigan. He is one of the decreasing number of Americans who does, in fact, have a connection to the labor movement.

His father was a member of the United Auto Workers (UAW) as a General Motors employee in Flint—the town whose mass layoffs became an infamous symbol of corporate cruelty thanks to Michael Moore's first film, *Roger & Me*.

Rennie's father had one job and got his pension thanks to the UAW. Rennie, by contrast, is just forty-four years old and has already had somewhere between eight and ten jobs—and he sees that he is not headed for the kind of guaranteed retirement his dad has.

He was a "blue badge" a few years ago but left Microsoft to work at a startup that soon went under during the dot-com crash. Now he is back as a permatemp. He works full-time as a programmer at the Microsoft division that engineers software for the Tablet PC, but he technically works for Volt—a temp agency. Mind you, he makes a good living—sixty dollars an hour. But he is a highly trained programmer, and now he only gets to work nine months out of twelve because of the forced hundred-day break.

Like most permatemps, Rennie has been trying to get back to full-time work—or, "go blue," as folks here say. Many lower-level permatemps like software testers don't have a prayer of realizing that goal. Earlier today, Doug told me that he had "applied for a hundred different full-time Microsoft jobs, but I've never even gotten an interview."

Rennie is one of the lucky ones—as a high-level programmer, at least he gets interviews. But he believes he is not much better off than people like Doug, because he says he has learned that the interviews are mostly for show. "I've interviewed for jobs, and they always say they are going to hire me, but before they get an offer on the table, the job gets outsourced or an H-1B gets brought in," he says.

H-1B . . . it is a bland, IRS tax form–ish kind of term, but it is uttered by Rennie in a disgusted tone, because it is at the heart of the third of the Fantastic Four: the Great Labor Shortage Lie.

For the better part of two decades, tech companies have insisted that there is a dearth of high-skilled computer programmers and engineers in the United States, and that this supposed shortage of workers is hurting business. This narrative is dutifully echoed by the media. *BusinessWeek's* headline in 2007 is typical of the coverage: "Where Are All the Workers?" the magazine asked, stating that "companies worldwide are suddenly scrambling to manage a labor crunch."

These claims have obstructed WashTech recruitment efforts by buttressing the Legend of Job Security. Specifically, the Great Labor Shortage Lie makes existing tech employees feel like they will never lose their job because they are supposedly a super-rare commodity.

There's just one snag: there is no labor shortage.

In 2007, a comprehensive study by Duke University researchers found "no indication of a shortage of engineers in the United States."

As *BusinessWeek* admits in that same story about a supposed "global labor crunch," many "so-called shortages could quickly be solved if employers were to offer more money." But, see, that's not happening. In fact, the magazine grudgingly acknowledged, "the strongest evidence that there's no general shortage today is that overall worker pay has barely outpaced inflation."

This is Economics 101. In the case of the tech industry, if companies were really facing a shortage of workers, they would be throwing competing offers for more money and better benefits at experienced people like Doug, Chuck, and Rennie—not relegating them to second-class permatemp status.

So what is the motivation for the Great Labor Shortage Lie? Why is it still being spread? To drive down wages, thus bringing us back to that H-1B thing.

To "fix" the purported shortage, Congress in 1990 created the H-1B program, which allows employers like Microsoft to bring in temporary foreign workers for high-skill jobs.

"They say they need H-1B's because they can't find a qualified American, but what they really mean is they can't find a cheap American," Rennie says.

His assertion is supported by the data. In 2005, the Center for Immigration Studies released a study of government statistics showing H-1B employees are paid an average of $13,000 a year less than American workers in the same job in the same state. Rochester Institute of Technology professor Ron Hira has documented cases in which companies use the H-1B program to import foreign workers at wages 70 percent less than prevailing American wages in the same occupation.

"These shills, these lobbyists, they always say, well, employers have to pay the prevailing wage for H-1Bs," Rennie says, his voice rising from a whisper, as if he wants everyone to hear him. "But you know, the prevailing wage can be anything they say it is."

That simple fact is supposed to be a secret. The legislation creating the H-1B program included vague language that seemed to protect American workers. One provision seemed to safeguard wages by telling companies to pay H-1B workers the industry's prevailing wage. Other language seemed to make companies prove they could not find a qualified American worker before they hired an H-1B. And still another provision seemed like it gave the federal government the power to police the program and make sure it isn't abused to screw workers.

But the operative word here is *seem*.

Though most major news organizations repeatedly claim the H-1B program forces firms to look for American workers before turning to an H-1B, even the government admits that's patently false. "H-1B workers may be hired even when a qualified U.S. worker wants the job, and a U.S. worker can be displaced from the job in favor of the foreign worker," wrote the U.S. Department of Labor in its official 2006 Strategic Plan. Likewise, the Government Accountability Office reported that in its surveys of employers, many "said that they hired H-1B workers in part because these workers would accept lower salaries than similarly qualified U.S. workers."

Such loopholes have spurred a whole cottage industry. Five of the top ten users of the H-1B program are Indian firms that use the visas to send foreign workers over to the United States to fill tech jobs. Corporate lawyers have developed consulting practices to help companies use the program to avoid hiring American workers. "Our goal is clearly not to find a qualified and interested U.S. worker," said one such attorney at a seminar on the H-1B program that was caught on video. "And, you know, that in a sense, that sounds funny, but it's what we're trying to do here."

Based on polling, Rennie isn't the only one who has caught on to the Great Labor Shortage Lie. A 2006 survey of 1,700 tech engineers found that only about half believe "there is a shortage of engineers at my company." A 1998 NBC News poll taken as Congress debated expanding the H-1B program found 72 percent of the country opposed allowing in more temporary high-tech workers. That followed a Harris poll that found 86 percent of Americans agreed that "U.S. companies should train U.S. workers to perform jobs in some technical field, even if it is faster and less expensive to fill the jobs with foreign professionals."

Today, Microsoft ranks third in the country among companies hiring H-1B employees, and so Rennie works with H-1B workers all the time. His anger is not the quasi-nationalism of Lou Dobbs, nor the xenophobia of the Minutemen. The rage is not directed at the H-1B workers themselves, but at people he feels are abusing the H-1B program and lying about it—and chief among them, he says, is Bill Gates.

In early 2007, the richest man in America brought his boyish happy-talk to the nation's capital, testifying before a Senate committee in an attempt to convince lawmakers to eliminate the cap on the number of H-1B visas the government issues every year. All three WashTech members I have met today brought up Gates's testimony on their own, making sure I understood what an atrocity they think it was. Here they are, working as permatemps, and the founder of their company had the nerve to spit out the Great Labor Shortage Lie by telling Congress he can't find qualified full-time workers.

Chuck called the testimony "loathsome and distasteful."

"I can't believe Gates went in front of Congress and said, 'Let in infinite number of H-1Bs because there's no programmers here,' that fucking liar," he said. "You know, how many people are still out of work or had to leave the industry?"

Rennie is even more strident.

"What Bill Gates is saying is that he doesn't want to pay for the American middle class anymore. He wants to pay more the standard of living over in India."

The centrality of Gates in the Great Labor Shortage Lie has opened a door for WashTech, because he puts a face to what the uprising is challenging.

"It is not possible to develop the necessary hostility against . . . a corporation which has no soul or identity," Saul Alinsky once wrote. "A target must be a personification, not something general and abstract."

WashTech appreciates this, as Tollefson cuts in to remind Rennie that the union has already started a fund-raising drive off Gates's testimony.

"We've dissected his speech and we're gonna do a newspaper ad where we show what Gates says and what the reality is."

The union plans to publish a full-page ad in *Roll Call,* the Capitol Hill newspaper, designed to pressure Congress to oppose Gates's H-1B request. It is a D.C.-centric move mimicking the tactics of the antiwar Players, except the proposed ad is not partisan at all. That's smart for two reasons. First, rank-and-file tech workers have mixed partisan loyalties, and they will probably be more willing to donate to something bipartisan. Second, the problem in Washington on all of these issues truly *is* bipartisan. Republicans may be the party of Wall Street, but Democrats—thanks to oodles of tech industry campaign contributions—have become the party of Silicon Valley.

"The people in the Senate were all praising Gates, telling him, 'Oh, you're such a great guy,'" Rennie says, his hand balled up in a fist, tapping his knee. "I just couldn't believe some of the stuff that was being said."

In particular, Rennie cites the last of the Fantastic Four—the Great Education Myth. Parroted by just about everybody who is anybody in business, politics, and media, this fairly tale tells us that if we just get everyone a college degree, all our problems with outsourcing, stagnant wages, and pension cuts will magically vanish as our knowledge economy booms.

In the white-collar world, this myth is employers' backstop for the other three story lines; if you get past the Marlboro Man Fable, the Legend of Job Security, and the Great Labor Shortage Lie and start moving toward the uprising out of economic fear and corporate loathing, you may be deterred by the Great Education Myth, which says all you have to do is go back to school and you'll be fine.

"At that hearing, Gates and all the senators were going on about how the answer for our economy is, 'well, we've gotta fix education'—and that's just a bunch of baloney," Rennie says. "Just a couple years ago, I got my master's degree, and, you know, I'm not seeing any return on it."

A lot of people are in the same boat. Between 2000 and 2004, census figures show that earnings of college graduates dropped by more than 5 percent. The *Financial Times* reports that "earnings of the average US worker with an undergraduate degree have not kept up with gains in productivity in recent decades," primarily because "a change in labor market institutions and norms [has] reduced the bargaining power of most US workers" (translation: the loss of unions has meant less leverage for workers). Even *Fortune* magazine concedes that "just maybe the jobs most threatened by outsourcing are no longer those of factory workers with a high school education, as they have been for decades, but those of college-educated desk workers [who] look more outsourceable by the day."

Tollfeson checks his watch, and signals to me that it is time to get going. As the three of us walk out of the building, Rennie's anger and passion turn back to the low-grade despair that has been running through all of these meetings today. Unprompted by me, he says that the only person who had the guts to ask Gates anything at the Senate hearing was Bernie Sanders, who—true to uprising form—garnered a bit of ink in tech trade publications for asking Gates about outsourcing.

"I wish we had a lot more people like Bernie Sanders in there," Rennie says, looking off in thought across the parking lot as the rain starts pouring harder.

But the Senate doesn't, and the effect of that void is not merely a lack of lawmakers asking questions at a specific hearing or even offering legislation. No, the real void and the potentially insurmountable obstacle for WashTech in building the white-collar uprising is something it cannot fully control. It can circumvent the physical obstacles to organizing through one-on-one meetings. It can slowly but surely break down the Fantastic Four and update the labor movement's image for the union-averse constituency it targets. But without the intangible of inspiration, it will be having a "fight with a windmill," as Saul Alinsky might say.

Whether antiwar protestors, third-party activists, state legislators, or Minutemen, those who become part of the uprising do so because they are sick and tired of a political system that ignores them. But for those folks like white-collar workers who may be less political by nature, that feeling of disenfranchisement can serve as a suppressant. Their apolitical, nonconfrontational disposition means that they, more than most other groups, need an inspiration that proves the value in joining the uprising. And without that inspiration, whatever uprising sympathies they may have are easily quashed under a sense of helplessness.

Rennie sums it up in distinctly Microsoft terms. "It's hard to change things when people turn on the television and see someone like Gates with all the congressmen fawning all over him."

9

THE BLUE-CHIP REVOLUTIONARIES

THIS PROBABLY SOUNDS ignorant, but I'll just admit it up front: before this late spring day, most of what I knew of Texas came mainly from the 2000 presidential campaign, and from *Pee Wee's Big Adventure* (perhaps not all that shocking since both of these pop culture spectacles revolved around immature, giggling manchildren and their antics in the Lone Star State).

During the 2000 election, ads seemed to be on every television in America making Texas out to be an environmental hazard from a post-apocalyptic sci-fi movie. For weeks leading up to this May 2007 trip, I imagined the sky in Dallas being a permanent yellow-brown, and for a time I considered bringing a gas mask, or at least one of those surgical face coverings.

The only part of me that's been looking forward to this trip is the magic-bullet skeptic in me—I hope to see the book depository and the grassy knoll, though within five minutes of getting off the plane in this hot, muggy, crowded, urban sprawl, all I can even think about on the historical score is what a bummer it would be to spend your last day of life in Dallas, Texas, whether you were JFK or Lee Harvey Oswald or anyone else.

Everything in Texas, I've been told, is big—especially in Dallas, a town known as "Big D." So it's no wonder that the beige, concrete monstrosity that is the Dallas/Fort Worth International Airport alone is probably three times the size of my town in Montana, and that the first thing I see on the highway is a church the size of a sports arena.

But maybe the biggest thing of all in Texas is ExxonMobil, whose shareholder meeting I will be attending tomorrow with some of the uprising's most skilled guerrilla fighters. This oil company is Texas big, and by that I mean that if the map of the continental United States represented all the corporations in the world by profit size, ExxonMobil would be the imposing Lone Star State right there in the middle.

Last year, the company set the world record for most profits ever recorded by a single corporation, raking in almost $40 billion. The *Washington Post* reported that ExxonMobil's total 2006 "revenue of $377.6 billion exceeded the gross domestic product of all but 25 *countries*."

During my ride to the hotel, I try to think about what these numbers really mean—in real-life terms.

This van I'm riding in, like the other cars crowding Interstate 35, probably filled up at one of ExxonMobil's 34,000 gas stations. Many of these vehicles are kept running with some of the thousands of barrels of lubricant the company produces every day. In fact, come to think of it, the plane I flew in on was probably fueled at one of ExxonMobil's 650 jet fuel facilities, while the snack I scarfed down in the airport, the carpet I walked on in the terminal, the road signs flying by at sixty miles an hour, and even the batteries powering the Ipod I am now listening to were probably all made possible in part by the twenty-seven million metric tons of petrochemicals ExxonMobil produces each year.

In Texas, ExxonMobil is such a pervasive part of the culture that the street signs here in downtown Dallas have Mobil logos over them (I'm not kidding—silver Pegasus emblems hang over downtown street signs). So when I see the group of shareholder activists I am meeting in the lobby of the Hotel Indigo, I don't know whether to cry or laugh—not at them, of course, but at the idea that a few shareholder activists could possibly mount an effective uprising to get the world's largest oil company to reduce its production of materials that emit greenhouse gases, the same materials that have made said company the wealthiest in corporate history.

My first thought is that the activists' crusade is the equivalent of the famous (and probably not altogether true) story of the horse-riding, saber-toting Polish cavalry suicidally charging out toward the wall of German tanks steamrolling in from the west during World War II.

But as I am about to find out, this is more American Revolution than it is World War II, only with a slightly different set of characters. Back in colonial times, it was a bunch of well-to-do East Coasters whose bourgeois resentment against the British Crown led them to throw tea over the side of a boat and organize an improbable war against England. Today, the group of revolutionaries sounds like the beginning of a stand-up comedy joke: a New Jersey nun, a Milwaukee priest, a New York retiree, a Boston environmentalist, a D.C. union official, a New England millionaire, a local politician from Connecticut, and a Philly Greenpeace activist all walk into a bar . . .

Only this is no joke.

This gaggle has come together, blue-chip stocks in hand, to file shareholder resolutions against ExxonMobil—a global force at least as powerful as the eighteenth-century British military. And if they are successful, they will have done a hell of a lot more than merely bring democracy to a single country—they will have helped save the planet from burning itself to death.

My DAD IS a kidney doctor. I am told that his field of nephrology is one of the nerdiest of the many medical disciplines (yes, it's true—there are fairly distinct nerd differentials within medicine). The field relies heavily on numbers, equations, tables, calculations, and the other various trappings of nerd-dom. One time when I was in high school, I accompanied my dad on his rounds at a dialysis unit, and within five minutes (and six references to something called "creatinine"), I felt like I was in a foreign country, utterly unable to comprehend what was going on, or to even communicate any questions without feeling like everyone around would think I was an idiot.

This is how I feel right now in Dallas.

I am in the lobby of the Hotel Indigo, sitting in a circle of shareholder activists and laughing along with their jokes about Securities Exchange Commission (SEC) enforcement . . . jokes that I do not understand in the slightest. I am nodding along as the group discusses "cross-investment asset classes" . . . a term I've never heard before and do not comprehend in any way at all. The shareholder movement is the nephrology of the uprising—maybe the nerdiest subspecialty within the already intensely nerdy world of politics.

I originally called the Interfaith Center on Corporate Responsibility (ICCR) in New York to start looking into this part of the uprising after reading a magazine article about "socially responsible" mutual funds. The thirty-year-old organization, I learned, helps coordinate investing for its 275 religious member organizations (churches, synagogues, hospitals, and foundations). That sounds quaint and small-time, until you find out that ICCR members control roughly $100 billion of stock holdings—a decidedly big-time amount.

ICCR put me in touch with a nun named Pat Daly. She runs an organization called the Tri-State Coalition for Responsible Investment, which describes itself as "an alliance of Roman Catholic institutional investors primarily located throughout the New York metropolitan area."

Daly's job revolves around the 1934 federal law giving shareholders with $2,000 worth of stock the right to file shareholder resolutions—most often directives to company management, which shareholders are asked to vote on. The more shares you have in a company, the more votes you get to cast on resolutions brought against the company.

In the last thirty years, these resolutions have been used by activists of all political persuasions to force corporations to do everything from disclosing company political contributions to divesting holdings in apartheid South Africa.

Sister Pat, as she is called by her colleagues, grew up in Queens and stumbled into the shareholder uprising through her work as a nun. She is part of the Dominican Order, originally founded by St. Dominic, one of whose central teachings, Sister Pat told me, was having the courage to "speak truth to the powerful." As a young nun in the 1970s, she first attended an annual shareholder meeting of a textile manufacturer then making head- lines for its union-busting activities and mass layoffs. Inspired, she became involved in using the modest $10 to $15 million in stock holdings of her community of nuns in Caldwell, New Jersey, to become more engaged in shareholder activism, ultimately taking the job of executive director of the Tri-State Coalition in 1994.

In her thick New York accent, she told me on the phone to meet her in Dallas and tag along as she and her merry band of activists file a package of shareholder resolutions at ExxonMobil's annual meeting. The resolutions this year, she said, would be aimed at compelling the company to come up with a plan to reduce the amount of greenhouse gases its products emit.

I tried not to react too skeptically when Sister Pat told me her commu- nity of nuns would be wielding just two hundred shares of ExxonMobil. "You'll see," she reassured me. "You can be a leader in this without neces- sarily owning a lot of stock."

I also had to hide my astonishment when she told me the exact sub- stance of her resolution. Unlike nearly every other big energy company on the planet, ExxonMobil officially refuses to invest any serious resources into developing alternative or renewable energy. This is a company that is so committed to making money selling oil for conversion into a greenhouse gas that it once underwrote an Epcot Center ride devoted to teaching kids about the supremacy of fossil fuels.*

Warming the planet, in other words, is ExxonMobil's whole business, and one it does quite well.

An independent study commissioned in 2004 found that over the

---

* The ride was called Universe of Energy and its primary feature was a giant reproduction of a *Brontosaurus* happily smiling, oblivious to the fact that millions of years later its rotted, liquefied corpse would be poured into a gas tank and burned to help an SUV pass a sixteen-wheeler on I-95.

course of its existence, this one company and its products have created about 20 billion tons of carbon—or roughly 5 percent of all human-generated carbon emissions in planetary history. It is today considered scientific fact that these same human-generated emissions significantly contribute to the global rise in temperatures over the past fifty years that is now threatening the Earth's ecosystem through intensifying droughts, floods, hurricanes, and other catastrophes.

Not surprisingly, ExxonMobil has spent millions funding front groups that have at times denied that the globe is warming, and at other times implied that oil companies like ExxonMobil are doing humanity a service by helping it warm. As just one example, since 1998, ExxonMobil has given $2 million to the Competitive Enterprise Institute (CEI)—a group that aired television ads promoting the benefits of emitting carbon dioxide. ("Carbon dioxide," said the ad. "They call it pollution. We call it life.") CEI's founder actually employed the "everyone loves tropical weather" meme as a scientific argument, claiming "most of the indications right now are [that global warming] looks pretty good" because it will mean "warmer winters [and] warmer nights."*

Strangely, none of this—not ExxonMobil's size nor its well-financed global warming denial machine—seemed to make Sister Pat question her resolution's prospects when we discussed it all on the phone. "The meeting is going to be fun," she told me. "You'll get a lot of good stuff down there."

So now, a month after first talking to Sister Pat, I'm here in Dallas, expecting a nun in the traditional church robes leading a group of tie-dyed shirts, ponytails, and Birkenstocks. Instead, I find Sister Pat wearing a black pants suit, surrounded by other business suits brandishing three-ring binders, making the group here in the lobby look like a gaggle of middle managers attending an insurance seminar.

Shareholder activism is a professionalized, technical, and esoteric uprising appendage—one with a very subtle strategy of influence that revolves

*Yay! Alaska will soon be the new Hawaii! Really—haven't you always dreamed of going surfing in the Arctic Ocean?

not around '60s-style protest, but around six sacred jujitsu teachings as opaque as Mr. Miyagi's "Wax on, wax off" lessons from *The Karate Kid*.

Luckily, Sister Pat and the group she's working with are taking sympathy on me, the perplexed moron, and explaining these teachings like a patient sensei.

WE ARE BEGINNING my training in the dark arts of shareholder activism in Sister Pat's rented beige Ford Taurus on a ride from our hotel over to a meeting with other allied shareholder activists at Dallas's Fairmont Hotel. While driving, she looks in the rearview mirror at me to explain:

THE FIRST RULE OF SHAREHOLDER ACTIVISM:
DON'T TALK ABOUT SHAREHOLDER ACTIVISM.

In the media vernacular, the term "shareholder activism" usually implies only efforts that are directly related to the use of shareholder resolutions. "But the first thing you have to understand is that most of our work is done in one-on-one meetings with the company," Sister Pat says, as she gets us lost in downtown Dallas.

I ask her to explain this further, because around this time of year when all the annual meetings happen, I always see a spate of news stories about how many shareholder resolutions lost. When I read these stories, I tell her, I always believed they proved that shareholder activism was interesting, straightforward, and utterly quixotic.

"No, no, that's the thing—we don't prefer to work through resolutions," Sister Pat continues. "Our strength is in dialoguing with the companies before it ever gets to the public activism and shareholder resolution part. The shareholder resolution is only the vehicle for us to get into the dialogue."

Other than the term *proxy*, which means a shareholder's actual vote on a resolution, the word *dialogue* is probably the most important term in shareholder activism's unique dialect. It means talking to and negotiating with company management. Unlike electoral politics's goal of destroying the opponent, shareholder activism is about constant dialogue with the corporate target, with activists pressuring management to modify its business practices.

Sister Pat is telling me that many companies often embrace this dialogue and begin to change well before resolutions are ever presented. This would explain why I have already found that the shareholder activists here don't themselves use the term *activism* all that much: because what these folks do is far more than merely file resolutions.

But, I wonder, why aim for dialogue? Why not just try to ram through resolutions and impose change on management? Shareholders are the owners of companies, after all, so why not just use your shares to get your way?

We are now turning a corner, and Tracey Rembert, riding shotgun, is alternately barking directions at Sister Pat while craning her neck to explain to me:

THE SECOND RULE OF SHAREHOLDER ACTIVISM: IT'S NEARLY IMPOSSIBLE TO WIN A VOTE ON A SHAREHOLDER RESOLUTION.

Rembert is the thirty-six-year-old pension expert for the D.C. office of the Service Employees International Union, whose pension fund owns about 100,000 shares of ExxonMobil. Formerly an environmental journalist, she is short with shoulder-length golden hair, wears small black-rimmed glasses, talks with a slight southern twang from her time growing up in South Carolina, and is wearing a purple shirt—the signature color of her organization.

As I am marveling at Sister Pat's New York–acquired ability to park the Taurus in a spot barely big enough for a bicycle, Rembert is telling me not to feel bad about having so many questions.

"Don't worry," she says. "My family doesn't quite understand exactly what I do either. All they get are the big parts. I overheard my mom tell a friend, 'Oh, Tracey faces down those big CEOs at shareholder meetings.'"

But, she says, the most important "facing down" happens during the dialogue, not during the shareholder meetings, because it's normally a foregone conclusion that a resolution will lose. Corporate management typically opposes all shareholder resolutions (not surprising, considering resolutions arise in response to management's refusal to dialogue with unhappy shareholders). Such opposition, she says, creates an insurmountable ripple effect, with the majority of big shareholders, like corporate pension funds and mutual funds, either not voting their shares, or consistently voting them against shareholder resolutions out of deference to management. This makes winning shareholder resolutions today next to impossible.

She tells me that I will soon meet the seventy-four-year-old shareholder activist Bob Monks—the guy *Fortune* magazine has called "the most important shareholder advocate of his generation."

Monks is an expert in "corporate governance"—the set of issues that makes shareholder resolutions so difficult. During a failed 1972 Senate run as a Republican from Maine, he saw pollution from a paper company foaming on the Penobscot River, and started asking questions about why the owners of the company—the shareholders—didn't have a say in stopping the destruction. Over the next decades, he became obsessed with this disconnection between company owners (aka shareholders) and company decision makers (aka management), and the all-too-cozy relationships between the managers of pension funds and the executives of companies the pension funds own stock in. These are precisely the relationships that make shareholder resolutions so impossible to win. Monks says part of the problem is horse trading, whereby one company's executives says to another company's executives that "my pension fund will not raise questions about your company if your pension fund will not raise questions about my company," Monks told *Fortune*. "They have neutered themselves intentionally." Other times, Monks says, mutual funds vote against all shareholder resolutions, because their directors are angling to manage corporate pension money or run 401(k) plans, and therefore don't want to antagonize the CEOs and corporate board members who dole out that management business.

As if those built-in obstacles are not enough, additional mechanisms rig shareholder resolution fights in a way that makes "Florida in the 2000 presidential election look like a model of vote-counting virtue," as Yale University stock expert Yair Listokin has said. Though voting proxies is known as "shareholder democracy," what goes on has very little to do with democracy in the common parlance, because one interested party—company management—has built-in advantages. Voting can go on for week, and votes are counted by the company itself. Executives can even check vote tallies as they come in, knowing that if they see a resolution winning, they will have time to rustle up more "no" votes.

"Ok, so if resolutions almost always lose, why is everyone here to file resolutions?" I ask Rembert and Sister Pat as we walk into the Fairmont Hotel bar. "Why do you do any of this in the first place?"

Sister Pat gives me that knowing smile a kindergarten teacher gives a wide-eyed child asking questions about simple arithmetic. Then, she tells me about:

THE THIRD RULE OF SHAREHOLDER ACTIVISM: SHAREHOLDER ACTIVISM ISN'T ONLY ABOUT RESOLUTIONS, BUT WITHOUT RESOLUTIONS, THERE IS NO ACTIVISM.

Crudely put, a shareholder resolution is to shareholder activism what a nuclear weapon is to foreign policy: a rarely used weapon whose coercive influence comes more from the fear it will be used than from its actual detonation.

Resolutions inherently threaten a public relations mushroom cloud for a company, with permanent fallout like the story folks are reminiscing about here in the bar when they greet Sister Pat—the one in which this unassuming Dominican nun became the public face of the successful campaign to embarrass General Electric into cleaning up one of the largest environmental disasters in American history.

Throughout the 1990s, GE fought the federal government's efforts to make the company pay to clean up the cancer-causing toxins known as PCBs (polychlorinated biphenyls) that it had been dumping in the Hudson River for three decades. At the urging of a group of churches in her tri-state coalition, Daly began using her coalition's GE stock holdings to engage in a dialogue with the company to push it to pay up. When that failed, she began filing resolutions each year asking GE CEO Jack Welch to disclose the amount of company money he was using to fight the federal government, through legal, lobbying, PR, and advertising expenses. Though the resolutions never passed, they attracted relentless media scrutiny that helped push GE to finally cave. By 2006, the company agreed to pick up the massive tab for cleaning up the Hudson, and also revealed that it had spent $800 million over fifteen years trying to avoid the inevitable financial responsibility for its mess.

The potential for such resolution-driven public relations disasters compels risk-averse corporations to dialogue with activists and often preemptively modify behavior to prevent embarrassing resolutions from ever getting introduced. And because of experiences like the GE cleanup, activists have gained grudging respect as advocates for change that will actually help the company's bottom line.

"If GE had listened to Pat earlier on, it wouldn't have spent all that money trying to stop the Hudson River cleanup and instead just cleaned it up and saved itself the money," Rembert says. "Every other company knows that and knows how bad the whole fight was for GE's reputation, and that's the kind of thing that gives our requests credibility in our meetings with management."

Sister Pat now chimes in with a bit more explanation, running her hand through her short gray hair.

"Look, we have become known as free consultants," she says. "These companies hire all sorts of consultants who really couldn't give a shit about the corporation, but we are shareholders who do care about the company's long-term profitability, and our campaigns have shown that we've got some experience pointing out major flaws in their business models."

Before I can process the reality that I just heard a nun say "shit," Rembert jumps in and says, "We have built up a good track record of showing the companies we own what problems are coming down the pike and how they can fix them."

That track record could never have been developed without the threat of using the nuclear weapon, because absent shareholder activists' ability to push the button, the companies have no incentive to listen at all.

Nonetheless, resolutions are not *really* like a nuclear weapon, but are merely "a shiny bomb case full of used pinball machine parts," to quote Christopher Lloyd from *Back to the Future*. If a particularly stubborn company that doesn't care about its own public image refuses to dialogue and change its behavior, it ultimately knows it can defeat any resolution in response. So why file the resolutions at all?

Sister Pat now explains:

THE FOURTH RULE OF SHAREHOLDER ACTIVISM: YOU CAN WIN, EVEN IF YOUR RESOLUTION TECHNICALLY LOSES.

GE agreed to Sister Pat's demands for disclosure in 2006—months after her resolution received an astounding 27.4 percent of the shareholder vote. In normal election terms, that sounds horrendous—a major party failing to break 30 percent in an election is universally recognized as one that got its ass whipped. So why would a company like GE, or any other company, react to resolutions that look to the casual observer like they were handily defeated?

Because, to adapt the old cliché, "close" counts in horseshoes, hand grenades, *and* shareholder activism.

The goal of shareholder activists is to change company behavior. The top priority of the executives who can change their company's behavior is preserving and increasing the company's stock price. Therefore, the way to change company behavior is to make company management believe that if it doesn't change its behavior, something bad will happen to the company's stock.

Shareholder resolutions do this in two ways, regardless of whether they win or lose. First and foremost, shareholder resolutions threaten a company's public image. As a top business consulting firm discovered in a late 2005 study, up to 27 percent of a company' stock price is attributable to intangibles like a company's reputation. Executives, then, know that shareholder resolutions that attract negative publicity to a company can seriously endanger that significant slice of a stock's price.

The second way shareholder resolutions make stock price–obsessed executives nervous is through their influence on other major financial players—the bankers, brokers, and analysts who collectively shape the company's stock price and market support. These all-important observers, unlike casual onlookers, know how the deck is stacked against resolutions, and therefore know a shareholder resolution that gets any significant support really may represent a bigger problem within the company—and that knowledge influences their articles, reports, and other assorted proclamations that determine investor attitudes and stock price.

Now it's easy to understand why Daly's 27.5 percent vote against GE knocked the wind out of the company. Similarly, it's simple to comprehend why, when a 1999 shareholder resolution encouraging Home Depot to improve its environmental practices garnered 12 percent of the vote, newspapers called it "an extraordinarily high amount for a resolution opposed by management" and the company soon changed its behavior. To get even that seemingly small amount of support signaled to the market gods that a significant number of major shareholders were angry enough to do something the system is designed to prevent.

Shareholder activists' most ardent enemies, like the Competitive Enterprise Institute (ExxonMobil's pro–global warming front group) grudgingly acknowledge this win-even-if-you-lose power of their adversaries.

"I really hate to say this, but I think [shareholder resolutions] are very effective even when they fail," said CEI's spokesman in 2001. "Corporate CEOs have nightmares over these resolutions because they generate negative publicity for the company and they irritate boards of directors and shareholders."

The key for activists, then, is beating expectations by making sure the resolutions they end up filing do more than just get crushed. If they do that year after year, they build up a menacing reputation for being able to humiliate companies if they refuse to dialogue. And they do that, says Rembert, by remembering:

THE FIFTH RULE OF SHAREHOLDER ACTIVISM:
A RESOLUTION CAMPAIGN IS A POLITICAL CAMPAIGN.

We are now sitting in a dimly lit corner of the Fairmont Hotel's bar. Above our heads the flat-screen TV pumps in a *Lou Dobbs Tonight* segment titled "God and Politics"—appropriate for the setting, considering the circle of activists here is an eclectic mix of religious leaders, politicians, and corporate governance experts like Bob Monks, who is holding court.

Wearing a light sport coat with an open collar, Monks has a soft voice and a rubbery face like a Richard Nixon caricature mask in a Halloween store. This is the man who, as a Reagan Labor Department official, crafted regulations requiring pension fund trustees to vote their fund's shares solely in the interest of pensioners. These regulations, aimed squarely at ending the kind of cronyish corruption Monks says makes shareholder activism so tough, provides the opening, albeit small, for groups like the one assembled here to mount their unique kind of political campaign. If they can convince a few key players to agree that a resolution is in the fiduciary interest of the company, they've got a chance to garner some real support—and shareholder votes—for their cause.

Who are these key players? Gulping down a glass of red wine as she tries to listen to Monks plotting strategy for tomorrow's meeting, Rembert whispers the letters *ISS* to me. It's short for something called Institutional Shareholder Services that keeps getting mentioned.

"ISS is the most important of the major institutional advisers whose recommendations on how to vote on shareholder resolutions are often followed by big institutional investors," she says. "When we decide to file a resolution, the entire campaign leading up to it is about convincing advisers like ISS and then individual institutional investors that supporting the resolution is in shareholders' fiduciary interest."

For institutional investors potentially sympathetic to the shareholder activists' cause, ISS's support for a resolution is the gold standard reassuring them the initiative is good for business. It also provides them the cover they need to prove they aren't violating their fiduciary responsibilities by going up against management in support of a resolution. On the other side, ISS support for a resolution may make hostile institutional investors feel vulnerable to legal questions about cronyism should they continue to blindly side with management.

But getting this seal of approval is only the first part of the resolution push—advertising the ISS endorsement (and other endorsements) to superwealthy individual shareholders, mutual fund managers, and pension fund boards is the other part, and that is what most resembles a traditional election campaign.

Rembert tells me SEIU, for instance, financed a direct-mail advertisement to about half of ExxonMobil's shareholders asking them to vote their proxies for Daly's global warming resolution, and citing ISS's support for it. That has been followed up by conference calls, PowerPoint presentations, and other kinds of one-on-one, hit-the-streets, knock-on-doors tactics of retail politics. The only difference is that it is Wall Street, and the knocking is on office doors.

The best pitches for any of these resolutions, Rembert says, are those designed to appeal to the widest interest, because a resolution, like the other uprising endeavors, is only as successful as the diversity of the coalition it can build. Monks's involvement in the greenhouse gas resolution is a good example. His wife is a descendant of the Carnegies, and he has made a fortune running a coal and oil company, yet he will be using the 125,000 ExxonMobil shares he controls through a trust fund to support the greenhouse gas resolution.

Certainly, Monks's support has something to do with his own personal sympathies with the environmental cause, but it is primarily motivated by his interest in corporate governance. Michael Boskin, an adviser to Rudy Giuliani's presidential campaign and ExxonMobil's Public Issues Committee director, has refused to even meet with the shareholders supporting the greenhouse gas resolution. This, despite the fact that meeting with shareholders is the core job description of his $75,000-a-year part-time gig on the board, and despite the fact that the shareholders supporting the resolution include the massive Connecticut and California state pension programs.

Boskin's behavior, to Monks, is the most offensive affront to good corporate governance: it is a company flipping off its owners. And Monks is responding by pushing his own corporate governance resolution and by voting his shares in support of Sister Pat's environmental resolution. Like other uprising endeavors, the most successful shareholder resolution campaigns replicate that kind of cross-cutting, cross-ideological appeal at all levels.

Now back in the car headed off to a working dinner, I feel like I finally have a grasp of the basics. But something is still bothering me. The work for this resolution is all done, and everyone here knows it will almost definitely lose. As Father Michael Crosby, who works with Sister Pat, joked earlier, the shareholder meeting tomorrow "is the liturgy—it's all happened before, but worked out in ritual." But then, if that's true, why are all the activists totally jittery and nervous?

Sister Pat concludes our lessons by coming full circle and explaining:

THE SIXTH RULE OF SHAREHOLDER ACTIVISM:
THEATER IS STILL IMPORTANT.

"The shareholder meeting is the theater when we cannot get movement from the company," she tells me, as we motor through the Dallas suburbs. "We don't prefer to work this way when we can sit down with executives, but we do it when we need to."

Though Sister Pat again insists that "dialoguing" is the objective and that "bringing public attention to issues through resolutions is not our biggest forte," the statement belies both her own personal claim to fame, and the very real drama that boils to the surface at these shareholder meetings.

During the pivotal 1998 GE shareholder meeting, CEO Jack Welch repeated his claim that the PCBs his company poured into the Hudson River do not cause cancer. Sister Pat then stood up to present her resolution, noting that the government "continues to list PCBs on its suspected-carcinogen list" and likening Welch to "the CEOs of the tobacco companies swearing that they were telling the truth." Welch freaked out and screamed at her—embarrassing himself and drawing another wave of negative headlines against GE's increasingly blatant cover-up.

Such spectacles, though rare, are essential to building public pressure on companies, and the fireworks once again hearken back to the original pioneer of political theater—a man who is one of the fathers of both the shareholder activist movement and the larger uprising.

"THE VAST MAJORITY of Americans, who feel helpless in the huge corporate economy, who don't know which way to turn, have begun to turn away from America, to abdicate as citizens," wrote Saul Alinsky in *Rules for Radicals*. "Proxies can be the mechanism by which these people can organize, and once they are organized they will reenter the life of politics . . .

they will have reason to examine, to become educated about, the various corporation policies and practices both domestic and foreign—because now they can do something about them."

He wrote these words four years after leading one of history's most famous shareholder proxy fights. His battle against Eastman Kodak in 1967 was inspired by the company's biased hiring practices, and specifically its refusal to hire more employees from Rochester's struggling African-American community. Alinsky and his organization, the Industrial Areas Foundation, had been asked by local African-American leaders to serve as a strategy team in making demands on Kodak, and just when the campaign seemed to be going nowhere, Alinsky stumbled on the idea of shareholder democracy by "part accident [and] part necessity," he would later write.

If anyone was going to figure out the power of shareholder activism, it was going to be Alinsky. For decades, the Chicago Svengali had refined the art of quietly commandeering the Establishment's power for his own causes, in some instances even getting politicians to let his political organizations serve as the delivery vehicle for government-funded social services. The use of longstanding but little-used legal provisions to create major battles with corporations was just the logical next step in pursuit of his axiom that "you can club them to death with their book of rules and regulations."

Today, many think the intersection of politics and religion begins and ends with the Christian Right's inroads into the Republican Party, but many Christian denominations, eager to do good with their money, have been financial supporters of shareholder activism. That also started with Alinsky. When he originally devised the shareholder proxy tactics, this Jewish son of Russian immigrants said, "We hoisted a banner with our slogan, 'Keep your sermons; give us your proxies,' and set sail into the sea of churches."

And when they left the port, they found a wind at their backs. On April 7, 1967, the *New York Times* ran a story headlined "Two Churches Withhold Proxies to Fight Kodak Rights Policy." The report noted that officials of the Episcopal Church and the United Church of Christ backed the social-justice goals of the initiative and "said it was the first time they had not signed over the votes on their holdings" to company executives. The campaign's goal was to get as many shareholders as possible to withhold their proxies from being automatically voted with management's positions, as was the custom at the time.

By the morning of Eastman Kodak's shareholder meeting in Flemington, New Jersey, Alinsky's coalition had amassed 40,000 proxies from both churches and from individual shareholders who had pledged to vote their shares for his campaign—more than enough for his Rochester organization to convert the normally mundane meeting into a national media spectacle. Kodak, which soon bent to public pressure and modified its hiring practices, would later admit that Alinsky's use of shareholder proxies made the company beg for mercy—literally.

"I'm not a praying man, normally, but I prayed the night before that meeting," said the company's CEO. "I went down on my knees."

As University of Wisconsin historian Sanford Horwitt wrote, Alinsky had "launched the first collective church effort to use stockholdings to influence corporate policy on social-justice issues," with the fight serving as the "forerunner and source of the corporate responsibility movement's increasingly ambitious campaigns in subsequent decades."

This story is now being confirmed to me here in Dallas by Father Michael Crosby as the group is conversing over dinner. Crosby is bald, talks with a nasal voice, and has a wry grimace on his face most of the time. He lives at a church in downtown Milwaukee that serves a few hundred indigent and homeless people every night. He originally was dispatched to Milwaukee in 1968 when the diocese asked him to help mediate racial tension in "a parish that was turning white to black," he tells me.

"I failed after five years," he says with a twinge of sadness, though he does proudly recount how, in 1969, he was arrested inside the Pentagon staging a pray-in against the Vietnam War while massive peace demonstrations took place outside.

By 1973, Father Crosby began refocusing his political engagement on shareholder activism, crediting Alinsky with kicking off the movement that would become his life's work. "Saul started what we're doing," he says, taking a sip of water. "After he did what he did in 1967 [with Kodak], a group of us worked to get the Catholic Church more involved after that."

Crosby tells me that his major qualm with Alinsky was how his campaigns against large institutions were waged through attacks on the individuals at their helms. That gets a nod of agreement from John Wilson, a droopy-eyed investment adviser for another group of churches working with Sister Pat.

"The whole point is to get into dialogues," he says, picking at his food. "If we make it personal, that makes it harder."

I'm surprised by these comments, because when I listened to the activists strategizing earlier today, they were worrying about the recent departure of ExxonMobil's longtime CEO Lee Raymond, whose relative fame and headline-grabbing retirement package (worth nearly $400 million) provided them a compelling public target for their criticism of the company. According to Sister Pat, Raymond "ruled the shareholder meeting with an iron fist," shouting down speakers, intensifying confrontations, and generally helping create a media spectacle. Raymond was, in short, the "personification, not something general or abstract" that Alinsky said organizers need in order "to develop the necessary hostility" for an uprising.

Still, it's probably true that a personal target is not *always* necessary. We're talking about ExxonMobil here—a company whose very name is associated with profiteering in the reptilian lobe of the public's brain. The company's infamous status as a polluter and profiteer makes it a magnet for shareholder resolutions. Its selection as a centerpiece target of the shareholder activist movement suggests these folks have Alinsky's deeper uprising goals in mind.

"People power is the real objective," Alinsky wrote in *Rules for Radicals*. "The proxies are simply a means to that end."

"Despite all the crap about 'people's capitalism,' the dominant controlling stock in all major corporations is vested in the hands of a few people we could never get to," Alinksy said in an interview, adding that the real significance of shareholder activism is its role as "an invaluable means of gaining middle-class participation in radical causes."

Selecting iconic companies like ExxonMobil and General Electric year after year and getting into high-profile screaming matches with famed CEOs like Jack Welch and Lee Raymond is, in Alinsky terms, not only about specific populist crusades to stop global warming and clean up the Hudson River—it is also about picking targets that will get the most publicity, in hopes that the media attention will not only draw attention to specific issues, but make the population aware of its own untapped uprising potential.

Today, $6 trillion of stock is owned by worker pension funds, meaning Joe and Jane Sixpack own a huge amount of Corporate America, and control an immense amount of untapped power to shape corporate behavior. Alinsky envisioned organizing these holdings into a "Proxies for People" movement that would help millions of individual shareholders use their proxies to exert popular power against the Establishment. And, as if somehow seeing the future of lower-intensity mouse-click activism, he prophesied that voting proxies—which is far less time-intensive than, say, protest marches—would be better suited to an increasingly complex world, and more culturally acceptable in a country where demonstrations like sit-ins have become stigmatized as uncouth, even among those with progressive sympathies.

"By assigning their proxies," Alinsky told an interviewer, "liberals can also continue attending cocktail parties while assuaging their troubled social consciences."

Such mass involvement in the growing shareholder activism movement hasn't happened . . . yet. But the possibility of such mass involvement is one of the reasons that Sister Pat, Father Crosby, and the rest of the activists assembled here select attention-grabbing targets: they know that if more people just find out that they have the basic tools to challenge Corporate America lying idly in their 401(k) plans, more people might be moved to start asking questions about how they vote those shares and take action.

This is probably why Alinsky said that "in all my wars with the Establishment, I had never seen it so uptight" as when it faces a shareholder revolt. It's also probably why companies like ExxonMobil seem so utterly frightened of their own shareholders, as I will soon find out.

WE ARE IN the car on our way to the ExxonMobil shareholder meeting to file the resolution against greenhouse gas emissions. We are probably burning ExxonMobil gasoline to get there, and we are definitely warming the earth with the carbon emissions coming out the car's tailpipe. But no one seems to be thinking about that. Everyone in the car this morning is tense, moving around in ways that I imagine boxers move around before a big prizefight. Shoulder shrugging, neck stretching, and brow wiping are plentiful.

The first thing I see as we approach Dallas's Meyerson Symphony Center is a wall of uniformed city cops. It is almost forty years ago to the day that Alinsky staged the first major shareholder revolt in New Jersey against Eastman Kodak, and the show of intimidating force at these things looks like it hasn't really changed since then. During that Kodak meeting, "police where everywhere—on the street . . . and atop buildings with rifles drawn," wrote Sanford Horwitt, the historian. The only difference here today is that weapons remain holstered, but the message is the same as it's always been: get too rowdy, and it's hammer time.

I can't say that I'm stunned by this militaristic scene, because shareholder activism is, at its core, direct action.

Most activism in America today focuses on indirect action that uses only the very narrow channels those in elected office have created for us—channels that allow us to meagerly beg them to do something on the public's behalf (think of nonthreatening activities like lobbying, writing letters, emailing, and so on). Direct action, by contrast, circumvents the political intermediaries that the Establishment relies on to calm things down. The public brushes aside the politicians entirely and takes matters into its own hands through union-organizing drives, strikes, boycotts, civil disobedience, ballot initiatives, and, yes, shareholder confrontations.

When direct action occurs, the Establishment's standard reaction has been to stop issuing flowery press releases and start talking with force. In the late nineteenth century, federal troops used bullets to put down mining strikes in the Rocky Mountain West; in the 1960s and 1970s, national guardsmen gunned down war protestors on college campuses; right now, a municipal police squad is stationed outside a Dallas meeting hall to let ExxonMobil company shareholders know exactly who is in charge. It's all designed to menacingly ask the uprising what a crazed, pistol-brandishing Robert DeNiro asked in *Taxi Driver:* "You talkin' to me?"

But the Dallas cops aren't the only projection of authority here today. Driving down the ramp into the underground parking garage, I see men with dark suits, earpieces, and ExxonMobil badges milling about. They are the company's private security goons and press spokespeople.

Like everyone, we are stopped at the parking gate by an ExxonMobil PR guy named Thom Gill. But unlike everyone else, he isn't asking for any documents from Father Crosby. "Go right ahead, Mike," he says, waving us through before Father Crosby can even roll his window down to identify himself.

Though Gill was smiling, it wasn't a friendly greeting. It was Big Brother's way to tell us that he—and the company—knows exactly who these activists are, and that's no conspiracy theory.

Back in 2005, the *Financial Times* reported that some of the biggest companies are now "hiring surveillance firms to find out who their share-holders are and which ones might cause trouble." Similarly, earlier in 2007, the *Wall Street Journal* reported that Wal-Mart had created a "Threat Research and Analysis Group" to direct "surveillance operations at critical shareholders," including municipal governments that hold Wal-Mart stock in retiree pension funds. As some of the best-known shareholder activists in America, this specific group I'm with has solid reasons to believe companies watch them. In fact, four years ago, Sister Pat's computer was stolen out of her car, and then a week later her small New Jersey office was broken into. Though nothing was taken, she told me that files obviously had been rifled through, Gestapo-style.

Parking the car, Father Crosby says to no one in particular: "I wonder if that friendly greeting from Gill was that chipper because he already knows our resolution got beat badly?"

We all laugh.

Nervously.

After going up an elevator, I head to the reception desk to pick up the badge that will let me into the meeting. I managed to get the pass by telling company officials I was an official adviser to one of the shareholder activists I'm with. Once through the metal detector being run by ExxonMobil's private security guards, I'm in the polished-stone lobby of the symphony hall with the rest of the group. But unlike them, I almost completely forget why I'm here, as my ten-year-old-in-FAO-Schwarz gene takes over. Humming "Welcome to our world of toys" in my head, I'm frantically filling a plastic bag with all sorts of free goodies sitting beside displays about the company's many successes.

Over at the display about oil rigs, I grab two pairs of yellow-tinted oil rig goggles. At the mock gas station set up to promote the company's foray into food products, I'm given a stainless steel coffee thermos. At the spread about how the company invests in education, I pick up ExxonMobil's math and science flip book for kids. And at the display on ExxonMobil's financial numbers, I acquire a free portable hard drive that I'm told contains an electronic presentation about Exxon's profits. While frolicking around in this goodie heaven, I am simultaneously stuffing my face with the Krispy Kreme doughnuts I snatched up at the full-scale mock-up of an On the Run—ExxonMobil's line of gas station convenience stores.

As I rejoin Sister Pat, Father Crosby and the rest of the shareholder activists marveling at this Disney World, I see the crowd parting as a head of slicked-back gray hair bounds through the room, followed by two bouncers in suits. The gray hair is moving toward us, shaking hands and laughing.

"Hi there—Rex Tillerson!" says ExxonMobil's CEO in a thick Texas voice as he thrusts out a beefy hand to me.

Wearing a charcoal gray suit, a yellow-and-black tie, and brand new shoes, Tillerson is known to some of these activists as "T-Rex," though the nickname doesn't do justice to his impressive interpersonal skills. He displays the jovial folksiness of Bill Clinton and the good looks of James Brolin, only with what appears to be a can of ExxonMobil lubricant combed through his coif. He turns from shaking my hand to enthusiastically greeting Sister Pat and Father Crosby by their first names, as if reconnecting with beloved relatives he had been desperately missing. And then, just as smoothly as he glided up to us, he glides away to greet others.

"That was very, very different," John Wilson whispers anxiously. He's concerned because the activists' suspicions appear to be on the mark. Whereas the prickly former CEO Lee Raymond was a perfect Alinskyian target for Exxon's critics to demonize as a scrooge caricature, Tillerson looks to be a smooth operator—the wily politician who slashes your chest open and rips your heart out all while biting his lower lip, slapping your back, and asking after your family.

Steve Viederman, a bearded sixty-ish New Yorker who is here on behalf of a small foundation, says, "Rex doesn't look worried at all."

At this, John Wilson laughs.

"If your whole job was to dig money straight out of the ground, you probably wouldn't look worried either."

BUT REX TILLERSON actually does look a little bit worried, now that he's up on the stage, facing down Sister Pat.

The first hour of the meeting has been an ExxonMobil infomercial. It started out with a stern reading of the meetings rules by ExxonMobil's corporate secretary, Henry Hubble—whose nasal voice, flushed cheeks, pasty skin, and grease-parted hair make him look like he just came from a casting call for a *Revenge of the Nerds* remake. Hubble warned the audience that "comments that are offensive or otherwise inappropriate will not be permitted"—it isn't clear what *inappropriate* means, but with so many bulging, pit-boss-looking private security people around, I'm pretty sure I don't want to find out what "not permitted" means.

Tillerson then took over by running through a slide show of the company's astounding financial numbers—more than $30 billion in profits on

$377 billion in revenues. We are treated to a slickly produced video about ExxonMobil's support of math and science education that includes all the cheap tugs at the heartstrings we've become used to as a nation of television watchers—piano music in the background, soft lighting, teary-eyed personal testimonials, the works.

Sitting down in the first level of the theater—the designated peanut gallery—I can see the approving smiles and head nods from the company board members. They are seated in a special balcony all to themselves, gazing down over the meeting like gods on Mount Olympus. ExxonMobil's board—like other corporate boards—is a mix of right-wing professors and top executives from other multinational companies, the former there to provide academic window dressing, the latter there to provide the broader business community's stamp of approval to all company decisions. And that stamp ain't small. Made up of current or former CEOs of IBM, Campbell Soup, Corning, PepsiCo, Chase Manhattan Bank, and ExxonMobil itself, the company's board represents firms possessing well over $1 trillion in total assets.

These board members all looked very comfortable in their box seats, until the shareholder resolutions began being presented and their facial expressions turned icy.

The process is, to my surprise, very straightforward. Tillerson introduces the resolution's sponsor, and after the presentation, simply refers the audience to the page in the meeting's brochure that outlines the company's official opposition.

Things started out with Monks's resolution to permit shareholders to cumulatively allocate their votes for board members, so, if they chose, they could allocate all of their votes to one board member, rather than having to distribute them to all of them. He makes a compelling case for his resolution, as only someone who has dealt with the issue firsthand could. Just a few years ago, Monks used Sears, Roebuck's by-laws to stage a nearly successful run for the company's board—a move that so rattled Sears's management that executives budgeted $5.5 million to campaign against him, filed a lawsuit to deny him access to a list of shareholders that he needed to solicit votes from, and hiked the number of votes he would need to get elected by almost 50 percent.

After Monks's presentation, the resolutions became more personally targeted at Tillerson.

First came Denise Nappier, the Connecticut state treasurer, who has been working with Sister Pat for months and who has been plotting with our group of activists here in Dallas. She delivered a thundering speech for her resolution to separate the positions of CEO and board chairman in response to the board's refusal to even meet with her, despite the fact that she controls $300 million of ExxonMobil stock in her role overseeing her state's $25 billion public pension fund.

After her, it was on to a package of resolutions aimed at reining in Tillerson's salary. The most compelling of these was the one from Steve Viederman, the New York activist, that would allow a nonbinding annual shareholder vote to either approve or reject the CEO's salary package. This "say on pay" concept has been adopted by many other companies under shareholder resolution pressure, and may end up being forced on all companies by the federal government, since the House of Representatives in early 2007 passed a say-on-pay mandate by a two-to-one bipartisan majority. In fact, ExxonMobil's former CEO, Lee Raymond, has been Exhibit A in the broader debate over executive compensation, having given himself a $400 million retirement package at the same time the company was running an $11 billion deficit in its worker pension fund—the largest single pension gap for any corporation on record.

Up to this point, the presenters have followed what is a predetermined script that frames their initiatives as coming from those utterly thrilled to own a piece of the wonderful company ExxonMobil and interested only in increasing the company's bottom line for the long haul.

"What a joy it is to be an ExxonMobil shareholder!" Monks exclaimed before eviscerating the board. Nappier repeatedly referred to ExxonMobil as "our company" and stressed that her resolution is "critical to the long-term value of our shares."

"We are share owners, not shareholders, but share owners," Viederman said. "And we take that responsibility seriously." Even the most overtly political resolutions about CEO pay were presented as spurred by a desire to increase the company's profits.

"We believe the historically high executive compensation level of our company diminishes shareholder value," said a presenter from NorthStar Asset Management. Reducing the disparity between the company's lowest salary and highest, she said, "will increase shareholder value by strengthening employee morale."

Such a presentation method is the same used in the run-up to the shareholder meeting, when these activists are frantically trying to convince nonpolitical, all-we-care-about-is-the-bottom-line investors and investment advisers like ISS that their proposals are truly the fiduciary interest of the company.

The big problem for activists, however, is that executives and board members got where they are by being, first and foremost, master number crunchers/manipulators, meaning these financial arguments are exactly the kind they know how to win. And that's why Tillerson looks so nervous right at this moment—because Sister Pat is veering off the regular script into uncharted territory.

WHEN TILLERSON ANNOUNCED Sister Pat's name, the murmuring crowd was suddenly blanketed by an "oh shit" silence—the same you hear at a ballpark when the announcer lets fans know the visiting team is sending in the feared reliever to shut the game down. From the activists who revere her, to Exxon's board members who probably despise her, to the rank-and-file shareholders who have heard of her reputation, to Tillerson who no doubt worries about her Jack Welch–ing him, this audience knows Sister Pat is the Closer.

She started off her presentation as the happy shareholder making the case that her greenhouse gas resolution is motivated by a desire to fatten the bottom line. "We are all shareholders [because] we've seen the success" of the company, she began.

"But what will our long-term health be when we are really faced with regulatory and other challenges around global warming?" she asked.

Now, though, as Tillerson stands at the podium shifting his weight, Sister Pat is unexpectedly turning her business seminar speech into a church sermon.

"This company and every single one of us are challenged by one of the most profound moral concerns," she continues. "We all want to be able to tell the children in our lives, and have those children tell their grandchildren, that we were part of the solution [to global warming], not part of the real problem, that we really stood up to the plate and turned this around. And that's why we want to be able to have our company show us its business plan, and how we are responding to the true moral challenge."

For some in the audience like the two middle-aged Texans sitting next to me, Sister Pat's plea hasn't been working. In their navy sport coats and khakis, they look as if they came to this event straight from a Republican Party fundraiser, and every time a resolution comes forward, they mutter angrily under their breath. There was an "Oh Jesus Christ, not this again" from one when the CEO pay resolution came up, and as Sister Pat is speaking, I'm treated to a "What do they want us to do, stop driving cars? Gimme a friggin' break!"

But when Sister Pat concludes her speech with that high and tight fastball about morality and our kids and grandkids, the audience—for the first time today—delivers a resounding applause, setting the stage for the contentious "discussion" period.

In this part of the meeting, the activists' goals change from trying to sway management and the few wavering shareholders in the room, to trying to mold public opinion at large. The discussion is structured as a Q&A with the CEO, but to paraphrase Upton Sinclair, every activist here knows it is "difficult to get a man to understand something when his salary depends on his not understanding it." The real goal is to land headlines in the paper to shape next year's battles.

Tillerson is deflecting questions from the audience with very little problem, until he makes the mistake of calling on Andrew Logan, the young representative from Ceres, a Boston-based network of investors, environmental organizations, and other public interest groups that has been working with Sister Pat and other shareholder activists on the greenhouse gas resolution. In addressing Tillerson and expounding on the dangers of global warming, Logan is using the inclusive language of "we" as fellow shareholders. He concludes by asking the CEO, "Why has our company seemingly put so much effort into making itself into public enemy number one on climate change?"

The question is delivered rather politely—smart, considering it's a "When did you stop beating your wife?" query whose aggressiveness needs no additional *umph*. A good politician would know to give an answer that avoided playing into this kind of gotcha trick. But Tillerson walks right into the trap, showing himself to be way less Bill Clinton deftly answering a question about sex, and way more John Kerry bungling a question about Iraq.

"We never set out for the company to be public enemy number one," Tillerson says, hand-delivering a defensive sound-bite that will end up being the lead quote from the meeting in tomorrow's national newspapers.

But he's not done.

"There's much we know and can agree on around the climate change issue, and there's much that we just don't believe we do know," Tillerson continues, as Logan struggles to contain a grin. "And we want to have a debate about the things we know and understand, the things we know about that we don't understand very well, and the things we don't even know about around this very complex issue of climate science. So that is what will continue to be our position."

If the answer sounds vaguely familiar, that's because you've probably heard something like it before. Defense Secretary Donald Rumsfeld became a late-night comedy show punchline when, trying to evade questions about the Iraq War, he said, "There are known knowns," "known unknowns," and "also unknown unknowns."

Tillerson concludes his answer by veering off his financial script and regurgitating Sister Pat's language almost word for word—proof positive that she really did rattle him.

"It's vital we understand the [global warming] issue better so that we can make wiser decisions," he says. "These *are* life-changing decisions for our children and our grandchildren, and we think you ought to be careful about that."

As Tillerson continues to get more off balance, he starts flinging out more red meat to the greed-is-good crowd, which still makes up the vast majority of those in attendance.

For instance, responding to a question about why ExxonMobil is the only major oil company to invest no money in developing alternative or re-newable energy, Tillerson states flatly that "the world, like it or not, is going to have to continue to consume largely—and live off of—fossil fuels."

And he gets backup from at least some in attendance. "I would like to recommend to all these people that have been complaining about how you all run your business, that they sell their shares and go ahead and buy Shell or buy BP and go to their annual meeting," says one wrinkled, sixty-ish guy from Corpus Christie toward the end of the Q&A session. "Then you can sit there and complain to them about why can't you be performing like Exxon."

Tillerson smiles as some hoots and hollers of support echo through the auditorium. But looking over, I see Sister Pat is also smiling, and I get the feeling she knows the damage has already been done.

"SEE THAT BIG black building out there with no signs on it? That's ExxonMobil's headquarters," Sister Pat tells us as she accelerates through rush hour traffic on I-35 back to the Dallas/Fort Worth airport.

The hint of triumph in her voice is pretty well justified. The black low-rise structure on the horizon of Irving, Texas, may house the largest and most profitable company in the world, but there's no sign letting passers-by know it's ExxonMobil's building for many of the same reasons Sister Pat and her fellow activists were so successful today.

ExxonMobil may be the most powerful company on the globe, and its executives may be some of the richest people in human history, but its dis-dain for its own shareholders, disregard for its environmental critics, and apathy toward the consumers it relies on has made the company the poster boy for an oil industry that is now toxically unpopular and looked at with suspicion by stockholders, financial managers, politicians, and the general public at large. That's why, as cars hurtle past its headquarters guzzling its fuel, ExxonMobil prefers to hide in obscurity. It's also why, despite the shiny trinkets, free doughnuts, slick infomercials, and other uprising suppressants deployed at the meeting, the company's executives saw a small group of well-organized, underfinanced activists humiliate them today.

When ExxonMobil's Henry Hubble announced the results of the voting, gasps rippled throughout the auditorium.

Monks's resolution to democratize board election received 32 percent of all shareholders' votes. Nappier's resolution to strip Tillerson of his dual role as chairman and CEO received 40 percent, and Viederman's "say on pay" resolution grabbed 41 percent.

But it was Sister Pat's greenhouse gas resolution, which nabbed 31 percent of the vote, that was most astounding. Unlike the corporate governance and shareholder empowerment resolutions, the climate change initiative cut straight to the heart of ExxonMobil's entire petroleum-based profit engine. Getting almost one out of three shareholder votes to support such a directive is a major referendum on the growing discontent that these activists are stoking.

At the end of any big campaign, everyone usually gets to enjoy a full evening of intoxication—the winners to celebrate, the losers to forget—before heading off to the airport for the next gig. Unfortunately, the activists' party at a local vegetarian restaurant lasted just forty-five minutes—enough time for Sister Pat to peruse the early news coverage of the meeting on a laptop computer while enjoying what she says is a "traditional" postresolution Margarita.

The general news stories were just like the ones I had read before I'd met these activists—the ones that lead casual readers to think resolutions being voted down are big losses. The *Fort Worth Star-Telegram* calls the meeting "uncharacteristically low-key" and claims Tillerson's smooth presentation style "may be working [because] none of the 15 shareholder proposals seeking to change company policies was approved." Similarly, Agence

France Press, whose copy is distributed to general-interest newspapers across the globe, says, "ExxonMobil shareholders voted strongly against several measures that dissident investors proposed to reform the climate policies of world's largest oil company."

Sister Pat and the rest of the activists are nonetheless thrilled because the news stories all include Tillerson's defensive denials. And they will be even happier later on when they read stories in the business press, the best avenue to create market pressure for future dialogue.

The leading oil industry trade publication will write that "greenhouse gas emissions and climate change were a top concern at ExxonMobil's annual meeting May 30." Dow Jones's MarketWatch news ticker will blare the headline "Tillerson defends ExxonMobil's greenhouse gas policies," noting that at the meeting, activists forced the company to agree "that some steps need to be taken to address global warming." And another leading publication that covers regulatory affairs for investors will cite the Exxon-Mobil meeting as proof that "shareholder activists are winning record levels of support for resolutions that would force U.S. companies to take action on greenhouse gas emissions."

Trying to stuff my ExxonMobil goody bag into my briefcase as we drive into the airport complex, I hear a ring. Kert Davies, a Greenpeace operative from Philadelphia, puts a cell phone to his ear. He's been coordinating with the shareholders down here in Dallas and is riding shotgun in the car with Sister Pat.

It's Bloomberg Radio, Davies tells us, and they want an interview with him about what happened at the meeting, but they need quiet background noise. On cue, Sister Pat frantically turns the car into a parking garage and pulls over to a deserted corner, leaving the car running to keep the air conditioner on in the searing, early summer heat.

Davies does a masterful job staying on message, even as Sister Pat and Rembert keep whispering in his ear. "This sends a big message to Exxon-Mobil that it needs to address climate change and that it needs to listen to its shareholders," Davies says confidently.

But does it?

Our entire economy is based on fossil fuels, and therefore producing greenhouse fumes—including the idling car we're sitting in now, the garage-worth of other cars surrounding us, and the planes crowding this airport. The pessimist in me feels a wee bit skeptical of the declarations of victory.

Then again, the enormous size that makes multinational companies like ExxonMobil seem so immovable is precisely why these seemingly minute victories are actually huge. If you get a giant corporation with global reach to change even a tiny bit, you have made a global impact. If, like these activists did today, you force the company that has produced 5 percent of all the human-created carbon emissions in history to even vaguely acknowledge that global warming is occurring, you have potentially started changing the planet. And the stubborn confidence of the shareholder activists indicates they know how important it is to make such planetwide progress for the uprising.

Still, as Sister Pat and the others bid me farewell in the terminal and tell me some of them are going on to Delaware for the upcoming General Motors shareholder meeting, I want to ask them how they can keep doing this? Even with the success, shareholder activism is a grind, and it must, at times, feel like "a fight with a windmill," as Saul Alinsky said. How can they keep slogging to these meetings, month after month? How can they motivate themselves to go back and forth and back and forth with bureaucrats, executives, and CEOs, year after year, meeting after meeting?

But I stop short, knowing that they ask themselves only one real question: How can they not?

10

CHASING THE GHOSTS
OF CHICAGO

R EX TILLERSON HATES me. At least I like to hope he hates me.

When I returned home from Dallas, the first thing I did was download his syrupy voice off the digital tape recorder I had smuggled into the ExxonMobil shareholder meeting. I then uploaded a few choice clips onto YouTube, the online audio / video website where users can share their own content. And within a few days, thousands of viewers had seen the ExxonMobil CEO make an evasive, Rumsfeldian ass out of himself on the subject of global warming.

Viewers did not find the clip by accident. The rudimentary video I made was posted on blogs all over the Internet. I coordinated my own little viral marketing campaign through email and through my own website, and I was pretty proud of myself when YouTube's page view counter showed me how many thousands of people had viewed the clips. I felt empowered that little ol' me could, with just a bit of effort, stick it to the CEO of one of the largest corporations on the planet.

But I didn't feel satisfied. What had I really accomplished? So what if the clip was played thousands of times in a few days? Sure, it might embarrass Tillerson a little bit. But I hadn't really developed anything lasting out of it. So what the hell was the point?

Such are the deepest, darkest, meaning-of-life questions that plague the Netroots—the Internet-based, left-leaning grassroots activists whose second annual YearlyKos Convention is taking place here in the heat of the broiling Chicago summer in 2007.

The Netroots, which is an amalgam of the word "Internet" and "grassroots," has many vocal promoters within its ranks and by the looks of the national reporters filing in to cover this convention, it has attained a level of Establishment respect. But it still has an unauthorized feel about it, even here in the Windy City's sleek, lakeside McCormick Place Convention Center.

The setting for this 2007 YearlyKos is a substantial upgrade from last year's debut (or what I remember of it, through a haze of hangover and cigarette smoke). Unlike the Riviera Hotel—the windowless ashtray of the Las Vegas Strip that was last year's venue—this facility resembles the airy, supermodern Cloud City set from *The Empire Strikes Back.*

From the looks of the crowd in the lobby, the Netroots itself has changed right along with its new convention digs. The scene appears much less MTV and more C-SPAN than last year—fewer jeans and T-shirts, many more sport jackets and khaki pants, and even some ties.

In recent months, political reporters have been lashing out at the Netroots, more bitter than ever that the Internet has stripped journalists of their monopoly on news. If online activists aren't being berated by pundits as ideological zealots, they are being belittled by reporters as immature children who should have no place in American politics. Epitomizing the vitriol, NBC News anchor Brian Williams recently complained that his news team is now going "up against people who have an opinion, a modem, and a bathrobe," and that's supposedly not fair because he's spent "all of my life, developing credentials to cover my field of work, and now I'm up against a guy named Vinny in an efficiency apartment in the Bronx who hasn't left the efficiency apartment in two years."

The goal is to disparage online activists as a mishmash of pathetic fifty-somethings who still live in their parents' basements; stoned college radicals typing between bong hits; hippie-turned-yuppie peaceniks; conspiracy

theorists; single-issue zealots; and the rest of America's all-grown-up mal-
contents who avoided going Columbine and instead directed their teen
angst into high school science clubs.

And yet, whenever this group of supposed weaklings, pansies, and
misfits raises serious money for political candidates or plays a decisive role
in helping a primary challenger like Ned Lamont in Connecticut or Jon
Tester in Montana, the media leads us to believe the Netroots is also
an all-powerful reactionary mob—one led by bloodthirsty twenty-first-
century Robespierres roving the information superhighway with virtual
torches and pitchforks, and looking for the next turncoat to drag off to a
cyberspace guillotine.

In truth, the Netroots is just a bunch of regular people. Nothing more,
despite triumphalist bloggers' boasts to the contrary. But also nothing less,
despite reporters' insults.

The Netroots may be geeks, nerds, and former *Dungeons & Dragons*
players, but so are a lot of Americans. The Netroots may sometimes behave
like an angry fist-shaking mob out for vengeance, but now and then, so
does America.

The Netroots, in short, is just as pissed off as the rest of the country.
What makes this group unique is how its outrage is expressed via personal
computers and blogs rather than vented through other conduits like voting
for right-wing Republicans, organizing unions, building third parties, joining armed militias at the Mexican border, or just tuning out over beers and
Baywatch reruns.

The Netroots perplexes so many political and media veterans because
its rise has contradicted the guru fetish—the underlying assumption running through our pop culture that assumes every phenomenon in politics is
the work of a small group of godlike geniuses. From the idolization of Bill
Clinton's campaign manager James Carville to the worship of Bush strategist Karl Rove, we are led to believe that only with the Svengalis' help can
the Unwashed Massses help themselves. But no one guru explains or controls online activism.

In earlier times, you had to be in Washington, D.C., or subscribe to expensive newsletters to get the latest political buzz about what's *really* going on in politics. But because everyone with a computer and an Internet connection can post anything they want from anywhere in the world, and because anyone with the same capacity can download that material, the market for political information has been equalized. You want to know what's going on in a state legislature? Get on Google and find the local blog that covers it. You want to know what's going on in Congress? You'll find blogs and websites out there not just about Congress, but about specific issues and bills.

The same phenomenon applies to political engagement. To solicit the government in the past, you had to write a letter, buy an envelope and stamp, and mail it. To create a petition, you had to knock on doors to collect signatures. To express the voice of thousands of people collectively, you had to physically show up for a march. You had to, in other words, expend the kind of time and energy many people simply do not have at their disposal.

Today, by contrast, if you have an Internet connection, you can sit in your house and do most of those things with the click of a button—no stamps, clipboards, or picket signs necessary. You can send an email to your congressman, you can create a virtual petition via a website, and you can create a group blog to organize and express the voice of thousands of people. You are limited mainly by your persistence, skill, and salesmanship, and far less by your geography or even your financial resources.

The result of that kind of power is self-organized activism as epitomized by events like YearlyKos—an event that is the physical, nonvirtual representation of group blogs' communal architecture. This event is run entirely by a swarm of volunteer Internet activists, without the top-down control of any traditional authority.

The conference schedule in my hand summarizes the phenomenon better than anything. Lots of politicians and executive directors from Washington organizations are certainly slated to give speeches here this year. But the program is dominated by panels and plenary sessions moderated and populated by grassroots activists. Behind the funny-sounding screen names and blog titles, these are the regular folks—the true outsiders—who make up the real soul of the Netroots.

ALMOST FOUR DECADES ago, the 1968 Democratic National Convention took place just north of where the YearlyKos Convention is being held. That event at first seemed destined to be an emotional ratification of Robert F. Kennedy's presidential campaign and its message of economic justice. Kennedy told a cheering California crowd that he looked forward to the convention just moments before he was brutally assassinated in a rain of bullets foreshadowing the convention's billy-clubs-and-cracked-skulls violence that Ron the Minuteman warmly reminisced about.

Surveying the gray and balding heads milling inside the convention center, I bet some of the folks here have firsthand memories of the fiasco. And sure enough, on the second day of the YearlyKos convention, I see Tom Hayden.

Next to Abbie Hoffman, the silver-haired sixty-seven-year-old Hayden is the best known of the 1968 protest leaders who were arrested and then acquitted in the gripping Chicago Seven trial. Cofounder of the American Left's iconic Students for a Democratic Society, one of Jane Fonda's husbands, and a former California state senator, he is a giant in the annals of contemporary uprising history. But as he stands here in a T-shirt and shorts chatting with me about his ongoing work against the Iraq War and for universal health care, no one passing by recognizes him. Not a single person.

Hayden's relative anonymity here says a lot about how the Netroots phenomenon is very much about the here and now.

OpenLeft.com's Matt Stoller and Chris Bowers, two of the most devoted scholars of the Netroots' short history, have written that many of the new activists brought into politics via the Internet originally began their political engagement in reaction to the 1998 Clinton impeachment. The theory makes sense considering that is exactly the event that launched MoveOn.org, one of the Netroots' foundational institutions. Among online activists, events before that 1998 witchhunt—from Hayden's work protesting the Vietnam War, to the great twentieth-century labor struggles, to NAFTA, to the Reagan revolution—are thought of as prehistoric and largely irrelevant.

Because of this, and because the Internet came of age as a political instrument during the ultrapartisan Clinton and Bush years, the Netroots possesses little coherent ideology beyond Partisan War Syndrome's crude belief that politicians labeled "(D)" in the newspaper are automatically preferable to those labeled "(R)." Markos Moulitsas, the founder of Daily Kos, has said "I'm not ideological at all—I'm just all about winning."

But winning what? That is more difficult to answer, considering who makes up the Netroots.

The crowd here at YearlyKos perfectly reflects the findings of the Pew Research Center's 2006 study, which found the Netroots skews white and is a "population disproportionately weighted towards the young, the relatively well-educated and the well-to-do." Blogger Chris Bowers adds that the Netroots tends to be people in "the creative class"—basically those holding well-paying, professional desk jobs with time to surf the Net regularly. And his analysis describes a population that makes for an uneasy fit into the broader populist uprising.

"Multi-ethnic, post-Vietnam, highly educated, raised in a major urban center"—these are traits that Bowers says define many in the Netroots. Parroting that demographic's political outlook, he claims that "coming from a little town in Arkansas is not a story many Americans can relate to anymore, because we just didn't grow up that way."

Such a bourgeois viewpoint dictates where the Netroots focuses its attention. Though there is little quantifiable data, any perusal of the most-trafficked blogs like TalkingPointsMemo.com, the Huffington Post, and ThinkProgress.org and any survey of MoveOn's campaigns reveals that the Netroots shares the traditional media's disinterest in the broader uprising's populist economic focus on issues like inequality, taxes, wages, and trade, unless those issues serve an overtly partisan cause in the day's media cycle. Online activists certainly are not hostile to such populist causes, but the topics that dominate blogs, MoveOn emails, and Netroots activities generally tend toward more headline-grabbing issues like presidential abuses of power, foreign policy missteps, or Fox News embarrassments.

That said, the Netroots' bourgeois proclivities—at least for the moment—are being overshadowed by its hyperpartisanship.

Almost everyone here at the YearlyKos Convention is a staunch Democrat. And while many of the people here and throughout the Netroots aren't necessarily populist ideologues and may not really feel comfortable with class-based campaigns, many of them are sympathetic to the uprising because they see it as a means to an end in the media-manufactured red-versus-blue world of American politics. As Senator Bernie Sanders said to me just before I left his office a few months ago, today's "definition of 'progressive' is anyone who rips apart the other side"—and, at least at this moment, the most effective way to "rip apart the other side" is to champion the uprising.

This is one of the reasons why Ned Lamont's primary run against Connecticut senator Joe Lieberman became central to the Netroots' identity—so important, in fact, that I see there is a whole session at the conference entitled "Ned Lamont for Senate: What Really Happened." Lieberman's worst offense in the eyes of this community was not his vote for the war—many other Democratic senators did the same and didn't face a Netroots-backed primary. His true crime was appearing throughout the media defending the Iraq invasion, berating the antiwar uprising, and therefore providing political cover to President Bush and Republican congressional candidates in the lead-up to the 2006 elections. To online activists, who raised funds and provided on-the-ground volunteer support to Lamont, the Connecticut primary campaign was not just an antiwar crusade. It was also a partisan battle to stop Lieberman from politically emboldening Republicans and polluting the Democratic Party brand with the taint of an unpopular foreign policy—and Lamont's primary success reaffirmed the Netroots' belief that antiwar populism makes for winning politics.

That conviction obviously benefits the uprising, and it is changing the incentives that determine politicians' votes and behavior. In years past, the system encouraged candidates to stay away from populist uprisings for fear of alienating the corporate interests that make big-dollar campaign donations. But a counterweight now exists. While corporate money still skews the system, more politicians now pay homage to the uprising as a way to ingratiate themselves with online activists, as the Netroots is brandishing significant fund-raising, publicity, and grassroots resources.

In 2004, Howard Dean almost nabbed the Democratic presidential nomination thanks to online organizing and the more than $20 million he raised through the Internet. Eventual nominee John Kerry raised a stunning $82 million online. In 2006, ActBlue, an online political action committee that bundles small-dollar online contributions, raised more than $17 million for key congressional races that flipped control of Congress to the Democrats.

But the Netroots is becoming more than just an ATM machine and media criticism soapbox whose effectiveness is limited to campaign contributions, page hits, and YouTube views. Online activists are starting to use the Internet for offline organizing.

In 2006, for instance, MoveOn created a phone calling program, whereby its members could log on to a website, download a list of voters in key congressional districts, their phone numbers, and a get-out-the-vote script. Volunteers ended up making 7 million calls, boosting turnout by about 4 percent among the voters it contacted, according to MoveOn's political director, Adam Ruben.

Similarly, Ned Lamont's Senate campaign designed a system it called the Family, Friends and Neighbors program. Those visiting the campaign website could click a link to look up the address of their friends and family in Connecticut and type in a personal message to them. The campaign then snail-mailed those personalized messages to recipients on the back of pro-Lamont postcards. The system generated more than 100,000 postcards and simultaneously built the campaign's get-out-the-vote list from scratch.

Pundits, of course, continue to call the Netroots a group of left-wing ideologues. Commentator Stu Rothenberg, the most practiced spewer of conventional wisdom in Washington (and that's saying a lot), recently hyperventilated that the Netroots is "measuring Capitol Hill behavior against a standard of ideological purity."

Yet online activists are not motivated by a doctrinaire attitude supposedly proven toxic by the McGovern Fable. The Netroots is not composed of ideologically zealous activists unconcerned with the potentially negative political ramifications of its advocacy. From what I've seen, it is the opposite: Netroots activists see ideology as the most pragmatic battering ram to crush partisan opponents and achieve partisan goals. Put another way, the populist uprising and the Netroots are—at least for now—benefiting from a marriage of convenience.

JUST OFF THE main convention hall is a slightly smaller room with lines of tables where organizations have set up displays. It is a Netroots flea market of sorts. Just take your pick—over there, buy a book deriding Fox News; over here, pick up a pin from Drinking Liberally, the group that organizes blogger happy hours at bars in cities across the country.

Walking among the tables, I realize the difficulty in trying to characterize the Netroots as a monolith.

Tens of millions of Americans are now using the Internet, and especially for political information. In 2006, the Pew Internet & American Life Project found that "on a typical day in August, 26 million Americans were using the Internet for news or information about politics." By mid-2007, *BusinessWeek* reported that there are 15.5 million active blogs.

So while the Netroots' left-leaning outlook puts Democratic politics first and sees uprising ideology mostly as a means of reaching partisan ends against a Republican White House, trying to generalize further about such a huge political frontier like this is nearly impossible.

The epiphany I come to after two days at YearlyKos is that the undefined nebulousness of the Internet is perhaps the whole point and the whole genius of it all.

Drifting from a panel entitled "Progressive Infrastructure" to a roundtable discussion on "New Innovations in the States" to a full-on, blogger-run Democratic presidential debate that ends up focusing on the corrosive influence of corporate money in politics, I start to believe that maybe on-line activism is actually the means to be used by the uprising, rather than the other way around. Without a cohesive ideology or even a singular goal beyond helping Democrats win elections, the Netroots is unlike anything else I have explored this year. The Internet is not its own outpost of the uprising. But the Netroots could turn the Internet into the connective tissue that ties all of the outposts to each other—the electronic version of the underground newspaper that has glued past uprisings together.

"I'm bill," he says greeting me like we are old friends.

I am standing in a hallway, getting ready to pack up and leave the McCormick Center for my flight home, and I have no idea who this guy standing in front of me is, though I have gotten used to this at the convention. Here, you finally meet the people you know only online by screen names and writing styles.

My face is blank.

"You know, Bill In Portland Maine," he says, holding up the laminated YearlyKos badge that is hanging around his neck and that indeed says "Bill In Portland Maine."

That moment you first meet someone whose blog posts you have been reading for a while is always a strange one. Your mental image of the person collides with the actual person standing in front of you. When I read Bill's regular postings at Daily Kos, I had unconsciously imagined him to look like a heavyset longshoreman. The real Bill In Portland Maine is frenetic, young, short, and spindly. He's wearing jeans and an open flannel shirt. I tell him I read his stuff on Daily Kos. He asks me about an article I had written a few months ago.

After we part, I walk out onto the street to catch a ride to the airport for my flight home. From the passenger seat in the cab, I look south down the lake thinking of the ghosts that haunt the horizon where one of history's great uprisings started. There in the stockyards and among the meat-packing plants, anger was first stoked into an uprising by muckraking journalists like Upton Sinclair and then organized into a multiethnic movement by Saul Alinsky and his renowned Back of the Yards Neighborhood Council.

From that experience, Alinsky learned why the everyday organizers—as opposed to self-centered leaders and gurus—are the real catalyst for uprisings.

Leaders, he said, "build power to fulfill desires, to hold and wield the power for purposes both social and personal." On the other hand, an organizer "finds his goal in creation of power for others to use," and to make that happen, organizers have to let people "play an active role in solving their own crises."

The Netroots' grounding in that democratic spirit Alinsky wrote about and the Internet's growing utility as an organizing tool is why YearlyKos and the Internet are so important to the uprising.

Out of all the political instruments that I have seen in my travels, none is more accessible than the Internet. Fire up a computer, write a call to action, post it to a website, and anyone can be Bill In Portland Maine—anyone can have a megaphone, and, better yet, anyone can start organizing on their own.

The cab speeds away from McCormick Place on Chicago's Stevenson Expressway, which heads southwest through the Back of the Yards neighborhood where Alinsky first got his start. Passing the aging apartment buildings and bungalows, I pull out the dog-eared copy of *Rules for Radicals* that I keep in my bag.

I flip it open to a random page, wafting that smell of aging, yellowed paper. And right there is an underlined sentence blaring Alinsky's most sacred principle of all:

A belief that if people have the power to act in the long run, they will, most of the time, reach the right decisions.

The belief that people—not dictators, not elites, not a group of gurus—should be empowered to organize and decide their destiny for themselves seems so simple, and yet is far and away the most radical idea in human history.

Putting that principle into action requires genuine courage and self-lessness, because participants in the uprising must make their own personal power (money, clout, notoriety, glory) a lower priority than popular control. Some Netroots institutions are more ready to wholeheartedly embrace this radical democracy than others.

Take MoveOn.org. *Rolling Stone* has described its leaders as possessing a "deep passion for populist democracy," and in interviews, the organization bills itself as a "direct democracy." But while it has recently launched an "Operation Democracy" tool, MoveOn still primarily makes top-down decisions. The organization certainly polls its members for their opinions, which is more democracy than most political organizations allow. But the choices offered in these polls are narrow, and the results are nonbinding.

More significantly, MoveOn sends its email out to the masses from a central command center run by a few people, rather than expanding tools to help its members communicate with each other. Additionally, the organization and its leaders have not submitted themselves to real popular control—MoveOn leaders are appointed without any popular input whatsoever. This model certainly helps MoveOn's top brass define the organization's messages and brand precisely as they see fit. But it is a structure that suggests MoveOn's leaders may not totally subscribe to Alinsky's beliefs, and that they rather believe that perhaps people shouldn't have the full power to act because they might not reach the right decision.

The Netroots really ensures that "people have the power to act" through online tools provided by groups like Democracy for America (DFA), the advocacy organization that sprouted out of the ashes of Howard Dean's transformative presidential candidacy. Through its DFA-Link program, any DFA member can build his or her own email list of other members and communicate directly with them, rather than relying on an intermediary. The system is being replicated on the state level. Colorado's ProgressNow.org, for example, provides web, blogging, and email tools for its users to self-organize and promote the causes they—not any central office—choose.

Then there is the Oregon Bus Project, the youth-oriented advocacy and get-out-the-vote group that relies on the Internet to communicate with its members. Every other year, Bus Project leaders ask its membership to attend a caucus to vote on what issues the organization should focus its resources on. The number of votes for members at this caucus is related not to how much money they contribute or how well known they are in the media, but to how much volunteer time they commit to donating to Bus Project causes in the coming year.

The same grassroots spirit was present at the YearlyKos Convention here in Chicago. Entirely funded, organized, and staffed by volunteers, its organizers took an "active role in solving their own crises." It is a spirit that is lacking in much of the rest of the uprising.

Indeed, from the antiwar Protest Industry to The Players to the Minutemen to the shareholder activists to *Lou Dobbs Tonight,* many uprising vehicles deny the people "a significant part in the action," to quote an Alinsky refrain. The vehicles either refuse to subject themselves to popular control or simply are not structured to allow it. Even the Working Families Party and the other more democratic outposts of the uprising like the WashTech union are somewhat insulated from true popular control and participation, whether by money, bureaucracy, election rules, or some combination of the three.

"Denial of the opportunity for participation is the denial of human dignity and democracy," Alinsky wrote.

The line in the book is slightly smudged on the page in front of me. The ink may be fading, but the words are as poignant a call for uprisings to embody true democracy as they were a quarter century ago when Alinsky first wrote them.

BETWEEN ALL THE interviews and the travel that has marked my yearlong tour, airport wireless networks have kept me connected to the uprising through email. The Internet's connective tissue at work, I guess.

Clicking around on my laptop while waiting for my flight here in Chicago's Midway Airport, I see these have indeed been busy weeks on the front lines.

First up is an email from the Working Families Party's executive director Dan Cantor. He tells me that the party quietly inserted language into a mundane elections bill in the Connecticut legislature that will now make fusion voting much easier in that state. I see the WFP also managed to beat back a bill in the Delaware legislature designed to outlaw fusion. These are significant accomplishments that could have lasting effects in two states that domicile and therefore regulate many multinational corporations.

Not a bad month, I start writing in a reply to Cantor, but then I check to see what's going on with the WFP in New York itself.

A Google News alert tells me that New York governor Eliot Spitzer—the WFP's sometime-ally who described himself as a "fucking steamroller"—has flattened himself and his administration. In their quest to end Albany's Three Men in a Room dictatorship, Spitzer's political aides allegedly compiled reports on Republican Senate Majority Leader Joe Bruno's use of state aircraft in a dirty-tricks scheme to plant negative newspaper articles about him. Now, in a story today headlined "DA Steamrolls Spitz," the New York *Daily News* reports that none other than Albany prosecutor David Soares—the WFP's original champion—is leading a criminal investigation into the matter. Amid the pandemonium, the distracted New York legislature scuttled WFP legislation to force businesses to give workers paid leave for family emergencies.

Back in Montana, the news is better. A friend emails to let me know that Governor Brian Schweitzer's administration is gearing up to mail out Democrats' chicken-in-every-pot property tax rebates. The antitax movement is so demoralized that Republicans are struggling to recruit a candidate to run against Schweitzer in the upcoming election.

Missing Big Sky Country, I can't resist the urge to click over to the Montana blog Left in the West just to see what's going on there. Scrolling through the diary entries, I see that Montana senator Jon Tester gave an impassioned speech at the state capitol in Helena declaring his support for legislation deauthorizing the Iraq War, but, according to an excerpt from the *Missoula Independent*, "he stopped short of calling for an immediate troop withdrawal or cutting off funding for the war." The noncommittal position, which is the stance of most of Tester's colleagues, is a disheartening symptom of the antiwar uprising's bigger meltdown.

Americans Against Escalation in Iraq (AAEI) and The Players in Washington have spent the summer berating Republicans in television ads and grasstop campaigns around the country. They're still going easy on wavering Democrats, as if Democrats don't already have the constitutional powers of the purse to bring the madness to an end. When Congress reconvenes in a few weeks, it will be more of the same. MoveOn will spend an eye-popping $65,000 on a single full-page *New York Times* ad—a huge expenditure that ineptly attacks Bush crony General David Petraeus with the clunky play on words "General Betray Us."

In the ultimate sign of how much of a joke both parties think the antiwar uprising has become, the House and Senate—including the majority of Democrats—will pass resolutions condemning MoveOn for the ad. A few months after that, John Bruhns, an Iraq vet who had been a key spokesman for AAEI (Americans Against Escalation in Iraq), will pen a scathing op-ed finally bringing all the conflicts of interest undermining the antiwar uprising out into the open. Deriding The Players as "anti-war phonies," he says "the war is used by [antiwar] organizations as ammunition against political foes" in a purely partisan campaign "just as bad as those who fight for a continuation of the war." Bruhns' op-ed comes the same week the *Washington Post* reports that AAEI's head, Tom Matzzie, will take a new job to run the Democratic Party's official presidential "money machine that will rival or eclipse what they created in 2004." The story confirms that The Players are no longer even bothering to pretend they ever saw a difference between antiwar objectives and Democratic Party loyalty. By the end of 2007, Harris Interactive will report that MoveOn is the least trusted advocacy organizations out of any surveyed in its nationwide poll.

The next email I get is from an acquaintance in the labor movement, forwarding me a recent newspaper article about accelerated job outsourcing to Latin America. The piece quotes WashTech's Marcus Courtney saying that continued congressional initiatives to pass more lobbyist-written trade deals will exacerbate tech workers' plight here at home.

At least WashTech has found a few high-profile political allies. One is their old friend Bernie Sanders. He has been spending his time in the Senate pushing a bill to prohibit companies that have announced mass layoffs from receiving any new H1-B visas. At the same time, Ohio senator Sherrod Brown is leading the charge against the package of new NAFTAs proposed for Colombia, Panama, Peru, and South Korea. If some of the rhetoric coming out of Iowa and New Hampshire of late is any clue, these efforts may find moral support even from some top Republicans.

In a sign of just how bipartisan the uprising is becoming, GOP presidential candidate Mike Huckabee told an Iowa audience recently: "If somebody in the presidency doesn't begin to understand that we can't have free trade if it's not fair trade, we're going to continually see people who have worked for twenty and thirty years for companies one day walk in and get the pink slip and told, 'I'm sorry, but everything you spent your life working for is no longer here.' . . . I'd like to prove that this presidency is not going to be just up for sale."

This kind of language has become commonplace of late, and has metastasized into something much more negative when it comes to Bush's controversial immigration reform bill. Though backed by a huge amount of corporate cash, it died on the Senate floor after a furious groundswell of opposition from groups like the Minutemen was amplified by conservative talk radio and the likes of Lou Dobbs, just as tensions at the border reached a boiling point.

Weeks after my visit to the Minutemen, a video was leaked onto YouTube showing a U.S. Border Patrol shooting and killing a twenty-year-old Mexican man who appeared to be trying to enter the United States illegally. Now as I click a link on a blog about immigration, I see the *Washington Times* website has an article saying that MS-13—the Latin American gang and drug cartel that so many of the Minutemen fear—is "unifying its violent members across the U.S.," according to an army intelligence presentation. The next day, the leader of a renegade Minuteman group emailed around YouTube video footage that appears to show an American vigilante sniper gunning down a Mexican at the border.

The last email I get is a press release from the Interfaith Center on Corporate Responsibility—the group that works with Sister Pat Daly on shareholder resolutions. This week the organization has been warning of a stealth government plot to legally bar shareholder activists from filing resolutions in the future. And sure enough, when I click onto the *Washington Post*'s business section, I find a story detailing a corporate-backed move by the Securities and Exchange Commission to do just this. The story specifically notes that the SEC's move could limit resolutions submitted by clergy and environmental groups demanding "action on such issues as reducing greenhouse gases." The effort is an obvious reaction to the uprising's success.

Exhausted, hungry, and with some time before my plane leaves, I turn the computer off and head over to the nearest restaurant I can find. When I sit down and open the menu, I see a picture of Harry Caray, another ghost of Chicago's past. The restaurant is named after the late broadcaster who was the jovial voice of the Cubs—the team that, much like the Philadelphia Phillies and the Boston Red Sox, has spent most of its existence as a cultural synonym for underdog.

The Cubs haven't won the World Series since October of 1908—a year Teddy Roosevelt was trust-busting in the White House, Upton Sinclair was muckraking, and the progressive movement was gaining momentum in its push for many of the consumer protection and workplace safety laws we now take for granted.

It was the year an Alabama coal mine played host to one of America's first major interracial labor strikes, and 15,000 female textile workers marched for voting rights, better pay, and an end to child labor in New York City's Bread and Roses protest.

That October, firebrand William Jennings Bryan was again the Democratic presidential standard-bearer, while populist Eugene V. Debs, who would soon be imprisoned under the Espionage Act for speaking out against World War I, was running a third-party presidential campaign on a 15,000-mile whistlestop train tour financed by thousands of small-dollar contributors. Just a few short months later, the National Association for the

Advancement of Colored People would be created, and one Saul David Alinsky would be born.

It was a milestone period in uprising history—one launching movements that shaped a century.

I sit back, take a deep breath, and rub my eyes. I hear feet shuffling in all different directions over the din of loudspeakers. The airport terminal is as chaotic as the new uprising I just surveyed through my laptop.

The activism and energy frothing today is disconnected and atomized. The only commonality in it all is rage.

The odds against converting that rage into a true populist movement are daunting, but the possibilities inspire that same anxious giddiness some of the passengers around me are feeling in the pit of their stomach right at this moment. As they prepare to board a plane to an exotic destination they have never before visited, they imagine the adventure in front of them.

I try to do the same right here in this restaurant with my eyes still closed.

I envision an organization with the vast membership and Internet savvy of a MoveOn that uses fusion voting to develop its own independent political machine like the Working Families Party, rather than playing Washington games in the media.

I think of a union like WashTech joining with shareholder activists and bloggers in a broad-based public campaign of direct action to fundamentally change business's most destructive practices—a campaign that doesn't rely on political intermediaries or on just a handful of powerful institutional investors, but instead leverages the holdings of millions of everyday individuals who now collectively own huge chunks of Corporate America in their 401(k) plans.

I picture state legislators in places like Montana exporting their successful fight against conservatives' dying antitax movement and pioneering a new politics—one that takes the anger of the Minutemen demographic and diverts it into a class-unifying economic agenda and away from class-dividing xenophobia.

I wonder: Are these visions of what can be? Or are they merely apparitions like those that haunt Chicago?

I hear the sound of a glass being put on the table and open my eyes to see the beer I ordered. I take a sip and glance over at a grimy newspaper someone left on the other side of the table. It is opened to the sports page, and when a headline drifts into view, I do a double take, grabbing the tabloid in a clenched fist and bringing it close to my face. If I'm reading the standings correctly, it looks like all the renowned underdogs are doing well. In fact, the Phillies, the Red Sox, and even the Cubs have a fighting chance to make the playoffs.

Maybe this is the uprising's moment after all.

notes

1: A Portrait of the Writer on a Bathroom Floor

6   **never before seen by the country's major polling firms:** Jeffrey Jones, Gallup Poll, "Congress Approval Rating Matches Historical Low," 8/21/07; Peter Baker, *Washington Post,* "Disfavor for Bush Hits Rare Heights," 7/25/07.

6   **"personally are more angry":** Thomas Hargrove and Guido Stempel, Scripps Howard News Service, "Was 9/11 an Inside Job?" 8/3/06.

8   **"left-populists and right-populists":** Ross Douthat, *Atlantic* blog, "Left-Populism or Something Like It," 9/3/07.

8   **throw him in prison:** Jim Lehrer, Online NewsHour, "The Origins of Labor Day," 9/2/01.

9   **"too responsive to public opinion":** David S. Broder, *Washington Post,* "A Mob-Rule Moment," 7/5/07.

9   **"it doesn't matter":** Ed O'Keefe, ABCNews.com, "Cheney: 'Full Speed Ahead' on Iraq," 11/3/06.

9   **"be overreacting to public opinion polls":** Jonathan Weisman and Shailagh Murray, *Washington Post,* "As Iraq Exit Plan Arrives, Democrats' Rift Remains," 3/8/07.

9   **"Kabuki dance":** Kate Zernike, *New York Times,* "Pelosi's Ascendancy in House Puts a Close Liberal Ally in the Spotlight," 11/25/06.

9   **"militate for more friction and fat everywhere":** Thomas Friedman, *The World Is Flat: A Brief History of the Twenty-first Century,* Farrar, Straus and Giroux, 2006, p. 258.

2: The Thrilla in Montana

12   **"job is to show no quarter to the Democrats":** Jennifer McKee and Mike Dennison, *Helena Independent Record,* "Covering the Caucus: Dems, GOP Pick Party Leaders," 11/28/06.

12 **"it's a war"**: Gwen Florio, *Great Falls Tribune*, "Keenan Hired as Advisor to House Speaker Sales," 12/30/06.

12 **"foaming-at-the-mouth Pomeranian"**: George Ochenski, *Missoula Independent*, "Ready for Battle State Republicans Declare War on Dems," 11/30/06.

13 **residue found in Holocaust gas chambers:** Ryan Parry, *Mirror* (UK), "Hitler Is Our Hero: 13-Year-Old Twins Whose Songs Inspire US Nazis," 10/29/05.

15 **"would get nothing"**: Jennifer McKee, *Montana Standard*, "Property Taxes Seen as Battle," 12/31/06.

16 **"right into their general fund in Fort Worth"**: Jennifer McKee, *Billings Gazette*, "Property Taxes Seen as Battle," 1/1/07.

17 **"I had to come down and represent them"**: Montana Senate Taxation Committee Hearing, 1/9/07; testimony from Kirk Hammerquist starts at 6:40 in audiotapes.

18 **"much more generous deduction"**: Gwen Florio, *Great Falls Tribune*, "Parties Split in Committee Session on Property Tax Cut," 2/2/07.

18 **defeat millionaire Jack McMullen:** Bill Delaney, CNN.com/All Politics, "Fred Tuttle: One Candidate Hoping to Lose This December," 10/22/98.

20 **invested in the company's stock:** CBS *60 Minutes*, "Who Killed Montana Power?" 8/10/03.

21 **digging up vermiculite:** Associated Press, "Burns: Asbestos Bill Not Dead, but Wounded," 2/15/06; *Washington Post*, "The Road to Riches Is Called K Street," 6/22/05.

21 **raw agricultural exports:** National Association of Manufacturers, "Facts About Montana Manufacturing," 10/07.

21 **Rockefellers used militiamen and machine guns:** PBS's *The American Experience*, "The Rockefellers: The Ludlow Massacre."

22 **Bush won ninety-seven of the nation's one hundred fastest-growing counties:** Michael DuHaime, "It's Not Where We Stand," Republican National Committee.

23 **"driving force behind modern populism"**: Paul Taylor, *Washington Post*, "American Politics' New Villain: Big Business," 2/1/87.

24 **"very high on social programs"**: Dirk Johnson, *New York Times*, "The Race for Congress: Republicans Set Sights on Montana, a Democratic Bastion," 10/22/88.

24 **a tax raiser:** *Oregonian*, "U.S. Senate: The Class of '89," 10/10/88.

24 **"between the conservationists and timber, mining and energy industries"**: Christopher Thorne, Associated Press, "Melcher Still on Capitol Hill, Talking About Farmers, Food and Animals," 3/7/02.

24 **Republicans had gained control of the state legislature and the governor's office**: Bob Anez, Associated Press, "Democrats Appear to Have at Least Tied with GOP in Senate," 12/3/04.

25 **affectionately called "The Life of Brian"**: *Missoula Independent*, "The Life of Brian," 10/19/00.

25 **mint farm from scratch in northwest Montana**: *National Journal's Almanac of American Politics*, 7/22/05.

27 **"engage in a crusade to politically destroy him"**: Mike Keefe-Feldman, *Missoula Independent*, "The Watchdog: Bigfork Sen. Bob Keenan on the Warpath," 02/24/05.

27 **clean it up and bill them for the work**: Jennifer McKee, *Billings Gazette*, "State to Fix Livingston Site, Then Bill BNSF," 3/17/06.

29 **"start from where the world is, as it is, not as [they] would like it to be"**: Saul Alinsky, *Rules for Radicals*, 1971.

32 **"a political unknown"**: Associated Press, "Political Newcomer Holds Sway as House Speaker," 01/14/07.

32 **remove provisions in state law that make Ku Klux Klan cross burning a hate crime**: Human Rights Network News, "Margins to the Mainstream: Right-Wing Conservatives Score a Few Wins," 2/07.

32 **never even headed a legislative committee**: Jennifer McKee, *Billings Gazette*, "New State House Speaker Outspoken," 1/5/07.

32 **crushing dissent from moderate Republicans**: Matt Gouras, Associated Press, "Legislative Leaders Picked with Control of House Still Unknown," 11/28/06.

32 **semiretired computer-salesman-turned-gentleman-farmer**: Associated Press, *Billings Gazette*, Political Newcomer Holds Sway as House Speaker," 1/14/07.

32 **first third-party legislator elected to the Montana legislature in almost eighty years**: Bob Anez, *Helena Independent Record*, "House Remains in GOP Control, Two Votes Separate Candidates," 11/9/04.

32 **Jore proudly says his beliefs are a form of "fundamentalism"**: Charles S. Johnson, *Missoulian*, "For Rick Jore, It's the Constitution Above All Else," 1/25/99.

32 **one of the founders of Project 7:** Montana Human Rights Network, "The Radical Right Wing's Collision with Mainstream Politics," 2006.

32 **"foment an anti-government revolution":** Reuters, "Montana Militia Busted," 3/1/02.

32 **"liberal socialists [who] have forfeited liberty and justice":** Montana Human Rights Network, 9/97.

33 **from $3 billion to $300:** Charles S. Johnson, *Helena Independent Record,* 2/18/07.

33 **ExxonMobil $300,000:** Gwen Florio, *Great Falls Tribune,* "Property Tax Relief Advances," 2/27/07.

34 **a quarter of the state's economy:** Evelyn Pyburn, *Big Sky Business Journal,* "Shadow Economy Keeps Business off the Books," 7/17/07.

35 **Of course not, he tells me:** Jackson ended up voting against HB 833, 4/18/07; Charles S. Johnson, *Helena Independent Record,* "Dems Win Tax Brawl in Senate," 04/18/07.

36 **aimed at out-of-state corporations and wealthy landowners:** Charles S. Johnson and Mike Dennison, *Montana Standard,* "No Budget Deal in Sight," 4/27/07.

43 **2,000-square-mile plot of land:** Michael Jamison, *Missoulian,* "Plum Creeks Steps Up Public Relations," 6/11/07 (1.3 million acres is over 2,000 square miles).

43 **bought mills to spin off a new timber business:** Michael Jamison, Missoulian.com, "Railroad Grant Paved Way for Huge Land Holdings," 2/4/07.

43 **tax-free dividends for its primarily out-of-state owners:** Mea Andrews, *Missoulian,* "Timber in Transition: Legislation Aims to Close Tax Loopholes," 2/7/07.

44 **"That is very disconcerting to business":** Montana Senate Committee hearing on SB3, 5/10/07 (Ricklefs's testimony is at 3:12 in the audio file).

46 **"ranked eighth best in the nation by the Tax Foundation":** Chris Atkins and Curtis S. Dubay, Tax Foundation, "State Business Tax Climate Index," 10/11/06.

47 **"The governor got everything he wanted and then some":** Matt Gouras, *Havre Daily News,* "Governor Got What He Wanted—But at What Cost?" 5/21/07.

48 **"the conservative mainstream in the Republican Party [will not] lie down to that":** Ibid.

48 **Democrats sweep local elections in Ravalli County:** Michael Moore, *Missoulian,* "Democrats, Independent Win Seats on Commission," 6/6/07.

48 **"liberal tree huggers":** Michael Moore, *Missoulian,* "Recent Elections Signal New Day in Ravalli County," 6/11/07.

48 **"a little lazy":** Charles Johnson, *Billings Gazette,* "State GOP Begins Its Repair Job," 6/17/07.

49 **56 percent disapprove of his tax policies:** *Newsweek* poll, 5/11/06.

49 **"The only Grover they know in Indiana is the fuzzy creature on *Sesame Street*":** Mitch Daniels, *Indianapolis Star,* "How to Fix Indiana's Busted Budget," 2/20/05.

49 **"taken out and horsewhipped":** *Columbus Dispatch,* "Critic Urges That 'Idiot' Taft Be 'Horsewhipped,'" 9/18/04.

49 **"he can get his residency requirements lined up":** Jennifer Harper, *Washington Times,* 3/1/05.

49 **"specific programs such as schools, roads and mental health":** Daniel Frank and A. G. Newmyer III, *Washington Monthly,* "Is Grover Over?" 3/05.

50 **much-needed transportation improvements:** Gregory Hahn, *Idaho Statesman,* "Otter Grows into Role as Governor," 7/5/07.

50 **64 percent of Montanans approve of the way Schweitzer is doing his job:** Charles S. Johnson, *Helena Independent Record,* "Schweitzer, Rehberg, Baucus Enjoy Good Ratings," 7/2/07.

51 **Republican voters back Schweitzer's rebate over the GOP legislators' plan:** Charles S. Johnson, *Billings Gazette,* "Voters Don't Like Legislature— But Favor Big Decisions," 7/1/07.

3: What Kind of Hardball Can Stop a War?

52 **burning through almost a quarter billion dollars a day:** Martin Wolk, MSNBC, "Cost of Iraq War Could Surpass $1 Trillion," 3/17/06.

53 **"think they know where it leads":** Matt Stoller, MyDD.com, "Ending the National Security State," 3/23/07.

53 **100,000 people out here in front of the U.S. Capitol:** Adam Schreck, Ashraf Khalil, and David Streitfeld, *Los Angeles Times,* "Thousands Join Bicoastal War Protest," 1/28/07.

54 **almost two-thirds of the protestors said they had no party affiliation or were members of a third party:** Scott McLemee, *Inside Higher Ed,* "Party in the Streets," 3/21/07.

56 **"turned a moderate movement into a full-scale revolution for change"**: PBS's *History Detectives,* "Feature—The March of 1913."

56 **bayonet and teargas the protestors, leaving scores dead and injured:** PBS documentary, "The March of the Bonus Army," 5/29/06.

57 **600,000 people rallied in Washington against the Vietnam War in 1969:** John Steinman, Bloomberg.com, "Washington Girds for War Protesters, Civil Resistance," 9/22/05.

59 **from a referendum on the war into a referendum on the antiwar movement itself:** Michelle Goldberg, Salon.com, "The Antiwar Movement Prepares to Escalate," 3/14/03.

61 **antiwar protests in the districts of pro-war Republican lawmakers:** Carl Hulse, *New York Times,* "Congress Not Expected to Vote on Iraq Policy Before Recess," 8/1/07.

61 **"make a splash in the media":** Elana Schor, *The Hill,* "Antiwar Group on March with Old-School Tactics, Online Savvy," 8/3/07.

62 **one-tenth of 1 percent of the whole country:** Media Matters for America reports that *Hardball* gets about 302,000 viewers a night. By contrast, the Census Bureau reports that the population of Bakersfield, California, is roughly 308,000, and the total national population is roughly 300 million.

64 **polls originally showed was ambivalent about supporting the unilateral invasion:** Weeks before the invasion of Iraq, polls reported that large segments of the public opposed the invasion. For example, *Newsweek*'s 3/9/03 poll showed that 43 percent of Americans said "removing Saddam Hussein from power is not worth the potential loss of American life and the other costs of attacking Iraq." CBS News's 3/5/03 poll showed 44 percent of Americans believing that "the Bush Administration has not presented enough evidence to show that military action against Iraq is necessary right now," and 60 percent of Americans saying "the United States [should] wait and give the United Nations and weapons inspectors more time." CNN's 2/26/03 poll found 59 percent of Americans either fully opposed an invasion, or would only support one with explicit United Nations approval.

64 **"ever since 2002":** Joe Klein, CNBC, 2/22/03; Joe Klein, Time blog post, "Now That I Have Your Attention," 1/8/07.

65 **"turn that public opinion into actual, legally binding policy":** Chris Bowers, MyDD.com, "Public Opinion and Political Power on Iraq," 5/22/07.

65 **"when an election year rolls around":** Chris Cillizza, *Washington Post,* "Tooting Democrats Horn," 7/19/07.

66 **staffers for the Democratic Senatorial Campaign Committee:** According to the Hildebrand Tewes website, Steve Hildebrand was the "Political Director at the DSCC in 97/98"; Paul Tewes "was the Political Director at the Democratic Senatorial Campaign Committee (DSCC) from 2003 to 2004 and was the National Coordinated Campaign Director for the DSCC the previous election cycle"; Cara Morris Stern "served as a spokesperson for the Democratic Senatorial Campaign Committee where she worked for three election cycles"; Ben Jones "provided research, message development, candidate recruitment services and assessment for the DSCC" from 2001 to 2005; and Sarah Berns "worked as a Research Associate at the Democratic Senatorial Campaign Committee where she provided key research for six Senate races"; Brad Woodhouse was "the Communications Director for the Democratic Senatorial Campaign Committee"; and Dave Hamrick "served as the Campaign Services Director for the DSCC."

66 **firm is being paid by various Democratic politicians:** The Hildebrand Tewes website lists U.S. senators Sheldon Whitehouse (D-RI), Maria Cantwell (D-WA), Daniel Akaka (D-HI), Robert Byrd (D-WV), and Kent Conrad (D-ND) among its political clients.

66 **North Carolina Democrat Erskine Bowles:** Mark Barrett, *Asheville Citizen-Times,* "Bowles, Dole Agree on Military, Security," 11/3/02.

66 **"supporting President Bush in the war on terror and his efforts to effect a regime change in Iraq":** Jim Morrill, *Charlotte Observer,* "Dole Links Bowles to Clinton on Iraq," 9/20/02.

67 **"Wynn is one of the war's leading critics":** Matthew Hay Brown, *Baltimore Sun,* "Rep. Wynn Faces Heat Over War in Re-election," 6/18/07.

67 **posted her photo on its website as Public Enemy #1:** Juliet Eilperin and Michael Grunwald, *Washington Post,* "Woman in the Middle," 2/21/07.

67 **"No one wants to end the war more than I do":** Bill Curry, *Hartford Courant,* "Lieberman Unshackled," 11/19/06.

68 **Senate Minority Leader Mitch McConnell of Kentucky:** Tim Starks, *CQ Weekly,* "The Anti-War Movement's Aggressive New Battle Plan," 4/16/07.

68 **"Democratic leaders can only accomplish what they have the votes**

for": Thomas Ferraro, Reuters, "Newly Empowered Democrats Draw Wrath of Voter," 6/18/07.

69 **"that's why you gotta go right at them":** Feingold conference call with reporters, 2/7/05.

70 **"the cranky left of the party in the primaries":** Kos, Daily Kos, "Midday Open Thread," 12/07/06.

75 **focused almost exclusively on Republicans:** Teddy Davis, ABCNews .com, "MoveOn Ad Hits McCain Saying Iraq Escalation Is 'Actually His Idea,'" 6/17/07.

75 **the ads against the two Democrats will only be aired on radio:** Todd Spangler and Justin Hyde, *Detroit Free Press,* "Levin in the Crosshairs," 5/17/07.

75 **"We don't want to be the party":** Farhad Manjoo, Salon.com, "MoveOn Moves in with Pelosi," 3/23/07.

77 **"cast further doubt on whether Democrats were the party of social order, even on the bedrock issues":** Marshall Witmann, DLC *Blueprint* magazine, "Out of Order," 5/31/05.

77 **"couldn't split with LBJ":** Mark Schmitt, *Decembrist,* "Who Is 'Serious' About Terrorism?" 8/11/06.

79 **"our job is to focus on the Republicans":** Jeffrey Birnbaum, *Washington Post,* "'The Other K Street'; In the Concrete Canyon of the Business Lobby, a Pocket of Liberal Activists Settles In," 5/7/07.

79 **selling out the organization's grassroots membership:** John Stauber, PRWatch.org, "96% of MoveOn Members Did Not Show Support for the Pelosi Bill," 3/23/07.

79 **"they would surely oppose it":** Farhad Manjoo, Salon.com, "MoveOn Moves in with Pelosi," 3/23/07.

81 **"the ones that we engage in wisely":** David Paul Kuhn, *Politico,* "Centrist Democrats Take on Left over Iraq," 7/31/07.

81 **"too little" or "about right":** Joseph Carroll, Gallup World Poll, "Perceptions of 'Too Much' Military Spending at 15-Year High," 3/2/07.

81 **"how 'wisely' we prosecute them":** Glen Greenwald, Salon.com, "Various Items," 8/1/07.

82 **longer than World War II:** National Public Radio's *All Things Considered,* "For U.S., Iraq War Is Now Longer Than World War II," 2/2/07.

82 **experts now say could top $2 trillion:** Reuters, 10/10/06.

84 **ballot initiative making it harder for workers to unionize:** Paul English, *Tulsa World,* "Demos Turn Back GOP," 11/6/02.

4: The Boss and His Fusion Machine

86 **100,000 votes:** Dave Leip's Atlas of U.S. Presidential Elections shows Nader received 97,488 votes in Florida.

86 **less than what Perot took out of Bush's numbers in those states:** Clinton won Nevada, Montana, Colorado, Louisiana, Ohio, Kentucky, Tennessee, Georgia, New Jersey, New Hampshire, and Connecticut—all states George H. W. Bush won in 1988, and all states where in 1992 Ross Perot's numbers were larger than Clinton's margin of victory.

88 **"worth while to work for the party":** William Riordan, *Plunkitt of Tammany Hall,* 1905.

91 **fusion tickets decided control of state legislatures:** Howard A. Scarrow, *Western Political Quarterly,* vol. 39, no. 4, "Duverger's Law, Fusion and the Decline of American Third Parties," 10/86.

91 **three-quarters of all states:** Peter H. Argersinger, *American Historical Review,* "A Place on the Ballot: Fusion Politics and Antifusion Laws," p. 289.

93 **"don't intend to fight all creation":** Peter H. Argersinger, The American Historical Review, "A Place on the Ballot: Fusion Politics and Antifusion Laws," p. 296, quoting a Michigan legislator in the *Detroit Free Press* from 1893.

93 **"the combination we detest":** *Madison Capital Times,* "Fusing a New Democracy," 1/12/06.

94 **Democrats dropped 122 electoral votes:** According to the National Archives and Records Administration, the Democrats' 1892 presidential nominee received 277 electoral votes, and the party's 1900 nominee received 155 electoral votes.

94 **put up obstacles to fusion in the interim:** Peter H. Argersinger, *American Historical Review,* "A Place on the Ballot: Fusion Politics and Antifusion Laws," pp. 298–302, reports that between 1892 and 1900, Illinois, Iowa, North Dakota, Pennsylvania, Wisconsin, Wyoming, Indiana, California, Nebraska, Michigan, Ohio, Oregon, and Washington all obstructed fusion. In 1892, the electoral votes in these states broke down 66 for Democrats, and 96 for Republicans: Michigan (5D, 9R); Illinois (24D); Iowa (13R); North Dakota (1D, 1R, 1P); Pennsylvania (32R); Wisconsin (12D); Wyoming (3R);

Indiana (15D); California (8D, 1R); Nebraska (8R); Ohio (1D, 22R); Oregon (1P; 3R); Washington (4R). In 1900, the electoral votes in these same thirteen states borke down 0 for Democrats and 164 for Republicans: Michigan (14R); Illinois (24R); Iowa (13R); North Dakota (3R); Pennsylvania (32R); Wisconsin (12R); Wyoming (3R); Indiana (15R); California (9R); Nebraska (8R); Ohio (23R); Oregon (4R); Washington (4R).

94 **"had presented the greatest threat":** Howard A. Scarrow, *Western Political Quarterly,* vol. 39, no. 4, "Duverger's Law, Fusion and the Decline of American Third Parties," 10/86.

94 **does in a handful of other places:** Ibid., p. 639.

94 **Supreme Court case attempting to legally invalidate fusion bans:** *Timmons v. Twin Cities Area New Party* (95-1608), 520 U.S. 351, 4/28/97.

95 **"where Clinton received low levels of support overall":** Alyssa Katz, *Nation,* "The Power of Fusion Politics," 8/25/05; WFP PowerPoint presentation entitled "An Introduction to Fusion Voting" cites a 2000 survey of New York state union members conducted by Peter D. Hart Research Associates.

95 **race he won by 55 votes:** Emi Endo, *Newsday,* "Working Families Party Is Working for Influence," 7/19/01.

95 **"That's the party that thinks wages should be higher":** Ibid.

96 **ten-year incumbent:** Rich Logis, *Journal News,* "Residents God Goodbye to Local Landmark, Valuables in 2002," 12/26/02.

96 **twenty-two votes:** Susan Elan, *Journal News,* "Bradley to Take State Assembly Office," 1/5/03.

97 **"won solely on a third party designation":** William Murphy, Curtis L. Taylor, and Luis Perez, *Newsday,* "3rd Party Nets Council Seat," 11/5/03.

97 **"Shockwaves Through Democratic Leadership":** Michele Morgan Bolton, *Albany Times Union,* "Soares Stuns DA Clyne: Albany Rival's Primary Win Against Former Boss Sends Shockwaves Through Democratic Leadership," 9/15/04.

97 **more important than the state's major newspapers:** Jonathan Trichter and Chris Paige, *New York Observer,* WCBS 2 News and WNYC Radio, Table 8, "New York City Mayoral Election Study: Second Democratic Primary Poll," 11/7/05.

98 **firms that do business with the local government:** Special election where WFP provided margin for victory of Democrats over Republicans took place in March 2001; Suffolk legislature passed living wage in July.

98   **bill helping the town avoid cuts to services:** *Journal News,* 10/20/04.

98   **Bloomberg's proposals to gut legal services for the poor:** Glen Thrush, *Newsday,* "Budget Cut Casualties: Legal Aid Supporters Protest Layoffs," 5/19/04; Frank Lombardi, *Daily News,* "Council Oks 47B Budget," 6/25/04.

98   **notoriously draconian Rockefeller drug laws:** Errol A. Cockfield Jr. and Zachary R. Dowdy, *Newsday,* "Hard-Won Reforms: Lawmakers Agree on Sweeping Changes to the State's Harsh Rockefeller-Era Drug Laws," 12/8/04.

98   **"instrumental" in passing:** Elizabeth Benjamin, *Albany Times Union,* "Spitzer's Bid Gets Early Edge," 1/23/05.

99   **50,000-vote edge in registration:** Bruce Lambert, *New York Times,* "Grucci Concedes Defeat in Long Island Congressional Race," 12/15/02.

102 **upper chamber by a Republican majority:** Seymour Lachman and Robert Palner, *New Press,* "Three Men in a Room: The Inside Story of Power and Betrayal in an American Statehouse," p. 88.

103 **his 18-vote reelection victory:** Lida Foderaro, *New York Times,* "3 Months + 18 Votes = Spano's 10th Term," 11/13/05.

105 **"No. Next question":** Daniel Trotta, Reuters, "Spitzer Stands by 'steamroller' Boast," 1/31/07.

105 **70 percent of the vote:** Associated Press, "Spitzer Elected New York Governor," 11/8/06.

107 **failed to win a single Long Island state senate seat in more than two decades:** Karla Schuster, *Newsday,* "Johnson Beats O'Connell," 2/7/07.

107 **1199, in fact, is financing television ads for the Republican candidate:** Elizabeth Benjamin, *Albany Times Union,* "SEIU/1199 Hits the Airwaves for O'Connell," 1/24/07.

113 **half of the 3,600 votes that provided Johnson his margin of victory:** According to official New York State Board of Elections results, Johnson received 27,632 votes to O'Connell's 23,995. Johnson received 1,529 votes on the WFP line.

113 **Cantor as one of the four big winners:** Karla Schuster, *Newsday,* "Johnson Beats O'Connell," 2/7/07.

116 **tax relief for working- and middle-class New Yorkers:** Dan Cantor and Bob Master, *Albany Times Union,* "To Do Health Care Right, Rich Must Be Taxed," 3/14/07.

118 **first time in three decades:** Lawrence C. Levy, *Newsday,* "The Little Political Party That's Shaping Big Agendas," 11/16/05.

119 **"institutional control over elected candidates":** Greg Sargent, *American Prospect,* "First Among Thirds," 4/16/06.

119 **"possession of child pornography":** Editorial, *New York Times,* "An Election Day Ballot Trap," 11/5/06.

122 **Fifty-seven percent of voters labeled the WFP a five or above:** Results from Benenson Strategy Group surveys of 1,461 likely voters in Ohio, Missouri, and Washington, 2/14/06.

122 **"a little more realistic as we mature":** Sarah Netter, *Journal News,* "Two Working Families Leaders Quit," 8/13/07.

5: The Permanent Barrier

125 **its own "permanent will":** Alexander Hamilton speech to the Constitutional Convention, 6/18/1787, as quoted in *The Works of Alexander Hamilton,* 1904.

128 **"proud to carry the progressive banner":** Jim Tankersley, *Toledo Blade,* "Candidate Brown Challenges GOP Establishment," 12/4/05.

128 **"progressive Democrat can win in a state like Ohio":** Peter Slevin, *Washington Post,* "Ohio Republicans Racing Storm Clouds," 3/26/06.

129 **"a campaign strategy even his supporters call a risk":** David Hammer, Associated Press, 7/13/06.

129 **seven in ten Ohio voters blamed these very trade pacts:** Associated Press, "Kerry's Support of NAFTA Could Pose Problem in Ohio," 4/14/04.

129 **"has voted Republican in congressional elections since 1938":** Tom Troy, *Toldeo Blade,* "For Weirauch, Brown Is Proof Democrat Can Win Area," 12/10/07; *National Journal's* "Almanac of American Politics," 12/5/07.

131 **Senate leaders crushed Clinton's health-care initiative:** Bob Franken, CNN's *Inside Politics,* "Health Care Reform Bill Dies in the Senate," 9/26/94.

132 **"cleaned up their environment":** Bill Clinton, Federal News Service, "Town Hall Meeting with Arkansas Governor Bill Clinton, Democratic Presidential Candidate," 6/12/92.

132 **"to drive it home over their dead bodies":** John R. MacArthur, "The Selling of Free Trade," 2000.

132 **"trade preferences to China when they're locking their people up":** Bill Clinton, 6/12/92.

132 **Brown ran hard for universal health care and against NAFTA:** Jim Sweeney, *Cleveland Plain Dealer,* "Brown Clobbers Oponent Mueller in 13th District," 11/4/92.

134 **"a nice little old man with a smile with toys in his bag, not a threat to anybody":** Cornel West on the *Tavis Smiley Show,* 1/12/07.

136 **3 percent of America's total voting-age population:** Forty-one senators from the least-populated states represent just 11 percent of the entire country, according to Census Bureau data. According to *Congressional Quarterly's* "Voting and Elections Collection: 2004 Presidential Election," in 2004, these 21 smallest states saw 14.2 million voters turn out. Half of this is roughly 7 million voters. According to the Census 2000 PHC-T-31 table, there are 209,279,149 Americans eighteen years of age or older; 7 million divided by 209,279,149 is roughly 3 percent. For more, read my Creators Syndicate column from 9/28/07 entitled "Tyranny of the Tiny Minority."

137 **arena of direct-election primaries:** Green, *Slate,* "My Vote Means Nothing; How Presidential Primaries Backfired," 6/11/07.

138 **40 percent of the votes needed to secure the Democratic presidential nomination:** Tom Curry, MSNBC, 10/23/03; Geoff Earle, *New York Post,* "Hills Plan Is 'Super,' " 03/13/07.

138 **voters in the two biggest Democratic states:** Tom Edsall, *Washington Post,* "Gore Sets His Sights on 'Superdelegates,' " 10/18/99. The DNC handbook shows 852 total "unaffiliated" (super) delegates—that's 852 out of a total of 4,367 delegates, or 19 percent of the total, and 40 percent of the total needed to win a majority. California has 6.599 million registered Democrats (42.5 percent of 15.5 million registered voters, according to California secretary of state totals). New York has 5.4 million total registered Democratic voters.

138 **"encouraged insurgent candidates":** Brendan Koerner, *Slate,* "Wait, Dean Has the Most Delegates,"1/24/04.

139 **within one House vote of stopping it dead:** House Roll Call Vote #443, 7/28/05.

142 **"time the Senate looks a little bit more like Montana":** Tester ad, "Real Montana," 10/30/07.

144 **eighteen-hundred-acre patch of high prairie:** Jennifer McKee, *Helena Independent Record,* "Big Sandy's Tester Sets His Sights on Washington," 5/21/06.

144 **converted his family plot into an organic farm:** Charles Johnson, *Helena Independent Record,* "Tester Ready to Lead Dems," 11/21/04.

144 **deregulated its energy industry:** Jonathan D. Glater, *New York Times,* "Under Deregulation, Montana Power Price Soars," 8/21/03.

146 **newspaper chain published a story about his having an extramarital affair:** Mike Dennison and Charles Johnson, *Billings Gazette,* "Morrison: Personal Conflicts Didn't Alter Investigation," 4/6/04.

146 **61 percent to 35 percent:** Charles H. Johnson, *Missoulian,* "Secret to Tester's Win: Large Margin of Primary Victory Surprises Political Observers," 12/8/07.

148 **to refuse to comply with it:** Jennifer McKee, *Helena Independent Record,* "House Condemns Patriot Act, 4/2/05.

148 **"I don't want to weaken the Patriot Act, I want to repeal it":** Gwen Florio, *Great Falls Tribune,* "U.S. Senate Candidates Trade Jabs," 9/24/06.

148 **ad attacking Burns for refusing to repeal the Patriot Act:** Tester ad, "Freedom First," 9/29/06.

154 **sugarcoating economic data:** Financial Services Committee hearing, 7/25/00.

154 **abolish the minimum wage entirely:** Financial Services Committee hearing, 7/18/01.

155 **"concern for the middle class and working families of this country":** Financial Services Committee hearing, 7/16/03.

158 **"were not worth the paper that they had been written on":** Richard Oppel, *New York Times,* "Companies Cash In on New Pension Plan," 8/20/99.

159 **"classic demagoguery":** Editorial, *Caledonian-Record,* 10/24/06.

160 **33 percent of the vote in the same county:** 1996–2004 data from the Vermont secretary of state's office; 1994 data provided by Sanders aide Phil Fiermonte.

160 **Sanders championed legislation to stop the kinds of schemes:** Albert B. Crenshaw, *Washington Post,* "Probe Finds IBM Altered Document: Treasury Inspector General Investigating Paper on Pensions," 6/18/04.

162 **"passed more roll-call amendments":** Matt Taibbi, *Rolling Stone,* "Four Amendments and a Funeral: A Month Inside the House of Horrors That Is Congress," 8/10/05.

162 **support from both Democrats and archconservative antigovernment Republicans:** Sanders press release, 6/15/05.

163 **"progress toward a rational world":** Saul Alinsky, *Rules for Radicals,* 1971, p. 76.

169 **"most widely quoted think-tank economist in the world":** Peterson Institute website.

172 **thirty-nine senators voted for a bill concretely demanding a withdrawal of troops:** Senate Roll Call Vote #182, 6/22/06. Democratic pickups in the 2006 election would likely add another six votes to this vote today, and based on the statements of Republicans like Olympia Snowe (ME), Chuck Hagel (NE), and Gordon Smith (OR), that's another three, meaning the "phased redeployment" position could have forty-nine solid votes in today's Senate.

174 **MoveOn did endorse the nonbinding bill:** Margaret Talev and Renee Schoof, McClatchy-Tribune News Service, "Senate Prepares to Debate Opposition to Bush's Iraq Policy," 2/1/07.

176 **"dramatic statement of senatorial disagreement with the president":** CNN, 2/1/07.

6: Mad as Hell, and Not Gonna Take It Anymore

178 **$1.7 billion fortress:** TimeWarner.com, "New Landmark Development at Columbus Circle to Be Named Time Warner Center," 9/19/03.

180 **closest to achieving the number one rank in its time slot:** Neilsen ratings (provided by MediaBistro.com) show that in the first quarter of 2007, Dobbs was 440 points behind first-place Fox News in the 6 p.m. time slot. That was the smallest gap from first place for any evening CNN show.

182 **"and trying to cover up the shooting":** Associated Press, "Border Patrol Agents Convicted in Wounding of Suspected Drug Smuggler," 3/9/06; Ruben Navarette Jr., *Tucson Citizen,* "Ex-Border Agents Deserve Sentences They Received in Shooting, Coverup," 8/1/07; Editorial, *Houston Chronicle,* "Misrepresentation: In the Case of Two Rogue Border Patrol Agents, the Truth Has Been Sacrificed to Unprincipled Lies," 8/8/07.

182 **Sacco and Vanzetti:** Annie Anderson, *In These Times,* "The Lessons of Sacco and Vanzetti," 3/27/07.

182 **were just doing their job:** Eunice Moscoso, *Austin American-Statesman,* "Lou Dobbs Special on Jailed Border Agents," 3/27/07.

183 **"He knew they needed him more than he needed them":** Luke Mullins, *American,* "The Secret Life of Lou Dobbs," 11/28/06.

183 **"editorial point of view":** Ken Auletta, *New Yorker,* "Lou Dobbs's Populist Crusade," 11/27/07.

184 **telling working folk to go to hell:** Lou Dobbs, CNN.com, "Dobbs: Bush, Congress Tell Working Folk to Go to Hell," 5/34/06.

184 **"And no one is noticing":** Lou Dobbs, CNN's *Lou Dobbs Tonight,* "Texas Court Issues Arrest Warrant for Tom DeLay; White House Under Pressure in CIA Leak Case; Report Says U.S. Still Not Taking Steps to Prevent Terrorist Attack; New Report on How Well Kids Are Doing in School; Administration Not Challenging China on Trade," 10/19/05.

184 **"increase the audience's intensity":** Ken Auletta, *New Yorker,* "Lou Dobbs's Populist Crusade," 11/27/07.

185 **"fascinated" by Dobbs:** Paula Froelich, *New York Post,* "Eyes on Lou," 8/18/07.

189 **"a somewhat flexible relationship with reality":** *Lou Dobbs Tonight,* "Border Insecurity; Criminal Illegal Aliens; Deadly Imports; Illegal Alien Amnesty," 4/14/05; Media Matters for America, "CBS Contributor Dobbs Defends False Leprosy Claim After Confrontation by CBS's Stahl" 5/11/07; David Leonhardt, *New York Times,* "Truth, Fiction and Lou Dobbs," 5/30/07.

189 **"the darling of the anti-immigrant movement":** National Council of La Raza, "A Response to Lou Dobbs: NCLR Supports St. Patrick's Day!" 3/06.

189 **"bash the undocumented":** U.S. Newswire, "Arizona Law and Education Center Today Issues Statement Calling for National Boycotts of AOL, Lou Dobbs and Kimberly Clark," 4/26/06.

189 **ties to white supremacist organizations:** Heidi Beirich and Mark Potok, Southern Poverty Law Center's Intelligence Report, "Broken Record: Lou Dobbs' Daily 'Broken Borders' CNN Segment Has Focused on Immigration for Years. But There's One Issue Dobbs Just Won't Take On," Winter 2005.

189 **"anti-immigration vigilantes as 'great Americans'":** Bill Berkowitz, CommonDreams.org, "Lou Dobbs' Dubious Guest List," 7/1/06.

191 **"We look to them for inspiration and innovation":** Lou Dobbs, CNN's *MoneyLine,* "Hail to the Chiefs," 7/4/01.

191 **"Robert Mosbacher, and other top financiers":** Howard Kurtz, *Free Press,* "The Fortune Tellers: Inside Wall Street's Game of Money, Media, and Manipulation," 6/5/01, p. 102.

191 **Shearson Lehman Brothers and Paine Webber:** Luke Mullins, *American,* "The Secret Life of Lou Dobbs," 11/28/06.

192 **"the worker be damned":** Associated Press. "CNN's Lou Dobbs Is a Man on a Mission," 4/9/04.

193 **promoted the same companies:** Zachary Roth, *Columbia Journalism Review,* "The Two Faces of Lou Dobbs," 6/17/04.

194 **"protect his market share":** Daniel Henninger, *Wall Street Journal,* "Lou Dobbs Takes On the World," 3/5/04.

194 **viewership start to increase significantly:** Ken Auletta, *New Yorker,* "Lou Dobbs's Populist Crusade," 11/27/07; Bill Carter and Jacques Steinberg, *New York Times,* "Anchor-Advocate on Immigration Wins Viewers," 3/29/06.

195 **"Wolf, back to you":** CNN, 2/8/07.

196 **lifetime member of the National Association of Hispanic Journalists:** Sridhar Pappu, *Mother Jones,* "Angry White Man," January/February 2007; Dan Gross, *Philadelphia Daily News,* "R. Crumb Draws a Show," 1/11/07.

198 **when reporting on the bill's provisions:** Lou Dobbs, CNN's *Lou Dobbs Tonight,* "Defeat of the Immigration Bill, That Everyone Loved to Hate, Begs the Question, What Next? Better Border Security?" 6/29/07.

199 **"dignity and honor to the White House":** George W. Bush, ABC News's *This Week,* 2/20/00.

199 **candidates who won in Republican districts largely ran against trade deals:** Public Citizen's Global Trade Watch, "Election 2006: No to Staying the Course on Trade," 11/8/06.

202 **"it will play well on Dobbs":** Luke Mullins, *American,* "The Secret Life of Lou Dobbs," 11/28/06.

202 **larger than her Illinois-based Republican predecessor used:** Jim Kuhnhenn, Associated Press, "GOP Bristles at Pelosi Plane Request," 2/7/07.

202 **her request was totally justifiable:** Jim Kuhnhenn, Associated Press, "White House Defends Pelosi Plane Request," 2/9/07.

203 **"textbook case of how not to conduct foreign policy":** Lou Dobbs, CNN's *Lou Dobbs Tonight,* "Defending the War; Iran's Role in Iraq; GOP Reps Break with Bush," 2/14/07.

7: Mainstreaming the Militia

208 **one of the most-trafficked routes:** Dana Harman, *Christian Science Monitor,* "Now Departing for Mexico," 7/7/05.

208 **"for every one they arrest, some estimate three to 10 get away":** *Santa Cruz Sentinel,* "Battle at the Border," 4/30/06.

208 **arrested inside the county itself:** Edward Sifuentes, *North County Times*, "Enforcement Effort Continues Against Illegal Immigrants," 6/30/07.

208 **elected a lobbyist for an anti-illegal immigration advocacy group:** Jeff Patch, *Politico*, "Lobbyist or Lawmaker: Bilbray Posts Stop Sign at Border," 5/2/07.

210 **"the entire right to fortify whatever point":** Yale University's Avalon Project, Treaty of Guadalupe Hidalgo—Article XVI, 2/2/1848.

210 **7 to 20 million illegal immigrants in the United States:** Brad Knickerbocker, *Christian Science Monitor*, "Illegal Immigrants in the US: How Many Are There?" 5/16/06.

211 **missive calling for the formation of an armed militia at the border:** Ignacio Ibarra, *Arizona Daily Star*, "Tombstone Paper Calls for Militia," 11/15/02.

211 **"I can only believe to be Chinese troops":** Gustav Arellano, *OC Weekly*, "See Tombstone, Nab a Mexican: Chris Simcox Wants 14 Million Americans to Visit Tombstone, Arizona," 3/6/03; Susy Buchanan and David Holthouse, Southern Poverty Law Center's Intelligence Report, "Minuteman Leader Has Troubled Past."

211 **1,900-mile U.S.-Mexican border:** Elliot Spagat, Associated Press, "Slow Pace of Border Fence Project in San Diego Raises Questions About Larger White House Plan," 7/13/07.

214 **"sucking the lifeblood from the productive middle":** Bill Berkowitz, IPS, "Hate Watchdogs See Darker Side to 'Minutemen,'" 8/4/05.

215 **immigrants cost taxpayers nearly $9 billion a year:** Edward Sifuentes, *North County Times*, "Cost of Illegal Immigration in California Estimated at Nearly $9 Billion," 12/5/04.

215 **"about $420 million more into state coffers than they take out":** Darryl Fears, *Washington Post*, "Texas Official's Report Ignites a New Border Conflict," 12/15/06.

216 **whites a minority in his town:** City of Bellflower demographics show Bellflower is 43 percent Hispanic and 30 percent white.

217 **impoverished, crime-plagued country:** Jay Root, McClatchy Newspapers, "Mexico Crime Continues to Surge," 9/22/07.

217 **target Minutemen for retribution:** Jerry Seper, *Washington Times*, "Gang Will Target Minuteman Vigil on Mexico Border," 3/28/05.

218 **50,000 members in the United States:** Mandalit del Barco, NPR's *All Things Considered,* "The International Reach of the Mara Salvatrucha," 3/17/05.

219 **"al-Qaida operatives and Latin American guerrillas":** Gustav Arellano, *OC Weekly,* "See Tombstone, Nab a Mexican: Chris Simcox Wants 14 Million Americans to Visit Tombstone, Arizona," 3/6/03.

219 **"refusing to assimilate":** Susy Buchanan and David Holthouse, Southern Poverty Law Center's Intelligence Report, "Minuteman Leader Has Troubled Past."

223 **local paper investigated the claims and found they were entirely false:** Tim Funk, *Charlotte Observer,* "Suggestion: Get Facts Before News Conference: Bad Info Given to Back Illegal-Immigration Bill," 11/14/05.

223 **"I don't have any information that it has actually happened":** Human Events Online, "Tex. Senator Shown Evidence of Arab Personal Effects at Mexican Border," 11/22/05.

223 **trumpet the revelations in advance of a congressional debate:** Fox News's *Hannity & Colmes,* "Exclusive! Rep. John Culberson," 11/21/05.

223 **the story was spread by websites:** Jon Dougherty, WorldNetDaily.com, "Lawmaker: Terror War Spilling Across Border; Concern Rising Following Arrest of al-Qaida Suspect in Mexico," 11/16/05.

223 **"We have no terrorist in our jail":** Samantha Levine, *Houston Chronicle,* "Smoking Areas Leave Lawmakers Burned up: The Air Quality in Some Parts of the Capitol Repels Texas Members," 12/11/05.

225 **turning their antigovernment ideology into violence:** Sharon Cohen, Associated Press, "Oklahoma City Aftermath: Militias Move Out of Spotlight, Feds Move In," 3/31/97; Robert L. Snow, *The Terrorists Among Us,* Da Capo Press, 2002, p. 101.

225 **"a growing acceptance of conspiracy theories":** Thomas Hargrove, Scripps Howard News Service, "Third of Americans Suspect 9-11 Government Conspiracy," 8/3/06.

225 **California governor Arnold Schwarzenegger and Texas governor Rick Perry publicly endorsed Minuteman patrols:** Susy Buchanan and David Holthouse, Southern Poverty Law Center's Intelligence Report, "Minuteman Leader Has Troubled Past."

226 **giving Minutemen official police powers:** Lara Jakes Jordan, Associated Press, "Sen.: Border Volunteers Should Be Deputies," 4/20/05.

226 **forty-seven Republican cosponsors:** Sara Ins Caldern, *Brownsville Herald,* "Lawmaker Proposes Creating Border Militias," 8/7/05.

226 **54 percent of Americans have a favorable opinion of the Minutemen:** Rassmussen Reports, "Most Say Volunteer Patrols Reduce Illegal Immigration," 9/22/05.

226 **a plurality of Americans believe the organization is just "concerned citizens":** CNN/Opinion Research Corporation poll, 10/12/07–10/14/07.

227 **"is easy to do":** Human Events Online, "Tex. Senator Shown Evidence of Arab Personal Effects at Mexican Border," 11/22/05.

227 **Central Intelligence Agency issued a threat report:** Pablo Gato and Robert Windrem, Telemundo and MSNBC.com, "Hezbollah Builds a Western Base: From Inside South America's Tri-Border area, Iran-Linked Militia Targets U.S.," 5/9/07.

227 **Hezbollah smuggling ring in Mexico:** Robert Mueller, FDCH Political Transcripts, "FY2007 Appropriations Hearing for the Federal Bureau of Investigation," 3/28/06; Fox News, "Some of Hezbollah's Volunteers May Be in U.S.," 7/19/06.

227 **"smuggled across our southern frontier":** Terence Jeffrey, Townhall.com, "Connect These Dots, Now," 11/17/04.

228 **"Hezbollah Invading U.S. from Mexico":** NewsMax.com, "Hezbollah Invading U.S. from Mexico," 07/27/06.

228 **threat to American national security:** Joseph Farah, WorldNetDaily.com, "Islam on March South of Border," 06/07/05.

228 **"have been linked to terrorist activities":** Chris Roberts, *El Paso Times,* "More Iraqis Cross Southwest Border Seeking Asylum," 8/22/07; WorldNetDaily.com, "Iraqi Terrorists Caught Along Mexico Border: American Intelligence Chief Confirms 'People Are Alive' as a Result of Capture," 8/23/07.

229 **harassing immigrants at day labor centers:** Jeffrey Ressner, *Time,* "How Immigration Is Rousing the Zealots," 5/29/06.

230 **"had guns pointed at them":** Michael Marizco, *Arizona Daily Star,* "Abusive Acts vs. Entrants Are Ignored, Activists Say," 3/29/05.

230 **"told authorities he was held against his will":** Arthur H. Rotstein, Associated Press, "Immigrant Says Minuteman Volunteers Watching Arizona Border Held Him Against His Will," 4/7/05.

231 **"campaign of violence and harassment"**: Susy Buchanan and David Holthouse, Southern Poverty Law Center's Intelligence Project, "Going Lawless: Border Guardians Leader Calls for Violence," 8/19/06.

231 **violent incidents aimed at U.S. Border Patrol agents had doubled**: Kris Axtman, *Christian Science Monitor*, "Rising Tide of Border Crime and Violence: Brazen Drug Criminals Now Smuggle People," 2/15/06.

231 **"to increased violence along the southern border"**: John Holusha, *New York Times*, "Violence Said to Increase on Mexican Border," 2/8/07.

231 **legislator received death threats**: E. J. Montini, *Arizona Republic*, "A Death Threat Falls in the Digital Forest," 1/30/07.

232 **"a committee of vigilantes"**: Karen Branch-Brioso, *St. Louis Post-Dispatch*, "Crossing Conflict," 5/3/04.

232 **"I'm damned proud to be a vigilante"**: Martin Wisckol, *Orange County Register*, "Event Turns Hostile; Anti-Illegal Immigration Activists, Protestors Clash," 5/26/05.

234 **"security measures on Canada and Mexico"**: Christopher Hayes, *Nation*, "NAFTA Highway to Hell," 10/15/07.

235 **third of all state legislatures**: Christopher Hayes, *Nation*, "The NAFTA Superhighway," 8/27/07.

235 **bring the superhighway through Kansas City**: Scott Rothschild, *Lawrence Journal-World*, "Proposed NAFTA Superhighway a Threat to Kansans, Boyda Says," 8/12/06.

236 **"social conservatives and economic and defense and libertarian conservatives"**: Matt Stearns, McClatchy Newspapers, "More Evangelicals Embracing McCain Immigration Stance," 4/3/07.

237 **Wallace for president back in 1968**: Kevin Graman, *Spokesman Review*, "Activist Speaks on Immigration Issues; Local GOP Hosted Minuteman Founder," 4/1/07.

237 **absorb Minuteman chapters into their party structure**: Edward Sifuentes, *North County Times*, "American Independent Party courts Minutemen," 4/3/07.

239 **"illegal aliens and illicit narcotics"**: United States Border Patrol—San Diego Sector, press release, "East County Agents Seize a Total of 731 Lbs. of Marijuana Over the Past Two Weeks," 9/5/00.

239 **almost 500 deaths annually**: U.S. Government Accountability Office, Report to the Honorable Bill Frist, Majority Leader, U.S. Senate, "Illegal

Immigration Border-Crossing Deaths Have Doubled Since 1995: Border Patrol's Effots to Prevent Deaths Have Not Been Fully Evaluated," 8/06.

240 **"pushing up the number of deaths":** Randal C. Archibold, *New York Times,* "At U.S. Border, Desert Takes a Rising Toll," 9/15/07; Ted Robbins, National Public Radio's *All Things Considered,* "Illegal Immigrant Deaths Burden Border Towns," 10/6/05; Robin Emmott, Reuters, "More Migrants Die as U.S. Tightens Border Security," 7/12/07; William M. Welch, *USA Today,* "Border-Crossing Deaths on Rise," 7/31/07.

241 **Polling data suggests he's absolutely correct about that:** Rasmussen Reports, "Immigration Matters: 60% Favor Sanctions for Illegal Hires," 9/17/06.

244 **"breath of life in a dreary, drab existence":** Saul Alinsky, *Rules for Radicals,* 1971, p. 113.

246 **"even greater illegal migration":** Charles Bowden, *Mother Jones,* "Exodus: Border-Crossers Forge a New America," 10/06.

247 **a "police riot":** *Time,* "Chicago Examined: Anatomy of a 'Police Riot,'" 12/6/68.

249 **into the heartland:** Haya El Nasser and Brad Heath, *USA Today,* "Hispanic Growth Extends Eastward," 8/9/07; Associated Press, "Report: Diversity Growing in Nearly Every State; Census Bureau Finds Minorities Are Bigger Share of Population in 49 States," 8/17/06.

249 **"gateway states such as Texas and Arizona":** Kansas City News, KMBC-TV, "Minuteman Groups Growing in Heartland: Group Hopes to ID Illegal Immigrants in Communities," 8/16/06.

250 **"impact on what have been their traditions":** Ryan Lizza, *New Yorker,* "Return of the Nativist," 12/17/07.

8: Dilberts of the World, Unite

253 **fast-growing metropolis:** Aubrey Cohen, *Seattle Post-Intelligencer,* "Seattle's Growth Is at Its Fastest in Decades: Healthy Job Climate Attracting Residents Statewide," 6/27/07.

253 **Silicon Valley, to Boston, to Austin, to Portland, to Seattle:** Matt Hudgins, *National Real Estate Investor,* "Former Dot-Com Markets Boom Again," 6/28/07.

254 **number of professional and high-skilled workers in the United States more than doubled:** Jim Grossfeld, Center for American Progress,

"White Collar Perspectives on Workplace Issues: How Progressives Can Make the Case for Unions," 2006.

254 **one-third of all employment growth between now and 2012:** Daniel E. Hecker, *Monthly Labor Review,* "Employment Outlook: 2002–12: Occupational Employment Projections to 2012," 2/04.

255 **6,000 employees at Microsoft known as "permatemp" workers:** Dan Richman, *Seattle Post-Intelligencer,* "Microsoft Ordered to Show Contractors Their Personnel Files," 1/26/00.

256 **no matter how permanent such employees are:** Dan Richman, *Seattle Post-Intelligencer,* "Microsoft 'Permatemps' Win: High Court Refuses Appeal; Firm May Owe $20 Million in Benefits," 1/11/00.

256 **regulatory change exempting high-tech companies:** Keith Ervin, *Seattle Times,* "Temporary Software Workers to Lose OT—Microsoft, Boeing Could Save Millions with State's Proposal," 12/5/97.

257 **changed by the then-Republican Congress:** William G. Whittaker, Congressional Research Service, "Computer Services Personnel: Overtime Pay under the Fair Labor Standards Act," 9/18/01. The report notes that "under the 1996 Fair Labor Standards Act amendments, a new categorical exemption was created as Section 13(a)(17)," which congressional Democrats noted "freezes the rate at which certain computer professionals are exempt from the minimum wage at $27.63 per hour."

257 **two Washington State unions supported the rule change:** Keith Ervin, *Seattle Times,* "Temporary Software Workers to Lose OT—Microsoft, Boeing Could Save Millions with State's Proposal," 12/5/97.

257 **signed a petition formally requesting union representation:** Leslie Helm, *Los Angeles Times,* "16 Microsoft Temps Organize into Bargaining Unit," 6/4/99.

257 **"$500 million from its annual tax bill":** Glenn R. Simpson, *Wall Street Journal,* "Irish Subsidiary Lets Microsoft Slash Taxes in U.S. and Europe," 11/7/05.

258 **two-thirds of all permatemps had been working full-time at the company for more than a year:** Ilana DeBare, *San Francisco Chronicle,* "Labor Group Wants to Organize Tech Temp Workers," 7/16/99.

258 **"bargaining unit under the federal labor laws":** Dan Richman, *Seattle Post-Intelligencer,* "Laws Need to Cover Temps, Labor Experts Say," 6/5/99.

258 **terminating the software project and firing all the permatemps:** Paul

Andrews, *Seattle Times,* "Microsoft Drops TaxSaver Software: Workers on Project Call Decision a Shock," 3/24/00.

259 **eighteen-day walkout that yielded major wage concessions:** Simon Romero, *New York Times,* "Accord Is Reached for Most Workers in Phone Walkout," 8/21/00.

259 *Seattle Times* **headline blared:** Paul Nyhan, *Seattle Post-Intelligencer,* "Unions Target Workers in the New Economy," 9/4/00; Alex Fryer, *Seattle Times,* "Strike Heralded as Dawn of New Age: Unions Look to Bring Professionals into Fold," 3/19/00.

259 **"unions have shaped solutions":** Paul Nyhan, *Seattle Post-Intelligencer,* "Unions Target Workers in the New Economy: Strike at Verizon Gives Hope to Organizers in High-Tech Industries in Puget Sound Region," 9/4/00.

259 **"against the idea of unions at his company":** Carolyn Said, *San Francisco Chronicle,* "Dot-Com Disasters Have Opened Door a Crack for Unions: Stock Price Crash Makes Employee Ownership Less Real," 12/3/00.

259 **"anti-union message to customers who inquire about the organizing campaign":** David Moberg, *In These Times,* "Amazon.com Workers on the Move: A Union Drive Launches at the Internet's Premier Retailer," 1/8/01; Steven Greenhouse, *New York Times,* "Amazon.com Fights Union Activity," 11/29/00.

259 **mowing down all four hundred workers:** Monica Soto, *Seattle Times,* "Amazon Cuts 1,300 Jobs," 1/31/01.

259 **union-free subcontractors of Northern Ireland and India:** Allison Linn, Associated Press, "Amazon Inks Deal with Northern Irish Customer Service Group," 7/25/01; *Economist,* "Back Office to the World," 5/5/01.

261 **Seattle voted to form a union and affiliate with WashTech:** Tricia Duryee, *Seattle Times,* "Bothell Cingular Workers Joining Union," 11/18/05.

261 **221,000 American tech jobs were eliminated:** Ron Schneiderman, Electronic Design Online, ID #10062, "IEEE Cites Outsourcing as Wages Drop and U.S. Loses 221,000 Jobs," 4/14/05.

261 **most significant income decline occurring in the upper-middle-class income bracket:** Rachel Osterman, *Sacramento Bee,* "Unionizing White-Collar Workers," 9/5/05.

261 **first drop in median income for tech workers:** Ron Schneiderman, Electronic Design Online, "IEEE Cites Outsourcing as Wages Drop and U.S. Loses 221,000 Jobs," 4/14/05.

261 **health-care premiums had increased, and their wages had either remained flat or dropped:** Evans/McDonough Company Incorporated, WashTech Tech Worker Survey 2005.

261 **between 2.0 and 5.5 percent of high-tech workers are unionized:** U.S. Census Bureau, "NAICS Sector: 54 Professional, Scientific, and Technical Services," last modified 1/23/01. Just 1.8 percent in professional and technical services are unionized: Bureau of Labor Statistics, "Union Membership (Annual): Table 3. Union Affiliation of Employed Wage and Salary Workers by Occupation and Industry," 1/26/07. Just 5.6 percent in computer services are unionized: Bureau of Labor Statistics, "Union Membership (Annual): Table 3. Union Affiliation of Employed Wage and Salary Workers by Occupation and Industry," 1/26/07.

264 **given to companies that outsource jobs:** Evans/McDonough Company Incorporated, WashTech Tech Worker Survey, 2003.

265 **"How to Stay Union Free":** Jackson Lewis advertisement for seminar on "How to Stay Union Free."

265 **"fighting and dying to defeat in Iraq and Afghanistan":** U.S. Rep. Charlie Norwood, *Washington Times,* "The Kennedy Bill Even Forces the Employer to Give the Worker's Home Address to the Union, So That the AFL-CIO's 'Fedayeen' Can Make a House Call on Reluctant Employees," 2/24/05.

266 **"there are actual union leaders wandering around":** Matt Bai, *New York Times,* "The New Boss," 1/30/05.

267 **certified bargaining unit under federal labor law:** Leslie Helm, *Los Angeles Times,* "16 Microsoft Temps Organize into Bargaining Unit," 6/4/99.

270 **board of major banking, insurance, and telecommunications corporations:** Bill Gates Interview with *Playboy,* July 1994; University of Washington website, About Mary Gates.

270 **countries like Germany, Sweden, Finland, and Canada:** *Economist,* "Ever Higher Society, Ever Harder to Ascend," 12/29/04.

270 **socialist countries in North America, Scandinavia, and continental Europe:** Jo Blanden, Paul Gregg, and Stephen Machin, Centre for Economic Performance, "Intergenerational Mobility in Europe and North America," 4/05.

270 **"has had a better chance at prosperity":** David Wessel, *Wall Street Journal,* "As Rich-Poor Gap Widens in U.S., Class Mobility Stalls," 5/13/05.

271 **"employers and employees are the same":** Seymour Martin Lipset and Noah Meltz, *The Paradox of American Unionism: Why Americans Like Unions More Than Canadians but Join Much Less,* Cornell University Press, 2004, p.128.

271 **"don't hate the boss, they want to be the boss":** Rachel Osterman, *Sacramento Bee,* "More Professionals Worry About Benefits, Unpaid Overtime and Outsourcing," 9/5/05.

275 **"statistically significant association between unions and productivity":** Industrial Relations Research Association, Proceedings 2004.

275 **27 percent more productive than their nonunion counterparts:** Jim O'Rourke, *Sun Herald,* "Unionists Prove Better Workers," 1/17/99.

275 **conduits between employees and management:** Harley Shaiken, Center for American Progress, "The High Road to a Competitive Economy: A Labor Law Strategy," 6/25/04.

276 **half of all tech workers surveyed do not believe outsourcing will affect their jobs:** Evans/McDonough Company Incorporated, WashTech Tech Worker Survey 2005, Slide 9.

276 **radically accelerate outsourcing in the coming years:** Paul McDougall, *Information Week,* "Why More U.S. Tech Jobs Could Be Lost to India in 2007," 1/10/07.

276 **42 million American jobs could be outsourced in the coming years:** Alan S. Blinder, Princeton University, CEPS Working Paper No. 142, "How Many U.S. Jobs Might Be Offshorable?" 3/07.

277 **encouraging those under them to hire foreign workers:** Roberta L. Wilson, WashTech News, "Deep Throat Move Over: Disgruntled IT Employees Expose All; 'Fair Globalization' May Be the Answer to Offshoring," 7/28/05.

277 **"technology positions are vulnerable to outsourcing":** Todd Bishop, *Seattle Post-Intelligencer,* "Microsoft Outsourcing High-End jobs, Union Says: WashTech Cites Work Documents It Received," 6/16/04.

277 **train their foreign replacements:** Associated Press, "U.S. Tech Workers Training Their Replacements," 8/11/03.

277 **80 percent of the region's tech companies were outsourcing jobs:** Brier Dudley, *Seattle Times,* "Large Companies in State Shift to Outsourcing, Survey Says," 10/21/04.

278 **"two heads for the price of one":** Helen Jung, Associated Press, "Tech Union Contends Microsoft Funneling Work to India," 1/24/03.

278 **"not a departure from the way we've always done business":** Todd Bishop, *Seattle Post-Intelligencer,* "Microsoft Outsourcing High-End jobs, Union Says: WashTech Cites Work Documents It Received," 6/16/04.

281 **"scrambling to manage a labor crunch":** Peter Coy and Jack Ewing, *BusinessWeek,* "Where Are All the Workers? Companies Worldwide Are Suddenly Scrambling to Manage a Labor Crunch," 4/9/07.

281 **"no indication of a shortage of engineers in the United States":** Vivek Wadhwa, Gary Gereffi, Ben Rissing, and Ryan Ong, Issues in Science and Technology Online, "Seeing Through Preconceptions: A Deeper Look at China and India," Spring 2007.

281 **temporary foreign workers for high-skill jobs:** Tom Abate, *San Francisco Chronicle,* "Reforms to the Work Visa Program Are a Small Part of the Overall Debate," 5/27/07.

281 **$13,000 a year less than American workers in the same job:** John Miano, Center for Immigration Studies, "The Bottom of the Pay Scale Wages for H-1B Computer Programmers," 12/05.

282 **70 percent less than prevailing American wages:** Ron Hira, *American Prospect,* "How 'Guestworkers' Promote Outsourcing," 8/6/07.

282 **official 2006 Strategic Plan:** U.S. Department of Labor, "Strategic Plan: Fiscal Years 2006–2011," p. 35.

282 **"accept lower salaries than similarly qualified U.S. workers":** Ron Hira, *American Prospect,* "How 'Guestworkers' Promote Outsourcing," 8/6/07.

282 **to the United States to fill tech jobs:** Marianne Kolbasuk McGee, *Information Week,* "Who Gets H-1B Visas? Check Out This List," 5/17/07; Mary Hayes Weier, *Information Week,* "Politicians Mull H-1B and L-1 Visa Reforms: Can They Tweak the Law Without Driving More IT Work out of the Country?" 5/26/03.

282 **"but it's what we're trying to do here":** Anya Sostek, *Pittsburgh Post-Gazette,* "City Law Firm's Immigration Video Sparks an Internet Firestorm," 6/22/07.

283 **"there is a shortage of engineers at my company":** EE Times, U.S. Salary and Opinion Survey, August 2006, p. 39.

283 **"less expensive to fill the jobs with foreign professionals":** Anne Kim and Mark Donnell, Third Way Middle Class Project, "Reforming and Expanding the H-1B Program," 1/17/07.

283 **Microsoft ranks third in the country:** Marianne Kolbasuk McGee, EE Times Online, "Who Gets H-1B Visas?" 5/17/07.

283 **testifying before a Senate committee:** Senate Committee on Health, Education, Labor, and Pensions Hearing, "Strengthening American Competitiveness for the 21st Century," 3/7/07.

283 **eliminate the cap on the number of H-1B visas:** Anne Broache, CNet News, "Gates Calls for 'Infinite' H-1Bs, Better Schools" 3/7/07.

284 **"A target must be a personification, not something general and abstract":** Saul Alinsky, *Rules for Radicals,* 1971, p. 133.

285 **earnings of college graduates dropped by more than 5 percent:** Peter G. Gosselin, *Los Angeles Times,* "That Good Education Might Not Be Enough," 3/6/06.

285 **"reduced the bargaining power of most US workers":** Krishna Guha and Alex Barker, *Financial Times,* "US Graduates Suffer Income Inequality," 5/4/07.

285 **"look more outsourceable by the day":** Geoffrey Colvin, *Fortune,* "The Poor Get Richer," 3/20/06.

9: The Blue-Chip Revolutionaries

288 **"exceeded the gross domestic product of all but 25 *countries*":** Steven Mufson, *Washington Post,* "Higher Oil Prices Help Exxon Again Set Record Profit," 2/2/07.

288 **ExxonMobil's 34,000 gas stations:** ExxonMobil Annual Report, 2006, p. 70.

288 **twenty-seven million metric tons of petrochemicals:** ExxonMobil Annual Report, 2006, pp. 85, 87.

290 **roughly $100 billion of stock holdings:** Interfaith Council on Corporate Responsibility website reports that "ICCR members include 275 Protestant, Catholic and Jewish institutional investors including denominations, religious communities, pension funds, healthcare corporations, foundations, dioceses with combined portfolios worth an estimated $100 billion."

290 **1934 federal law:** Joan Lowy, Scripps Howard News Service, "Religious Shareholders Take the Environment on Faith," 9/3/01.

291 **Tri-State Coalition in 1994:** Hugh Morley, North Jersey Media Group, "Keeping Faith: Guiding Corporate America Is N.J. Nun's Mission," 5/25/03.

291 **refuses to invest any of its resources:** James R. Healey, *USA Today,* "Alternate Energy Not in Cards at ExxonMobil," 10/28/05.

292 **5 percent of all human-generated carbon emissions:** Friends of the Earth press release, "Study Assesses ExxonMobil's Contribution to Global Warming: First-of-Its-Kind Report Paves Way for Legal Action," 12/29/04.

292 **"warmer winters [and] warmer nights":** Judd Legum, ThinkProgress.org, "CEI Founder on Global Warming: 'It Looks Pretty Good . . . We're Moving to a More Benign Planet,'" 5/17/06.

295 **failed 1972 Senate run:** Marc Gunther, *Fortune,* "Investors of the World, Unite! It's Up to Institutional Owners to Fix Corporate America, Says the Dean of Shareholder Activists," 6/24/02.

296 **time to rustle up more "no" votes:** Geoff Colvin, *Fortune,* "A Tie Goes to the Managers," 5/28/07.

297 **avoid the inevitable financial responsibility:** Mark Pattison, Catholic News Service, "Religious Groups Force GE Disclosure of Money Spent to Avoid Cleanup," 1/25/06.

298 **27.4 percent of the shareholder vote:** Tri-State Coalition for Responsibile Investment press release, "Religious Shareholders Force Disclosure by GE That Company Spent Tens of Millions to Delay Clean-Up of Hudson River, Other PCB Site Discharges," 1/10/06.

298 **significant slice of a stock's price:** Pete Engardio and Michael Arndt, *BusinessWeek,* "What Price Reputation?" 7/9/07.

299 **company soon changed its behavior:** Joan Lowy, Scripps Howard News Service, "Religious Shareholders Take the Environment on Faith," 9/3/01.

299 **"irritate boards of directors and shareholders":** Ibid.

301 **$75,000-a-year:** ExxonMobil's proxy statement, p. 15.

303 **"because now they can do something about them":** Saul Alinsky, *Rules for Radicals,* 1971, p. 178.

303 **delivery vehicle for government-funded social services:** Wendy Plotkin, H-Net/H-Urban Seminar on History of Community Organizing and Community-Based Development, "Alinsky and Back of the Yards Neighborhood Council," 8/6/96.

303 **"set sail into the sea of churches":** Saul Alinsky, *Rules for Radicals,* 1971, p. 173.

304 **"I went down on my knees":** Sanford D. Horwitt, *Let Them Call Me Rebel: Saul Alinsky: His Life and Legacy,* 3/31/92, p. 497.

305 **"proxies are simply a means to that end":** Saul Alinsky, *Rules for Radicals,* 1971, p. 181.

306 **$6 trillion of stock is owned by worker pension funds:** According to the AFL-CIO's Office of Investment, "Some $6 trillion of workers' capital is invested in public-sector, single employer or multiemployer Taft-Hartley pension funds, Taft-Hartley multiemployer health and welfare funds, employee stock ownership plans, 401(k) and other defined-contribution retirement plans, profit sharing and stock plans, as well as individual savings and union reserve funds."

306 **"assuaging their troubled social consciences":** *Playboy* interview with Saul Alinsky, 3/72.

306 **"had never seen it so uptight":** Saul Alinsky, *Rules for Radicals,* 1971, p. 175.

307 **"atop buildings with rifles drawn":** Sanford D. Horwitt, *Let Them Call Me Rebel: Saul Alinsky: His Life and Legacy,* 3/31/92, p. 498.

308 **"which ones might cause trouble":** Deborah Brewster, *Financial Times,* "Boards Seek to Keep Tabs on Activists," 12/9/05.

308 **"hiring surveillance firms to find out who their shareholders are":** Ann Zimmerman and Gary McWilliams, *Wall Street Journal,* "Inside Wal-Mart's 'Threat Research' Operation," 4/4/07.

310 **more than $30 billion in profits:** ExxonMobil Annual Stockholder Report, pp. 20–22.

311 **well over $1 trillion in total assets:** According to *Fortune* magazine's 2007 rankings of America's largest corporation, IBM ($107 billion in assets), Campbell Soup ($7.8 billion), Corning ($13 billion), PepsiCo ($29.9 billion), and J. P. Morgan Chase ($1.3 trillion) have combined assets; *Fortune,* annual ranking of America's largest corporations, 4/30/07.

312 **hiked the number of votes he would need:** Gary Strauss and Jeffrey Potts, *USA Today,* "Sears, Shareholder Face Off," 5/9/91; Robert A. G. Monks and Nell Minow, Lens Investment Management, "Sears Case Study."

312 **$400 million retirement package:** Robert Trigaux, *St. Petersburg Times,* 4/24/06.

312 **single pension gap for any corporation on record:** David Henry, *BusinessWeek,* "Shortfall at Exxon; All Those Profits—But Underfunded Pensions," 5/29/06.

315 **lead quote from the meeting in tomorrow's national newspapers:** Bob Cox, *Knight Ridder Tribune,* "Exxon Mobil Chief Cools Global-Warming Dissent," 5/31/07.

315 **"also unknown unknowns":** Donald Rumsfeld, Pentagon briefing, 2/12/02.

318 **"top concern at ExxonMobil's annual meeting May 30":** Starr Spencer, *Platts Oilgram News,* "ExxonMobil Holders Vote Down GHG, Pay Proposals," 5/31/07.

318 **"some steps need to be taken to address global warming":** Dow Jones *MarketWatch,* "Updates, Advisories and Surprises," 5/30/07.

318 **"take action on greenhouse gas emissions":** *Environmental Finance,* "GHG Resolutions Get Highest Votes at GM, ExxonMobil," 6/7/07.

10: Chasing the Ghosts of Chicago

321 **"hasn't left the efficiency apartment in two years":** Brian Williams, speech at New York University as quoted by NYU's Journalism blog We Want Media, 4/4/06.

324 **in reaction to the 1998 Clinton impeachment:** Chris Bowers, MyDD .com, "Teenagers and Adults: The Emerging Anti-Netroots Narrative," 5/2/06; Matt Stoller, TPMCafe.com, "What Is This New Movement?" 1/15/07.

325 **"relatively well-educated and the well-to-do":** Lee Rainie and John Horrigan, Pew Internet and American Life Project, "Election 2006 Online," 1/17/07.

325 **"we just didn't grow up that way":** Chris Bowers, MyDD.com, "The End of the 1960s?" 12/14/06.

327 **$82 million online:** Glen Justice, *New York Times,* "Kerry Kept Money Coming with the Internet as His ATM," 11/8/04; Alexis Rice, CampaignsOnline.org, "The Power of the Internet," 11/04; Fredreka Schouten, *USA Today,* "Internet Critical Tool for Political Cash," 12/18/06.

327 **$17 million for key congressional races:** Scott Helman, *Boston Globe,* "Internet-Based PAC Driving Democratic Push: Small Donors Fuel Big Support Drive, 8/7/07.

328 **"using the Internet for news or information about politics":** John Horrigan, Pew Internet and American Life Project, *Reports: E-Gov & E-Policy,* "26 Million Americans Were Logging on for News or Information About the Campaign on a Typical Day in August, the Highest Such Figure Recorded by the Pew Internet Project," 9/20/06.

328 **15.5 million active blogs:** Heather Green, *BusinessWeek* blog, "With 15.5 Million Active Blogs, New Technorati Data Show That Blogging Growth Seems to Be Peaking," 4/25/07.

330 **"play an active role in solving their own crises":** Saul Alinsky, *Rules for Radicals,* 1972, p. 80.

330 **"most of the time, reach the right decisions":** Ibid., p. 11.

331 **"deep passion for populist democracy":** Tim Dickinson, *Rolling Stone,* "The Online Insurgency," 2/24/05.

332 **"Denial of human dignity and democracy":** Saul Alinsky, *Rules for Radicals,* 1972, p. 123.

333 **make fusion voting much easier in that state:** According to the Connecticut Working Families Party website, Connecticut governor Jodi Rell signed SB1311 in the summer of 2007. The bill "includes language that dramatically expands the ability for minor parties to use fusion voting."

333 **beat back a bill in the Delaware legislature:** Patrick Jackson and Kathy Adams, *News Journal,* "'Fusion' candidate ban fails in House: Opponents of Bill 'Ecstatic' at Victory in Face of Lobbying from Democratic Party," 7/1/07.

333 **give workers paid leave for family emergencies:** Jay Jochnowitz, *Albany Times Union* blog, "Not Smart=?" 7/18/07.

333 **"stopped short of calling for an immediate troop withdrawal":** Jay Stevens, Left in the West.com, "On Tester's Call to Deauthorize the Iraq War," 7/5/07.

334 **clunky play on words "General Betray Us":** CBS/AP, "New TV Ad Slams Petraeus," 9/13/07.

334 **resolutions condemning MoveOn for the ad:** Senate Roll Call Vote #344, 9/20/07; House Roll Call Vote #910, 9/26/07.

334 **"just as bad as those who fight for a continuation of the war":** John Bruhns, *Philadelphia Daily News,* "The Anti-War Phonies," 11/19/07.

334 **"eclipse what they created in 2004":** Chris Cillizza, *Washington Post,* "Matzzie to Head Democratic Soft Money Effort," 11/12/07.

334 **least trusted advocacy organizations out of any surveyed:** Harris Poll #123, 12/11/07.

334 **exacerbate tech workers' plight here at home:** Tom McGhee, *Denver Post,* "S. America Speaking the Language of Outsourcing U.S. Companies Looking to Cut Costs and to Attract Latino Customers Are Drawn to Cheap Labor and Spanish Speakers," 8/8/07.

335 **bill to prohibit companies that have announced mass layoffs:** Patrick Thibodeau, *ComputerWorld,* "Senators Seek to Bar H-1B Use by Firms That Lay Off Workers," 6/7/07.

335 **"this presidency is not going to be just up for sale":** Andy Karr, *Newton Daily News,* "Huckabee Touts Self as Family Values Candidate at Newton Stop," 4/30/07.

335 **trying to enter the United States illegally:** Greg Gross, *San Diego Union Tribune,* "Border Patrol Video of Shooting Leaked to Internet," 4/30/07.

335 **vigilante sniper gunning down a Mexican:** Casey Sanchez, Southern Poverty Law Center's Hatewatch, "Shooting at Mexicans: Chilling Video Exposed," 8/10/07.

336 **press release from the Interfaith Center on Corporate Responsibility:** PRNewswire, "Groups to SEC: Hands Off Shareholder Resolution Process for Investors," 7/24/07.

336 **"action on such issues as reducing greenhouse gases":** Carrie Johnson, *Washington Post,* "SEC Proposal Raises Profile of Investors," 7/26/07.

336 **one of America's first major interracial labor strikes:** Feminist Majority Foundation, Women's History Month, Women's History Facts; Brian Kelly, *Race, Class, and Power in the Alabama Coalfields,* 1908–21, University of Illinois Press.

336 **New York City's Bread and Roses protest:** United Nations Cyber School Bus, "International Women's Day 2003."

336 **15,000-mile whistlestop train tour:** J. Robert Constantine, *Monthly Labor Review,* "Eugene V. Debs: An American Paradox," 8/1/91; Elizabeth Schulte, *Socialist Worker,* "The Presidential Campaigns of Socialist Party Leader Eugene Debs: When 1 Million Voted for Socialism," 10/1/04.

336 **National Association for the Advancement of Colored People:** NAACP website.

acknowledgments

THIS BOOK COULD not have been possible without the unrelentingly supportive group of people that believed in this project and sustained me in what was a grueling year.

To all the sources named and unnamed in *The Uprising*: This book is about something you are all building and shaping, and this book could never have happened without you taking the time to let me into your lives.

To Jim Grossfeld, Dave Neiwert, Chris Slevin, Robert Greenwald, and others who were my de facto proofreaders, research support, and fact-checkers: Thank you for taking the time to educate me about your areas of expertise.

To Jeff Weaver: Thanks for believing in me eight years ago and giving me a shot on Capitol Hill. And thanks for the intern badge this year.

To my college journalism professors John Kupetz and John Reque: I hope the writing and reporting in this book make you proud—it is the product of your tutelage not only in the mechanics of writing, but in what journalism is supposed to be about. Thank you for your wisdom, and for your feedback during the writing of this book.

To Chris Hayes, Aaron Kleiner, and Matt Villano: Writing starts with talking and thinking aloud. Thank you for spending countless hours brainstorming with me about this project over coffee, over the phone, and over IM at all hours of the day and night. The book is better for it.

To Mike Levy: You were my resident historian on the project. Since eighth-grade basketball in the pit, you have always been my teammate. This project was no exception. Thank you for being on call for me twenty-four hours a day even as you were representing our country on the other side of the globe in the Peace Corps.

To Joel Barkin: Next to me, you probably saw the most drafts of this book, as you were willing to read iteration after iteration after iteration and give me feedback. Thank you for your devotion to this project, and for your persistence as one of the most important leaders of the uprising.

To Craig Chanoff: Since nursery school, you have been like a member of my family—always supportive, no matter what. Thank you for letting me use your apartment as my own personal hotel during the writing process, and more important, for your support and friendship over the last quarter century.

To Lucinda Bartley: Draft after draft after draft, back and forth we went. You never complained or tired of helping me. Thank you for making this book the best it possibly could be. Plain and simple, this book would not be what it is without your passion for it, and your willingness to throw all of your tremendous editing skills into it.

To Rachel Klayman: Thank you for believing in this project from the beginning, when it was just an idea. And thank you for being an unrelenting advocate for this book from start to finish.

To Will Lippincott: You are my Jerry Maguire. Thank you for being my ambassador and, more important, my friend.

To Danielle Locke: I was a little nervous asking you to read the book and give me your feedback, feeling like I might be imposing a burden on a busy full-time mother with two young children, and especially on a busy full-time mother who is not all that interested in politics. But your enthusiasm for the project and your incredibly helpful feedback immensely enriched the final product. I can't thank you enough.

To Monty: Thank you for literally being at my side or at my feet for almost every single hour I spent writing this book. Dogs—and particularly golden doodles—are really a man's best friend.

To Jeff, Kate, Steven, Nate, and Zach: Thank you all for making the phrase "you are your brother's keeper" a reality in how you keep me with such a strong support system.

To Mom and Dad Lipp: You have embraced me as a son, with all of the stress that comes with writing books like this. Thank you for being there for me in so many ways.

To Mom and Dad Sirota: You are my editors, my proofreaders, my end-note compilers, my advisers, and my parents. Thank you for being all of those things all at once.

To Emily: My soul mate. Thank you for being my inspiration and my partner.

index

a b o u t　t h e　a u t h o r

DAVID SIROTA is a political organizer, journalist, and nationally syndicated newspaper columnist who has worked in state and national politics
all over America. His first book, *Hostile Takeover* (2006), was a *New York
Times* bestseller, and his column runs weekly in, among others, the *Denver
Post,* the *San Francisco Chronicle,* and the *Seattle Times.* Sirota blogs at
credoaction.com/sirota. He is a senior fellow at the Campaign for America's
Future and is the founder of the Progressive States Network—both nonpartisan research institutions. He lives in Denver, Colorado, with his wife,
Emily, and their dog, Monty.